Attrition

Aspects of Command in the Peloponnesian War

ATTRITION

ASPECTS OF COMMAND IN THE PELOPONNESIAN WAR

by

Godfrey Hutchinson

SPELLMOUNT

To my wife Sheila and my children Miles, Nikki and Paula.

British Library Cataloguing in Publication Data:
A catalogue record for this book is available
from the British Library

Copyright © Godfrey Hutchinson 2006

ISBN 1-86227-272-7

First published in the UK in 2006 by
Spellmount Limited
The Mill, Brimscombe Port
Stroud, Gloucestershire. GL5 2QG

Tel: 01453 883300
Fax: 01453 883233
E-mail: enquiries@spellmount.com
Website: www.spellmount.com

1 3 5 7 9 8 6 4 2

The right of Godfrey Hutchinson to be identified
as the author of this work has been asserted by him
in accordance with the Copyright, Designs
and Patents Act 1988

Printed in Great Britain by
Oaklands Book Services
Stonehouse, Gloucestershire GL10 3RQ

Contents

Acknowledgements	vi
Introduction	vii
Glossary	xvi
Maps and battle plans	xviii
I Greek Navies and Naval Actions early in the War	1
II The Siege of Plataia	25
III Demosthenes, the North-West, Aitolia and the Battle of Delion	36
IV Sphakteria, 425 BC	53
V Brasidas	65
VI The Battle of Mantineia, 418 BC	100
VII The Great Sicilian Expedition, 415–413 BC	118
VIII The Elusive Checkmate	172
Appendix 1: An Outline of the Pentecontaetia	215
Appendix 2: Speeches	227
Appendix 3: Calendar of the War	246
Select Bibliography	256
About the Author	258
Map of mainland Greece	259
Index	260

Acknowledgements

I am particularly grateful to John Lazenby, lately Professor of Ancient History at the University of Newcastle upon Tyne. He it was who reinforced my view that much of 20th-century scholarship showed a somewhat unfair antipathy to the Spartans and the Spartan way of life. He was not without criticism of them himself, but in a very balanced manner (see the Preface and text of his *The Spartan Army*). I hope that I have proved to be as objective as my mentor when touching on such matters in this much broader study. I thank him also for reading the initial drafts of this book and for the suggestions he made. While many were persuasive there remain points of difference and emphasis in some areas. I take full responsibility for the retention of these in the text.

My thanks to the staff of several university libraries for their assistance in locating articles and volumes in their collections.

The author created the maps and battle plans and took the photographs, unless otherwise indicated.

Godfrey Hutchinson
Staindrop, England
2006

Jacket images: Front flyleaf, a replica of a 4th-century BC bust of the remarkable politician and commander, Alkibiades, inscribed 'Alkibiades, son of Klinios, Athenian'. This is an idealised image of a Greek male and Alkibiades is a convenient subject for such a study, renowned for his good looks. His remarkable life would see him not only conspire with the Spartans but also lead the Athenian war effort and die in exile, murdered by order of the Persian governor at Phrygia. Front of jacket, a beautiful example of Attic red-figured pottery by Phindias of around 500 BC in the National Archaeological Museum, Athens. Back of jacket, top, an early photograph of the remains of the defensive wall at Mantineia, setting for the Spartan victory in 418 BC (LOC). Below, the 5th-century BC coastal fortifications at Aigosthena.

Introduction

The Peloponnesian War of 431-404 BC has fascinated scholars and laymen alike for centuries, not merely because of its longevity and complexity, but because of the treatment given to it by Thucydides, who set out the basic principles which most historians follow today. For his time he was unusually meticulous in checking his sources and few over succeeding centuries have matched his achievement. He lived through the conflict himself, had first-hand experience of the plague in Athens, knew eye-witnesses to much that he described, and before his exile, heard himself some of the great speeches he reports.

The war itself was one which need not have happened. Few other than the Spartan king Archidamos had the foresight to realise that it would be so long, and even he, had he lived, would have been surprised that twenty-seven years would pass before the conflict was resolved.

Essentially this was a war between a land power, Sparta, and a sea power, Athens, the former striving to achieve parity and then superiority over the latter in the element of its opposition. Perikles was intransigent in not coming to an accommodation with Sparta at the outset. He put faith in sea power and in creating a fortress of Athens, impregnable to the landward, supplied by sea and dominating that element. He had no plans to achieve the kind of parity on land which the Spartans were to seek at sea. Therein lies the dilemma. Despite later offers of peace from the Spartan side during the war, Perikles had set them on a course whereby the Spartans were obliged to continue hostilities after each rebuttal of their peace proposals. His successors were to view things differently.

Not that Perikles did not prosecute the initial stages of the war with great vigour. As long as he avoided direct confrontation with Spartan-led Peloponnesian forces in the field he could inflict considerable damage on both property and prestige. He followed this strategy in the belief that the Spartans would tire of achieving little or nothing that could hurt Athens and would eventually come to terms. Those who followed after his death abandoned this strategy and sought outright victory even when presented with peace proposals by the Peloponnesians. Perikles' strategy had no plan for total victory and was one of aggressive defence only. This could well have achieved a temporary peace but hostilities would have inevitably resumed. To deny an enemy the opportunity to win a war with no clear course of action by which one's own side could achieve victory was a hollow undertaking – and an unusual military circumstance.

Thucydides chronicled all but the last few years of the struggle with great objectivity. He leaves his readers often to draw their own conclusions and his narrative illuminates life in his time. Sometimes there appear to be fundamental contradictions or conflicts of thinking, for example in the democracy of Athens and the treatment meted out to her empire.

As its title suggests the present study seeks to give an outline of the major events organised into the periods dominated by particular commanders. Comparison can sometimes be made between chapters which have a common base or theme, such as the two dealing with sieges, that of Plataia and Syracuse. Although the scale of each was very different it is as well to compare the activities of the Spartans in the former with the Athenians in the latter. For some unaccountable reason unsupported by sources, the Athenians had gained a reputation for being pre-eminent at that time in conducting sieges. They certainly could build walls very quickly but other than that there is little to suggest that they were any better than the Peloponnesians, who appear to be more thorough. The anonymity of the leaders at Plataia is in contrast to the succession of named famous leaders at Syracuse.

The incredible seamanship of the few ships under the inspired Athenian admiral Phormio early in the war can be set against the guile and meticulous preparation of Lysander in its closing stages. The broader strategic vision of Demosthenes, which sought to nullify Boiotian involvement in the war and to cause a direct threat to Sparta at Sphakteria, can be set against the Spartan counter-attack led by the greatest commander of the war, Brasidas. His strategy put Athenian colonies and client states at risk in the northern Aegean. The Spartan lack of support for Brasidas was significant. But there were two key turning points in the war. The first was the battle of Mantineia wherein the Spartans were brought to the point of risking all in a land battle. Admittedly it was not against Athenians but against Argives and their allies. Had the Athenians fully supported a land engagement their presence would have swelled the ranks of the Argives out of all recognition. The second was the total annihilation of Athenian forces at Syracuse.

Before this great conflict Greek warfare between city-states was seasonal, short in duration and conducted in almost ritualistic fashion. The agricultural needs of the homeland often determined the length of operations carried out by the invader. Battles took place on the flat ground of a plain between two phalanxes of heavy infantry. Any auxiliary forces present were virtually negligible in their impact on the conflict except occasionally in pursuit. The winning side lost far fewer men than those who were defeated, most casualties occurring in the pursuit rather than in the battle itself. Battles were often conducted in two phases. This came about because of the inclination of each side to drift to its right in order that the unshielded side of each right wing could gain greater protection. Thus in the advance each left wing often became outflanked. In the first phase the right wings of both sides enveloped and destroyed their opposition. The second phase occurred when the right wings of each side regrouped to fight each other to a conclusion.

It is hard to account for some of the lost opportunities that occurred in these contests. It may seem obvious that the side enjoying early success on its right could then take its remaining opposition in flank and roll up the line. In the surviving descriptions of battles success on one wing often led to an overlong pursuit of the defeated, as happened at Mantineia.

Reasons can be advanced for the dominance of Spartan-led forces in the field. The most obvious is their life-long training for conflict; but this is not enough. Pursuit by Spartans was noticeably briefer and this may have been a tactical decision. The common messes attended daily by the citizen body wherein they shared a meal would have been the opportunity for discussion of the tactical possibilities, and perhaps it was there that the tactic was decided upon. The habit of only conducting a short pursuit meant early regrouping. If the enemy broke, the integrity of the victorious line could still be preserved, such was their discipline. It is noticeable that Agis, whose light shone dimly as a commander in his early campaigns, was alert, or perhaps was alerted by another, to the danger to his left at Mantineia. The success of his opposition's right at that battle was followed by an over-enthusiastic pursuit not dissimilar to that of the Thebans at Koroneia in 394 BC. The disciplined and limited pursuit by the Spartan-led right and centre allowed for manoeuvres to be completed in both cases in advance of those of the enemy right. Tactical awareness on the field of battle, given the restricted view enjoyed by the commander, was part and parcel of Spartan life. This accounts for the successes enjoyed by commanders other than the kings such as Brasidas, Gylippos, Hegesandridas and Lysander and for the threatening, though eventually unsuccessful, manoeuvres of Mindaros. While the first two enjoyed their triumphs on land, the last three had to contend with the less familiar element of the sea.

The defence of a successful flank seems to have been given greater consideration by the Spartans but was also prosecuted by the Theban commander Pagondas at Delion. Of Athenian commanders, Demosthenes' use of pre-laid ambushes offered a counter to a perceived weakness in his line of battle.

The Peloponnesian War saw year-round conflict in all types of terrain. Its compass was enormous for its time. The whole manner of the conduct of hostilities gave rise to new and untried methodologies. Campaigns lasted much longer, bringing with them new problems of logistics. For a war of such longevity formal land battles were few and far between. As it progressed atrocities increased and a moral decline becomes evident on both sides. The conflict became one of attrition punctuated by acts of barbarism. The war seemed never-ending and can be seen with hindsight as a tragedy for Greece. Human nature is exposed in the raw. Frailty and bravery often go hand in hand in Thucydides' history and none who read it can be unaffected.

Thucydides (c.460-399 BC)

Thucydides was an Athenian citizen whose family probably originated from the northern Aegean or Thrace. We glean from his writing and the manner in which he couches some of his pronouncements that his background was aristocratic. Living in a democracy he is happier, however, when it is led by a fellow aristocrat such as Perikles rather than under characters such as the demagogue Kleon. He was probably a mature man of 30 when the war began and, given that he lived throughout its duration, he was possibly a little over 60 when he died in the early years of the Spartan Hegemony. Of the manner of his death we know nothing which can be relied upon. He was the son of Oloros, an uncommon name at Athens. Given that the family had possessions and mineral rights on the mainland near Thasos his clan may well have originated there.

He would have been brought up like any other of his class to be a leader of the people. He survived the plague which struck Athens early in the war. His description of its symptoms and the development of the disease are comprehensive and clinical. His position in Athenian society is confirmed by his election as a general and he served at Thasos near his family possessions, where he had influence over the inhabitants of the area. His misfortune was to come too late to save Amphipolis from Brasidas. He did, however, save its port, but was exiled for twenty years for the loss of the city. A misfortune for Thucydides but fortunate for us, in that we would otherwise have been deprived of his history, which became the occupation of these years.

Other sources

Because Thucydides did not complete his history we rely for coverage of the final years on other writers. Xenophon, Diodoros and Plutarch are those to whom we must turn for information. Xenophon the Athenian is particularly useful in that he was a younger contemporary of Thucydides growing to manhood as the war progressed. He himself became an extremely capable commander, being first a general and then commander-in-chief of the 'Ten Thousand' who had to fight their way back to Greece from the heart of the Persian Empire. Among his many entertaining works his *Hellenika* is less a history than a personalised record of events. Initially this work was a continuation of Thucydides' history. As his work progresses beyond the war and into the next century Xenophon often displays biased opinions but is wholly sound on all matters military.

Less reliable on tactics is Diodoros, a Sicilian who lived during the last century BC. From his *Universal History*, Book XIII is useful. His stock rose some years ago when fragments of an unknown but obviously talented historian came to light in Egypt. The Oxyrhynchos historian as he is known has not been identified but his work appears to have been written in the 4th century BC and to have been one of Diodoros' sources. So on points of conflict between Diodoros and Xenophon, the latter's reliability was put in doubt for a time. However, common sense has seen the pendulum swing back. It is up to the reader to scrutinise all evidence and weigh the possibilities carefully.

The Boiotian Plutarch was born in the 1st century AD. His biographies of great Greeks and Romans known as *Lives* draw on a wide range of sources, some now lost. Despite the fact that his intention is not historical, his writings provide details that support Xenophon's accounts and provide insights into areas which the latter chose to ignore.

List of main sources

Thucydides	*History*
Xenophon	*Hellenika* (mainly Books I & II)
Diodoros	*Universal History* (mainly Book XIII)
Oxyrhinchia	*Hellenika* (mainly the Cairo and Florence fragments)
Plutarch	*Perikles*
	Nikias
	Alkibiades
	Aristides
	Lysander
	Lykourgos
	Kimon
	Artaxerxes

Secondary sources

Aristotle	*Athenian Politics*
Herodotos	*Histories*
Pausanias	*Description of Greece*
Xenophon	*Spartan Constitution*
Euripides	*Herakles*
Plutarch	*Themistokles*

Occasional differences in spelling between the main text and the passages of the Loeb translation of Thucydides quoted, e.g. 'k' in place of 'c' can be accounted for by my preference for a more direct treatment of the language rather than a latinized one. Thucydides' *History of the Peloponnesian War,* translator. C F Smith, Loeb Classical Library, 1919, is now published by Harvard University Press.

Ancient source references are given within the text and those to modern works in the notes at the end of each chapter.

The main combatants

It must always be borne in mind that, although there were many differences between Athens and Sparta, firm personal friendships existed between the citizens of both states, for example Perikles and King Archidamos. Sparta was admired by some of those Athenians who held the democracy in which they lived in mild distaste. Indeed, Athenian sons were sometimes sent to Sparta to participate in its rigorous system of youth training known as the *agoge.* One of our sources, Xenophon, when exiled from Athens, chose to serve with the Spartan army and live on an estate given to him by the Spartans for his services. So it is best to avoid a 'black and white' attitude to the two city states.

Living within a democracy it is much easier for us to understand the similar structures enjoyed by Athens. Those of equal rights, freedom of speech, obedience to the law framed by the citizens themselves, public positions open to all and awarded on the basis of ability to rich and poor alike, an expectation for all citizens to participate in public matters, and ample opportunity and time to take part in more leisurely activities. Voting at assembly was restricted to males who had been born free and had completed two years of military training.

Usually there was a minimum of four meetings per month, although additional meetings could be called if circumstances demanded. Numbers attending were variable but for a meeting to be viable, 6,000 citizens had to be present to debate business. Any citizen could propose items for debate via the Council of 500. This body was made up of fifty citizens selected by lot from each of the ten tribes each year. They were given payment for their services which was reviewed at the end of their term of office. Their main duties were to prepare agendas for the assembly, collect taxes and supervise elections to the senior magistracies. The *strategoi,* or generals, were chosen annually at assembly. Prominent and successful individuals could be re-elected and therefore could pursue a foreign policy which, to all intents and purposes, was in their hands. They too were subject to scrutiny both during and at the end of their tenure. Other magistrates (*archons*) took control of religious, civil and criminal issues. A range of minor appointments covering civic activities involving finance, markets, prisons, weights and measures, etc. were made in groups of ten, reflecting the tribal base. The society was underpinned by a considerable slave population owned by individual citizens.

The structure of Spartan society is fascinating. Its governance can best be described as a mixed constitution. The rights of a citizen could well be described as being democratic. But the citizen body was massively outnumbered by others within the population, so, in a sense, governance could also be described as oligarchic. One obviously unusual feature was that there were two kings. Following progressive reforms through the late 7th and early 6th centuries BC, Sparta had reached a system by the 5th century that contained checks and balances between the various levels of its constitution. The prime cause for these developments was the subjugation of Messenia, which doubled the area under Spartan control, giving her citizen body the freedom to concentrate on becoming the finest infantry in the Greek world. It also gave her the problem of a huge state-controlled slave (*helot*) population that had to be constantly kept under control. While the helots created the produce that gave the military caste the time to follow its pursuits and to pay the requirements of the communal messes, that very citizen body became increasingly paranoid about the possibility of an uprising. Athens was not slow to exploit these tensions.

Spartan citizens or Spartiates (*Spartiatai*) were taken from their homes at the age of 7 and inducted into the *agoge*, the formal mode of military training. Up to the age of 20 they were trained to a level of physical endurance unparalleled in the ancient world. At around 20 they became eligible for military service (*eirenes*) but had to wait until 30 to become full citizens and members of the assembly (*ekklesia*). Agendas for voting upon at assembly were prepared by a council of elders (*gerousia*) made up of the two kings and thirty citizens over the age of sixty, the age at which military service ceased to be a requirement. Membership of this body was granted by the assembly, whose level of applause for candidates was the measure for selection. This group also acted as a criminal court. Five *ephors* were appointed annually from the citizen body. Their powers and responsibilities were formidable. They had charge of much of foreign policy, were in control of the secret police (*krypteia*), decided which year groups should go to war, and were, together with *the gerousia*, the supreme court within the constitution. As important was their power to call the kings to account for any action of ill-repute. At the end of their tenure of office they were called upon to account for their actions.

The kings, coming from the Agiad and Eurypontid royal houses, acted as high priests and supreme commanders of the army. By the period under discussion it had become the custom for only one of the kings to be away on military duty at any one time. Two *ephors* normally accompanied the king on campaign. While the king held the power of life or death over those he led in the field he could on his return be censured and punished for any misdeed while absent from Sparta. The kings conducted all sacrifices and had two *pythoi* whose duties were to keep records of oracles and to consult at Delphi. For their duties the kings were maintained at state expense, being given double portions in the mess (*syssition*) possibly to allow them to host foreign guests or friends. A corps of young men in their prime acted as the king's bodyguard when on campaign.

Below the citizen body were several groups of 'inferiors': *Partheniai*, sons of Spartiates born to slave women, *Hypomeiones*, probably those who failed to sustain their civic obligations and had lost status, *Mothakes*, of inferior origin, sometime *helots*, who were companions to sons of Spartiates and shared the experience of the *agoge*, *Tresantes*, a group who had temporarily lost citizenship for some misdeed, and *Neodamodeis*, or 'new citizens' who had been enlisted from the *helot* population on the promise of freedom as a reward for military service.

The remainder of the Dorian population, *Perioikoi*, 'those who lived around,' mainly resided in townships with their own local autonomy but were subservient to the needs of Sparta.

While it has been necessary to give more detail on the less familiar aspects of Spartan society, it is as well to draw attention to the confusing terminology used in our sources. While Spartiates signify full citizens or Equals, Spartans or Lakedaimonians can be used to describe both them and also, on other occasions, broader sections of, or indeed the whole of, the army from the country of Lakedaimon. When leading their allies the whole army may be described as Peloponnesian, the elements within it only becoming clear if listed in orders of battle.

There were very clear differences between the lives of Athenian and Spartan women. While neither had a vote, the former were legally under the control of first, their father, and then their husband, the choice of whom was made for them. An Athenian woman of good status needed to be chaperoned by a male member of the family when away from home. She remained in the women's quarters unless summoned and her duties were to maintain the household. Her skills were mainly domestic. Only the less privileged females had the opportunity to work, perhaps in the market. Spartan girls, on the other hand, were organised into groups similar to the boys and took part in many sporting activities and vied with boys in choral and dancing festivals. Although they lived at home their lives were much freer than those of their Athenian counterparts. Their wishes were considered in the matter of marriage and it is significant that by the mid-4th century a little under half of landed property was under the ownership and control of matriarchs.

Finally, to the military resources at the outset of hostilities. In the case of Athens the figures decline as the war progresses. As has been stated above, this started as a war between a sea power and a land power. Athens could field an army of around 12,500 heavy infantry, about 1,000 cavalry and 200 archers from her own resources while having a reserve for home defence. She could supplement her forces from her allies and use the large financial reserves derived from her empire to hire mercenaries. Athens had an overwhelming superiority in naval terms, well over 300 triremes with significant reserve fleets from her allies and subjects. Her city and port were strongly fortified with walls linking one to the other.

Had the occasion arisen, unfortified Sparta could easily have raised an army of over 30,000 heavy infantry from the League she led, together with over 2,000 high quality cavalry from Thebes and her central Greek neighbours. There was no shortage of skirmishers and light-infantrymen. Her great weakness was maritime. The League could assemble around 100 ships at the start of the conflict, the largest contingent coming from Corinth. But the disparity in ship numbers was not the only problem. The navy, unlike that of Athens, was hampered by a shortage of good seamen other than the mercantile Corinthians. Experience in the techniques of naval warfare developed by the Athenians was lacking, and that experience would take time to acquire. The diminution of funds on both sides led to hopes that their erstwhile adversary Persia would provide the necessary shortfall. Despite Alkibiades' machinations on behalf of the Athenians, it was to Sparta that the old enemy gave decisive support.

Glossary

Agoge	System of training common to all Spartan citizens.
Archon	Nine magistracies existed at Athens under this name. The most important of the nine was the eponymous archon. He presided over the festival of the Great Dionysia and dealt with family disputes. The year was named after him in the calendar. The *basileos* archon retains an echo of kingship in its name. He acted in the role of the ancient priest-king, having responsibility for the 'Mysteries'and all other religious celebrations. The *polemarch* was responsible for those religious activities and rites associated with warfare. The remaining six acted as judges.
Ekklesia	The Athenian civic assembly.
Ephors	The most powerful Spartan magistracies.
Helots	Slaves under the organisation of Sparta. Originally within Lakedaimon but later embracing the population of Messenia following its subjugation by Sparta.
Hoplite	Greek heavy infantryman.
Hypomeiones	Inferiors within the Spartan social structure, including *Mothakes, Partheniai, Tresantes.*
Lochargos	The commander of a section of the Spartan army generally agreed to have been 640 men at full strength. The unit was called a *lochos* and equated to half a *mora*.
Lakedaimon	The area settled and controlled by the Spartans, who with the other elements of the population are sometimes called Lakedaimonians.

GLOSSARY

Mora	A unit of 1,280 men within the Spartan army. There were six *morai* by the end of the fifth century.
Neodamodeis	A new citizen. Helots were sometimes given their freedom after serving in the Spartan army. Although free they had no rights in the Spartan assembly but most probably were autonomous in their settlements, much in the same way as the *perioikoi*.
Paean	A rousing religiously based form of singing employed by *hoplites* as they entered battle or celebrated victory.
Peltast	A light infantryman used initially as a javelin throwing skirmisher. Iphikrates was to modify the arms and mode of fighting in the early 4th century.
Perioikoi	Literally, 'dwellers around'. The locally autonomous population of Lakedaimon that was called for service in the Spartan army, usually against opposition which did not come from the neighbouring states of the Peloponnese.
Peripoli	Young Athenians who served as defenders of the city walls of Athens or patrolled the state boundaries.
Phalanx	A formation of *hoplites* of variable depth which made up the battle line. While the usual depth was eight, the Thebans experimented with a range, the greatest being of 50 men at Leuktra in 371 BC.
Polemarch	The commander of a *mora*.
Spartiate	A Spartan citizen with full civic rights. One of the ruling class.
Strategos	A general.
Syssition	A Spartan communal military mess. There were several of these and all Spartiates were required to attend on a regular basis to take a meal with their fellow citizens.

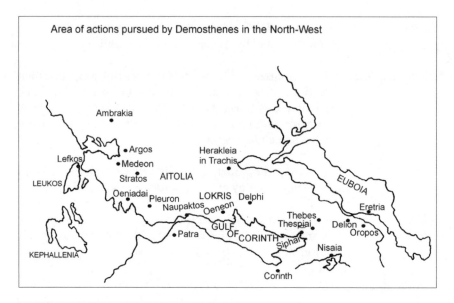

Area of actions pursued by Demosthenes in the North-West

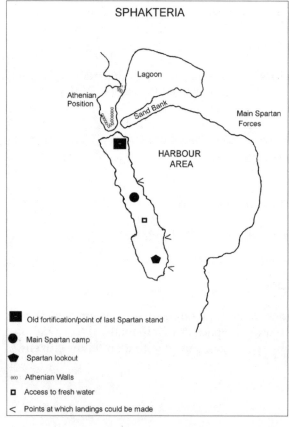

SPHAKTERIA

■ Old fortification/point of last Spartan stand

● Main Spartan camp

⬠ Spartan lookout

ᴑᴑᴑ Athenian Walls

◻ Access to fresh water

< Points at which landings could be made

Above: *Area of actions pursued by Demosthenes in the North-west. (See Chapter III, page 36)*

Left: *Sphakteria. (See Chapter IV, page 53)*

Opposite above: *the environs of Amphipolis. (See page 89)*

Opposite below: *The Theatre of Brasidas' Operations. (See Chapter V, page 65)*

MAPS AND BATTLE PLANS

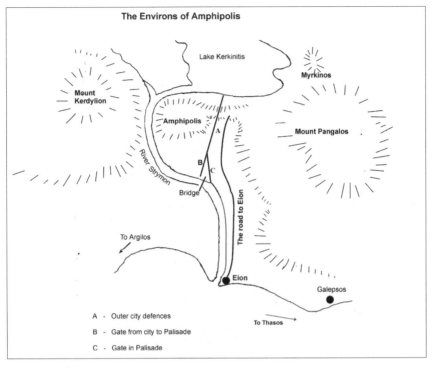

The Environs of Amphipolis

Lake Kerkinitis

Myrkinos

Mount Kerdylion

Amphipolis

A

Mount Pangalos

B

C

River Strymon

Bridge

The road to Eion

To Argilos

Eion

Galepsos

A - Outer city defences

B - Gate from city to Palisade

C - Gate in Palisade

To Thasos

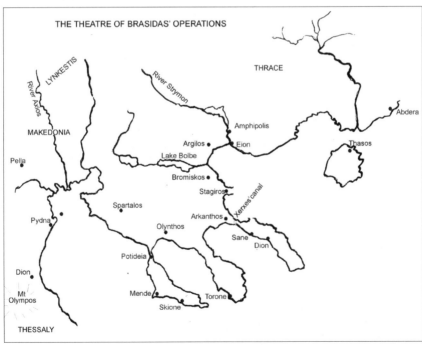

THE THEATRE OF BRASIDAS' OPERATIONS

LYNKESTIS

River Axios

River Strymon

THRACE

Abdera

MAKEDONIA

Amphipolis

Pella

Argilos

Eion

Thasos

Lake Bolbe

Bromiskos

Stagiros

Xerxes' canal

Spartalos

Arkanthos

Pydna

Olynthos

Sane

Dion

Potideia

Dion

Mende

Torone

Mt Olympos

Skione

THESSALY

xix

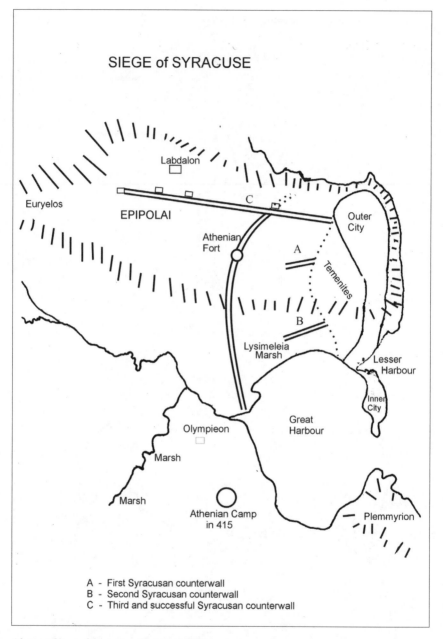

Above: *Siege of Syracuse. (See page 131)*

Opposite above: *Battle of Mantineia phase 1. (See Chapter VI, page 100)*

Opposite below: *Battle of Mantineia phases 2 and 3.*

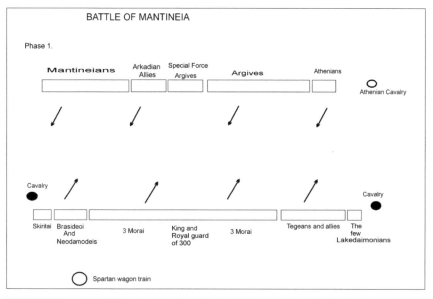

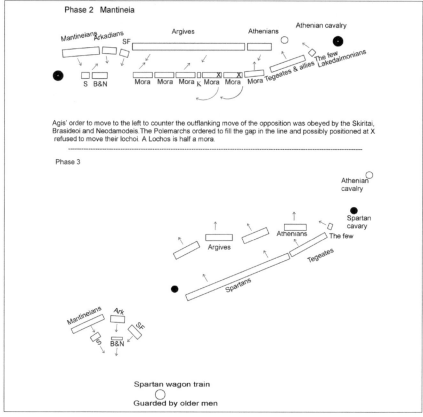

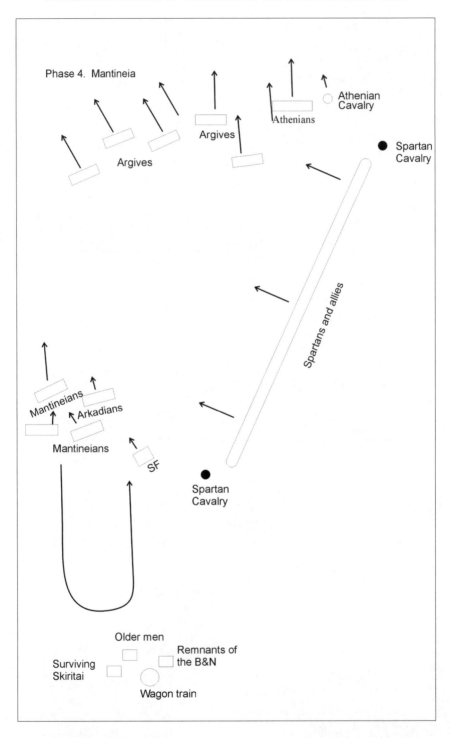

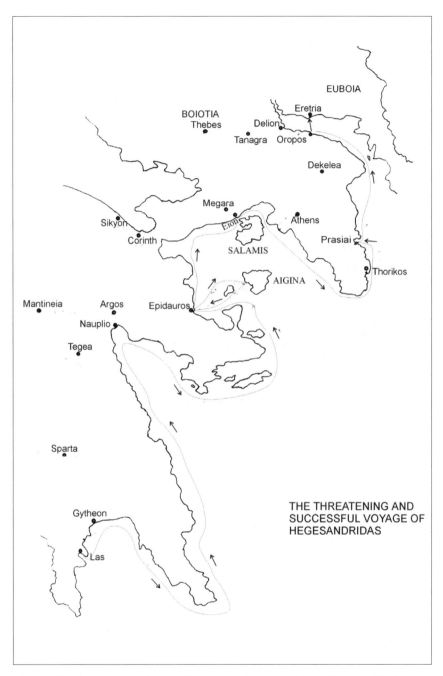

Above: *The threatening and successful voyage of Hegesandridas. (See page 173.)*

Opposite: *Battle of Mantiniea phase 4.*

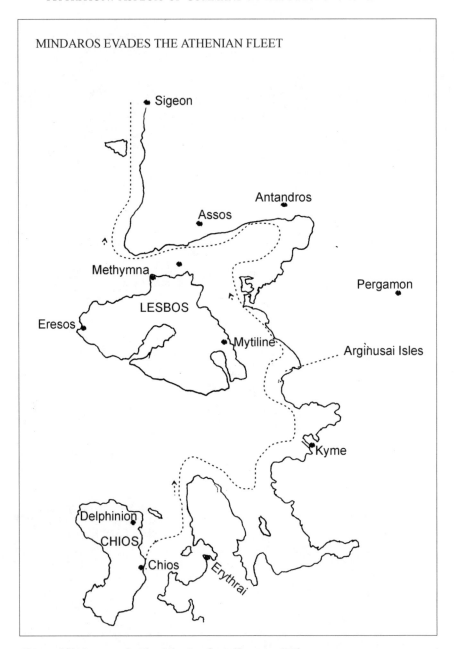

MINDAROS EVADES THE ATHENIAN FLEET

Above: *Mindaros evades the Athenian fleet. (See page 177)*

Opposite above: *Battle of Kynossima. (See page 179)*

Opposite below: *Battle of Arginousai. (see page 199)*

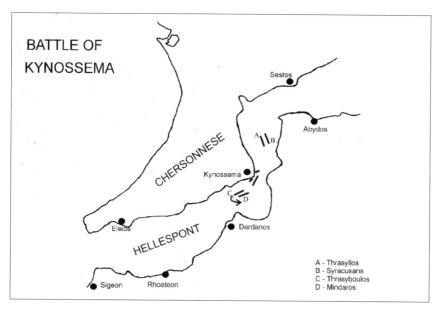

BATTLE OF
KYNOSSEMA

Sestos

Abydos

CHERSONNESE

Kynossema

A ‖ B

C
D

Eleios

Dardanos

HELLESPONT

Sigeon   Rhoeteon

A - Thrasyllos
B - Syracusans
C - Thrasyboulos
D - Mindaros

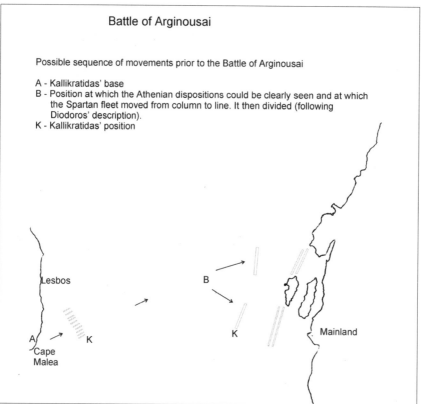

Battle of Arginousai

Possible sequence of movements prior to the Battle of Arginousai

A - Kallikratidas' base
B - Position at which the Athenian dispositions could be clearly seen and at which
the Spartan fleet moved from column to line. It then divided (following
Diodoros' description).
K - Kallikratidas' position

Lesbos

B

A
Cape
Malea

K

K

Mainland

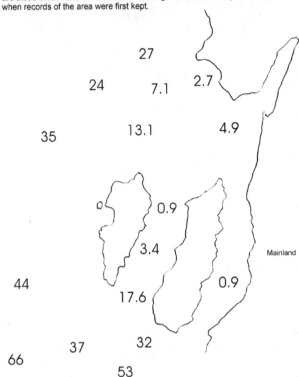

Depth of waters around Arginousai Isles

It is obvious that any possibility of passage between the islands or between the mainland and the islands was denied to triremes. The depths in metres are those which have been consistent throughout the last 200 years the point when records of the area were first kept.

Left: *Depth of waters around Arginousai Isles.*

Below: *Area of Propontis. (See page 206)*

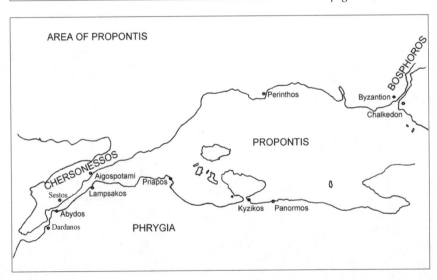

I

Greek Navies and Naval Actions Early in the War

At the outset of the war the antagonists were ill-matched for anything other than a stalemate. Athens, a sea power, was supreme in her element, and Sparta commanded the best land forces in the Greek world. So long as Athens followed the Periklean strategy of refusing large land engagements and indulged in harassment of the coast of the Peloponnese the hostilities would continue to meander frustratingly for her enemies. For Sparta her only solution to this massive problem was to become a sea power herself. This she eventually did but it took more than twenty years to achieve.

The outbreak of hostilities saw Athens as the most practised in action and best equipped of all states in the Aegean in terms of naval warfare. It was this experiential and technological divide between the enemies which had to be addressed before Sparta could compete on even terms. In so doing the Peloponnesians developed vessels and tactics which eventually secured victory and which the Athenians could not match. It is surprising that during the war Athens did not attempt to counter the technological developments of her enemy but continued to rely on fleets and tactics which eventually became virtually obsolete.

From the outset, Athens was supreme at sea and that supremacy stemmed from the condition and light structure of her vessels and the aggressive use to which they were put. Ostensibly the Athenian trireme was a floating battering ram. While one could argue that construction could be copied or shared by an enemy, it does not take into account the skills of the rowers, or of those practised commanders who called for the various manoeuvres to be carried out, or the rapid response of the oarsmen to such orders. Athens, with the tribute from her empire, could afford not only to build successive fleets but could sustain large numbers of skilled oarsmen with which to man them. It was such skills through practice and experience that the Peloponnesians had to acquire before any success was to be achieved.

All Greek navies had triremes, indeed the Corinthians were the first to build this type of vessel, and, as its name implies, there were three levels of rowers. For the Athenians the lowest level was manned by fifty-four *thalamitai* (θἀλἁμτης -an oarsman serving on the lowest bench with the shortest oar and the least pay), fifty-four *zygitai* (ζὐγίτης – an oarsman on the middle bench placed on a major crossbeam in the construction of the vessel), and sixty-two *thranitai* (θρᾶνίτης – the most important of the trio, having the longest oar and seated in an outrigger fitted to the topmost part of the hull). The *thranitai* were the key oarsmen regulating the combined strokes of those on the two levels below. They were the only oarsmen who could view what was happening and obviously gave warning to those below of impending impact in times of engagement. So with a complement of 170 rowers, four to six archers, ten marine hoplites, steersmen and sail handlers, each ship would have been a crowded place with regular landfalls a necessity.

Adverse weather conditions made for summer campaigning at sea and the heat taxed the strongest of rowers. Fleets would of necessity skirt the coastline and cross open seas by the shortest route so that periods of time on shore could be guaranteed. This explains why Athenian fleets going to Sicily circumnavigated the Peloponnese and crossed to the Italian coastline from Kerkyra before continuing southwards to their destination. Although it was possible for the crew to eat aboard it was preferable to go ashore for meals. Ships secured a safe anchorage or were beached by rollers each night with the men sleeping ashore. Although this procedure may be questioned one has only to look at the activities of Iphikrates in the early part of the next century when he circumnavigated the Peloponnese. Admittedly he established a good system of lookouts but the lack of earlier evidence should not obviate the possibility of precedent, in this case particularly in the Peloponnesian War.

The trireme itself was usually 120 feet long and no more than sixteen feet wide.[1] Apart from its bronze ram, its construction was surprisingly light and allowed the crews to comfortably beach the vessels using wooden log rollers. This was important, for speed was of the essence. Dry but not over-dry ships rather than those which had become waterlogged by constant use at sea were more manoeuvrable and this produced a pattern of use which was to be tactically important. The problems encountered with the Megaran ships by Brasidas and his companions will be observed later. These had been too long out of water (Thuc. II. 14. 3), and being over-dry, leaked. Nikias, in a letter to the Athenians (VII. 12. 1-5), points to his dilemma in both maintaining his fleet at the ready because of the danger of attack and seeing them becoming increasingly water-logged, thereby limiting their manoeuvrability. Lysander, by contrast, in taking over command from Kratesippidas, made arrangements for his fleet to be in top condition:

> As for Lysander, when he had finished organising his fleet, he hauled ashore the ships which were at Ephesos, now ninety in number,

and kept quiet, while the ships were being dried out and repaired. (Xenophon, *Hellenica*, I. 5. 10)

With its strongest section at the prow the targets for attack were amidships and the stern, and it was in safeguarding these that tactical manoeuvre was an imperative. The speed of such manoeuvre was all important and a reduction in overall weight assisted. Ideally ships were stripped to the bare essentials before any engagement. As attack or retreat was usually made under the power of oars, masts, sails, food supplies, reserve armaments, rollers, etc. were placed onshore. This required a base camp from which to operate. It will be seen in later chapters that onshore facilities were all-important to success at sea and that sometimes the loss of a camp could nullify any seaborne success.

The two main manoeuvres were known as the *diekplous* and *periplous*. In facing an enemy line of ships the former was achieved by sailing through the line and turning to attack an enemy vessel amidships. The latter, as implied by the prefix *peri*, entailed an outflanking of a wing so that the attack was made by sailing round the opposition line to attack either the stern or side of a vessel. The *periplous* was usually a more concerted manoeuvre involving more than one vessel. The *diekplous* more often would have been the manoeuvre of an individual ship unless there was sufficient water between several opposition vessels to permit such an attack by more than one. The employment of each manoeuvre depended entirely on the disposition of an enemy line. The *periplous* was more often the outcome of the admiral's planning and the *diekplous* that of an opportunist captain.

Thucydides was himself the commander of a fleet and is a good source for viewing the tactical continuum of naval warfare of this period. Initially some means of denying the Athenians space for manoeuvre was sought to offset the abilities of the Athenian crews and the Syracusan experience gives examples of the eventual success of this tactic. Later, Persian funding allowed the Spartans to hire experienced crews and to train others on a long-term basis. This brought parity in the abilities of the oarsmen on each side and success went to the commander who planned the best action.

From the start the other Peloponnesians relied heavily on Corinthian expertise. The other sea power of any consequence, Syracuse, did not assist until its forced involvement much later proved pivotal. Syracusan success during the siege eventually stemmed from the tactic of sustaining pressure on the Athenian fleet until it became nearly unseaworthy, of denying it room for easy manoeuvre and of strengthening the hulls and modifying the prows of their own ships (VII. 62. 3), after the manner of a recent Corinthian technological experiment. This permitted the tactic of ramming any part of the opposing vessel including its prow. Banks of oars thus became even more vulnerable, much to the discomfort of the

3

oarsmen. The result was to create what was effectively a land battle at sea, with the redesigned Syracusan prows causing damage also to the exposed position of the highest Athenian bank of rowers. Without a complete and balanced line of *thranitai* an Athenian trireme would be helpless.

One may question why the Athenians did not adopt this structural change for its own fleets but it can be argued that so long as they engaged in open waters and did not allow themselves to be denied space, the superior manoeuvrability of their vessels stood them in good stead. In the last phase of the war, the so-called Dekelian War, when the greater part of hostilities took part in the Eastern Aegean, speed of developments may have forced technological considerations into the background. What is observable, however, is the number of engagements that took place very close to shore, often with the involvement of land forces in support. This last factor suited the Peloponnesians well and, as will be seen, the last battle of the war was to all intents and purposes won on land.

Experienced pilots were critical to the success of any navy and at the start of the war Athens had an abundance. However, as discontent within her empire erupted from time to time, the Peloponnesians were able to use those of the disaffected possessing these skills who came over to their side. Such was the case of the Samian exiles at Anaia who supplied much needed pilots to the Peloponnesian navy early in the struggle (IV. 75. 1).

As remarked earlier, with Persian finance supporting the Spartans in the last years of the war, it became much easier to retain and recruit experienced crews.

Prior to battle, screens were hoisted to the sides of vessels as a protection against missiles (Xen. *Hell.* II. 1. 22.).[2] At close quarters grappling hooks were thrown onto the opposing vessels if capture was a probability. To combat this, animal hides were stretched over the prow and the upper parts of the hull so that any such device might slip away. This was to be the preparation for all the Athenian ships in the last naval action of the Siege of Syracuse (Thuc.VII. 15. 3).

Timing and speed were of utmost importance in a ramming attack, for it was one thing to disable the enemy and reverse the oar stroke to be able to back water and disengage, and quite another to find the prow fixed in the target vessel. To further avoid the possibility of entanglement the bronze of the prow did not come to a point but had a spread facia.

Damaged vessels were more often than not taken by the victors for repair, refitting and reuse. The capture of undamaged ships i.e., by an action onshore was the ultimate bonus in any victory as it augmented the fleet of the victor and diminished that of the vanquished.

In the mid-5th century there were three significant naval powers in Greece: Athens, by far the most efficient and strongest, Corinth and Kerkyra. All three could put to sea with a fleet well in excess of 100 vessels. Farther west Syracuse in Sicily was emerging as a potent force but needed the experience of the dangers of the later Athenian expedition against her to propel this state to the first rank of naval powers.

Although not within the confines of the Peloponnesian War itself the Battle of Sybota is described in reasonable detail by Thucydides and is cited as being one of the causes from which that conflict sprang. This battle between Kerkyra and the Corinthians in 433 BC, a mere two years before the official outbreak of hostilities, serves to show the unsophisticated tactics employed at this time by non-Athenian fleets.

A fleet of 150 gathered for the attack on Kerkyra. The armada was made up of ninety vessels from Corinth, twelve from Megara,[3] ten from the island of Leukas,[4] ten from Elis, twenty-seven from Ambrakia[5] with one from the city of the Anaktorians. Xenokleides is named among the commanders as being the senior of five Corinthian admirals. The other contributors to the allied expedition had their own, unnamed commanders but one must assume that Xenokleides was admiral in chief. From Leukas the allied fleet sailed north and across to the mainland making a base camp not far from Ephyre, south of the Cheimerion promontory. It is worthy of attention that in almost all sea operations landfall was never far away. It is also useful to look at the maps of the area in conjunction with the following description.

There is a marginal problem with the exact location of the islands of Sybota. Those identified as such today lie almost twenty miles south of modern Igoumenitsa. However, the Thyamis river which flows to the sea a little north of Igoumenitsa has, over the centuries, deposited silt which, by the 19th century, had become a marshy plain and advanced the coastline considerably.[6] Subsequent control of the waters has led to an improving arable area. Within that plain are some hills near the present coastline which would have been islands in the 5th century BC. These are sometimes referred to as the original Sybota islands and their position is almost directly across from the city of Kerkyra and in good alignment with Cape Leukimne where the Kerkyrans stationed their supporting land forces together with 1,000 allied Zakynthian hoplites. There is little to choose between the two positions in terms of a defence of Kerkyra. The location most favoured is that of the islands as they are today. Perhaps the most persuasive support for this view is not only Thucydides' description of the anchorage for the Corinthians (I. 46. 4), but the presence of a settlement near the present Sybotan islands which also carries the name Sybota. As some Greek place names have an incredible longevity the continued presence of a place carrying that name in the area almost wholly convinces. One cannot be sure, however, that the name persisted through time from its first mention to the present day and, in this case as in others, no proof exists.

To the action itself. On learning of the location of the Corinthian fleet the Kerkyrans set sail with 110 ships and made their base on one of the

Sybota islands. With them went ten Athenian vessels under the command of Lakedaimonios which had been sent to Kerkyra in accordance with the defensive alliance made that year. Lakedaimonios had specific instructions not to engage with any Corinthian ship unless Kerkyra itself was in danger. In merely posing a threat the Athenians sought to sustain the peace treaty with the Peloponnesians. The battle which followed was the greatest in terms of vessels ever to have taken part in an action between Greeks up to that time.

The Corinthians set out from their first camp with three days' provisions and sailed north during darkness, presumably supported by a parallel advance on land by their mainland allies which Thucydides described as having gathered in force (I. 47. 3). At dawn both sides sighted each other and came into battle line. The Corinthians had their allies on their right wing and part of the centre while they themselves made up the remainder of the line out to the left wing. The Kerkyrans drew their fleet up in three sections each under one of their three commanders, Mikiades, Aisimides and Euryvatos, the right wing having the Athenian contingent at its extreme point.

At this juncture in the description Thucydides points to the crudity of the tactics employed on both sides:

> ...they joined battle and fought, both having many hoplites on the decks as well as many archers and javelin men, for they were still equipped rather rudely in the ancient fashion. And so the sea-fight was hotly contested, not so much by reason of the skill displayed as because it was more like a battle on land...still more because they trusted for victory to hoplites on the decks, who stood and fought while the ships remained motionless...they fought with fury and brute strength rather than with skill. (I. 49.1–3)

In the early part of the battle the Athenians did not engage but threatened support for any point where the Kerkyrans were being worsted. The allied right wing of the Corinthian fleet was routed and pursued by twenty vessels to the mainland which then sailed on to destroy the Corinthian camp. The mainland allies of the Corinthians had moved to the north in conjunction with the fleet to Sybota and were not therefore present to defend the camp. On the other wing, however, victory went to the Corinthians and it was when the Kerkyrans were in flight that Athenian ships took a positive and active part in covering their retreat. Still unaware of the defeat of their own right wing, some of the victorious Corinthians of the centre and left, rather than taking the disabled ships of the enemy in tow, committed the atrocity of killing those men who were now in the water. Usual practice would have been to take them prisoner. In indulging themselves in this carnage these Corinthians also accidentally killed those men they came upon from their own defeated right wing. In total, more than 1,000 men were taken prisoner. The Kerkyrans lost seventy ships and the Corinthians thirty.

With the Kerkyrans pursued to the shore, the Corinthians collected the damaged ships of both sides together with their own dead and came to anchorage at Sybota, a harbour on the mainland. From the evidence it seems highly likely that the Kerkyrans had been chased back to their own island north of Cape Leukimne, if not to the environs of Kerkyra itself. This is supported by the fact that when their fleet took to sea once more in response to the second intended attack by the Corinthians they took with them the ships which had not taken part in the first engagement

The Kerkyrans were surprised that, just before the onset, the Corinthians started to back water. They had done so on sighting a twenty-strong squadron of Athenian ships which had been sent as a reinforcement to their original ten. The exact number was not known by the Corinthians and they may have assumed that the fleet was much larger. The Kerkyrans did not pursue even when they became aware of the approaching Athenians for it is apparent that they too did not recognise the identity of the fleet. Indeed, later that night when the Athenian ships sailed into the Kerkyran base at Leukimne, the Kerkyrans were initially alarmed and thought that an attack was being made against them.

The following day all seaworthy vessels set out together with the thirty Athenian ships and made for the Corinthinian anchorage at Sybota. The Corinthian fleet organised in line in open water but obviously had no intention of engaging if it could be avoided, hampered as it was by the necessity of guarding prisoners. In choosing their anchorage the Corinthians had overlooked the need to ensure a ready supply of timber for repairs and so they resorted to diplomacy. Sending a small negotiating party across to the Athenians the Corinthians accused them of intent to break the treaty between Athens and the Peloponnesians. The Athenians gave answer that, far from breaking that treaty, they were standing by their defensive alliance with the Kerkyrans. They added that so long as the Corinthians made no attack against those allies they were free to go unhindered.

Those Corinthians who were sent to negotiate with the Athenians did not carry the emblem of a herald. To have done so would have been to acknowledge that a state of war existed between the two city states: this despite the fact that fighting had already taken place between the two, thus breaching the treaty.

> ...for they were afraid that the Athenians would consider that the treaty was broken, since they had come to blows, and would not let them sail away. (I. 52. 3)

Thereafter the Corinthians set up a trophy at mainland Sybota for their victory. After they had departed, the Kerkyrans set up their trophy on one of the Sybotan islands because of the Corinthian retreat near nightfall and their refusal to come to battle on the following day. The Corinthians had left the area of action in the hands of the Kerkyrans. They too were able to retrieve their dead.

In essence the entire proceedings had lacked imagination. Manoeuvres were minimal. Other than coming into line for the battle and in pursuit, the action had been stationary. The number of hoplites and light-armed combatants involved on both sides was more akin to a land battle. It is clear that enmeshed within the melee the orders of commanders on both sides would have been lost in the noise, even if any were given. It is likely that each ship's captain or pilot acted on his own initiative.

The only question which unfortunately will not be resolved from the description of Sybota is the actual activity of the ten Athenian ships at the extreme end of the Kerkyran right wing. While all else was stationary these vessels were mobile. Thucydides comments: 'The Attic ships, if they saw the Kerkyrans pressed at any point, came up and kept the enemy in awe' (I. 49. 4); and later:

> But the moment the Athenians saw that the Kerkyrans were being hard pressed, they began to help them more unreservedly, and though they at first refrained from actually attacking an enemy ship, yet when it was conspicuously clear that they were being put to flight and the Corinthians were close in pursuit, then at length every man put his hand to work, and fine distinctions were no longer made; matters had come to such a pass that Corinthians and Athenians of necessity had to attack one another. (I. 49. 7)

Why were the Corinthians 'in awe'? Detail of Athenian movements and some indication of the manpower aboard the Athenian ships given would have been helpful. Given their orders to refrain from direct engagement it is unlikely that they carried as many men as their allies. Of significance is that even when they did come directly into action none of their ships appears to have suffered damage. Were any of the Corinthian losses the result of an Athenian attack? Rowing power and speed of manoeuvrability would have been the Athenian trump cards.

Some of the possible answers concerning manoeuvres will be answered in the next section. It is highly unlikely that the passage of four years would have brought about significant changes in the Athenian approach to naval warfare.

The first sea operations of the Athenians after the outbreak of war were largely concerned with ravaging the coast of the Peloponnese and ensuring the security of Euboia. The latter was important to them as a source of food supplies. Thirty ships were dispatched to raid the coast of Opuntian Lokris which lies opposite Euboia. Thronion, just north of

8

modern Karmena Vourla, was captured and later a naval base was established farther south at Atalante. To consolidate security further Athens expelled the population of the island of Aigina lying as it does strategically between the Peloponnese and Attika. Thereafter, the Spartans settled them at Thyrea. Naval activity also occurred around Kephallenia and Leukas but the most telling of their early moves was made during the winter of 430–429 BC.

Phormio, who had in the previous summer assisted the Akarnanians in a local dispute, was sent by Athens with a small fleet of twenty ships to Naupaktos. To sail round the Peloponnese during this season would not necessarily have been safe or comfortable. Weather conditions would have been variable and any landfall on enemy territory would have to have been carefully chosen. It may well be that Phormio during his earlier campaign of the summer had reached the opinion that a permanent naval station at Naupaktos would cause discomfort to the enemy and had persuaded Perikles and others of the Assembly to his viewpoint. The Athenians had settled some Messenians there c.460 BC, after they were permitted to leave Ithome by the Spartans (see Appendix 1). Their presence at this location was to prove extremely helpful to Athens. The purpose behind Phormio's establishment of this base became all too apparent. Situated near the narrows of the entry to the Gulf of Corinth his presence there was a constant threat to any Peloponnesian fleet seeking to reach the open sea. With this fleet on station Corinth was faced with an almost insuperable problem. Dragging ships over the *diolchos*[7] at the Isthmus was out of the question because of Athenian dominance of the Saronic Gulf and the waters around the eastern Peloponnese. Now its other exit to the open sea posed a problem. Further, any Peloponnesian fleet seeking to send men to the northwest or to Kerkyra had to contend with this Athenian presence.

Thus, when in 429 BC the Ambrakiots, together with their allies to the north, requested support from Sparta in their attempt to subdue Arkanania, this seemed an opportune moment to counter Athenian influence in the area. Knemos, who in 430 BC had led an unsuccessful attempt to capture the island of Zakynthos with 100 allied ships and 1,000 Lakedaimonian hoplites, was still admiral. It must be understood that a commander could by virtue of his office operate both on land and sea should the occasion arise.

The Ambrakiots correctly surmised that a combined attack by both land and sea would lead to a division of Arkananian manpower thus rendering the operation much easier. Thereafter, if successful, the subjugation of Kephallenia and Zakynthos would have easily followed. This in turn would have made it more difficult for the Athenians to circumnavigate the whole of the Peloponnese and put at risk any foray which might be attempted from Naupaktos. In the longer term success in Arkanania would have led to great discomfort for the Athenian naval station at

Naupaktos. Kerkyra, with its considerable fleet, would have been isolated and threatened.

Knemos managed to evade Phormio's squadron and cross over the seaway outside the Corinthian Gulf with his 1,000 hoplites on a few ships acting as troop transports.[8] Although Thucydides does not mention the landfall it is likely to have been in Ambrakiot territory, perhaps even at the landward end of the Ambrakiot Gulf, so that an easy junction could be made with the allies. Wherever that meeting point happened to be Knemos received considerable reinforcements in the form of what Thucydides describes first as Hellenic forces, Ambrakiots, Leukadians and Anaktorians and 'barbarian' allies consisting of Chaonians, Thesprotians, Molossians, Atintanians, Paravaians, and Orestians (I. 80. 5–6).

An interesting addition to this army would have been the 1,000 Makedonian troops from Perdikkas, had they arrived on time: interesting, because the king had sent them on this mission without Athens knowing of the matter. Athens had obliged Perdikkas to enter into alliance with her in 432 BC (I. 61. 3), and was to have his help against the Chalkidians in the following year (II. 29. 6).

At the time of Knemos' departure from the Peloponnese orders had been sent to the Corinthians, Sikyonians and presumably the Megarans to send the allied fleet to join those vessels from Leukas, Anaktorion and Ambrakia which had stationed themselves at Leukas in anticipation of their arrival. Assuming that this fleet was well on its way or for want of dependable intelligence on its position and readiness, Knemos started his advance southward. This was much too precipitate and negated the basis of the original plan of a co-ordinated land and sea operation. He should have waited until all components were in place and at the ready. He may well have felt unduly confident because of the army of several thousand men which he then had at his disposal. Had he waited the force would have been augmented by the additional 1,000 Makedonian late arrivals.

Advancing quickly without encountering opposition the Spartan-led forces arrived in the environs of Stratos, the capital of Akarnania and its largest city. The latter part of the advance would have been very easy for the army over an area which was, and still is, rolling lowland. That advance had been unopposed. The Akarnanians, being relatively unthreatened on their coast, had sought to avoid any land engagement by remaining to defend their various settlements. Their forces had not been split as originally envisaged.

Nevertheless, recognising that their predicament could worsen should additional ships arrive they sent to Phormio at Naupaktos to request his help. This was a reasonable request to make of an ally but it placed Phormio in a predicament. To have left his station and sailed to the northwest would have put Naupaktos at risk of being taken. His decision to stay where he was proved to be correct. Nothing would have been achieved

10

by sailing to the Arkananian coastline where little or no danger seemed to threaten from the small enemy fleet already in those waters; and to have taken a land force northward would have denuded Naupaktos of its defenders. It was far better to stay where he was in the hope of hampering the large reinforcing fleet.

Back in Akarnania, Knemos, notionally commander-in-chief, was to have unforeseen problems. Advancing toward Stratos in three columns his plan was to make camp near the city and attempt a negotiated surrender prior to any attack on its fortifications. With the left column comprising Ambrakiots and Peloponnesians under Knemos and the right of Leukadians and Anaktorians, Thucydides is specific in describing the centre column as being non-Hellenic or barbarian and led by the Chaionians.[9] Thucydides describes the advance of the wings as being well ordered (II. 81. 4), and mentions a little earlier that there were occasions when each column was not in sight of the others. The Chaionians in their eagerness to prove themselves doughty warriors hurried forward and, without even attempting to encamp, made an impetuous attack on the city. The Stratians had read their intention well and had manned ambuscades on the periphery of the city so that the barbarians were caught between those placed in ambush attacking their flank and rear and a frontal attack from the city itself.[10] The barbarians suffered considerable losses and took flight. They were eventually taken into the lines of the other two allied columns which came together into a single encampment.

Knemos was therefore presented with another setback. The Stratians were unlikely to enter into any negotiations on the subject of surrender after their success. He was also probably aware that the fleet from Corinth had not appeared and that soon he would be faced by a force of Akarnanians coming to the relief of Stratos. The Stratians, being renowned slingers, kept up such a barrage of missiles that it was necessary to remain in armour. When night fell Knemos withdrew about six miles to the west to the Anapos River from where, the following day, he took up his dead under a truce, thereby conceding defeat. Thereafter, he led the army south to the territory of the Oiniadai where the allies dispersed to their own territories.

In what should have been a land and sea operation the débâcle at Stratos was played out probably at about the same time that the fleet from Corinth came into contact with Phormio (II. 83. 1). Knemos' impetuosity and lack of full control of those forces under his command had led him to evacuate them from the field of operations, threatened as he was by a population which had nothing to fear from any serious diversionary attacks from its coastline. He had not waited until all facets of the overall plan were in place. Whether he neglected to do so was because he assumed that the fleet would arrive in due course, or because he did not wholly agree with the plan, which may have been made by others, can only be guessed at.

He may well have been swept along by the enthusiasm of his allies who had come in such considerable numbers. Whatever the case, he had lost his opportunity and had to abandon any idea of taking Stratos by assault, given that the Akarnanians were mobilising to his rear.

And what of the Corinthian fleet? There can be no doubt that its preparation was expedited but such was Knemos'speed of movement that he had made no allowance for the necessary time for its assemblage, outfitting and provisioning. Having already commanded a fleet, Knemos, unlike other Spartan commanders, had little excuse for this omission.

Thucydides makes it clear that the Corinthian and allied fleet was not prepared for action at sea nor did they envisage an attack from the twenty Athenian vessels stationed at Naupaktos (II. 83. 3). They had a fleet of forty-seven ships but as Thucydides states '...were not equipped for fighting at sea, but rather for operations on land.' So these were troop transports whose role was to take forces for a coastal attack on Akarnania. These vessels would not have been suitable for anything other than a defensive sea action unless it was fought in restricted waters where lack of space for manoeuvre would have made conditions similar to a land battle.

To have anticipated opposition from the small Athenian squadron at Naupaktos would have made the Corinthians a little more circumspect in their preparations, but this was still early in the war and the Peloponnesians had not yet fully appreciated the skills and seamanship of the Athenians. They presumed that the great disparity in the number of ships available to each side would deter the Athenians from any action.

Thucydides, himself a naval commander, is fully conversant with the niceties of tactical manoeuvres at sea and his description of the action hereafter is succinct. Phormio kept the fleet under observation as it sailed along the northern coast of the Peloponnese. Thucydides here indicates what was to be the tactical basis of any sea operation by the Athenians throughout the entire war and which proved their eventual downfall, 'preferring to attack them in open water'(II. 83. 2).

So long as the Peloponnesians were near the southern coastline of the Corinthian Gulf they were relatively safe and could make landfall quickly. They were shadowed by the Athenian ships which coasted along the northern shore, both fleets being in sight of each other. Having passed through the narrows between Rhion and Antirhion, a distance of perhaps three-quarters of a mile and where a regular ferry service operates today, the Peloponnesians continued to hug the coastline until they came to Patras. From there they attempted to sail north towards the Akarnanian coast but were dissuaded from doing so by the sight of the Athenians approaching from the direction of Chalkis and the Evenos River.

In view of this the Peloponnesians decided to make their move by night and sought secure anchorage. Although Thucydides makes no mention of it there must have been a moon that night, otherwise what followed would have been nigh impossible to accomplish.

It goes without saying that Phormio would have maintained observation of the enemy fleet so that their attempt to bypass his fleet was detected. It is also likely that Phormio allowed the Peloponnesian fleet to make some progress before making his move so that the following action could take place at the midpoint of the much broader waterway.

As a defensive measure the Peloponnesians made a wide circle of their vessels with the beaks of their prows pointing outwards and their sterns towards the centre of the circle. They were sufficiently close to deny the Athenians the opportunity to sail through their line and ram the stern or side of any ship in the manoeuvre known as the *diekplous*.
Within the circle the lighter boats and five of the quickest vessels were stationed to give support at any point of the circumference which might be attacked.

This form of defence could well have worked in a more sheltered location. The Corinthian commanders Machaon, Isokrates and Agartharchidas had little alternative given the composition of their fleet; just as in convoys of the Second World War, all were obliged to move at the pace of the slowest vessel.

Let there be no doubt that within the Peloponnesian fleet there were fine seamen. The Corinthians in particular had an impressive mercantile record and it was only in terms of aggressive tactics that they were less well versed than the Athenians. To adopt and maintain the circular form of defence required skill and control. To sustain it as they did for some time demonstrates the skill of trimming each individual vessel's position and the oar control necessary. The size of the circle for such a defence is critical. Discounting the 'light boats which accompanied them' (II. 83. 5), possibly as supply ships and subtracting from the fleet the five 'swiftest ships', which were within the circle, the circumference was made up of forty-two vessels. The nature of the formation required the sterns to be closer one to another than the prows. Sea room for each stern would, of necessity, have had to be enough to employ the oars from time to time to maintain position.

The tapering towards the stern starts very close to its rear and therefore it is better to take the likely measurements of a ship's width (16 feet) together with the likely distance of the projecting oars on either side (13 x 2 = 26 feet) which gives a total of 42 feet. Obviously there needs to be water between each vessel so that the oars do not foul each other. It is unlikely that an additional distance of less than 15 to 20 feet on each side could be countenanced even by the most skilled sailors. Thus with each ship and its oars taking up 42 feet and a distance of clear water between each being 20 feet, the circumference of the inner circle made by the sterns would have been 2,604 feet or 868 yards. With a vessel length of 120 feet the outer circumference at the prow would have been approximately 1,120 yards. The distance between prows would have been almost 80 feet but still insufficient for any attack to be safely carried out. While the formation held there was little an antagonist could do other than to threaten. The calculations here give the closest operable distances between vessels and were most likely to have been more generous in reality, giving an even greater circumference to the formation.

Phormio deployed his twenty ships in column and had them sail continuously around the circle, threatening attack. This caused the circle to contract until sea-room between vessels became scanty, evidence that the psychological aggression was working, particularly at night. The measurements given above are likely to have been nearest those of the contracted formation. The relentless circling of the Athenian ships would have been not unlike that of American Indians attacking a circled wagon train and probably involved exchanges of missiles. It must have gone on for some considerable time and the reason for it became apparent in full daylight, the action having started in the half-light preceding dawn. Here we have a splendid example of a commander's knowledge of local conditions being used to advantage. Phormio knew that a wind regularly rose at this time and assumed that it would disrupt the Peloponnesian formation, thus making it easier for an effective attack to be launched. With the coming of the breeze and the consequent heavier seas the now restricted Peloponnesians began to foul each other. Amid the confusion and shouting no orders could be heard, as each of the Peloponnesian ships attempted to keep clear of, or disentangle itself from, its neighbour. This was the moment when Phormio signalled the attack and the ramming of exposed Peloponnesian vessels began. Several ships were either sunk or disabled, including one command vessel. The Peloponnesians made no attempt at resistance but fled for safe haven to Patras and Dyme, twelve of their number being overtaken and captured by the pursuing Athenians. Most of the crews were taken from those Peloponnesian ships which had become casualties of the Athenian attack. They were taken first to Molykreon where a trophy was set up nearby at Rhion[11] and then on to Naupaktos.

Following the departure of the Athenian fleet, those surviving Peloponnesian vessels at Patras and Dyme made for the Elean naval docks at Kyllene where they were joined by Knemos with his ships and those of the Leukadians.

It would appear to have been an excellent victory for the Athenians but as has been more than hinted at in the description of the battle, it was not an encounter between equals. At first sight the disparity in numbers of vessels in each fleet would seem to give the Peloponnesians an overwhelming advantage. However, twenty seaborne missiles, which to all intents and purposes the Athenian triremes were, greatly outweighed the aggressive capabilities of the Peloponnesian fleet in open seas. The only possibility of victory for the latter would have come had it trapped the Athenian fleet near the coast, denying it sea-room to exploit its superior seamanship and converting the engagement into a land battle across decks. Nonetheless, Phormio's tactics and knowledge of local conditions had produced the desired result; and even better was to come.

News of the engagement led the Spartans to send three commissioners or advisers to Knemos with orders to prepare for another sea battle. Thucydides neatly sums up the Spartan attitude:

> For the issue of the recent battle seemed to them utterly incomprehensible, especially since this was their *first attempt* at a sea fight, and they could not believe that their fleet was so greatly inferior, but thought that there had been cowardice somewhere, failing to take account of the long experience of the Athenians compared with their own brief practice. (Author's italics, II. 85. 2)

It would have been obvious to them that the naval station at Naupaktos was a much bigger threat than had at first been anticipated.

Phormio was a realist and knew that there would very likely be another test of strength that would prove more difficult than the first. He sent with his report of the victory a request that Athens send him reinforcements. The response of the Athenians is still impossible to understand and suggests that the majority did not yet fully appreciate the strategic significance of their new naval station.[12] They did indeed dispatch a further twenty ships but sent them first on a mission to Crete. Needless to say this reinforcement did not arrive in time for the anticipated naval action.

The three Spartans sent to Knemos by the home government were Timokrates, Brasidas and Lykophron.[13] Their orders were to ensure that adequate preparations were made for another sea battle. They in turn sent to their allies for further ships to enlarge the fleet and for supporting land forces to meet with the fleet at Panormos, a place which commanded a view both of Naupaktos and Anthirion on the opposite shore. Phormio took up a position with his fleet near the latter, a move mirrored by the Peloponnesian fleet which then sailed a short distance west to Rion on the Achaean coast.

As has already been noted, the distance between the two is about three-quarters of a mile and constitutes the narrowest part of the Corinthian Gulf, as well as being its outlet to open waters to the west. Thucydides remarks (II. 86. 5) that both fleets spent six or seven days practising manoeuvres and presumably improving rowing standards. He follows this by pointing to the desire of the Peloponnesians to keep the coming action within a restricted area rather than undertake it in more open waters which would favour the Athenians. The Peloponnesian commanders came to the decision to seek an engagement largely on the grounds of anticipated Athenian reinforcements. Sufficient time had passed for such intelligence to have reached them.

It is notable that immediately prior to the exhortatory speech to their men only Knemos and Brasidas are mentioned from among the Peloponnesian commanders. The first part of the speech relates to the previous sea fight. It may reflect the views of the Corinthian commanders who had been present on that occasion or may have been Knemos' thoughts on the matter. But the latter part has a resonance of some of the later speeches of Brasidas. He, more than any other Spartan commander, is credited with a gift for words unusual among his fellows. Unless this is an unlikely fiction by Thucydides it would appear to be an amalgam of the words of the two commanders. This in itself was unusual in that Spartan commanders on land, Brasidas being the exception, rarely indulged in such addresses.

Phormio's twenty ships faced the seventy-seven of the enemy and it was extremely important for him to sustain the morale of his men facing such odds. His speech stressed the superior abilities and earlier success of his men. Later, he clearly defines his aims and what he expects of his men.

> As for this contest, I will not risk it in the gulf if I can help it, nor will I sail into the gulf. For I am aware that a confined space is not an advantage to a fleet of a few ships with better sailors and experienced crews, when it is opposed to a large number of ships which are badly managed. For one cannot charge properly upon an enemy ship to ram her side, through not having a clear view of her a long way off, nor can one retire at need when hard pressed; and there is no chance for such manoeuvres as breaking through the line or whirling round to ram, though these are precisely the proper tactics of fast sailing ships, but the sea-fight would have turned into a land-battle, and in that case it is the larger fleet that wins...As for you, keep good order, stay near your ships, give heed sharply to the word of command, especially since the two fleets are at watch so near one another; and when it comes to action, give regard to discipline and silence. (II. 89. 8-9)

The initiative lay with the Peloponnesian commanders. Phormio was not in any position to instigate an attack. With his twenty vessels his posture had to remain defensive until such opportunity to damage the opposition presented itself, possibly from their errors. On the other hand the Peloponnesians could not afford to wait too long and Phormio's understandable reluctance to make any move led them to the following plan.

In a feint which suggested that the Peloponnesians were going to make an attack on Naupaktos, their fleet sailed east along the coast moving farther within the restrictions of the Corinthian Gulf. The formation of their fleet is worthy of note. Having anchored the night before their move in a line four deep, bows facing seaward, they set out at dawn. The whole fleet moved away from the shore, then, with sufficient water, all turned to the right and proceeded now four abreast along the coast. Phormio could not afford not to give protection to Naupaktos and he was forced to respond by moving his fleet formed in single file in the same direction along the opposite shore, supported by his Messenian land forces. Thus far the Peloponnesians had retained the initiative and drawn the Athenians into more restricted waters. It must be remembered that none of the Spartan commanders, including Knemos, had been part of the preceding action of their fleet and the orderliness of their formation is reminiscent of their disciplined approach to warfare on land.

This disciplined approach to the manoeuvre of numbers was evident in the sudden turn to the left at a given signal from the Peloponnesian command which brought the fleet into formation for an attack on the Athenian fleet. Thucydides (II. 90. 4) is clear that the Peloponnesian fleet came 'into line' and this might not have been four deep. Each group of four could have distanced themselves from the next as they moved eastwards. This would give sufficient sea-room for a wheeling manoeuvre of each group of four to be made so that an attack in line-abreast could be quickly made. An alternative analysis of this manoeuvre could be as follows. The left turn brought the Peloponnesian fleet into a position for launching an attack on the Athenians with a battle line four deep, each ship within the groups of four being abeam one from the other. This would have given a defence against any Athenian attempt to effect a *diekplous*, the ships behind the front line being a threat to any such attempt. The line would have been shortened and would have presented a front slightly shorter than that of the Athenians, e.g., seventy-seven divided by four. Had this been the case it may have accounted for the fact that eleven of the Athenian ships managed to evade the attack and make for Naupaktos. Given the superior seamanship of the Athenians at this time, such an 'escape' could be envisaged. On balance, the Peloponnesian fleet must have come into line to a depth of four vessels to preserve their safety from a counter-attack.

The intention was to cut off the opposing vessels and the initial shock to the Athenians must have been considerable. If any fault can be levelled at the Peloponnesians it must be in the fact that eleven Athenian ships escaped the onslaught and ten reached Naupaktos, where they formed up with their prows defensively facing seaward. They had been able to do so at the time of the turning movement of the Peloponnesians and this suggests an insufficient overlap, the Athenian crews, being better rowers, having gradually pulled ahead of the Peloponnesian fleet.

Those nine Athenian ships which had either been forced onshore or crippled had all their men killed who were unable to reach the safety of land.

Captured and disabled ships were taken into tow, one of which still had its full complement of men. However, the Messenian land forces recaptured some of the ships by boarding them and fighting from the decks.

Those Athenian ships which eventually reached Naupaktos had been chased by twenty of the Peloponnesian vessels. The single Athenian vessel which had not yet reached Naupaktos was being hotly pursued by a Leukadian ship which had pulled well ahead of the main body in its chase. This was commanded by the Spartan Timokrates who probably commanded the right wing of the Peloponnesian fleet. He was now being a little over-zealous in leading from the front and might well have been lured into a trap. It is unlikely that the Athenians at this stage in hostilities could be outrowed. Their single ship may well have assumed the role of a rearguard while its fellows reached refuge, thereby enticing the foremost of the opposing vessels sufficiently far from its allies that a counter-attack could be made. As both boats neared Naupaktos the Athenian vessel sailed around a merchant ship which lay at anchor and rammed Timokrates' vessel amidships. That it was able to do this implies a quickening of the stroke rate near the time when it would have been obscured by the merchantman. The remainder of the pursuers, now described by Thucydides as being in no disciplined order, were completely thrown into confusion. Their dismay increases the probability that Timokrates was indeed their commander. Far from continuing their enthusiastic singing of victory paeans which they had struck up during the pursuit, this section of the Peloponnesian fleet was in total disarray. Some ships came to a stop as their rowers arrested their forward movement, intending to await the other section of the fleet, while others continued onward, coming to grief on rocks near the shore.

A disciplined attack by the Athenians created mayhem and after a short but futile resistance the Peloponnesians made for the safety of Panormos. In the confusion the initially victorious vessels of the Peloponnesian left and centre must have been caught up in the pursuit. Thucydides reports that not only were six ships captured but that the Athenians retook those of their own vessels which were being towed away as trophies of the first part of the action.

The immediate aftermath saw the discovery of the body of Timokrates in the harbour of Naupaktos. At the loss of his ship he had committed suicide. Both sides set up trophies on opposite shores each denoting their success in the varying stages of the battle, but it must have been obvious to both that the Athenians had once again triumphed. The reason that the Peloponnesian fleet sailed from Panormos to Corinth by night was because they were concerned that Athenian reinforcements might arrive.

This action was not one which demonstrated Phormio's tactical competence. He had been forced against his will to move within the confines of the Corinthian Gulf for the protection of Naupaktos. What does reflect to his credit is the belief he instilled into his men that they were indeed superior at sea. Sustaining morale in the extremes of adversity and keeping their skills honed is a gift few commanders possessed.

One would have thought that the Spartans would have entrusted future sea operations to those commanders such as Knemos, Brasidas and Lykophron who had some experience. However, responsibility for defeat had to be apportioned and the commander-in-chief Knemos appears to have been the target, for he is never mentioned again in Thucydides' narrative.

A temerity is discernible hereafter in Spartan naval operations. Phormio's successes with his few ships had done an immeasurable service to Athens and had severely dented the confidence of Sparta. It was reluctant to attempt confrontation at sea and this left that element almost wholly in the control of its adversary. Only when the revolt of Mytilene and all cities on Lesbos except Methymna provoked a major problem for the Athenians did they make a positive move. This occurred in the following year of 428 BC, when Mytilenean ambassadors arrived to persuade the Spartans and their allies to send assistance to them.[14]

To keep the Peloponnesians preoccupied Athens had sent thirty ships to make raids around the Peloponnese under the command of Asopios, the son of Phormio, as he made his way to Naupaktos taking with him twelve of the fleet. From there he made an attempt on the territory of Oiniadai, supported by the Akarnanians. He was not successful in the enterprise and, having dismissed his land forces, made a raid on Nerikos on the island of Leukos. There he evidently failed again and had to acknowledge defeat by being obliged to recover his dead under truce.

This must have been heartening for the Peloponnesians and they entered into an alliance with the Mytilenians knowing that by doing so they could well have a large and effective fleet at their disposal for use in the Aegean. Orders were sent out to all allies to gather with two-thirds of available forces at the Isthmus. In this endeavour the Spartans were the speediest, which is understandable as they had others to gather in the harvest on their behalf. Some of their allies proved tardy. Thucydides states at III. 15. 2, '...they were busy gathering in their harvest and were in no mood for campaigning'.

The Spartans wanted to launch a simultaneous land attack along with their sea operations. Finding themselves virtually alone among the alliance present at the Isthmus they set about building the transports which would carry the ships from the Corinthian Gulf over the *diolchos* to the waters on the Athenian side of the Isthmus.

The Athenians wished to dispel any idea that they were weakened at this time and manned 100 ships from all but the two richest propertied classes, the knights and the *Pentakosiomedimni*. With these they made raids around the Peloponnese to such effect that the Spartans returned home

thinking that the Lesbian ambassadors had misled them. With the immediate danger receding, the Athenian fleet returned home.

The Spartans would now be aware of the expenditure necessary to
maintain fleets at sea. The drain on the Athenian treasury was considerable. It cost one talent each month to keep a warship at sea and during
this short period Athens had sustained 250 vessels in an aggressive posture. This, together with the toll of the plague, which had decimated the
enclosed Athenian population, proved to be a great strain.

However, with news coming from Lesbos that all was not going well for
the Athenians there, an additional 1,000 hoplites were despatched 'who
also served as rowers' (III.18. 3), a strong sign that all was not well with
Athenian finances. To expect heavy infantrymen to row themselves to the
proposed area of action was highly unusual at this time. Further, a small
fleet under the command of Lysikles was sent out to extract contributions
for the war, particularly from the littoral of Asia Minor. Inland in Karia
they were attacked and Lysikles was killed.

The Spartans had appointed Alkidas admiral in 428 BC but he was not to
set sail with the intention of helping the Mytileneans until the following year.
With forty-two ships the expedition set out from an unspecified location.
His sailing coincided with the almost annual summer invasion of Attika. A
hint here that Archidamos was in failing health is given in the report that it
was led by Kleomenes in place of the under-age joint king Pausanias. This
proved to be a more extensive invasion and could have served their fleet
well in keeping Athenian attention riveted on matters at home.

However, Alkidas, with the fleet, is described by Thucydides (III. 27. 1)
as 'loitering on the way' (ἐνεχρόνιζον) and at III. 29. 1 '...the Peloponnesians
in the forty ships, who ought to have arrived speedily at Mytilene, wasted
time (ἐνδιέτριψαν) and on the rest of the way proceeded at a leisurely speed
(σχολαῖοι).

It is one thing to be cautious, and one could argue that Alkidas ensured
that the fleet arrived safely in the operational area, but it is another to tarry
to such an extent that the purpose of the expedition was, in part, nullified. The Athenians had taken control of the island. Alkidas' subsequent
actions tell us a great deal about the man's abilities and character.

From Delos the Peloponnesian fleet moved to Mykonos and then to
Ikaros, where Alkidas heard of the fall of Mytiline which had occurred
seven days earlier. An ambivalent phrase in Thucydides at III. 29. 1 is translated in the Loeb edition as: 'They were unobserved by the Athenian home
fleet *until* they reached Delos.' An alternative to this would be: 'They
arrived at Delos unobserved by the fleet at Athens.' This carries a different meaning and accounts for the readiness of Alkidas to sail possibly via
Chios (see below) to Embaton in the territory of Erythrai on the Ionian
coast. The present author is in no doubt that Alkidas would have 'cut and
run' had the meaning expressed by the Loeb translation suggested that

his presence had been discovered. Indeed, it is difficult to be certain of the point at which Alkidas could have been sure that he had been detected.

There a certain Elean commander, Teutiaplos, proposed that the fleet should sail directly to Mytilene using the element of surprise as an advantage to mount a night attack against an Athenian force, which could well be off its guard and dispersed. This was extremely sound thinking under the circumstances, having a high probability of success. Alkidas refused to countenance such an operation and, as a substitute, some Lesbians who accompanied the fleet proposed that they take a city on the coast of Ionia or make Kyme farther north in Aeolis the target. By doing so Ionia would revolt, there being evidence that Spartan-led forces would be welcomed. The Athenians would thereby lose revenue from this source, be obliged to spend monies on the expense of a blockade, and run the risk of the Persian satrap, Pissuthnes, joining in the hostilities against them. This, too, Alkidas rejected.

Either of these two very sound proposals would have sustained the initiative. Had both been followed in sequence and been even partially successful Athens would have been placed under extreme duress. The problem was the quality of the commander-in-chief. No doubt this was the farthest he had ever been from Sparta and his insecurity shines through like a beacon. His subsequent activities are those of an unthinking, unfeeling, cowardly bully.

Retreating from his forward position at Embaton he sailed south along the coast putting in to Myonnesos where he executed 'most of the captives' he had taken. Coming next to Ephesos he was berated by exiled Samians for his execution of these men; on the grounds that he showed a strange way of freeing the Greek world by doing such things to men who were not so much enemies as coerced allies of Athens (III. 32. 2). At least Alkidas took heed of this advice and set free the remaining Chians and others held captive.

Prior to his visit to Ephesos his fleet had been sighted at Klaros by the two state triremes of Athens, the *Salaminia* and the *Paralos*. Knowing that they would inform Paches, the Athenian commander at Mytilene, of his position, he was very eager to return to the Peloponnese. Thucydides is explicit in his description of Alkidas' flight from the area (III. 33. 1). Unusually, sailing across *open* sea without any intention of touching or encamping on land, Alkidas made haste to reach safe haven. This must have been an uncomfortable voyage for those aboard but satisfactorily quick for Alkidas in his haste to avoid contact with an Athenian fleet. Paches was unable to overtake him and gave up the pursuit at Patmos. Alkidas, with his fleet wholly intact and undamaged, arrived back in the safer waters of the Peloponnese.

His failure to contest the Athenian control of Lesbos led to the summary execution in Athens of Salaithos, the Spartan who had been sent out earlier to Mytilene to reassure the citizens of the coming of the fleet and to give assistance in the defence of the city. Unease in sea operations is understandable for Spartan commanders at this time but cowardice is surprising. Alkidas was obviously proud to hold command but was too timorous to exercise it.

The Spartans appear to have been far more tolerant of the obvious shortcomings of their commanders than the Athenians and it is quite astonishing to see Alkidas retained in his position as admiral thereafter.[15] Admittedly he had Brasidas appointed as adviser and with this support there is a notable improvement. At least he did eventually come to action.

Notes

1. A modern reconstruction of an ancient trireme has been successfully carried out. Sea trials showed it to be fully capable of those manoeuvres and speeds alluded to in our sources. See J S Morrison, J F Coates and N B Rankov, *The Athenian Trireme*, Cambridge, 2000.

2. Also at Xen. *Hell.* I. 6. 19, but here the purpose of raising the screens was for disguising the purpose of the mission.

3. Megara had two main ports: Nisaia sited opposite the island of Salamis and Pegai on the Corinthian Gulf. It is likely that the Megaran ships came from the latter port although it is not impossible that if they came from Nisaia they were hauled over the *diolchos* at the Isthmus.

4. To call Leukas an island is not strictly accurate. A narrow isthmus existed in the 5th century BC which joined the 'island' to the mainland. It was across this isthmus that Peloponnesian forces took their vessels either to shorten their journey or to avoid the open sea and the likelihood of meeting an Athenian fleet (see Thuc. III. 81. 1 and IV. 8. 2). Today the area is one of marshland and sandspits through which a canal runs. This canal may have had two ancient precursors, in the time of Augustus and further back in the 7th century BC, constructed by the original Corinthian colonists. The need to keep the waterways open and free from silt suggests that by the time of the Peloponnesian War no canal was available and ships had to be taken over the short stretch of intervening land.

5. There is a numerical error in the Loeb translation which suggests the complement as being seventeen vessels rather than the twenty-seven indicated in the original ʹεπτὰ καὶ ἐίκοσι.

6. Much the same has happened on the Aegean coast between Euboia and the mainland south of Lamia. A visit to Thermopylai will give graphic illustration of how silt from inland waterways can alter a coastline. An army

would have little trouble moving over the fertile coastal plain which has been built up over the centuries since the battle.

7. A paved way running from the Gulf of Corinth across the Isthmus to the Saronic Gulf. It was used for moving ships from one seaway to the other.

8. D. Kagan, *The Archidamian War*, Cornell Univ. Press, p.108. 'The wily Phormio may have deliberately allowed the fleet of Knemos to go by in order to engage only part of the Peloponnesian force. Had he tried to stop Knemos he might have had to deal with reinforcements from Corinth and Sikyon. When at last he chose to engage the reinforcing fleet the Spartans were fighting in Akarnania.'
   Thucydides is quite explicit (II. 80. 2) that the troop transports of Knemos were *few* in number and there can be little doubt that they eluded Phormio either by stealth or by his ignorance of their sailing. The distance from Corinth, where the main fleet gathered, to the open sea at the outlet of the Gulf is at least eighty miles, whereas Phormio was relatively close to the route taken by Knemos. It unlikely that the Corinthian and allied vessels could have rowed non-stop the required distance in anything under nine to ten hours. They were essentially troop transports and not stripped down for direct naval combat. Given that Knemos did not wait for the allied fleet, and that this took a little time to assemble and equip, Phormio had ample time to deal with the *few* without endangering Naupaktos.

9. βαρβάρων, barbarians. This name was assigned to all who did not speak Greek as their native tongue.

10. Stratos is situated close to the Acheloos River and covers a considerable area spanning four ridges, which makes any approach to it uphill. The remaining courses of the 5th-century walls indicate that this had been a strongly fortified location of considerable importance.

11. Thucydides obviously means Rhion on the southern shore of the Corinthian Gulf, from where a car ferry now operates to Antirhion on the opposite coast west of Naupaktos. A toll bridge now also links the two landfalls.

12. Kagan pp. 111-113 questions the diversion of the reinforcing fleet and the reason for it. He also correctly points to the paucity of information given by Thucydides concerning its detour. At the same location he cites the scathing comments of B W Henderson in *The Great War between Athens and Sparta*, London 1927, pp 103-104, and the suggestions of A W Gomme, *A Historical Commentary on Thucydides Vol. II*, Oxford, 1956 p.221, that the diversion to Crete was in the interests of protecting trade links from piracy. Kagan then follows with a suggested solution which, though plausible in itself, does not satisfactorily explain the lack of recognition on the Athenians' part of the urgent requirements of Phormio's position.

13. It may well be that the Lykrophon mentioned here is one and the same as

the Corinthian commander who appears at IV. 43. 1 and IV. 44. 2. There is no further evidence to support this identification, so it remains doubtful. Although at II. 85. 1 Thucydides states that the Spartans sent three commissioners to the fleet, there would appear to be no reason why all should have been Spartans. With Corinth as a major ally and provider of ships it would seem sensible to have sent a Corinthian well versed in naval matters, an area in which Sparta was less knowledgeable.

14. Mytilene's plans for revolt were made known to the Athenians by some representatives or *proxenoi* of Tenedos, a small island to the north of Lesbos; this at a time when Mytilene's defensive preparations were unfinished. After an initial resistance against the Athenian fleet sent against them, the Mytileneans managed to gain a respite by asking to have their case heard in Athens. They had little hope that the protestation of innocence would be successful and therefore sent to the Peloponnesians for succour.

15. In 426 BC the Spartans founded the city of Herakleia some four miles from Thermopylai. Alkidas, the former admiral, was one of the three founding governors. The site was probably less than two miles from the sea and a short crossing to Euboia. Naval dockyards were begun at the coast and the pass of Thermopylai secured. The obvious intention was to cause problems for the Athenians by raids on Euboia and disrupt any Athenian naval activity in this area. Further, it was located strategically, in a position from where support could be given for actions in northern Greece, Makedonia and Thrace. Initially, the foundation held great promise and attracted large numbers of settlers. However, such was the harshness and mismanagement of the governors that the dockyards were not completed and plans for aggression towards the Athenians were forgotten. The foundation did not last long.

> One of the principal causes…was that the governors sent out by the Lakedaimonians themselves ruined the undertaking and reduced the population to a handful, frightening most of the settlers away by their harsh and sometimes unjust administration, so that at length their neighbours more easily prevailed over them. (III. 93. 3)

This foundation could have served the Spartans well as a base from which expeditionary forces could have been sent northwards to support or continue the activities of Brasidas in the dislocation of the north Aegean segment of the Athenian empire. To those who might suggest that the passage of such forces through Thessaly would be very difficult, the author would counter that a Spartan-led army supported by Boiotian cavalry would have succeeded in their objective and have only suffered harassment. It is therefore all the more discreditable that the Spartans enjoyed the product of Brasidas' success on their behalf without him receiving any additional support from his home state.

II

The Siege of Plataia

The eventual outbreak of war was provoked by Thebes' attack on Plataia.[1] For Thebes, an ally of Sparta and Plataia, an ally of Athens, to be in open conflict, was a breach of the Thirty Years' Peace and marked the beginning of the Peloponnesian War.

Some interesting 'civilian' tactics emerge from Thucydides' description of the early stages of the Plataian episode. He assumes his reader will understand the 'command' element in the actions of the Plataeans but at this distance in time a little additional assistance is required.

A group opposed to Plataia's continued alliance with Athens and led by Naukleides arranged to pass control of their city to Thebes. Two Theban Boeotarchs (generals), Pythangelos and Diemporos, with about 300 men were let through the gates during the night.[2] Instead of making the city secure by taking the likely opposition captive, they attempted by proclamation in the marketplace to win over the Plataians by persuasion. Initially, the Theban proposals were accepted, largely through fear and under the assumption that the number of interlopers was far greater than it was. With the realisation that the Thebans were few in number, the greater part of the populace who wished to remain in alliance with Athens sought the means to concentrate their strength. This they did by breaking through the dividing walls between houses, avoiding the need to use the streets openly, presumably finding it easy to persuade others of like mind to join them. Their first action was to place wagons in the streets to act as barricades. An attack was made just before dawn so that the Thebans would not be able to see their way clearly through unfamiliar and blockaded streets.

In the darkness and with rain falling, the Thebans, in close order, resisted the first attacks of the Plataians. However, when an obviously concerted attack was made, the Thebans broke and ran. Thucydides is specific in his description here that the noise of this attack added to the Thebans' confusion. They became thoroughly disorientated by the uproar (θορύβῳ) of their attackers on the ground together with the shrieking and loud crying (κραυγῇ καὶ ὀλολυγῇ) of the womenfolk and slaves acting as missile throwers on the rooftops.[3] Theban lives were lost as they sought to escape down unfamiliar byways made slippery by mud and often blocked by barricades. Thucydides makes it clear that there was no moon and that the confusion must have been total: a typical example of the difficulties encountered by armed forces when embroiled in street fighting.

The gates through which the Thebans had made their covert entry were now closed by the Plataians. A minority of those Thebans who jumped from the city walls survived the leap and a few others were lucky to escape through an unguarded gate before this avenue was also closed to them by their pursuers. Throughout the city those who had lost contact with the main body were killed throughout the city. That main body rushed through what appeared to be city gates but which were doors to a large building near the city wall and were trapped. Discussions then took place as to what should be done with the Thebans. One of the options proposed was to burn them to death. However, at this point negotiations between the adversaries led to the unconditional surrender of those Thebans who were within the building and those who had survived in the streets.

What has just been described was not just a fortunate sequence of events for the Plataians. Thucidides makes the point early in the narrative,

> ...while they were negotiating the terms they perceived that the Thebans were few in number, and thought that by an attack they might easily overpower them...So it was determined to make the attempt and they began to collect together... (II. 3. 2–3)

This small group must have quietly agreed the proposition and the means by which their party could be gathered together in secret so that detailed planning for an attack could be made. The tactical use made of the darkness, the positioning of barricades and missile throwers, the closing of the gates, the synchronisation of the tumult, all point to control and that control must be discovered within command. And whoever held that command must also have taken steps to restrain any likely support for the Thebans within the city.

But where was this command? Obviously those who negotiated with the Thebans would be the elected representatives of the community. Among them one or more annually elected generals (*strategoi*) would be present and thereafter, when the decision to resist was taken, control of the conduct of operations would be in their hands.[4]

The main body of Thebans coming in support of those who had gained entry to Plataia had been delayed by the adverse weather conditions and had difficulty in making a crossing of the Asopos river. Their late arrival was greeted by the news from the survivors of their lack of success. The Plataians sent out a herald to pre-empt the likely intention of the Thebans to take hostages from the population living outside the city walls. They were warned not to cause any injury if they wished to keep alive their captive fellow citizens and promised that if they withdrew these men would be restored to them. The Thebans were accused of impiety for making an attack in time of peace.

Here, Thucydides makes clear the Theban claim that this arrangement was made under oath by the Plataians, a point which the latter subsequently denied. Whatever the case, once the Thebans had withdrawn, keeping their side of the agreement by not causing any damage, and those outside the city walls had been safely gathered in, the Plataeans killed all 180 prisoners.

Tactically this was a foolish act. The Plataians had given up a major bargaining counter. No single person is identified as having given the order proposing the deaths of the Thebans and this leads one to wonder whether the killings followed a hasty meeting of the assembly in which a majority desire for revenge overcame the wiser counsels of a minority, or, worse still, was the product of mob violence.[5] It is therefore difficult, in the absence of evidence, to come to any firm conclusion as to why the Plataeans acted in such a precipitate way. Those who had negotiated the agreement with the Thebans, and these must surely have been the figures who had taken the leading role in organising the attack on the Thebans to regain control of the city, now found that their side of the bargain had been broken. It is unlikely that they would have been the instigators of such violence and it seems more probable that on this point their leadership was temporarily disregarded.

Two messengers had been sent to Athens. The first, immediately after the Theban entry to the city and the second, when the Plataians regained control. On the arrival of the first the Athenians arrested all Thebans currently within Attica and sent a herald to the Plataians instructing them not to take any hasty action with regard to the Theban prisoners. However, the messenger arrived at Plataia after the fateful action. An Athenian force brought supplies to the city, left a garrison and took back with them to Athens the women and children and those men deemed unsuitable for the city's defence.

As the first invasion of Attica by Sparta and her allies took place the Boiotians, having supplied the normal contingent of two-thirds of its fighting force to the army under Archidamos, laid waste the countryside of Plataia with the remainder (II. 12. 5).

The year 429 BC proved to be momentous, bringing with it the death of Perikles from the plague and seeing Archidamos leading his army not against Attica but into the territory of Plataia. The plague had raged in Athens since the previous year and this may be one of the reasons why the Peloponnesians avoided making another expedition against its territories. It was also an opportunity to try to resolve what had become an irritant, the problem of having a city with an Athenian garrison in Boiotia.

The Plataians immediately sent to Archidamos reminding him of the oaths made at the time of the Greek victory over the Persians; that the

Plataians should be permitted to be independent and never enslaved. This reminder of the Battle of Plataia (479 BC) served also to bring to mind the fact that the Thebans had fought on the side of the Persians. The exchanges that followed between the king and the representatives of the Plataians show a commander both pious in terms of sacred oaths and ready to offer the Plataians an honourable escape from their impending calamity. Archidamos' reply showed his readiness as a commander to eschew force if his ends could be achieved through diplomacy. The purpose of the war, he said, was to free those peoples who had become subject to Athens and who had sworn the same oaths as the Plataians to uphold the right to independence. He went on to suggest that they should themselves be taking part in this movement for liberation. Archidamos further suggested that it would be acceptable for the Plataians to be friends with both sides but to help neither militarily. The Plataians returned from the city after debating his proposals there with the message that they could not accede to his proposal. Their position was precarious in that their families were in Athens and they could not enter into an agreement without the permission of Athens. Further they believed that if they accepted the plan, when the army of Archidamos had left their territory, the Athenians would come and overturn the agreement or the Thebans would take the opportunity to make another attempt on the city. Archidamos countered these fears by pledging to enter into an arrangement with the Plataeans whereby they could leave their city and territory in trust to the Spartans only and live wheresoever they wished for the duration of the war. They were to make an audit of all their possessions, show the Spartans the boundaries of their lands, and enumerate their trees. All would be cared for and the land cultivated by the Spartans with an agreed rental paid until their return, at which point they would receive back all that had been held in trust for them.

This was a truly remarkable offer and was recognised as such by the Plataians who asked Archidamos for a truce and freedom from any depredations to their crops while they sent an envoy to Athens to receive permission to accept the proposals.

Whether purely from self-interest with respect to their garrison or with a genuine belief that they could give the Plataians further support, the Athenians persuaded the Plataians to stand by their alliance. After hearing the reply from the walls of the city Archidamos is reported as having

> ...stood forth calling the gods and heroes of the country to witness in the following words: "Ye gods and heroes who protect the land of Plataea, be our witnesses that we did no wrong in the beginning, but only after the Plataeans first abandoned the oath we all swore did we come against this land, where our fathers, invoking you in their prayers, conquered the Persians, and which you made auspicious for

the Hellenes to fight in, and that now also, if we take any measures, we shall be guilty of no wrong; for though we have made them many reasonable proposals we have failed. Grant therefore your consent, that those be punished for the wrong who first began it, and that those obtain their revenge who are seeking to exact it lawfully.[6] (II. 74. 3)

Unlike later historians such as Xenophon, Thucydides does not often refer to those matters of religious practice or piety which were the day-to-day responsibility of commanders on behalf of their troops. When he does it is usually in connection with a Spartan commander and often only in a brief reference. Examples of this can be found at V. 54. 2, V. 55. 3, and V. 116. 1, where Spartan armed expeditions were abandoned because of adverse boundary sacrifices. There is more than a hint that the Spartans were possibly the most scrupulous of the Greeks in matters of religious observance.

Archidamos' intention now was to take the city by storm. In order to keep the Plataeans trapped, a stockade was built encircling the city. The timber came from trees felled in the locality. With so many men on hand Archidamos decided that a mound should be raised against the city walls.[7] The earth was held in place by a lattice-like structure made of timber taken from the slopes of Mount Kithairon. So continuously working in relays over a period of seventy days and nights the mound gradually rose, while at the same time the Plataians raised the height of that portion of the wall against which the mound was being built. They did this by taking stone and brick from nearby houses and holding these in place within a wooden framework protected from fire arrows by leather hides. Obviously this alone was not sufficient and the defenders adopted a new tactic. Removing a lower section of the wall against which the mound abutted, they proceeded to bring the earth within the city perimeter. When this was discovered, the Spartans filled the offending area with clay-packed reed mats, preventing easy access to loose earth so that it became very difficult for the Plataians to continue this practice. The Plataians now directed their attention not to abutment of the mound but to its foundations. They dug a tunnel underneath the mound and for a considerable time were successful in withdrawing sufficient quantities of earth without being detected. The building rate of the mound slowed as all new materials brought up settled to fill the space which was constantly being renewed below.

Work now ceased on the superstructure of the walls and a further defensive wall was set up. This ran from either side of the superstructure where the city walls were at their original height and was built in a crescent shape. The thinking behind this was that the Peloponnesians would have to erect a second mound once they had breached the first line of defence. Further, they would have had have great difficulty in doing so because those building would be exposed to flank attacks from both sides of the crescent, working as they would be within it. The Spartans now brought up battering rams, one of which was deployed on the mound and others at various other parts of the walls.[8] The one on the mound successfully broke down a substantial part of the superstructure. However, the defenders countered the threats by either pulling up the engines of war after successfully attaching a noose to each or dropping huge logs suspended by chains onto the points of the battering rams, thereby disabling them.

Whether this response was solely the product of Plataian ingenuity is questionable. It is highly likely that whoever was the Athenian garrison commander would draw on the experience of his men, for the Athenians were reputed to be the most proficient in terms of siege warfare; although this claim was based more on their ability to build walls quickly than anything else found in the evidence. Viewing the operations which the Spartans and the Boiotians put in place at Plataia, these would seem to be more sophisticated than anything the Athenians had achieved hitherto.

Being on the receiving end for once, the Athenians would have been very much to the fore in suggestions for counter-measures. It is as well to recall that the Spartans themselves had called upon the Athenians at the time of the Messenian revolt which had centred on Ithome (464 BC) on the grounds that they were known for their skills in siege operations (I. 102. 2). The dismissal of the Athenian force from Ithome supposedly because of fears that 'democratic' views would be contagious eventually led to the downfall of Kimon, a man who had striven hard to maintain good relations between Athens and Sparta. It is difficult, however, to assess the veracity of this claim. Neither Herodotos nor Thucydides gives any substantial evidence for Athenian pre-eminence in this area of expertise other than the fact that they were involved in sieges to a greater extent than any other Greek state. In what follows the reader will see that the Spartans appear quite sophisticated in this skill. The later account of the siege at Syracuse shows the limitations of the Athenians in their siege tactics.

As a final throw before settling to a sustained siege, the Peloponnesians decided to attempt a conflagration of the city, and hoped that a favourable wind would assist their enterprise. A siege was an expensive operation and this was to be only undertaken as a last resort. The space between the mound and the wall was filled with kindling and it is suggested that combustible materials were actually thrown into the city itself (II. 77.3). Pitch and sulphur were added and the fire started. A breeze had in fact sprung up and the fire was initially of great proportions but, as luck would have it, a thunderstorm quenched the flames and the hopes of the Spartans for a swift resolution. With the failure of this last attempt the Peloponnesians settled down to a siege of the city (429 BC). The greater part of the army was now sent back to their homes and the remainder, with the Thebans, worked from May to September completing a circumvallation.[9] A wall was erected surrounding the city with the responsibility for different sections being shared out amongst the allies. Ditches were made both inside and outside the wall, the clay from which was used to make the bricks of the circumvallation. Thucydides is quite explicit in the details he gives of the construction:

> It had two encircling lines, the inner looking towards Plataea, the outer to guard against attack from the direction of Athens, and the two circuits were distant about sixteen feet from one another. This interval of sixteen feet had in building been divided up into rooms assigned to the guards; and the whole structure was continuous [i.e., the two walls were joined together by a roof], so as to appear to be a single thick wall furnished with battlements on both sides. And at every tenth battlement there were high towers of the same width as the wall, extending both to the inner and outer faces of it, so that there was no passage left at the sides of the towers, but the guards had to go through the middle of them. Now at night when the weather was rainy the guards left the battlements and kept watch from the towers, which were not far apart and were roofed overhead. (III. 21. 1–4)

This was a sophisticated and well planned structure suited to its siege purpose and eminently defensible against attack from any relieving force. When it was completed around September, arrangements were made for the Thebans to watch over half the circumference and the Peloponnesians the other half. Thucydides enumerates the total number within the city as 400 Plataeans, 80 Athenians and 110 women who had remained to prepare the provisions (II. 78. 4).

The decisions taken ultimately by Archidamos the commander must be applauded. He had arranged for the comfort and security of his own men and at the same time cut the Plataians off from the outside world.

Two years later, 427 BC saw food supplies running low and no sign of any help coming from Athens despite the fact that she was vigorously prosecuting the war elsewhere. It had always been unlikely that Athens would risk sending a relief force to central Greece, decimated as she had been by the plague and knowing that Sparta and her allies would mobilise very quickly at news of such an event. The Plataians can be admired for their loyalty, but, apart from the garrison of eighty Athenians, no assistance was forthcoming from her ally.

A plan was devised for a breakout. This suggestion came from two men, Theainetos the soothsayer and Eupompidas, one of the commanders. Initially, the plan was for all to take part but second thoughts about the enterprise led many to conclude that the chances of success were slim and only 220 decided to make the attempt. Again we are given the kind of detail by Thucydides which would have been welcome in other parts of his narrative. Scaling ladders were constructed to the height of the circuit wall. In the construction of these the numbers of bricks in the wall were counted many times by several of the Plataeans for accuracy. This implies a standard size for bricks and the counting was possible because the side of the wall facing the city was of course unplastered.

The attempted breakout took place on a night which saw rain and wind with no light from the moon. Even though they were lightly armed, they kept some distance one from the other so that arms and accoutrements would not clash as they crossed the ditch and came to a section of the wall between two towers. Constant observation must have made them secure in their minds that the battlements would not be manned in adverse weather conditions, the defenders watching from the shelter of the towers. As can be seen the escape had been meticulously planned. Whether conceived by a single unknown person or more likely by committee, the following shows a well sequenced plan carried out with great discipline.

Only the left foot of each man was shod to avoid slipping in the mud. Acting in relay, the first group set up the ladders, then twelve men armed only with daggers led by Ammeas climbed up, thereafter splitting into two groups to secure each of the two towers adjacent to their ascent. Those who followed carried javelins and were in turn followed by men who carried their shields. Unfortunately, the garrison was alerted by a falling tile dislodged from the battlements by one of the escapees. At this moment the towers had not been taken, for Thucydides notes that the sentries on the towers became aware of their presence (III. 22. 4). The alarm was raised and men ran to their positions. The weather conditions aided those making the breakout and, to add further to the confusion, those left in the city made a diversionary attack on the walls at a point opposite that at which the genuine attempt was being made. All this shows splendidly sequenced objectives, well planned even to the detail of surefootedness, which also indicates the Plataians had decided to make their attempt when such an inclement night arrived.

Thucydides' comment that the sentries remained at their posts (III.22.6) is perhaps indicative of good discipline rather than his suggestion that they feared leaving their posts to render support to some as yet unknown position. In any case a special force of 300 men had been established for just such a purpose, presumably by Archidamos before he left (III.22.7). It was this force which emerged outside the circumvallation and proceeded towards the area of disturbance. It seems logical, therefore, that those defenders should hold their positions. An agreed form of fire signals had been in place from the start of the investment. These were immediately used to summon help from Thebes, showing planning which must have taken into consideration all expected eventualities. This too had been anticipated by the Plataians and Athenians. Those in the city saw to it that other fire signals were raised above the walls to join those of the besiegers, thereby confusing the desired message. This was done in the hope of gaining additional time for the escape to be carried out before any support arrived. It was a vain ploy, for even if a confused signal was seen, the recipients would be likely to go to investigate even if only to clarify its meaning and origin, and they would do it in force.

The Plataians then secured the flanking towers, killing the guards and manning the entrances so that none could come from below to the assistance of the beleaguered besiegers. This proved to be the second planned objective of the unidentified commander of the escape. From this position it proved easy to give covering fire to protect the main force as it mounted the wall secured between the two towers. The majority clambered over the outer wall, initially taking up a position by the ditch, from where they protected the crossing of the wall by the remainder of the escapees, firing arrows and hurling javelins at anyone who came in support of the besiegers.

When all those who had been in possession of the flanking towers had just come down from the walls to the ditch, the special force arrived at the scene carrying torches. This illuminated them as a target for the party of escapees gathered at the side of the ditch and the latter poured arrows and javelins at their exposed target under the cover of darkness, before crossing over to the other side through deep, icy water. From there the Plataeans began to march in the direction of Thebes and not in the expected direction of Athens. In so doing they were not pursued but had the advantage of seeing the torches of their would-be pursuers moving towards Kithairon and Druoskephalai on the Athens road. After about half a mile they turned off the road to Thebes and made for the hills around Erythrai and Hysiai and thereafter came safely to Athens. The escape had been achieved by men equipped as light infantry and not as hoplites. They proved much more mobile and managed to keep their enemies at a distance. The lightness of their equipment would also have been advantageous on their march to Athens.

Those few who did not go over the wall assumed that their fellows had been killed or captured. It was only the next morning, when the Plataians within the city asked for a truce so that they could take up their dead, that they were given proof of the great escape.

The foregoing narrative outlines well organised activities on both sides, which were the obvious outcome of firm command. While it is easy to identify Archidamos and his actions up to the point of the siege, it is unfortunately impossible to identify those commanders he had left behind to conduct the siege. To ascribe command positions to those named on the Plataian side other than Eupompidas is to be faced with the same problem as for the besieging forces.

Although it is frustrating not to be able to give praise or blame to those who took the lead in the actions described, Thucydides' narrative does clearly outline the tactics employed as a product of firm command. On the Plataian side the influence of the Athenian garrison commander in all the activities which took place must be considered. It is significant how much the Spartans had learned about siege warfare since the siege of Ithome in the 460s.

The summer following the escape (427 BC) saw the surrender of Plataia. The remaining defenders were virtually starved into submission. At a point when an attack on the walls proved irresistible, the Spartan commander did not press on to capture the city but sent a herald to offer terms. He was under orders to do so (III. 52. 2) so that it could be said that the Plataians had come over willingly to the Peloponnesians and the city would not, at a time of negotiated peace, have to be handed back to the Athenian alliance. After a strange trial there followed the execution of the remaining 200 Plataians, together with twenty-five Athenians, the other fifty-five members of the garrison having presumably taken part in the escape. The women were sent into slavery and, after using the precincts for a year as a domicile for those Plataians who supported Thebes and for those who were political exiles from Megara, the city was razed to the ground.

Notes

1. An outbreak of hostilities between Sparta and Athens would seem inevitable to Thebes at this time. Those allied to each side would be drawn into the conflict. Plataia, an ally of Athens, was situated close to the road that was Thebes' line of communication with her southern allies in the Peloponnese. For strategic reasons it seemed best to pre-empt an Athenian invasion of Boiotia by taking control of the city, thereby maintaining Thebes' means of contact with her allies. That its location was recognised as being of great strategic importance can be demonstrated by the immense effort made by the Spartans to capture the city after being drawn into the conflict.

2. Herodotos VII. 233 suggests that there were 400 men under the leadership of Eurymachos. He, however, is described by Thucydides (II. 2. 3) as being the Theban who had planned the initial operation with the Plataians opposed to the continuance of their alliance with Athens.

3. This seems to have been a common response in urban areas. See W D Barry, 'Roof Tiles and Urban Violence in the Ancient World', *Greek, Roman and Byzantine Studies* 37 (1), 1996.

4. In many city states appointments to command positions were made by election, like those of magistrates. These were usually annual appointments and an individual could well be a general one year and then return to the ranks as a hoplite the next. In the Classical period there are obvious exceptions to this such as Sparta, Macedonia and Thessaly where the kings,

or in the case of the last, the Tagus, were looked to as commanders. In a war such as the one under discussion, which required activity in several locations simultaneously, temporary command positions were made, in addition to those of the kings.

5. This atrocity more than any other action seems to set the tone for the decline in morality that characterised the war. Archidamos' later plea and very reasonable offer to guarantee the safety of the Plataians is in stark contrast. At the time when the atrocity took place it must be assumed that the Plataian leaders of the community had momentarily lost control of the populace.

6. P B Kearn, *Ancient Siege Warfare*, (p. 103) makes a telling point which adds more flesh to note 5. 'They shouted their defiance from the walls. The immunity of a herald was one of the most sacred conventions of diplomacy and warfare in Greek society. The Plataians' fear for the safety of their herald reveals just how deep the fear of treachery had become and is a sure sign of the collapse of conventional standards.' See also D Lateiner, 'Heralds and Corpses in Thucydides', *Classical World*, 71, 1977, pp. 97–106.

7. It is highly likely that the labour would have been undertaken by helots. There would have been a considerable number of them, as indicated by Herodotos (IX. 10. 1). In his description of the 5000 Spartans marching north to Plataia in 479 BC he says they were accompanied by some 35,000 helots.

8. Thucydides is clear in his description of these engines of war. Hitherto there would appear to be no explicit description of the use of battering rams in Greek sources. Had Archidamos specified the need for protective coverings for the rams he might have been more successful. Similarly, siege towers and archers would have dissuaded the Plataians from their successful attempts to disable the machines. He could well have followed the Plataian example of using sappers.

9. This appears, at first sight, to be rather a long time, but Thucydides' detail clearly demonstrates that this was a highly sophisticated circumvallation and it could well have taken the length of time described. The decision to conduct a siege meant that the besiegers were resigned to a long-term operation. In any case, the supplies of the Plataians would be diminishing meantime and the building could be done in a leisurely manner. No further assistance from the Athenians appeared imminent.

III

Demosthenes, the North-West, Aitolia and Delion

In Demosthenes we encounter one of the most able of Athenian commanders. He possessed a characteristic essential to all who aspire to be successful: the ability to learn from experience and mistakes. This chapter deals with only two, but important, episodes early in his activities within the Archidamian War. He is also to be encountered in the chapters on Sphakteria, Brasidas and Sicily.

He is first mentioned as joint commander with Prokles of thirty ships in an expedition around the Peloponnese in 426 BC, at the same time that a larger fleet of sixty ships and 2,000 hoplites under Nikias went first to Melos, then to Tanagra in Boiotia and later farther north to raid the coast of Lokris. The initial aims of these missions were obviously to cause annoyance by hit and run despoiling of coastal crops and settlements, although Nikias' force came to battle at Tanagra with success. The disposition of the command appointments is interesting and one wonders if Thucydides omitted to name a colleague or colleagues of Nikias who, after all, was in charge of a force more than double the size of that of Demosthenes and Prokles.

As a preparatory comment on Nikias' style of command it must be said that, although successful in the field, nothing substantive was achieved, and this seems to characterise much of this commander's operations and may well explain his caution at the siege of Syracuse (see Chapter VII).

As for Demosthenes, what is certain is that the thirty ships and whatever number of unspecified troops they were carrying were part of a plan agreed with the Akarnanians. The enterprise, that of the destruction of Leukas, gives rise to the question of why two such disparate forces should be sent out by Athens on what could be argued was a mismatch of resources dedicated to specific tasks. We know that Melos, a Dorian colony, was later utterly and savagely subjugated by an Athenian force of only thirty-eight vessels, 1,200 hoplites, 300 archers and an additional 1,500 allied hoplites under the command of Kleomedes and Tesias (418 BC, V. 84. 1). Again, as a prelude to chapter VII, one can argue that Nikias, in most of his operations, did just enough to satisfy some of the aspirations of his fellow citizens. However, he never achieved any success in battle that could be regarded as truly significant in terms of altering the direction of the war. In all he acted without committing himself to the danger of failure in his enterprise. When finally faced by an enemy that matched his own in numbers he was more often than not reactive rather than proactive.

Returning to Demosthenes, he and his colleague did damage at Ellamenos in the area of Leukas. They then directed their efforts against Leukas itself and were supported in this by the whole of the Akarnanian forces except for those of Oiniadai in the south, whose sympathies lay with the Peloponnesians. They were reinforced in this enterprise by men from the pro-Athenian islands of Zakynthos and Kephallenia, and by an additional fifteen ships from Kerkyra.

The mobilisation of such a large force must have been prearranged and was not a matter which could be organised opportunistically. The Leukadians did not offer battle and, at the point when the Akarnanians proposed the building of a circumvallation in order to put Leukas under siege, Demosthenes was approached by the Messenians based at Naupaktos with a counter-plan for the large force he then commanded. Their proposal was for an invasion of Aitolia. It had its merits not least in relieving Naupaktos of the constant threat the Aitolians posed for this Athenian naval base.

Demosthenes saw strategic possibilities beyond this laudable aim. If he subdued the Aitolians he could then enlarge his army from their number and, together with the pro-Athenian Phokians, threaten Boiotia from the west. This, if successful, would neutralise a major ally of the Spartans and secure the north of Attika from attack. (See map, page xviii.)

He agreed to the plan of the Messenians. Undeterred by the Akarnanian refusal to be involved, disappointed as they were that the investiture of Leukas was not being carried out, he went with the Messenians, Zakynthians, Kephallenians and 300 Athenian marine hoplites to Oineon in allied Ozolian Lokris.[1]

The Messenians supplied Demosthenes with the basic intelligence that by moving quickly he would be able to overcome this warlike people piecemeal. The Aitolians lived in widely separated, unwalled villages and fought as light infantry.[2] If picked off one by one in quick succession, those in the settlements would have no opportunity to coalesce. In an area not normally in anything more than occasional contact with other Hellenic areas, rumours abounded. Typically, the more remote the tribe the less Greek they seemed. Indeed, the Eurytanians were deemed to use a language which was unintelligible and to eat their meat raw (III. 94. 5).

It had been arranged that the Lokrians would supply significant numbers of men, not least because they were armed in the same manner as the Aitolians and, more familiar with the territory. They were to join

Demosthenes 'in the interior' (III. 95. 3), a vague and unspecified location but undoubtedly known to both Lokrians and those who were to guide the main expedition.

Initially, all went well, with targeted and successful attacks made against villages over the first three days of the incursion. No details are given of these engagements, but they proved so successful that Demosthenes was persuaded by the Messenians to press on with his invasion. In so doing he neglected to wait for the Lokrians who would have supplied him with the light-armed troops that were a necessary addition to the force required to subjugate the area.

Thus far Demosthenes had made two errors, the first in alienating the Akarnanians, a factor which luckily for him did not later prove insurmountable. The second was being too impetuous, swept along by his early successes, to await the light-armed troops that would have been appropriate to his needs and the security of those already under his command.

It was after the successful taking of Aigition that Demosthenes encountered strong opposition. The inhabitants had taken to the nearby hills and the Aitolians at large had come in support of their brethren. Thucydides (III. 97. 3) describes the tactics typical of these light-armed combatants. They attacked at the run and poured javelins into the ranks of their enemy and retreated when the Athenians moved towards them, only to return to the attack when the Athenians desisted from pursuit. The terrain would be helpful to javelineers. Throwing a missile downhill added impetus and the extra poundage thereby added to the cast could be critical. It is likely that the heavy infantry of the Athenians were in their usual close order and a welcoming target for such tactics. The lighter-armed Aitolians would be in open or loose order and, without the panoply of a hoplite, would have been much fleeter of foot than the Athenians and their allies. Thucydides reports that the attacks, pursuits and retreats went on for a long time, greatly to the advantage of the Aitolians.

To counter such tactics an army needed peltasts and cavalry where conditions of terrain were suitable for pursuit uphill. Demosthenes would appear to have had neither. Even so, these units would have had to be deployed in a manner conducive to success. The later example of the Lechaion, where cavalry supported by the younger and obviously fitter and fleeter Spartan hoplites were worsted by peltasts, serves as an example of poor command of adequate forces.[3]

Without the assets of peltasts and cavalry the only adequate reply lies with a corps which can supply a response in kind to a missile attack. Demosthenes did have archers with him and Thucydides notes that they did sterling service in restraining the Aitolians from closer combat. However, with the death of their commander and their subsequent dispersal, the attacks became more onerous for the now near exhausted Athenian and allied heavy infantry. At length they broke ranks and fled.

The area was unfamiliar to them and the Messenian guide with the invaders had been killed. The pursuit was relentless and in an unfamiliar terrain the Athenians fell foul of any natural impediment.

A large number of the allied army sought refuge in a forest, not having found a path suitable for them to leave the area. Here they were forced into the open again in no defensive order by fire which had been set to the woods by the Aitolians. The death of the Messenian guide Chromon left every man seeking his own sanctuary and carnage ensued as the Aitolians fell upon the disorderly rabble. Many fell in the scramble to reach the safety of Oineon and while Thucydides records only that 'Many of the allies were slain' he does give the figure of approximately 120 Athenians as being among the fatalities. He further goes on to note that these men were young and of good families. The plague at Athens would have made the senior politicians there very sensitive to the numbers available for service. Prokles, the colleague of Demosthenes, was also a casualty. It is no wonder that the latter chose not to return to Athens after reclaiming the dead under truce and returning to Naupaktos. The wisdom of his self-preserving action is reflected in the record of Athens towards its unsuccessful commanders.[4]

The upshot of Demosthenes' foray into Aitolia was a second ambassadorial visit by the Aitolians to Corinth and Sparta with a request to send an expeditionary force against Naupaktos. This time they received a positive response, no doubt heartened by the news of the Athenian disaster. The Spartans arranged for 3,000 allied hoplites, 600 of which came from the newly founded Spartan colony of Herakleia, to be sent under the command of the Spartan Eurylochos supported by Makarios and Menedaios to the muster point at Delphi. From there a herald was sent to the Ozolian Lokrians, notionally the allies of Athens, to attempt to induce them to revolt and, more importantly, to secure safe passage through their territory to Naupaktos. With Amphissa agreeing to the Spartan request through fear of their Phokian neighbours, many Lokrian settlements offered hostages to the Spartan-led army. These were placed in Kytinion, a city in Doris, the reputed homeland of the Dorians, north of Boiotia in central Greece.

Eurylochos then moved towards Naupaktos, with his Aitolian allies subjugating the two Lokrian settlements of Oineon and Eupalion, which were disinclined to cooperate. They overran the unfortified outskirts of Naupaktos and pillaged the surrounding countryside, going on to reduce Molykreon nearby. While this was going on, Demosthenes managed to persuade the Akarnanians to supply him with 1,000 hoplites, this despite the bad feeling which he had aroused in them for his lack of support in the siege of Leukas. One can imagine his argument would rehearse the problems which would arise for the Akarnanians if Naupaktos fell. It is to his credit that he was able to persuade them to support him. He and the hoplites were transported to Naupaktos by ships from the Akarnanian fleet, there being no Athenian vessels on station at that time. His arrival with the reinforcements was timely because there was an insufficiency of men to guard the extensive fortifications of the inner city (III. 102. 4). Having discovered that it was impossible to storm the city with any chance of success, Eurylochos moved on to the area of Kalydon and Pleuron which was suitable for the deployment of a hoplite phalanx. So far all was in order, although Eurylochos had left an enemy force in his notional rear at Naupaktos, which could have caused him problems.

At this time the Ambrakiots persuaded Eurylochos to make a joint attack on Amphilochia, which was a small area to the north of Akarnania, and on Akarnania itself. This request came in late summer and the initial attack was made in the winter of 426–5 BC. The fact that Eurylochos remained with his army from late summer until this time is worthy of attention. Questions arise concerning such a long delay and as to why the campaign started in winter, still an unusual time for opening hostilities. The Spartan commander was not one of the kings and may therefore have had to ask for endorsement of the proposal from the home government. Considering the record of failure of the Peloponnesians in this area up to that time, the matter required careful consideration. However, Sparta was not half a world away and the interval of inactivity is too great simply to explain away by saying the decision makers there pondered long on the matter. It also seems difficult to countenance the need for three or four months to mobilise on the part of the Ambrakiots, considering they were the instigators of the proposal. Thucydides gives us no help in this matter; but to launch an offensive in winter at this time was an unusual move.

During his sojourn, with his troops quartered in the region of Pleuron, Kalydon and Aitolian Proschion, Eurylochos dismissed his Aitolian allies. Whether he anticipated their return once hostilities were resumed, or the Aitolians were satisfied that Naupaktos was now much less of a problem and had requested their return to their homeland, one can only guess. No doubt there were crops to be gathered and stores to lay in for winter in Aitolia. An additional factor would have been the major problem of the commisariat for a large body of men over several months. It is to Eurylochos' credit that he was able to come to some satisfactory arrangements in this matter which was unusual for the time. The quartering of his men at disparate locations minimised the effect on any one particular place and it is likely that the troops helped their hosts with their harvesting and any other work that needed to be undertaken in return for their hospitality.

At the outset, the Ambrakiot force of 3,000 hoplites took control of Olpai. In response the Akarnanians sent a force to defend Argos, their main army encamping meantime at Krenai hoping to prevent the junction of Eurylochos' army with that of the Ambrakiots. The Akarnanians also sent to Demosthenes at Naupaktos requesting that he take overall command and despatch the twenty ships now on station there. With the mixed population of the region we find that the Ambrakiots residing at Olpai had also sent for aid from their countrymen in fear that Eurylochos would not be able to pass the Akarnanians undetected. This meant that significant forces were moving from north and south towards the target area, although Eurylochos was unaware of the fact, otherwise it is likely that he would have attempted a junction prior to taking action. He, on learning of the opening of hostilities, and because the enemy concentration was to the north, advanced through a relatively undefended Akarnania. His route is clearly defined by Thucydides. Moving past Stratos they passed through Phytia, around Medeon, through Limnaia and into the allied region of Agraion from where they succeeded in eluding detection to rendezvous with the Ambrakiot army already at Olpai.

Demosthenes had also arrived at about the same time in the Ambrakian Gulf with 200 Messenian hoplites and sixty Athenian archers. The twenty Athenian ships brought reinforcements to Argos and blockaded Olpai. Most of the Amphilochians were pinned down by the Ambrakiots but some had managed to join the Akarnanians at Argos. Demosthenes took this combined force and encamped near Olpai. Thucydides describes the opposing armies being divided by a large ravine. The terrain was not wholly conducive to a hoplite engagement and this accounts for the five days of inactivity that followed. The sixth day saw both sides coming into battle order, with Demosthenes taking the issue of terrain seriously in his planning. Being aware that his army was smaller than that of the Peloponnesians and fearful of being outflanked, he placed 400 mixed hoplites and peltasts in a position of ambush to counter this threat.

Thucydides gives enough detail for us to envisage the course of the engagement. Unusually for a commander of this period, Eurylochos had positioned himself on the left wing opposite Demosthenes and his Messenians. Eurylochos' forces had formed up with Ambrakiots and Peloponnesian troops intermingled. Only the Mantineians were in a discrete unit adjacent to Eurylochos in his position at the extreme point of the left wing.

Opposing them the Akarnanians had taken their places in tribal units with Amphilochian javelineers presumably taking position on the wings. The camaraderie of tribal units in the case of the Akarnanians and the disposition of the Mantineians as a unit can be seen as crucial to the outcome of the battle.

It was abundantly clear that Eurylochos enjoyed a considerable overlap on his wing and in the opening moves of the combat he attempted the obvious encirclement of the opposition before coming to close. In the advance they had passed the position of Demosthenes' arranged ambuscade. Prior to direct engagement with Demosthenes, the Peloponnesians suddenly found themselves assailed in the rear. The attack must have been fierce for the Peloponnesian left wing broke and fled, the sight of which caused dismay to a significant part of the rest of their line. They too broke ranks and fled while their left wing was decimated. On the other wing, however, the Ambrakiots had early success and pursued the opposition to Argos from where they returned to find the victorious Akarnanians reformed and ready to engage them. Opposition was brief and, in the rout and rush to reach Olpai, many Ambrakiots perished. Thucydides notes (III. 108. 3) that by virtue of their ordered retreat the Mantineians suffered much less than their Ambrakiot allies, underlining the principle of interdependency which safeguarded hoplite formations. This interdependency could only be fostered in the long term within like-minded communities with common interests and attitudes.

The survivors were now under a state of siege at Olpai. The Athenian fleet served as a blockade and no escape could be achieved or help received from the seaward side. Demosthenes and his allied army were encamped around the landward side. The situation of the Peloponnesians was desperate. Menedaios had taken command now that both Eurylochos and Makarios had been among the fatalities. He sued for a truce to recover the bodies of those who had fallen, thereby admitting the obvious fact of the defeat. This was granted and the Athenians and their allies set up the usual trophy denoting their victory. Menedaios' request that his army should be allowed to retreat was denied.

Here Thucydides gives us a further glimpse of Demosthenes the strategist. The refusal to allow the enemy to withdraw under truce was hedged by a secret agreement to permit Menedaios, the Peloponnesian commanders and the Mantineians to leave clandestinely and quickly. The purpose of this agreement was to leave the Ambrakiots and the mixed group of mercenaries isolated. These mercenaries, mentioned for the first time by Thucydides at III. 109. 2, cannot be identified. Their existence is conjectural. What was subtle in the agreement is that, by permitting those from the Peloponnese to leave unhindered, provided that it was in a manner unbeknown to their allies, Demosthenes would successfully bring discredit upon them. They would be seen by their allies as abandoning them merely to save their own skins in an act of dishonour. Demosthenes reasonably thought that such an act would not only disaffect those in that region who had supported the Peloponnesian cause but might also cause strains elsewhere within their alliance in the future.

Later, he was perhaps disappointed that such disaffection as there was as a consequence of the flight of the Peloponnesians was confined to the north-west. Here, too, the result was a little muted, but the fact remains that the hitherto dependable Oiniadai were later forced into the Athenian alliance by the rest of the Akarnanians (IV. 77. 2). Sparta thereby lost her bridgehead to the north-west.

As those who had been promised unhampered withdrawal planned how this could be done without arousing the suspicion of their allies, Demosthenes received intelligence that the army from the city of Ambrakia summoned by those in Olpai was now moving through Amphilochia. Had this news also come to be known to Menedaios the result for Demosthenes could well have been disastrous. He did well to keep the information from the enemy and some insight from Thucydides into his intelligence security methods would have been illuminating. His response to the news was to occupy forward positions along their presumed route in the form of ambushes and manning of hilltops adjacent to the passage of the enemy. At that time he would no doubt be extremely anxious for the withdrawal of the Peloponnesians to get under way.

The escapees had come to the conclusion that the best way to effect their salvation was to pretend to be foraging for fuel and cooking herbs.[5] Not everything went as planned. Those who were party to the plan were observed by the Ambrakiots they were abandoning and they too, in a body, ran to join them. The Akarnanians were correct in thinking that all were not party to the agreement and went after the entire body of fugitives. Even when their own commanders tried to remind them that there was an agreement under the terms of the truce for the Peloponnesians to leave, they were so incensed by what they thought was duplicity that some even threw javelins at their leaders. Eventually, the Peloponnesians were permitted to go on their way and pursuit was made of the Ambrakiots. Even then Thucydides notes that there was some confusion as to the identity of the pursued (III. 111. 4). Three hundred Ambrakiots were killed while the remainder of the sanctioned escapees reached safety with the neighbouring Agraions.

The advance of the second Ambrakiot army had now reached Ithome and had encamped on the lower of the two massifs. The higher one was occupied shortly after the Ambrakiots' arrival by those units sent earlier to the area by Demosthenes. They had done this at night undetected by the Ambrakiots. Demosthenes then divided his army and led half under the cover of darkness by the lower route to the area between the hills, while the other half went by the higher road through the Amphilochian highlands. Although the distances were relatively short, the planning to arrive in time for a coordinated dawn attack required care.[6]

When the attack was launched, Thucydides states that Demosthenes had placed the Messenians in the van specifically to mislead guards at positions forward from the encampment, by speaking to them in the Dorian dialect (Δωρίδα τε γλῶσσαν). The ruse may have depended on the Messenians being taken for Mantineians or other members of the Peloponnesian allied forces. It is otherwise difficult to accept that the guards thought that these were 'their own men' (III. 112. 4) unless they assumed this to be an advance party from Eurylochos' army. Certainly, it was necessary to avoid the possibility of an Athenian betraying the attack. The Ambrakiots were still unaware of the defeat of the Peloponnesian army to the south and would be expecting early contact with these forces. As it was not yet first light the Ambrakiot guards were deceived.

With the coming of dawn the attack was made with the Ambrakiots still asleep. Their slaughter can only be imagined as they gave what little resistance they could, relatively unarmoured and in no form of order. The greater part of their number were killed within their encampment while the remainder fled through the mountains All routes taken were manned by Demosthenes' men and the allied Amphilochians knew the terrain better than the Ambrakiots. The latter therefore fell easy prey to the prepared ambushes. When they lost their way they were overtaken by the Amphilochians who, as light infantry, were better suited to the conditions. Thucydides' point that these light-armed troops were pursuing hoplites must be taken as referring to the combat experience of the adversaries. Those fleeing lacked all the aspects that defined the hoplite: the close battle order of the phalanx; many would not be wearing the full panoply of a heavy infantryman such would have been their haste, and those who were would be slowed down by its weight; and they would be defending themselves in unsuitable conditions and be subject to missiles rather than close combat. Some who managed to reach the coast chose to swim out to the Athenian fleet. Here Thucydides waxes poetic:

> ...thinking in the panic of the moment that it was better for them to be slain, if slain they must be, by the crews of the ships than by the barbarian and detested Amphilochians.' (III. 112. 7)

Realistically, these fugitives would have the hope of being taken prisoner by the Athenians rather than being killed. Indeed it was their only hope for survival.

Trophies were set up and the dead stripped of their arms which were taken to Argos. There the following day a herald arrived from those Ambrakiots who had managed to reach the safety of Agraion territory. He had come to claim the bodies of those who had been killed in the flight from Olpai and had no knowledge of the disaster which had overtaken his countrymen the day before. Confusion ensued between the herald and the person who questioned his amazement at the number of arms gathered there. The herald had expected to see those of around 200 men (Thucydides III. 111. 4). Then, as the fact of the second battle was revealed to him, the herald realised that more than 1,000 of his comrades had fallen. Appalled by this revelation he left without thought for the completion of his mission.

Thucydides graphically illustrates the disaster that can befall a community which suffers such a loss of manpower.[7] The city itself was now at the mercy of its enemies. Had the Akarnanians agreed to an attack upon it as proposed by Demosthenes, there is little doubt that it would have fallen. For very sound reasons the Akarnanians and Amphilochians chose instead to make a defensive alliance with the Ambrakiots on the departure of the Athenians. This avoided having the Athenians in control of another city uncomfortably close to their territory.

Without doubt, Demosthenes' generalship had achieved a remarkable rehabilitation of his reputation. He could now safely return to Athens. To dissect the elements of his success one has to point specifically to his care and attention to the setting of ambuscades, initially to offset the danger of the Peloponnesian overlap and later with the intention of hindering the advance of the second Ambrakiot force. The deployment of his battle line in tribal units recognised the esprit de corps of such groups. His advance at night prior to the second battle was well timed and led to a complete exploitation of surprise. His use of Messenians in penetrating the outposts of the Ambrakiots was crucial to delivering his attack at close quarters. Finally, the pursuit was left to the Amphilochians, who, as light infantry or peltasts, were ideally suited to the rough terrain. This last point was a lesson well learned from his Aitolian experience.

Eurylochos was unfortunate. He had enterprisingly taken up his position in the first battle unusually on the left wing so as to be opposite the command position of the enemy. The terrain had allowed his opposing commander to lay the unexpected ambush which came into effect as he was creating a decisive overlap on the left. To have done this he would have had to order his men to move to the left, a move not wholly comfortable to a phalanx whose tendency was to move to the right to protect the unshielded side. He is to be given credit for achieving this, and it says much for the discipline which he exerted over his troops. The disposition of his line could have been better, however. Apart from the Mantineians who fought as a corps, the rest of his troops were intermingled and the loyalty factor so important to the integrity of a battle line was diminished.

Mention has been made of Demosthenes' skill as a strategist. His later occupation of Pylos was a masterstroke and could well have won the war for Athens had it not been for the later activities of Brasidas (see chapters IV and V). The idea of neutralising Boiotia during the conflict continued to be a preoccupation and we must recognise Demosthenes' grasp of the possibilities to do harm to the enemy in mainland Greece, which went unrecognised by the majority of his compatriots. Just as Brasidas recognised an opportunity to weaken Athens' hold on her allies to the north-east, he saw that by forcibly detaching the Boiotians from the Peloponnesian alliance a significant change in the balance of power would emerge. Had he been successful, the almost annual invasion of Attika by the Spartans would have been less secure, with either a belligerent to their rear or no support.

Demosthenes was the colleague of Hippokrates at Megara (see Chapter V). They were obviously like-minded people and together they hatched a plan for the invasion of Boiotia. Demosthenes had persuaded Hippokrates to his view that an attack from two directions would divide the Boiotian forces and lead ultimately to its subjection. This was a more sophisticated endeavour than that which came awry on Demosthenes' progress through Aitolia. They must have been given support from the Athenian assembly for their enterprise. Both generals were in contact with citizens of several Boiotian cities who wanted to change their form of government to one of democracy. The plan was to take Siphai, a city to the south of Thespiai on the coast of the Corinthian Gulf. The city was to be betrayed to the Athenians by their sympathisers. At the same time Chaironeia near the Phokian border was to be betrayed. The Athenians were to occupy the sanctuary of Apollo at Delion and fortify it. All actions were to be carried out simultaneously.

With Phokian allies to the west of Boiotia, an attack from its underbelly and another towards its sanctuary to the east of its territory would have necessarily led to a division of Boiotian forces. Demosthenes had set out earlier than his colleague and had arrived at Naupaktos with a fleet of forty ships on which he proposed to transport an army of Akarnanians and allies to Siphai. The operation was planned to take place in winter, an indication that this war was departing increasingly from the accepted and almost ceremonial hoplite engagements of former times. Open hostilities were now all-year occurrences.

Despite the supposed agreed date for simultaneous operations, Demosthenes arrived too early at Siphai. The time between the making of the plan and its execution had been too great and knowledge of it had been received by the Spartans, who had given warning of it to the Boiotians. A Phokian, Nikomachos, who obviously sympathised with the Peloponnesian cause, was the source of the intelligence. Whether he still lived in Panopeus is not clear, but that was the community from which he came. Panopeus lies adjacent to Chaironeia and he may well have heard of the plan in that vicinity. The Boiotians threw garrisons into both Siphai and Chaironeia and those within the cities who sympathised with the Athenians were unable to act on their behalf. This was not known to Hippokrates who had secured Delion and was fortifying it. He was not to know that, with matters settled in the two western cities, the Boiotians had withdrawn their forces from them and could now present a united front. They were mustering at Tanagra as Hippokrates was busy with his build-ing work at Delion. Hippokrates' fortifications were of wood and stone with a ditch surrounding his pallisades. It took the Athenians the best part of five days to complete the work. Hippokrates ordered his men to return to Athens leaving only a garrison to secure the place.

The Athenian muster contained *metics* or resident aliens who, because they enjoyed certain privileges in the city, were now expected to do military service. The reduction in Athenian manpower caused by the plague made reliance on this group essential if a significant force was to be raised.

The light infantry of the Athenians continued towards Athens on their withdrawal while the hoplites moved two kilometres to the south, no doubt waiting for their commander-in-chief who was still at Delion making last-minute arrangements with the garrison he was to leave there.

The Boiotian federation forces, each with its own Boiotarch or commander, were initially reluctant to take the field against the Athenians now that they had withdrawn from Boiotian territory. This was a technicality. The Athenians still held Delion and the fact that their army was now over the border in Oropos did not alter the fact that a hostile incursion had been made. Pagondas, the Theban Boiotarch, was able to persuade his other Boiotarch colleagues that the invasion needed a strong response. It is illuminating to see the growing primacy of Thebes in the politics of Boiotia.

Pagondas then ordered an advance against the Athenians. They arrived at a place where, because of a hill between the two forces, neither could see the other. Although the exact location of the battle is under dispute, the countryside is not a particularly difficult one in which to make troop movements. News of the Boiotian move was made known to Hippokrates who, still at Delion, sent orders to the Athenians to form into battle line. He left 300 cavalry at Delion for its defence and for the possibility of attacking the Boiotian rear should the opportunity arise. Thucydides does not make it wholly clear that the force left behind by Pagondas to neutralise this cavalry contingent was of a similar kind and strength. Theban cavalry were better than those of the Athenians and this makes the selection of cavalry the more likely (IV. 93. 2).

Here, in the narrative, we are given the numbers and disposition of combatants on each side. The Boiotian line was arranged as follows. The right wing was taken by the Thebans and their allies. This comment at IV. 93. 4 shows that there were still tensions within the growing federation of the Boiotians and although Thebes would appear to be paramount, their influence over some cities was not as secure as they would wish. The centre was taken by the Haliartians, Koroneians, and Kopeians together with those other peoples who lived around Lake Kopais.[8] The left wing was manned by Thespians, Tanagrians and Orchomenians.[9] Within the line itself the units were allowed to array themselves as they wished. It is important to note, however, that the Theban depth of phalanx was twenty-five, as opposed to the average eight ranks of the usual battle line. This increased depth became a feature of Theban deployment culminating in the phalanx depth of an extraordinary fifty ranks at Leuktra under Epameinondas in 371 BC.

In excess of 10,000 light armed troops, approximately 7,000 hoplites, 1,000 cavalry and 500 peltasts are the numbers given for the Theban army.

The distinction between light-armed troops and peltasts is very fluid during much of the 5th and early 4th centuries. At this date Thucydides is probably distinguishing between the Thracian type peltast and that mixture of troops who did not have the whole panoply of the hoplite, e.g. slingers, spearmen, javelineers or stone throwers.

The Athenian army would have been smaller in total. The greater part of their light forces had already started on their return to Athens. The majority of these had no arms in any case and probably would have been an encumbrance to Hippokrates had they been present. The Athenians matched the opposition in the number of hoplites. Their deployment eight deep would have more than matched the Boiotian phalanx, given that the Theban contingent at twenty-five deep could have had a front three times longer had they arrayed themselves at the same depth of eight ranks. Cavalry covered both wings.

Hippokrates had arrived to join his army. Where he intended to make his command point is not known. It is likely to have been towards the right wing. Here we encounter one of those interesting details which Thucydides throws up from time to time. Hippokrates was going down his line encouraging his men before the coming conflict and is reported to have reached the centre when the Boiotians started their advance down from the crest of the hill where they had marshalled their forces. This would have caught Hippokrates away from his desired position and may have contributed to his death in the second phase of the battle. He may well have had to stay where he was at the centre considering that the meeting of the opposing forces was done on the run ('ἀντεπῇσαν δὲ καὶ οἱ Ἀθηναῖοι καὶ προσέμειξαν δρόμῳ, IV. 96. 1).

The extremities of all wings found that local conditions were against them so that the cavalry on both sides and the light-armed troops of the Boiotians did not come into combat initially. As it was winter, the streams and waterways were fast flowing and presented an obstacle to those troops on the wings. The conflict, therefore, had to be mainly contested between the hoplite forces of both sides, which Thucydides describes as pressing shield against shield. As often happened in a hoplite battle the right wing, where the elite troops were usually positioned, more often than not worsted the left wing of their enemy; and this proved to be the case here. The Athenians were victorious against the Boiotian hoplite left wing. Historically, the Thespians were doughty fighters and they found themselves surrounded by the Athenians, those of their allies on each side having been put to flight. Their contingent was cut to pieces.

Thucydides mentions that in the confusion of the hand to hand fighting which ensued some Athenians killed their fellows. This success by the Athenians would appear to have happened early in the battle, for now the remaining centre and right of the Boiotian army were threatened by the Athenian victors with an attack on their exposed flank and rear. Those who had been able to take flight found refuge with the more successful areas of their line. The Thebans, possibly because of their greater depth and weight in the phalanx were enjoying success against the Athenian left wing. As Thucydides describes the Thebans pushing the Athenians back 'step by step', it is obvious that the Athenian line held together and was not broken immediately. Only with the increased impetus which a depth of twenty-five ranks gave once on the move against a depth of only eight, did the Athenian line break. Pagondas had sent two cavalry squadrons around the hill to bring succour to his own beleaguered left. These appeared together with some Lokrian cavalry who had lately come up at the same moment as the break was made in the Athenian line. Those victorious Athenians on the right who had worsted their enemies and who could have come to the support of their fellows in an attack on the Theban flank or rear, assumed another army was approaching and took to their heels.[10]

What followed was a typical rout. Once the defensive cohesion of a phalanx was lost, an individual hoplite was at the mercy of his pursuers. Arms and armour would be discarded in the scramble to reach safety more quickly. Those who had kept their arms would be encumbered and slower moving. In retreat they would be ineffective, showing their backs to the pursuers. Obviously in some instances knots of men, in some form of order, saved themselves, but the overall picture would have been one of mayhem.

Pagondas had made a wise move. The cavalry and presumably many of his light-armed troops had not been able to take part in the battle because of the terrain and its impediments. His order to the two cavalry squadrons and the timely arrival of the Lokrians brought into play the very troops tailor-made for pursuit and attacks on a disorganised enemy. What is intriguing is that he was in a position to see the likely danger and make his order for the redeployment of the cavalry, presumably positioned to his right. As a general usually fought with his men and once the engagement was under way was unable to make the kind of redeployment described, marks this out as a highly unusual event.

Perhaps his position in the deep phalanx was sufficiently far back to allow him to merely push and to give his attention to matters other than personal combat. Thucydides gives him the credit for this move. However, it is not beyond the bounds of possibility and more probable that the *hipparch* (cavalry commander) of the squadrons on the right, finding his men unengaged because of the topography, used his initiative to counter the threatening development on the Boiotian left by leading the cavalry upstream to a fordable point and behind the hill to make his surprise attack.

Thucydides records (IV. 96. 7) that the fugitives scattered widely, some reaching safety at the sea near Delion or Oropos and others on Mount

Parnes. They were helped in this by the onset of darkness, for the battle had started late in the day. Those near the coast were taken off by ship the following day. The Athenian losses in the battle were more than 14% of their forces, the greatest casualties sustained in any hoplite battle.

Nonetheless, a garrison remained at Delion within Boiotian territory and it was this which caused the Thebans to refuse to give up the dead to the Athenian herald. The Thebans placed a guard over the corpses and the main body moved to Tanagra where plans were made for an attack on Delion.

Pagondas decided to attempt to take the place by storm. His army had been reinforced by the Peloponnesian garrison from Nisaia, which was accompanied by some Megarans. Corinth had also sent 2,000 hoplites but they arrived after the battle. These, together with darters and slingers from a little to the north on the Malian Gulf, who had been requested by Pagondas, now joined the main force in front of Delion. The key to its weakness lay in the wooden construction of its defences. After the more straightforward forms of assault had proved ineffectual, an interesting device was brought up to the walls on carts. It proved to be a form of flame thrower. Its construction is clearly described by Thucydides:

> Having sawed in two a great beam they hollowed it throughout, and fitted it together again nicely like a pipe; then they hung a cauldron at one end of it with chains, and into the cauldron an iron bellows-pipe was let down in a curve from the beam, which was itself in great part plated with iron...They inserted a large bellows into the end of the beam next to them and blew through it. And the blast passing through the air-tight tube into the cauldron, which contained lighted coals, sulphur, and pitch, made a great blaze and set fire to the wall, so that no one could stay on it longer, but all left it and took to flight. (IV. 100. 2–4)

In this way Delion was taken. Thucydides does not give the number of fatalities but records that 200 prisoners were taken, the remainder having reached the coast and been shipped to Athens.

Within the course of seventeen days Pagondas had rid Boiotia of the Athenian menace. Now that Delion had been retaken and no live Athenians remained on Boiotian soil, the Athenians were allowed to reclaim their dead. It being winter, decomposition would not be too advanced. In the battle itself just under 1,000 Athenians had lost their lives. This, together with the fatalities of the Delion garrison and the 200 Athenian prisoners taken, together with an unspecified number of light-armed forces and baggage carriers, was a significant setback. Hippokrates himself was one of the casualties. The Boiotans had lost about 500 of their number but these had been mainly Thespians and Orchomenians.

Notes

1. The fifteen Kerkyran ships had returned home with their men. Whether they too were angered by Demosthenes' abandonment of the subjugation of Leukas is conjectural.

2. Largely because of the terrain, which was mountainous and not conducive to hoplite engagement, the peoples of this region were armed in similar fashion to the Thracian peltasts, using missiles and javelins as their main mode of attack.

3. See Hutchinson, G, *Xenophon and the Art of Command*, p.106.

4. For the summary and unjust treatment of Athenian commanders after the Battle of Arginusai, see Hutchinson G. *op.cit.*, p.111 and Xen. *Hellenika*, I. 7. 34.

5. Even today those Greeks living in or near open countryside will collect wild herbs for cooking on a regular basis. The author has been the recipient of such gatherings.

6. Night marches show even more sophisticated planning in the next century. The judgement of time required, topography and intelligence of enemy practices are clearly evident in the Theban attack on the Spartan force holding a position on the Oineion mountain range. Their arrival was timed so that an attack could be made at the end of the night watch (Xen. *Hellenika*, VII. 1. 15–16).

7. Athens itself had suffered manpower losses due to the plague, but its population was much larger than that of most city states and its defences far better than average. In the conduct of warfare, the growing habit of depopulation can be found. The Spartan treatment of the remaining Plataians at the end of the siege pales beside the conduct of the Athenians in their treatment of defecting allies (subjects) or those who were unwilling to become subservient to her. The slaughter by the Athenians of all males from adolescent age upward, and the enslavement of females and their children, was relatively commonplace as the war progressed.

   A more subtle and cynical method of reducing a city's manpower has been detected by Victor Hanson in his 'Hoplite obliteration: the case of the town of Thespiae' in *Ancient Warfare*. On page 213 he writes, 'It seems that the traditionally independent Thespians were intentionally stationed at the most dangerous spot at Delion out of general enmity on the part of the Thebans. The town itself was targeted the next year out of national rather than factional rivalry, once it was clear that a third of the landowning males of the town were gone and its hoplite force permanently weakened.'

8. This area is now drained and affords modern day Thebes and the villages around an area of rich agricultural land. One site of extraordinary interest which was at the edge of this lake is the enigmatic site of Gla. This is the

51

biggest Mycenean site thus far discovered and, because it is not the stuff of legends or the discovery of gold, is not the subject of the kind of mass tourism which besets Mycenae or Tiryns. Its demise is shrouded in mystery and was the subject of conflagration. Well worth a visit; one may well be the only person on the site for a whole day.

9. The Orchomenians had long challenged the primacy of Thebes. In due course, because of the pressure from Thebes, the Orchomenians sought succour from the Spartans who used their city as a base from which to operate against Thebes in the 4th century BC. It is no surprise, given Victor Hansons' theory in note 6 above, that they were placed with the Thespians in the more dangerous area of the line against the command position of the opposition.

10. V. D. Hanson in *The Wars of the Ancient Greeks*, p.115, rightly points to the intelligent use by Pagondas of cavalry as a defence against his Theban phalanx being taken in the flank and rear. He is incorrect, however, in calling this force a *reserve*. To use the term is to misinterpret the action. There are two distinct forms of reserve. Both require the force to be uncommitted to the first phase of engagement as part of the battle plan. The first may be designated to a 'specific subsequent mission, which is essential to the successful outcome of a major operation or battle.' These are sometimes called in the modern day *echelon forces*. The second may be given no specific orders other than to be held *in depth* to react to some unforeseen development in the ongoing action of others. This last force is given no mission but has planning options. The cavalry in question within this battle fits neither of these categories. It had not been active in the first phase largely because of difficulties of terrain. It had been planned for it to engage from the start of hostilities and therefore was not a reserve. They had not been designated as a reserve to fulfil a specific role as part of the battle plan. They were redeployed during the course of the action. For probably the first description of the use of true reserves in ancient warfare see Xen. *Anab.* VI. 5. 9. See also pp. 76 and 89 for 'special forces' and reserves in *Xenophon and the Art of Command* by Godfrey Hutchinson.

IV

Sphakteria 425 BC

In this chapter the focus is on the actions of Demosthenes and Kleon. The former had been given permission to come out of private life after his return to Athens from his activities in the north-west and to make use of the fleet of forty Athenian ships on its way to Sicily around the coast of the Peloponnese. The later arrival of Kleon was more an accident of political manoeuvre than a direct award of command in the normal manner.

The Athenian fleet had sailed around the Peloponnese and their commanders, Eurymedon and Sophokles, wished to move quickly to Kerkyra where an allied Peloponnesian fleet of sixty ships had arrived to help the exiles of that island. Such had been their orders. Demosthenes wanted them to make a landing at Pylos prior to this. Thucydides (1V. 3. 1–2) suggests that Demosthenes had a preconceived plan to establish a base at this point or somewhere on the Messenian coastline. He had probably put the details of his suggestion to the Athenian Assembly and was granted permission to make use of the fleet. The original idea for such an enterprise and indeed the specific location may have come from his Messenian associates who had served under him from their base at Naupaktos in his earlier campaigns. Their resistance for ten years at Ithome was a day's march from the environs of Sphakteria and they knew their territory well. This can be adjudged a continuance of the Periklean policy of harrassing the Peloponnesian coastal areas. To attempt to make a permanent base was not a departure from Periklean policy, particularly when one compares the activity of Perikles himself in 430 BC. At that time, while the Spartans were ravaging Attika to the south of Athens, Perikles, having refused to allow the army to leave the city to engage the enemy, had organised a fleet of 100 vessels and a force of 4,000 hoplites and 300 cavalry to sail to the Peloponnese.[1] After attempting to take Epidauros, he laid waste its territory and those of Troezen and Halieis, and sacked Prasiai.

Perhaps because on that occasion Perikles did not establish a garrison at the place he took, he was not seeking a semi-permanent base in enemy territory. It was clear that his target had been Epidauros. Situated as it was within easy reach of support from Athens from the sea and adjacent to Argos which, at this time, was neutral to the conflict, a base at Epidauros could have threatened both Corinth and Sparta and detached Epidauros from the Peloponnesian alliance.

One only need look at the figures of the forces involved to be convinced that this had been conceived as a significant operation. They were almost equal in infantry, and in cavalry were superior to, the forces sent out initially by the Athenians for the attempted capture of Syracuse. Taking Perikles' statement 'but the opportunities of war wait for no man' (I. 142. 1) suggests more flexibility in his strategy than is often credited. And the statement has a bearing on the activities of first Demosthenes and later Kleon.

To return to Demosthenes, it so happened that despite objections to his idea, a storm forced the issue and a landfall was made at Pylos. Demosthenes suggested that it would be a good idea to fortify that location. Very few places could have afforded a better anchorage for a fleet in bad weather. The small promontory occupied by Demosthenes and his men overlooked a large area of relatively deep water, sheltered from the open sea by an island running parallel to the shore-line. The northern outlet to the open sea was much narrower than that to the south. The whole region was well wooded at that time. At the northern end of the sheltered waters was a lagoon almost adjacent to the eventual Athenian position. A remnant of this progressively silted up area is still to be seen and its presence has suggested to some that it could well have been the anchorage for the Peloponnesian fleet when subsequent hostilities commenced. This is highly unlikely. The shoreline of the bay itself is, and was, ideal for the beaching or anchoring of a fleet. The Athenians had to sail around the Peloponnese to reach Kerkyra, being unable to use the Isthmus crossing in Corinthian-held territory. (See map, page xviii.)

Demosthenes' previous experience of working with the Messenians at Naupaktos had made him very much of their persuasion and he saw that a fortified area in Messenia could provoke problems for the Spartans. The location of Sphakteria is within a day's journey of Ithome, the place where the helots resisted the Spartans for ten years. The latter had allowed them to go free on the advice of an oracle after the ten year stand-off (see Appendix I) and they had been settled at Naupaktos by the Athenians whose active allies they now were.

No one took Demosthenes' suggestion seriously until the very fact of the continuing bad weather led the hoplites to fortify the area at which they had landed merely, as Thucydides suggests, to keep themselves occupied. Whether this was only a time filling exercise or one which recognised that the Spartans would eventually come against them is debatable. On balance, the latter has more credibility. Leaving Demosthenes with five ships and a garrison, the Athenian fleet continued its journey to Kerkyra.

The annual invasion of Attika by the Spartans proved only to be of fifteen days duration. The news of the occupation of Pylos, together with a lack of provisions shortened the incursion. The Lakedaimonian army now moved to the vicinity of Pylos and news of the Athenian move against Pylos was sent to the Peloponnesian fleet of some sixty ships off Kerkyra. Meantime Demosthenes had sent two ships to ask the Athenian naval squadron at Zakynthos for help.

Thucydides indicates that the Spartans intended to attack the hastily made Athenian fortification at Pylos by both land and sea and to block the entrances to the safe anchorage offered by the protection of the island of Sphakteria (IV. 8. 4–5). Thucydides gives an approximation of the number of vessels which could pass through the channel between each end of the island and the mainland as being two ships in the strait between Sphakteria and Pylos and nine ships at the other end of the island (IV. 8. 6).[2] An eminently defensible anchorage, or so one would have thought, which was improved further by the occupation of the island itself by the Spartans, who sent over hoplites commanded by Epitadas. Those on the island numbered 420 heavy infantry accompanied by their helot servants.[3] The Spartan plan would appear to have been to deny any relieving Athenian force coming by sea both the island and the safe anchorage. By safeguarding these they could look forward to quickly taking the unsupported Athenian force at Pylos by siege.

It is obvious from Thucydides' description that he had not visited the region, nor were his sources entirely correct in the topographical account which he followed. Not only is the island itself bigger than he suggests. His estimate of the length of the island is fifteen stadia, which is approximately one and three-quarter miles, whereas it is almost a mile longer. The water passage, the Sikia, between the northern point of the island and Pylos is very narrow and passage through it could well have been effectively blocked by two or three vessels. However, the southern entrance to the bay is far, far wider than he suggests. Even by using the bulk of the Peloponnesian fleet, which they could ill afford, it would have been very unlikely that entrance to the bay could have been impeded.

It seems clear when one visits the area that the bay, protected by the huge screen of Sphakteria, was an ideal location for a safe anchorage. Boats could easily be brought ashore on the gently sloping coastline to be quickly relaunched when necessary.

It is easy to appear wise after the event and many might question why heavy infantry was sent by the Spartans to the island. Thucydides describes it at IV. 8. 6, as being uninhabited, without roads and covered with woodland, much as it is today; not ideal conditions for troops normally deployed in close formation. This is to deny the Spartan practice of using their younger and more agile hoplites in sallies from their lines against enemies much in the manner that others used light infantry. The Spartan hoplite was the best trained and most adaptable of heavy infantry in the Greek world at this time.

While these preparations were going on, Demosthenes assumed correctly that the Spartans were preparing to attack his position both by land

and sea and made his own arrangements. Pulling ashore the three remaining vessels to a point close to his fortifications, he had them safeguarded by a stockade. Arming their crews as best he could and reinforced by the timely arrival of some forty Messenian hoplites who had obviously been undertaking coastal raids, he positioned his forces at the strongest positions of his landward fortifications. These last it should be remembered had been hastily built without tools to shape the stones (IV. 4. 2).[4]

The seaward side presented very difficult terrain for an enemy attack and was not so well fortified. However, it seemed obvious to Demosthenes that this would be the point recognised by his enemy at which an assault should be made. To counter this threat he selected sixty hoplites and some archers and took them out of the encampment to the very sea edge to repel any possibility of a landing being made. His preparations had been well made. The Spartan combined land and sea attack, which lasted for the best part of two days, proved unsuccessful.

One of the problems for the Peloponnesians was that their fleet of forty-three vessels had a restricted approach to the shore and only small numbers could make the approach at any one time. They were obliged to divide their ships into a series of groups each taking it in turn to attack the shoreline. This had the disadvantage that they could not overcome the Athenians by force of numbers but had the unwanted advantage of allowing each group a rest period between attacks. This last factor allowed the overall attack to be sustained for such a long time. It is to the Athenian defenders' credit that they were able to resist such a prolonged and fatiguing onslaught and to Demosthenes' for sustaining their morale.

To have achieved success the Peloponnesians needed to ground their ships so that their hoplites could operate on firm ground. The reason for the failure of the seaward attack is made clear by Thucydides:

> Brasidas showed himself the most conspicuous of all. Being captain of a galley, he noticed that the captains and pilots, because the shore was rocky, were inclined to hesitate and be careful of their ships, even when it seemed practicable to make a landing, for fear of dashing them to pieces. He would therefore shout that it ill became them through being thrifty of timber to allow their enemy to have built a fort in their country; nay, he urged, they must break their own ships so as to force a landing; and the allies he bade, in return for great benefits received from the Lakedaimonians, not to shrink from making them a free gift of their ships in the present emergency, but to run them aground, get ashore in any way they could, and master both the men and the place. And he not only urged on the rest in this way, but compelling his own pilot to beach his ship, he made for the gangway; and in trying to land he was knocked back by the Athenians, and after receiving many wounds fainted away. (IV. 11. 4–IV. 12. 1)

The next Spartan plan seems to have been directed to preparing for an assault using siege engines. Following their initial failure they had sent some ships to Asine (near modern Koroni) to collect timber for the manufacture of these engines. While waiting for their return the Athenian fleet from Zakynthos arrived along with the squadron from Naupaktos and four ships from Chios. With no offer of a sea battle being made by the Spartans and Sphakteria and the mainland bristling with hoplites, the Athenian fleet withdrew to an anchorage on the island of Proti a few miles to the north of Pylos.

It had obviously been decided by the commanders of the Athenian fleet to offer battle in open waters or, if that was refused, to force entry into the harbour and make an attack on the Peloponnesian fleet. When they arrived they discovered that not only was the Peloponnesian fleet at the harbour shoreline but both entrances were unguarded. The Peloponnesians were busy making ready to man their ships and Thucydides states that they were preparing to meet any Athenian vessels within the area of the anchorage, there being a sufficiency of room for their purposes and less for the seamanship of the Athenians to exploit. The seeming failure to guard the entrances would appear to have been a ploy. Whereas it was unlikely that the Peloponnesians would have any success in the open sea against the highly skilled manoeuvring of the Athenian fleet a more restricted area would suit them better. It is likely that the Athenian attack was a little earlier than anticipated and came before the Peloponnesians were fully prepared. The action which followed saw the Peloponnesians utterly routed by the swift onslaught with many crews taking flight. The Spartan soldiers on the shore rushed into the water in an attempt to stop their ships from being towed away and were successful in saving all those which had not been taken at the first attack. They in turn inflicted considerable damage on the Athenians until the engagement was broken off. With the Athenians in possession of the waters of the harbour the men on Sphakteria were isolated and cut off from their fellows.

Here we are given an insight into Spartan attitudes to its citizenry.[5] Magistrates were sent down to Pylos from Sparta with full powers to decide on what should be done next. With a naval patrol sealing off any contact from the shore with those on the island, they came to the decision that rather than have their men die from starvation or eventually at the hands of an overwhelmingly superior force, they should request a truce during which envoys could be dispatched to Athens.[6] The terms accepted by the Spartans were onerous. In return for the maintenance of the status quo in terms of the men on Sphakteria, the latter were to be allowed to receive some food and wine. However, the Peloponnesian ships which had taken part in the recent engagement were to be surrendered to the Athenians, together with all others around the coasts of Lakonia. No attacks were to be made from either side during the truce, at the end of which the ships would be returned. In all sixty ships were handed over and the envoys were conducted to Athens in an Athenian trireme.

The offer of peace made by the Spartan envoys was rejected largely due to the vehement opposition of Kleon[7]. On their return to Pylos the truce ended and the Athenians refused to return the Spartan fleet, claiming that a raid had been made on their garrison which therefore broke the terms of the truce. The Spartans vigorously protested at this behaviour, claiming it to be wholly unjust.

Hostilities were resumed and a further twenty ships were sent by Athens to bring the number of its fleet to seventy. In fine weather the whole fleet was anchored on all sides of the island at night. In more adverse weather conditions the fleet came wholly into the bay. During the day two ships sailed continuously around the island in opposite directions. Constant attacks were made against the Athenian position from the landward side. Discomfort was felt by both besieged forces.[8] Those on the island were sustained only by those volunteers, helots among them, who had been offered their freedom, who sailed from other points of the Peloponnese in small boats carrying supplies to the seaward side of the island, often when the wind strength made it imperative for the Athenians to seek safer anchorage on the eastern side of the island. Others skilled in swimming, for the greater part underwater, set out from the Spartan-held shore towing food supplies behind them. The Athenian garrison suffered from a shortage of water and the Athenian fleet had no nearby landfall at which to take their meals.

Although it was only July, Athens feared the approach of winter and with no sign of further approaches from Sparta, and news of the discomfort of their own men and the knowledge that food supplies were getting through to those on Sphakteria, opinion in Athens changed to one of regret at not having accepted the peace proposals. Kleon intervened once more because he was being criticised for being the main instigator of the rejection of those proposals. He denounced the reports from Pylos as lies and suggested that an expeditionary force be sent forthwith to capture Sphakteria. In so doing he suggested that this was what he would have suggested had he held command and that the present generals, and Nikias in particular, were not man enough to risk the task. His bluff was called and Nikias suggested that he, Kleon, should be asked to go and offered to resign his command so that he could take his place. The more Kleon tried to wriggle out of the consequences of his proposal, the more the Athenians urged him to lead the expedition in place of Nikias.

Hoist by his own petard, Kleon, in a fit of bravado, declared that he would not take a single Athenian with him but only the Lemnian and Imbrian troops now in Athens, together with some light troops from Ainos and a body of 400 archers.[9] Further, he made the boast that he would bring back the Spartans on Sphakteria as prisoners or kill them on the island within twenty days, a claim which was received with great mirth. Thereafter, he selected Demosthenes as his colleague, largely on the grounds that he had heard that he intended to make an attempt on the island himself. That decision had been made on two counts. First, because a fire had denuded the island of its scrub and woodland, thereby removing the danger to his men of operating on unfamiliar ground covered by obstacles to both contact and to vision. Thucydides suggests that memories of his disastrous experience in Aetolia made him wary of operating in wooded areas (IV. 30. 1). Second, his men were now experiencing such discomfort in their cramped conditions that they were ready for anything which might improve their lot. Their garrison area was so restricted that Thucydides states that some Athenians used to land on the island to take their meal, protected by a picket, and it was one such group which had accidentally been responsible for the conflagration.

Accident it may have been, but in the light of Demosthenes' intention and his Aetolian experience it may be that the firing of the island was an eminently sensible action to take. As commander he could now see the movements of his enemy and Thucydides mentions that Demosthenes discovered that there were more men on the island than he had hitherto assumed.

The fact that there was a fire is not in dispute. Neither is the fact that its result worked to the Athenian's advantage. If Thucydides had an opportunity to verify his statement with Demosthenes himself or another present at Pylos, his account is correct. Given that such opportunities existed one must weigh the possibilities carefully.

Reinforced by neighbouring allies and by the troops newly arrived with Kleon, preparations were finalised. A herald was sent to the Spartan camp on the mainland asking for the surrender of the men on Sphakteria. They were to be held prisoner in good conditions until such time as peace negotiations were completed. The Spartans would have none of this and on the next night 800 hoplites of the Athenian forces were ferried across to both the seaward and landward sides of the island where successful landings were made and the guard of thirty men killed before they had time to arm themselves. The landings had been made on the south part of the island, the main body of Spartans being encamped beside their water supply on the flatter central area. To their north, the highest point of the island facing Pylos was guarded by another contingent of Spartans. In this, an area with cliffs to the side facing Pylos and a steep approach to the summit from the south, there was an old fort which the Spartan commander Epitadas intended to use only if hard pressed.

As dawn was breaking, the second phase of landings was carried out. Messenians, around 800 archers and the same number of peltasts and the upper two tiers of crews from just over seventy ships, all organised into groups of 200, occupied the high points surrounding the main body of Spartans. The oarsmen were armed as well as they could be, but with nearly 8,000 of them present, along with the more formally armed contingents, the whole force must have been in the region of 9,000 or more men.[10] At a ratio of about 18 to 1 in the Athenians' favour this looks like overkill.

The Athenian force of hoplites advanced north towards the Spartans who immediately came into battle line and in turn advanced with the intention of joining battle with a force of hoplites double their own number. Their advance was checked by missile attacks from the flanks and rear and they were unable to come into contact with the Athenian heavy infantry who had halted and remained where they stood in good order. Repeatedly, the Spartans put the missile throwers to flight, but in such terrain and carrying much heavier armament they were unable to cause them any serious damage. The usual Spartan tactic of leaving the ranks to attack the nearest of the enemy before returning to their position did not achieve any lasting success.[11] As time went on, the Spartan hoplites tired and were frustrated in their efforts to come to grips with an enemy who poured missiles through the blinding dust of the ashes of the recent fire which filled the sky. Their armour afforded insufficient protection from javelins or arrows and, with the shouting of such a large enemy force making commands incomprehensible, their only option was to close ranks and retire to the fortification at the highest point of the island.[12] The very fact that the Spartans were falling back, even in good order, spurred on the opposition and a number of Spartans perished before they achieved their objective.

There, in a strong position and without the fear of being outflanked, the Spartans withstood the Athenian onslaught for much of the remainder of the day. What appeared to be a stalemate was only broken by the suggestion of Komon the Messenian commander.[13] He requested that he be allowed to lead some archers and peltasts to the rear of the Spartan position. At that time no such route was known. The starting point of this enterprise was beyond the view of the Spartans and must have involved something akin to traversing a rock face at times, such is the difficulty of the terrain. The attempt was successful and the appearance of another force to their rear marked the beginning of the end for the Spartans. Having broken through the defences the Athenian commanders stopped short of annihilating the remaining Spartans and offered them the opportunity to surrender.

Epitadas, the Spartan commander, had been killed and his deputy, Hippagretas, lay wounded though presumed dead. So it fell to Styphon as acting commander to suggest that he send a messenger to the mainland to ask advice from the commanders of the main Peloponnesian forces about what they should do. The Athenian commanders would not allow any Spartan to leave the island and sent instead heralds of their own. After several conferences, the final instruction from the mainland to those Spartans on the island was: 'The Lakedaimonians bid you decide your case for yourselves, but do nothing dishonourable' (IV. 38. 3).

After deliberating, the Spartans gave up their weapons and in due course the 292 survivors out of the original total of 420 heavy infantry were taken to Athens. Of these prisoners, 120 were Spartans, the remainder being *hypomeiones*.[14]

It would appear at this stage of the war that both sides feared the reputation, rather than the actuality, of the other. At sea the long dominance of Athens led to a feeling of gross inferiority among the Peloponnesians each time they engaged. A sea battle was almost won before the parties met, such was the temerity of the Peloponnesians in the face of the Athenian reputation. Only certain individuals such as Brasidas refused to be swept along by the prevailing assumption that Athens would always be victorious. At the onset of the attack by the Athenian fleet at Sphakteria many of the Peloponnesian crews had fled rather than contest the issue. It was the land forces who, in part, saved the day for Sparta in the latter stages of the engagement and limited the damage done by the Athenian fleet in the shallows of the harbour at Sphakteria. Here, the fear of Spartan supremacy on terra firma had its effect on the Athenian psyche. That recognition of Spartan skills in land engagements led to the preparation by the Athenian generals of an overwhelming force to deal with fewer than 500 Lakedaimonian hoplites. That it took almost a whole day to overcome this small number confirms their reputation, except at the point when the Spartans chose to withdraw to the fortification on the higher ground. At this point, with the Spartans at last giving ground, the morale of the opposition rose, only to fall once more when the determined resistance of the Spartans within the fortified area prolonged the action further.

Demosthenes had planned well. He left nothing to chance and used forces well suited to the terrain. The shock at the Spartan surrender which passed through the Greek world was based on the assumption that the Spartans would have fought on to the last man and never have considered giving up their arms. But what is actually astonishing is that such a small force, suffering from hunger and exhaustion, could have held out for so long against such odds. Denied the opportunity of a formal land battle, the commander of the onshore forces of the Peloponnesians proved unimaginative throughout.

So it was that Kleon made good his boast. After Sphakteria, Sparta was very much on the defensive. Without a conclusive agreement, the prisoners were held in Athens. Sparta had little to bargain with and Athenian demands were high. The threat that the prisoners would be put to death if Attika was invaded blunted Spartan belligerence. Pylos was strengthened and manned by a garrison from which the Messenians from Naupaktos operated, causing much damage to the Spartan-controlled hinterland. Helots were encouraged to desert with the real prospect that an uprising among this section of the populace might bring about a return of their homeland, Messenia. The greater part of the Peloponnesian fleet was still in Athenian hands. The capture of the island of Kythera by Nikias a year later (424 BC) offered another haven for helot deserters and another base from which predatory raids on the coastline of Spartan-held territory could be made. Such were the depredations that Sparta was obliged for the first time to raise a force of cavalry and archers to attempt a form of mobile defence. Repeated embassies were sent from Sparta to Athens but to no avail as Athens escalated her demands on each occasion. Spartan morale reached its lowest point. There seemed no relief or solution to their ever-growing problems.

It is at this point that a charismatic figure, mentioned earlier in this chapter, emerges to restore the fortunes of Sparta.

Notes

1. Seaborne raids on the coast of Lakonia proved to be of great nuisance value and were pursued for many years. It was an aggressive defensive tactic which wore down Spartan morale so long as Athens held complete control of the sea. The facility to arrive in force and ravage an area and re-embark before Peloponnesian forces could arrive denied the possibility of any formal engagement on land to the Spartans.

2. This has led to considerable debate as to whether the large bay was the anchorage for the Spartan fleet or the lagoon to its north adjacent to the Athenian position. However, W K Pritchett in *Studies in Ancient Greek Topography I*, settled the issue by showing that the rise in sea level since that period had created the lagoon and no anchorage at that point would have been available.

3. Each hoplite would have at least one servant, thus the total number on the island would have been a little short of 1,000 men. This is a sizeable group to keep provisioned and points to the magnitude of the problem when the Peloponnesians lost control of the seaway. The hoplites were a mix of Spartiates and 'Inferiors'. J F Lazenby's *The Spartan Army* makes the valid point that the nearest of the *perioikoi* would have come from the Messenian area (p.114 and note 4 p.195). Lazenby also advances a persuasive argument for the choosing by lot to have been done from the *lochoi* not by individuals but by *enonomotia*, a unit of thirty-five men, i.e., thirty-five men from each of the twelve *lochoi*. In this Lazenby follows and develops a suggestion made by A J Toynbee in *Some Problems of Greek History*, pp.376–7.

4. Athenian hoplites were the best builders of walls in the ancient world. They could put up a circumvallation in a surprisingly short time when undertaking sieges. Normally building tools were part of the equipment of any Athenian force. It would appear that this was not the case with this fleet or that when the men built the walls, initially out of boredom, the tools were still aboard ship. Although rudimentary, the Athenian defences proved effective. Demosthenes had recognised the need for a defensive wall, but the two commanders Sophokles and Eurymedon, were against it. Obviously their impatience to proceed with their assignments at Kerkyra and Sicily

blurred their judgement. On leaving they should have given tools for defensive repair and improvement to the garrison remaining at Pylos if they had them on the ships.

5. Spartiates were the full citizens of Sparta having voting rights. At the time of Sphakteria the decline in their numbers may well have been under way. Helot desertion and the disruptions of war may well have led to Spartiates not being able to meet their mess contributions, thereby reducing the number of those who could continue to claim full citizenship. Therefore the term Spartan broadens in its meaning.

6. Sparta, being such a close-knit society, would have concerns for the safety of its citizens. A large proportion of the *Spartiatai* would have relations on the island. It was one thing to die a glorious death in battle but quite another to face an ignominious death by starvation. The number of full Spartan citizens appears small but when set against the probable number of 4,000 Spartiates then in existence, it represented a significant proportion.

7. These negotiations and those later when Kleon was given command are lucidly presented in *The Archidamian War,* D Kagan pp. 231–244.

8. P B Kern, *Ancient Siege Warfare,* p.116, correctly emphasises the change from the besiegers becoming the besieged.

9. That these light-armed forces were conveniently at Athens at that time may indicate that Demosthenes had requested reinforcements of a particular type best suited for the attempt he was about to make on the island.

10. The crews of triremes were organised in three tiers and totalled 170 rowers, ten marine hoplites, possibly four to six archers, and up to sixteen other personnel for streerage, sail management, etc. Taking two levels of rowers, i.e. fifty-four + sixty-two from over seventy ships gives a total of well over 7,000 men. Add to these the availability of marines, archers and reserve oarsmen and the final total is around 8,000 men.

11. The Spartan army was much less reliant on light-armed troops than those of other city states. It fell to the younger and more mobile hoplites to make sudden sorties from the ranks against any light infantry which came against them.

12. It was surely the volume of shouting which disconcerted the Spartans and made orders impossible to hear. This was not a formal engagement in which orders would already have been passed down the line, but one in which they were obliged to constantly adapt both formation and response to ever-changing conditions. In such circumstances it is understandable that they became disorientated. In addition, this was an attack planned to be at long range. Demosthenes' experience in Aetolia had given him a well learned lesson. There may well have been serious conclusions drawn from the Athenian success on Sphakteria. Euripides' play *Herakles,* written after 424

BC, contains an interchange between Lykus and Amphytrion which points to the heart of the matter. Both are speaking of Herakles:

Lykus:

In other matters he was no hero – he was nothing!
His left arm never held a shield; he never faced
An enemy's spear. He used a bow – the coward's weapon,
Handy for running away. The test of courage is not
Skill with a bow, but the firm foot, the unflinching eye
When the spear drives its hurtling furrow through the ranks...

Amphytrion:

...And then you sneer
At that superb discovery, the bow! Listen:
I'll teach you a little sense. A man with spear and shield
Is slave to his own arms. Suppose, to right and left,
The next man loses courage, he lets himself get killed
Through others' cowardice; if he breaks his spear-shaft, how
Can he defend himself? He's lost his one resource.
While a skilled bowman has two great advantages:
First, he can shoot a thousand arrows, and still have more
To defend himself with; secondly, his fighting's done
Well out of reach – he wounds a watchful enemy
From perfect safety, with invisible stabs, and gives
No chance of striking back. In war it's common sense
To strike at every enemy within range, and keep
Your own skin whole. So in this argument my words
Contradict yours, and prove the exact opposite.'

(*Euripides. Medea and other plays*, trans P. Vellacott, Penguin Classics, 1963, pp. 158-9)

13. Named by Pausanias at IV. 26. 2, but not by Thucydides.

14. Spartan society was becoming a little more fluid than hitherto and it may be that with the gradual loss of Spartiate status new designations, as became obvious later, were appearing in the citizen ranks, e.g:
Hypomeiones, or inferiors to the full Spartiate or *Homoioi*;
Mothakes, another class of inferiors who were brought up alongside the sons of full Spartiates;
Tresantes, those who were designated as cowards, usually in battle. These 'tremblers' lost their full citizen status although it is hinted that they could regain their former position by some act of heroism;
Neodamodeis, technically a term meaning new citizens. However, this designation was usually given to emancipated helots who had given good military service to the State.
Despite the term 'citizen', this group, like those listed above, had no voting rights in the Spartan Assembly.
See also *The Spartan Army* by J F Lazenby, pp. 14ff & 45–46, where it is argued that those others with the Spartans were *hypomeiones*.

V

Brasidas

Brasidas was arguably the greatest commander to emerge from Sparta in this war and certainly the most problematic to the Athenians. To cite Lysander, the eventual victor, as being greater because of his achievements is to devalue the humanity and honesty of purpose shown by Brasidas, traits not notably present in Lysander. That both were for the prosecution of the war against Athens is beyond dispute, but the conditions under which each operated were very different. One wonders how well Lysander would have fared had he been limited to an army made up of a significant proportion of helots, lacking reinforcement or material support from home, and without a Persian paymaster or viable fleet.

Brasidas first comes to our notice in Thucydides' history at II. 25. 2, in the summer of 431 BC, as the commander for the defence of a district in the Peloponnese in which an Athenian incursion took place. At that time the Athenians were instigating their policy of raiding the coasts of the Spartan-held territories of the Peloponnese. Thucydides informs us that an Athenian fleet of 100 ships, reinforced by a further fifty ships from Kerkyra, were conducting this policy. Although specific in the total number of vessels, he says nothing about their dispositions. It is unlikely at this early time of the conflict, when Athens was pre-eminent in naval strength, that all 150 ships would have stayed together. Rather, two or three sub-groups would have been formed to make those raids sporadic and difficult for the Spartans to counter.

The landing at Methone in the south-west of the Peloponnese was fortuitous. Thucydides describes it as having no garrison and a weak wall, a prime target for a successful seaborne raid. The description of Brasidas' first known action in this war is typical of the commander we come to know. Taking only 100 hoplites, a force which could not have been pitted against the superior odds of the Athenian forces of perhaps several hundred hoplites, had the fleet been split into two, he quickly arrived at the beleaguered locality. He chose a time when the Athenians were foraging for supplies or ravaging the countryside and made a speedy passage through their disorganised lines. Their attention would, in any case, have been directed towards the city itself, and the expectation of any activity to their rear would have been minimal. He managed, with the loss of a few men, to reinforce the city with a garrison and thus thwart the plans of the Athenians, who sailed on to the coast of Elis.

His next appearance is as one of three commissioners from Sparta to Knemos, the naval commander, whose defeat at the hands of Phormio had provoked these appointments. That defeat had brought suspicion of negligence to the minds of the Spartans, they not yet having appreciated the significant difference in naval skills between the Athenians and the Peloponnesians. The duties of the commissioners sent in the summer of 429 BC were to correct the shortcomings of their forces. It is obvious that Brasidas was the person with the positive ideas.

The Peloponnesian fleet had far outnumbered the Athenian fleet of twenty ships. However, when looking at the total of forty-seven for the Peloponnesian vessels, one has to take into consideration that many were troop transports lacking the manoeuvrability of their opponents. Brasidas and his colleagues, Lykrophron and Timokrates, were adamant that a further test of strength should be made and that their troops would eventually arrive in the north-west combat area.

This is the only instance of the mention of training in the various descriptions concerning Brasidas (II. 86. 5). Thucydides records that both Athenian and Peloponnesian fleets undertook training for about a week on opposite shore-lines near the mouth of the Corinthian Gulf. No doubt the Peloponnesian efforts would have been at the instigation of the commissioners, including Brasidas, but one can assume that the chastened Knemos acknowledged the need, even with the additional vessels which had brought his fleet to a total of seventy-seven. A Peloponnesian army was in support of their fleet on the south shore of the Gulf. Although some initial success was achieved by the Peloponnesian fleet, the eventual victory went to the Athenians once more and the Peloponnesian fleet retired to Corinth. For a detailed description of the battle see chapter I.

Considering his later actions, it seems typical of the man that even after this setback, with the remainder of the fleet having returned to base and winter coming on, Brasidas, together with his co-commanders, should look for other opportunities to cause immediate harm to Athens.

On a suggestion which Thucydides ascribes to the Megarans (II. 93.1), a plan to take Peiraeus, the port of Athens, was made. The idea itself was brilliant and it is a pity that its originator is not named. Had it succeeded the war might well have ended much sooner. It is easy with hindsight to suggest that it could well have been better to wait until the following year. Then all the crucial elements could have been verified as being in order and in place; but that would be to ignore two paramount issues in any commander's thoughts, surprise and opportunity.

The Athenians enjoyed such an overwhelming superiority at sea that their harbour at the Peiraeus was undefended at that time. With the hoplites and oarsmen of the Peloponnesian fleet now at Corinth and not disbanded, it was proposed that they march across the Isthmus to the Megaran port of Nisaia.

Each oarsman took with him his oar, cushion and the leather thong he used as a rowlock. Having arrived at their destination, forty vessels were put at their disposal for the project. Here lies a contradiction in the sequence of Thucydides' narrative and the common sense, opportunism and adaptibility which the many participants in the enterprise must have displayed.

Had all gone as planned, the northern coast of Salamis would have obscured the initial approach. In any case, any fleet within those waters would have been presumed to be Athenian. Thereafter, the short journey down the eastern side of the island before crossing to the Peiraeus would have taken little time. Although this route is conjectural it is much shorter than following the mainland coastline. Indeed, Thucydides notes that the fleet made towards the nearest point of Salamis and suggests that this was instead of making straight for the Peiraieus, a curious comment when to do so would be to start on much the quickest route. He claims (II. 93 .4) there was mention of a wind which stopped the fleet. This is an invalid reason for a change of objective in that, although rowers may have found it harder work, they still could have reached their objective. A more cogent reason is mentioned towards the end of the description, namely that the boats themselves were not watertight (II. 94. 3). This factor may well have been recognised early in the operation leading to an adaptation of the plan, a matter usually disregarded because of its late entry in the narrative.[1] It is the timing of such a discovery which is important and the odds are for that discovery to have been made early, thus leading to the change of the plan to an attack against Athenian-held Salamis. The key clue lies in the words 'since they were appalled by the risk', early in the description (II. 93. 4). The reason may well have been their lack of confidence in the safety of their vessels.

When out of the water for any considerable length of time triremes dried out, leading to substantial leakage through their seams when refloated. On the other hand, a trireme that was waterlogged was difficult and slow to manoeuvre, leading to a periodic need to put the ships in dry dock. A fine balance had to be maintained in a long campaign to sustain the maximum fighting capability of a vessel. Obviously, the lighter the vessel the greater its manoeuvrability. This appears to be the key factor. According to our source the decision to attack Salamis rather than the Peiraeus was made early. The difference in distance between the primary objective and its replacement is easily appreciated from a glance at the map.

It was recorded that the march to Nisaia had taken place at night. Therefore it can be assumed that the journey to Salamis was also taken under cover of darkness. The attack was successful in that the three ships stationed near a fort of Boudoron on the promontory, to threaten any vessel entering or leaving Nisaia, were captured, their crews being absent. This shows a lax overconfidence on the part of the Athenians. If only three triremes were to do their job satisfactorily a constant watch should have been in place. It would have been foolhardy for the Peloponnesians to bypass this small squadron, which could later have caused much annoyance to their rear. It could well have been their original intention to disable these vessels before proceeding on their mission.

Much of the island was pillaged. Fire-signals warned the Athenians of the attack. Many Athenians thought that the Peiraeus had been captured and those at the harbour itself thought that Salamis had succumbed and the enemy was about to sail into their harbour. Thucydides states that this might have actually happened had there not been a wind, which we have already discounted; or if there had not been temerity in the Peloponnesian forces (II. 94. 1). That caution was soundly based considering the adverse condition of their ships.

The modified plan proved extremely successful and much booty and many prisoners were collected. At news of a relief force approaching Salamis, the Peloponnesians returned to Nisaia.

As a consequence the Athenians made modifications to their harbour, making the entrance narrower and establishing a permanent guard, thereby making a similar attempt extremely difficult. Thucydides' description of the Athenian mobilisation makes it clear that the boats to be manned to go to the relief of Salamis were onshore. Thereafter, they always maintained manned vessels already in the water.

Should we conclude that this was an opportunity lost? That having alerted the Athenians to their lack of security the Spartans had made their enemy aware of a weakness which could otherwise have been exploited in the future? For the able commander to wait for such future opportunities is to prevaricate. Brasidas and Knemos were correct in taking advantage of any opportunity to harass the enemy. They could not know of the fleet's condition until after they were committed. Perhaps the most important aspect to consider is the morale of the men of the Peloponnesian fleet in the aftermath of their two encounters with Phormio's much smaller fleet of twenty ships. No doubt they were dispirited. Any commander worthy of his position will do his utmost to bolster morale. Faced with the two disappointments which many had suffered at the hands of Phormio's fleet, it was incumbent on the Spartan commanders to restore their men's self-esteem. It is understandable therefore that they should grasp the opportunity offered to them by the Megarans. Even with the modified plan their success struck terror in the hearts of the Athenians such as had not hitherto been experienced (II. 94. 1). So the Peloponnesians could be dismissed to their homes with that vitally important feeling of success and self-satisfaction which could lead them to expectations of further successes in the future. This is undoubtedly one outcome of successful command.

Our next encounter with Brasidas is when he was sent as an adviser to Alkidas, the commander of forty vessels. The latter had been a lame duck commander, choosing to avoid contact with the enemy and failing to fulfil his remit to bring aid to the beleaguered Lesbians who had rebelled against Athens in anticipation of Spartan support. He had cut and run from the opposition, arriving back at the Peloponnese, where the Spartans now wanted his fleet to exploit the opportunities presented by the revolution on Kerkyra. They joined Brasidas at Kyllene together with thirteen triremes of Leukadian and Ambrakiot origin in the summer of 427 BC.

Despite his poor showing Alkidas remained admiral of the fleet, now boosted to fifty-three in number, but this time bolstered by the energetic advice of the officially appointed adviser, Brasidas. Although some negativity is still to be detected in the conduct of Alkidas, this proved to be a more successful enterprise against the enemy. The fact that he came to battle must have been to some degree a consequence of Brasidas' urgings.

After four or five days of revolutionary activity, the democrats held the upper hand in Kerkyra, supported by the Athenian commander Nikostratos. The Spartan fleet had arrived at Sybota opposite the southern tip of the island of Kerkyra and at dawn set sail for the city. Its appearance caused great consternation. Contrary to the advice given to them by the Athenians to allow them to sail out first with the Kerkyran fleet following in order, the Kerkyrans hastily manned sixty vessels and sent them off as soon as their complement was satisfied. This meant a disorderly assemblage of ships in no immediate battle order. Such was the disarray that Thucydides reports that two ships deserted to the Peloponnesians while the crews on others fell to fighting among themselves (III. 77. 2).

The arrangement of the Peloponnesian fleet for the engagement is worthy of scrutiny. It is bolder and has more purpose than anything Alkidas had done hitherto. It shows a clear analytical assessment of the prevailing conditions and appears to be out of character with Alkidas' previous thinking in any of his command decisions. Although Thucydides makes no mention of the originator of the battle plan, it is highly likely that Brasidas was sufficiently persuasive in his position as adviser for the arrangement described to have been put in place. Only twenty vessels were set to oppose the disorganised force of sixty Kerkyran ships, the remaining thirty-three were set against the Athenian squadron of twelve, which contained the premier vessels, the *Paralos* and *Salaminia*, often used for business of state. This shows imaginative thinking, of which, on the evidence of Alkidas' previous service as a naval commander, he was incapable.

Needless to say, the Peloponnesian fleet opposed to the disorganised Kerkyrans was successful. The Athenian fleet chose not to attack the enemy centre but made a foray against its wing, sinking one ship and forcing it into a defensive circle as had been the case in the first Peloponnesian engagement against Phormio off Naupaktos.[2] This obviously brought back memories of that disastrous occasion, so that that section of the Peloponnesian fleet ranged against the Kerkyrans disengaged and came to the support of their fellows. Seeing this, the Athenians, keeping their prows towards the now united enemy, backed water and retired from the conflict slowly enough to allow the Kerkyrans to make for home and safety.

The decision to move the whole fleet against the Athenians was critical in that it placed superior numbers against superior seamanship. Although the Peloponnesians had won the battle at sea, they did not follow it up but returned to their mainland base with the thirteen ships they had captured. At this point (III. 79.3) Thucydides mentions that Brasidas urged his superior, Alkidas, to attack Kerkyra on the following day while all there was in total confusion. However, true to form, Alkidas avoided direct confrontation and chose to attack Leukimne on a pillaging expedition, thereby losing the initiative gained by the naval action. The chance of winning control on land soon passed. A report was received warning of the approach of sixty Athenian ships and Alkidas, this time with good reason, immediately withdrew from the area by hauling his ships over the narrow Leukadian isthmus to avoid contact with the approaching fleet.

So an opportunity was lost to gain control at Kerkyra. Brasidas had urged it but had to bow to the authority of his superior officer in the matter. The Athenians would have found it difficult to dislodge the Peloponnesian forces had they achieved entrenched land positions as a result of Brasidas' recommendation.

It is a pity that Thucydides did not name the commanders of the two squadrons of the Peloponnesian fleet. One can assume that Alkidas was the admiral in charge of the larger number of vessels that was forced into a defensive formation. Brasidas, as his adviser, was likely to be with him, for earlier he had been described as being on board the admiral's vessel (III. 76. 1).

At IV.11.4 Thucydides reports an action typical of Brasidas leading by example. This was in the summer of 425 BC when a combined Spartan land and sea operation was made against the Athenian fortified position at Pylos with the intent to dislodge the force. The Athenian commander, Demosthenes, aware that access to his position was possible from the seaward approach, posted sixty hoplites and some archers along the limited shoreline approach to impede any attempt to land. Indeed, the possible landing area was so limited that the Spartan vessels had to make their approach in small squadrons. Brasidas, serving as a captain of a trireme, became aware that the Peloponnesian ships were therefore not fully committing themselves to the attack for fear of causing damage to their vessels. His reaction was to urge the allied forces to sacrifice their ships for the sake of all that they enjoyed from Sparta and not to allow the fear of damaging some wood stop them from running their vessels aground on the shore. Not content with mere words, he ordered his steersman to make for the shore and there, in an attempt to force a landing, was severely wounded. On fainting from loss of blood he fell into the bow of the ship, his shield slipping from his arm into the sea, later to be retrieved by the Athenians as a trophy.

Some may think this a foolish act of bravado, but leadership by example was, and still is, considered important. A foolish act of bravado is usually a spontaneous emotive reaction to a set of unforeseen circumstances. In this case, however, Brasidas had clearly evaluated what was impeding success in the operation. He had rightly come to the conclusion that the captains of the fleet were giving precedence to the safeguarding of their equipment, their ships, over their objective, the securing of a landing and the taking of the enemy position. He had made his case to the allies and presumably thought that he then had their support. Following his individual action he would have anticipated others similar to his own. These were the actions and thought processes of a valuable commander.[3]

Brasidas was obviously one of those rare commanders who felt it incumbent on himself to take immediate and positive action if he perceived either a threat to the Peloponnesian alliance or an opportunity to do harm to the enemy. Spartan commanders, once beyond their homeland boundaries, held supreme authority, and once Brasidas had achieved such an appointment, it can be perceived that his actions did much to redress the balance between Sparta and Athens at a time when it tilted very much in the latter's favour. His analysis of prevailing conditions would often lead him to grasp an opportunity which might not present itself again. His overall view of strategic elements was soundly based.

He appears to have been given his command in response to requests from some of the cities in Chalkidike who wished for support from Sparta in their proposed revolt against Athens (IV. 80. 1). These cities promised to help to maintain an army. The case for such an expedition was further strengthened by Perdikkas, king of Makedonia. He was uneasy in his relationship with the Athenians and wished for support in an expedition to subdue his neighbour Arrhabaios, king of the Lynkestians. With this in mind Perdikkas offered substantial financial support. This suited Sparta well, drained as it was by the coastal raids on its territories by the Athenians and facing increased danger of a helot uprising. Insecurity and low morale were commonplace. The shock of Sphakteria had led to a loss of confidence and those Spartans who favoured a more aggressive prosecution of the war were in the minority. However, all hoped that such an expedition would divert the attention of Athens and, if successful, provide a bargaining counter with which the return of the Spartiate prisoners could be negotiated.[4]

Brasidas is said by Thucydides to have volunteered for the command (IV. 81. 1). This would have been entirely in character. He was given 700 helots as hoplites, thus removing some possible trouble makers from the Peloponnessos (IV. 80. 5). The remainder of his troops he engaged as mercenaries.

In 424 BC, while raising troops around Corinth for his northern campaign, he heard that Megara was beset by an Athenian attempt to gain control there. He was quick to take action. Had he not done so the Boiotians would have been isolated from the Peloponnesian alliance, Megara being the normal route to the south for land forces from Boiotia. Loss of Megara would have limited movement between the Peloponnese and Boiotia to the sea. Moving forces by ship would have proved perilous at a time when the Athenians were a threat in all waterways. It was opportune that it was Brasidas, with forces, who was at Corinth at that very moment.

To digress a little, the desire of the Athenians to isolate Boiotia loomed large in what is described as the Archidamian war, i.e. the first ten years of the Peloponnesian war. We have Demosthenes' attempt to gain control of Aitolia, then his attempt to attack the under-belly of Boiotia in conjunction with Hippokrates' direct invasion of the Delion area. This was mistimed and led to the defeat of Hippokrates at Delion, and the action presently under discussion, which was under the joint command of both generals.[5]

The ground for an action against Megara had already been laid by Nikias' capture of the island of Minoa in 427 BC. This was done to deter a repetition of Brasidas' attack on Salamis which, with better vessels, might well have arrived at the Peiraeus (see above).

Minoa no longer exists. The island had been very close to the mainland and it would appear that at that time only a narrow channel divided it from the mainland. The description at III. 51. 3–4 makes it clear that the channel between the island and the mainland was silting up. So what was an island not very distant from Nisaia has now become a promontory and part of the mainland itself.

The revolution in Megara which had seen the democrats oust the oligarchs had not put a stop to the regular invasions of their country by the Athenians. Those oligarchs established themselves in Pegai, the port of Megara on the Corinthian Gulf from where they continued to be a thorn in the side of the ruling party. A desire among the citizenry to put a stop to one of Megara's problems by recalling the exiled oligarchs led to some alarm among the leaders of the democrats, who entered into secret negotiations with Demosthenes and Hippokrates, both elected as generals in 424 BC. Their goal was to betray the city to the Athenians and plans were laid to that end. It is obvious from this that the general populace was not of a mind to change its loyalties in the war despite the hardships suffered. The leaders of the popular party did not feel they were sufficiently entrenched to use the power of persuasion to achieve their end.

The capture of the long walls down to the sea from Megara to Nisaia was to be the first objective, so that the Peloponnesian garrison stationed at the port would be unable to assist the upper city.

In preparation for the achievement of their objective the Megaran conspirators had established the practice of nightly taking a boat loaded on a cart through the gates on the pretence that they were going to evade the Athenian blockade (IV. 67. 3). On the night designated for the coup the 600 Athenian hoplites under the command of Hippokrates had taken up a position in a ditch not far from the walls; and even nearer, Demosthenes lay in wait with a force of Plataians and *peripoloi*.[6] With the gates opened and the cart within the aperture, Demosthenes and his force ran forward while at the same time their Megaran accomplices killed the guards. After defeating the Peloponnesians who had come to close the gates against the Athenians, the main body entered and secured possession of the walls, with the garrison retreating to Nisaia thinking that all Megara had gone over to the Athenians. Success had been with the leaders of the democrats thus far, but the next stage in their plan came to grief.

It had been arranged that with the approach of 4,000 Athenian heavy infantry supported by 600 cavalry from neighbouring Eleusis, they would exhort their fellow Megarans to march out to battle. In the meantime they manned the gates themselves and anointed all prospective participants in the coming conflict with oil so that by that very difference they would be recognised and not harmed by the Athenian army in its attack.

Obviously this was too much for one or more Megarans to stomach. The idea that their fellow citizens would be killed, whatever their political viewpoint, was not to their liking and the plot was revealed to the opposition. Cleverly, the opposition did not reveal their knowledge of the intelligence they had received, but argued successfully against marching out to face the Athenians on the grounds that at times when their strength had been greater they had not countenanced such a military response to an Athenian attack. Their view prevailed, and by carefully keeping a watch on the gates of Megara they thwarted the plans of the enemy.

The Athenians, disappointed that the plan had not reached its final objective, sent for workmen from Athens to build a cross-wall cutting off Megara from Nisaia. The Peloponnesian garrison surrendered on seeing the near completion of these works, still under the impression that the Megarans were now against them and not having any hope of being provisioned.[7]

So with Nisaia taken and Megara under threat, Brasidas sent a message to the Boiotians to meet him at Tripodiskos, a village between Pegai and Megara. Quickly moving with 2,700 Corinthian hoplites, 400 Phliasians, 600 Sykonians and the helot forces he had gathered himself, he marched to his meeting point. He had expected that Nisaia would still be in Peloponnesian hands but, hearing news to the contrary, he approached

Megara secretly with 300 chosen men. He asked the Megarans to allow him to enter the city, assuring them that he was confident of retaking Nisaia. However, the Megarans were unwilling to agree, being at that time in a state of political ferment and preferring to await the result of a likely confrontation between Peloponnesian and Athenian forces.

The day after his return to Tripodiskos saw the arrival of the Boiotians at dawn. They had made good time, worried as they were about an adverse outcome, which would isolate them from their allies should Megara fall. Their army had been at Plataia and 600 cavalry and 2,200 hoplites were dispatched to meet Brasidas, the main body returning to their homes. Brasidas now had a force of some 6,000 heavy infantry with the afore-mentioned cavalry in support. The first action took place in the plain which reaches down to the sea. Here the Athenian light-armed troops were scattered over the plain foraging with their hoplites around Nisaia and by the sea. Hitherto no help had come to the Megarans on any previ-ous Athenian invasion of their territory, so it came as a complete surprise when the Boiotian cavalry appeared and ran down many of the dispersed light infantrymen, eventually driving those remaining down to the sea. The Athenian cavalry made a counter-attack, killing the Boiotian hipparch and those of his followers who had come very close to Nisaia.[8] In reality the action was a stalemate but the Athenians claimed victory because the Boiotians claimed the bodies of their fallen in a truce, thereby conceding the field to the Athenians by common custom.[9]

So it was that the Athenians retired to Nisaia, rejoining the main force, while Brasidas advanced between the sea and the city of Megara and offered battle. This was an astute move. Brasidas was now in a position to protect Megara. To take the city the Athenians would first have to defeat his army, which was unlikely given the disparity in numbers.[10] Not to make the attempt would leave the Athenians without any credibility among those in the city who supported them. The balance of the argument rested with the likely losses to be sustained on each side. The Athenians calculated that they would lose a disproportionate number of their best men, whereas the allied forces of the Peloponnesians and Boiotians would lose only a fraction of their available forces. No attack was made by either side and the upshot was that Brasidas' bluff succeeded. He was credited with a victory because the Athenians chose not to engage. Without any loss of men he had saved Megara and on entry to the city his talks with his supporters there left the democratic element muted.

Brasidas had succeeded in the time-honoured manner of the best of commanders: to achieve one's objective by manoeuvre rather than by engagement.[11] There was no doubt in the minds of the Megarans about who had triumphed in the war of nerves. The morale and loyalty to their commander of Brasidas' forces would no doubt have been enhanced by the evidence of his tactical thinking, making those who were to travel north with him trust his judgement the more, knowing that their welfare was an important element in his planning.

With the Athenian refusal to come to battle and their withdrawal, Brasidas and his men were welcomed into Megara. Securing the city for the Peloponnesian alliance, Brasidas dismissed the allies and went back to Corinth to complete his preparations for his expedition to the north.

Shortly after the Megaran affair Brasidas moved north with 1,700 hoplites to commence his campaign. Thucydides gives this number (IV. 4. 78) and later (IV. 80. 5), makes mention that 700 of them were helots equipped as hoplites, the remainder of the recruits being Peloponnesians serving as mercenaries. These helots proved to be the lucky ones. On their eventual return from the north in 421 BC, they were given their freedom and settled alongside the already existing Neodamodeis at Lepreon.[12]

Brasidas' route would have taken him through the allied area of Boiotia and possibly Lokris and Doris before his arrival at Herakleia in Trachis. This was a colony set up by the Spartans two years earlier in 426 BC.[13] There he made contact initially with the northerly Achaians and those Thessalians who were friendly towards Sparta, to seek safe conduct through Thessaly. The majority of the Thessalians were pro-Athenian and some attempted to stop his march near Meliteia. Having persuaded his opposition that he had no intent to harm any part of Thessaly, he took the opportunity on their departure, following his promise not to go any further, to press ahead with his journey before additional forces could be gathered against him. He did not wait for any response from the party opposed to his journey and, with forced marches, arrived at Dion in the territory controlled by the Makedonian king Perdikkas.[14]

It has already been observed that, as a subordinate commander, Brasidas was quick to respond to developing conditions either by direct action himself, as was the case with Methone and Pylos, or to give advice to his commander, exemplified in the naval actions in the Corinthian Gulf and off Kerkyra. One can appreciate the appetite he would have had for the suggested attack on the Peiraeus. Now he had his own command and had already demonstrated his credentials to his enemy and the allies at Megara. Naturally, news of his appearance in the north would cause some concern to the Athenians, particularly those such as Demosthenes and his colleague who had been outwitted by him at Megara.

A force of 1,700 hoplites could not be defined as an invasion force on its own, rather an annoyance within an area notionally under Athenian control. However, should Brasidas win over the support of Thrakians and the Greek cities within the area, the numbers would rise significantly. With his arrival the Athenians could only guess that some cities within the immediate area of his likely operations had invited some form of support from Sparta; and at that time they were unsure of the position of Perdikkas. This point is made in defence of Thucydides himself, who at that time was commanding a squadron of ships at Thasos and who was later exiled for only partly forestalling Brasidas.

Thucydides reports that all in the area were keen to have Brasidas act in their interests. The Chalkidian representatives who were with Brasidas advised him not to remove immediately all curbs on Perdikkas in his dealings with his neighbours, so that he would be more committed to the common objective of acting against Athens. Perdikkas on the other hand wanted to bring Arrhabaios, who was the son of the king of the Lynkestian Makedonians, Bromeros, under his control. This, together with what the envoys of Perdikkas had said in Sparta prior to the expedition, gave Brasidas pause for thought. The envoys had suggested that adjacent areas around Perdikkas' kingdom could well be brought over to the alliance. Arrhabaios himself had already contacted Brasidas requesting that he act as arbitrator between himself and Perdikkas. Therefore, when Brasidas was persuaded to join Perdikkas in the latter's expedition against Arrhabaios, he told Perdikkas that, prior to the opening of hostilities, he wished to attempt to bring Arrhabaios over to the Spartan alliance. This was a sensible approach. However, it did not suit Perdikkas' agenda and he informed Brasidas that he had not been invited to the north with half of the commissariat being paid for by Perdikkas for him to be negotiating with Perdikkas' enemy. Nonetheless, Brasidas did what he thought was prudent and, after discussion with Arrhabaios, desisted from attacking Lynkestis, leading Perdikkas to cut his support for the Lakedaimonian force from half to one third.

Brasidas' next move was to march against Akanthos with his Chalkidian allies. His arrival in their area was just before the grape harvest, a factor which proved decisive. One wonders whether the timing of his appearance was deliberately at harvest time. As in many cities at that time there were two parties, one democratic and one which supported a more oligarchic form of government. This ambivalence and the fear for their threatened harvest was enough to allow entry for Brasidas, so that he could address the assembly. Thucydides states that his entry was at his own request with the promise that he would come alone. A brave thing for any commander to undertake, but it is as well to remember the honour code of guest-host relations Greek to Greek. In addition, Brasidas may well have made some pledge about his visit and this would be regarded as sacrosanct.

His reported speech is in two parts: first expressing disappointment at his forces being excluded from the city when they had come as liberators, and second, warning that, if he was rejected, he would have to regard them as hostile and lay waste to their lands. The fear for their harvest seemed to loom large in the Akanthian deliberations for, on hearing a reiteration of the promise that they would be independent if they revolted, they allowed entry to Brasidas' army. Their example was followed by Stagiros a little to the north of Akanthos.

Winter was now upon him, but Brasidas had garnered allies from Thrace and marched against Amphipolis. This was an Athenian colony situated at a strategic position in relation to Thrace, where Seuthes had just succeeded Sitalkes as king of the Odrysians. Thucydides indicates (IV. 103. 2) that Brasidas must have been in touch with certain of the citizens of Amphipolis. He comments that he had been in contact with some citizens of Argilos, a township nearby, who resided in Amphipolis and who were part of a larger group within that city who wished to go over to those opposing Athens.

The importance of the strategic position of Amphipolis cannot be over-emphasised, commanding as it did the easier east–west coastal route from Chalkidike to Thrace at the passage of the river Strymon to the sea. With Perdikkas to the west of Chalkidike, overland access to the area could only be made via Amphipolis or circuitously from the north, an approach through hostile territory unlikely to be attempted by even the most desperate of Athenian commanders. If Brasidas was to secure this position, the intervening area of Chalkidike could be reduced piecemeal by picking off one city after another in a region which lay between the then friendly Perdikkas and Amphipolis.

Before continuing with the description of Brasidas' well planned approach to Amphipolis, we must consider what might have been his overall aim and the prevailing conditions.

The Odrysian empire is described by Thucidides (II. 96) as extending from the whole of the Black Sea coastline up to the mouth of the Danube westwards to the Strymon river. At this time the Greek cities on the Aegean seaboard from Abdera to Byzantion found themselves not only having to pay tribute to Athens but also for some years previously having to make payment to first, Sitalkes, and then his successor, Seuthes. This may have accounted for the reduction in tribute asked by Athens of Abdera from 15 to 10 talents in 432/1 BC.[15]

Amphipolis had been founded by Athens in 437/6 BC to counter further Thracian expansion. In addition, its hinterland was rich in forests for ship-building. Indeed, after its capture, Brasidas set up a building programme for triremes on the Strymon river (IV. 108. 6). It was a prime target for Brasidas if he was to gain control over Chalkidike. Although not discussed by Thucydides, Brasidas, on settling affairs in Chalkidike, may well have intended moving eastward by both land and sea along the Aegean seaboard, persuading or reducing those cities subject to Athens until he reached the Hellespont. Losing control of this waterway would have been a serious setback for Athens, relying as it did on its trade with the Black Sea area. He would have had two Athenian naval bases to contend with, Thasos and Ainos, both having a harbour and safe anchorage. On the capture of Amphipolis Brasidas should have been in receipt of significant reinforcements from Sparta.

Brasidas' march on Amphipolis started from Arnai, a town which has yet to be identified, but which must have been south or west of Bromiskos, for Brasidas arrived at this last place in time to take supper before proceeding with the march northward during the night. Marching conditions could not have been comfortable, for Thucydides declares: 'The weather was bad and somewhat snowy' (IV. 103. 2). He says Brasidas wished to make haste because of the conditions.[16]

This implies that the climatic conditions were part of the planning. Concealment of approach was a prime issue in his attempt to take Amphipolis. The decision to time the arrival at the destination during darkness was another. To time a march in adverse conditions required knowledge of both route and topography. We are not aware that Brasidas himself had been in the environs of Amphipolis up to this time, but from the fact that he had contact with the Argilians resident in Amphipolis we can assume that he had more than adequate intelligence.

In darkness the Argilians passed their city into Brasidas' hands on his arrival and guided his army to a bridge on the Strymon river. Its guard was overcome partly because of the bad weather and also because of treachery. Having achieved a crossing, Brasidas was now in control of all Amphipolitan property outside the walls. Thucydides (IV. 114.3) states that if Brasidas had marched straight to the city he would have taken it and yet follows this by saying that none of the plans laid earlier was carried out by those in the city. This leaves us in little doubt that Thucydides was wrong in his assumption that Brasidas could take the city. Without the planned help of those within who would open the gates to him and did not because of fear of the opposition (IV. 114. 4), he had to satisfy himself with the control of the surrounding area.

We learn more of Thucydides from what follows thereafter. He was commander of a fleet at Thasos, an island not very distant from the area of action. Thasos was the main Athenian naval base along the Thracian seaboard. It, together with Ainos, had the best harbours and anchorages in the area. Thucydides' family possessed the right to work gold-mines on the mainland and had sound relations with those who held significant positions within the area. To him fell the responsibility of reacting to the developing situation.

According to Thucydides Brasidas was aware of the nature of his likely opposition and Thucydides suggests that it was because of that knowledge that moderate terms were proposed to the people of Amphipolis. Be that as it may, the evidence shows that Brasidas was always even-handed and moderate in his negotiations. His fine reputation coming down to posterity was won in part by that aspect of his character and it is Thucydides himself who attests to the fact.

The other interesting aspect of Thucydides' description is his evaluation of the possibilities open for himself. He hoped at most to secure the city of

Amphipolis before it surrendered or to save Eion, the port of Amphipolis. This is an important statement to consider when taken alongside his claim that his influence on the mainland could bring considerable allied forces to the succour of Amphipolis.

Brasidas' appearance provoked surprise and confusion. Without the help of his confederates within the city, its capture would be delayed. He was aware that salvation from elsewhere could soon be at hand for the city and probably knew that Eukles, the Athenian commander there, had already sent for help. Whether because of this, or more likely because he was the exemplary type of commander who sought to achieve his end by means other than direct combat, his next step was to offer moderate and attractive terms to the inhabitants. If they came over to him, resident Amphipolitans *and* Athenians could retain their property and citizen rights in an independent city allied to Sparta. Those who wished to leave could do so within five days taking their possessions with them. The Athenians were a minority within the city and many Amphipolitans had relatives among those who had been captured outside the walls, so these terms proved very persuasive.

Thucydides arrived just after Amphipolis went over to Brasidas, but in time to occupy Eion, its seaport. Thucydides should be regarded as having been successful in the prevailing situation. The Athenian general, Eukles, commanding the defences of the city, had lost control of the populace in face of Brasidas' moderate proposals and there was little that Thucydides could do to remedy this. His later exile from Athens for his failure to protect Amphipolis was excessive.

At 1V. 107. 2, Thucydides remarks that Brasidas *suddenly* (ἄφνω) launched an attack on Eion. Again the element of surprise is implicit in Brasidas' planning. This proved to be a two-pronged assault by both land and water, with vessels sailing down the Strymon in an attempt to capture the entrance to Eion. Both were repelled; but this did not deter Myrkinos, a city just to the north of Amphipolis, from coming over to Brasidas along with Galepsos and Oisyme, cities to the south and east. Preparations were now made for the building of triremes.[17]

Perdikkas now arrived and this reinforcement, together with Brasidas' moderation, led many cities to seek to make terms with him, thus creating a major problem for the Athenians. The heavy Athenian defeat at Delion (see Chapter III) was another setback for the Athenian cause at this time. Brasidas sent a request to Sparta for reinforcements:

> ...the Lakedaimonians, however, did not comply with his request, partly on account of the jealousy of the foremost men, partly also because they wished rather to recover the men taken on the island (Sphakteria) and to bring the war to an end. (1V. 108. 7)

If this comment is true, it is an indictment of those in charge of policy within Sparta. Here, for the first time, was a man who had taken the initiative from the enemy and was threatening the very core of its power base – the continued loyalty of those on the Aegean littoral. He had done so with a relatively small force, part of which comprised helots the like of whom the Spartans were only too eager to see outside the Peloponnese at that time. The fact that it is reported that some of the Spartiates were envious of his success suggests small-mindedness rather than conservatism. The second and third points, their desire to get back those men captured at Sphakteria and achieve a peace agreement, are understandable. However, their objections that Brasidas' luck might not hold, or that by achieving further successes he might prejudice the likely return of the prisoners sound hollow and timid. To deprive a successful commander of reinforcements impeded his powers of consolidation and limited his capacity to manoeuvre. It is important to assess Brasidas' achievements against such a background. To fight a formidable enemy was problem enough; to lack the support of one's own side in so doing was disgraceful. Here was a man who, single-handedly, had tilted the balance of the war in Sparta's favour being left to his own devices through envy, self interest and a fear that luck would not hold. To have given Brasidas reinforcements would have diminished the possibility of the latter and pressed the Athenians even harder. If one considers these facts, together with the conduct of Brasidas following the armistice, a balanced view is attained.

Brasidas' reputation went before him and many of the cities of the peninsula of Akte welcomed him as he continued to campaign through the winter of 424/3 BC. Those who did not, namely Sane and Dion, had their lands ravaged. These two were near the head of the peninsula and were strategically important. They may well have been persuaded not to capitulate because the Athenians sent men at this difficult time of the year to boost the garrisons of cities which had, as yet, not gone over to Brasidas. This, and the following spring, were the critical times at which Spartan reinforcements should have been dispatched. Nonetheless, by switching his aim to the strategic location of Torone Brasidas maintained the initiative, the prime objective of any commander. With his arrival just before dawn at a point about a quarter of a mile from the city, twenty men armed with daggers were sent forward. Their approach was covered by darkness and seven of their number, led by the Olynthian, Lysistratos, were let in by Brasidas' sympathisers within the city. It would appear that the other thirteen men were too fearful to continue with their mission (IV. 110. 2).

The seven proceeded through the wall facing the sea, climbed the hill with their Toronaian collaborators and killed the guards at this, the highest watch point of the city, before breaking open the postern gate facing Kanastraion, the most easterly prong of the three peninsulas of Chalkidike.

While this was going on Brasidas had quietly advanced a short distance, from where he sent forward 100 light infantry (peltasts) to await the opening of the gates. There appears to have been some delay to the expected moment for entry and these peltasts were now very close to the walls. That delay may well have been caused by the Toronaians having had to spend time cutting through the bar of the gate to the market place.[18]

All had been achieved without the other guard points or the townsfolk noticing. The peltasts were allowed in at several points and at the same time a fire-signal was made so that Brasidas with the main force could raise a cry and rush forward to compound the confusion of the surprised citizens. Entry was made via gates and by scaling scaffolding already in place for the repair of a damaged section of the wall. All high points within the city were secured. The fifty or so Athenians who had been asleep in the market-place fled either by the land route or by the two guard ships to the citadel, which occupied a narrow strip of sea-girt land and was probably secured by a wall. There, at Lekython, they and those Toronaians who had fled with them, joined the garrison.

Brasidas offered the Toronaians the opportunity to return to their property without impediment and ordered the Athenians to evacuate the garrison under truce. The latter would not leave and asked for a day's truce. Brasidas offered two days and used this time to make fortifications of the nearby houses while the Athenians saw to their defences. The content of the speech Brasidas made to the assembled citizenry is again a model of moderation.

> He said that it was not just either to regard as villains or as traitors those who had negotiated with him for the capture of the town – for they had done this, not to enslave it, nor because they were bribed, but for the welfare of the city – or to think that those who had not taken part would not get the same treatment as others; for he had not come to destroy either the city or any private citizen. He explained that he made his proclamation to those who had taken refuge with the Athenians for the reason that he thought none the worse of them for their friendship with these; and when they had proved his countrymen, the Lakedaimonians, they would not, he thought, be less but rather far more kindly disposed toward them than toward the Athenians, inasmuch as their conduct was more just; whereas now they had been afraid of them through inexperience. Moreover, he told them all to prepare to show themselves staunch allies and to be held responsible for whatever mistakes they might make from this time on; as to their former actions, it was not the Lakedaimonians who had been wronged by them, but the Toronaeans rather by others [the Athenians] who were stronger, and it was pardonable if the Toronaeans had made any opposition to him. (IV. 114. 3–4)

This was to be the tenor of all Brasidas' dealings with civilian populations. He had taken on board full commitment to the image of Sparta as
the liberator of Greece. No doubt his presence and actions in the northern
campaign were a model for all Spartans to follow. His was a strategy
which avoided sieges, costly endeavours in terms of time and money.
Rather, preparation by way of dialogue with those malcontents within
a city leading to their aid in its capture proved a better way. In any case,
Brasidas' resources were still extremely limited. Lack of knowledge of the
Spartan character led most in the area to think that Brasidas was typical
of all their commanders.

The need to protect limited forces helped to define his choice of action.
It was much quicker and safer to take an objective by deception than by
siege. Speed was important to his northern campaign. A rolling succession
of achievements following hard on each other, together with the understanding, compassion, clemency and integrity Brasidas displayed in his
dealings with the populations of those cities which had come over to him,
was proving unstoppable. Although Spartan morale at home was at its
lowest ebb, it is hard to comprehend Spartan timidity. The failure to grasp
the unexpected opportunity created by Brasidas and to send reinforcements to him so that the momentum of his campaign could be sustained
was a huge miscalculation.

With the ending of the truce at Torone, the Athenian garrison successfully resisted the first day of attacks made upon them. The following day
the Athenians made preparations to thwart a fire-throwing engine which
was to be brought against the more combustible parts of their defences.[19]
Having built a wooden tower on top of a house, they proceeded to load
it with all conceivable containers capable of holding water. They did not
take into account the strength of the structure below and the house col-
lapsed under the enormous weight of both men and water. Those of the
defenders at some distance from the spot thought from the noise that their
defences had been breached and made off in their boats, followed closely
by those who had been defending areas adjacent to the collapse. Brasidas,
coming to the conclusion that divine intervention was to be thanked for
such good fortune, gave the thirty *minas* promised to the first man to climb
the wall to the temple of Athena, which was sited within Lekython and,
thereafter, made the whole area a sacred precinct.

Here Thucydides makes direct reference to Brasidas' careful planning.
'Then for the rest of the winter he proceeded to set in order the affairs of
the places that he held and *plot against the other towns.*' (Author's italics, IV.
116. 3.) This is a direct allusion to Brasidas' favoured method of attempting
to achieve his objectives by means other than force.

The appearance of another Peloponnesian army at this juncture coming as reinforcement to Brasidas could well have been decisive, but the
Spartans now had bargaining counters to offer in exchange for the cap-

tives of Sphakteria still held in Athens and did not want the opportunity to be lost. A truce was made between Sparta and Athens in 423 BC. Athens was a very willing party because under its terms Brasidas would theoretically not be allowed to persuade any more of its 'allies' to secede and it would give them time for retrenchment. Their recent land defeat by the Boiotians at Delion had left them not a little disorientated. Equally, the willingness of Sparta to enter into such negotiations at a time when Athens was on the back foot after a series of setbacks shows the degree of Spartan demoralisation.

The terms negotiated for a year's truce need not concern us here but, at the point at which the ceremonial libations were being made in confirmation of the final agreement, Skione, a city on the most westerly of the three peninsulas, offered itself to Brasidas. He immediately sailed over from Torone to applaud the citizens for having crossed to his side voluntarily. The manner of his journey is worthy of note.

Following some distance behind what is described as a 'friendly' trireme in a smaller fast vessel of one bank of oars, he sought to minimise any possibility of capture. His reasoning was that if a larger vessel than his but smaller than the trireme appeared, the 'friendly' trireme would act as a protection. If, however, another trireme appeared, it was more likely to attack the trireme rather than the smaller vessel. It must be remembered that the Aegean waters were still firmly under Athenian control. The 'friendly' trireme may have been from Torone. Its description means it was not one Brasidas had ordered built at Amphipolis.

Brasidas was given a rapturous welcome, garlanded and given a golden crown. He left a small number of men at Skione, a force which had been carried by the trireme. Returning to Torone he recrossed soon after with forces he intended to use in conjunction with those of the Skionians to attempt the capture of Mende, a town farther to the north, and eventually that of Poteidaia.

Once again Thucydides gives us an insight into Brasidas' methods '...besides, he was negotiating with these towns with a view to their betrayal.' (IV. 121. 2.)

The location of Poteidaia at the entrance to the Pallene peninsula was important strategically. It had been taken by the Athenians after a prolonged siege as recently as the winter of 430/29 BC, its survivors ordered to disperse from the city, to be replaced by Athenian colonists. Under such circumstances its loyalty to the Athenian cause could not be doubted and Brasidas must have held very little hope of winning it over by ruse or persuasion and known it would have to be the target for an assault.

It was at this time that the Athenian Aristonymos and the Spartan Athenaios arrived in the area to announce the terms of the armistice. All was agreed except for the calculation made by the Athenian that Skione had revolted *after* the deadline. Brasidas disagreed, probably on the grounds that the intentions prior to the act of revolt were sufficient evidence of disaffection. He refused to give up the city. Impressed by Brasidas' defence of Skione, the citizens of Mende now came over to his side.

Expecting an attack to be made upon these cities, Brasidas arranged for their women and children to be taken to the safer location of Olynthos with a protective force of 500 hoplites and 300 peltasts under the command of Polydamidas. This concern for the civilian population contrasts sharply with the later treatment by Kleon of the citizens of Torone after its capture. He enslaved the women and children and shipped 700 surviving men to Athens to unrecorded fates.

Perdikkas would appear to have required Brasidas to fulfil some agreed obligation at this point. Although Thucydides baldly states the facts of the expedition (from IV. 124. 1), he gives no reason why Brasidas should allow himself to be removed from his very important operational area, which he knew would soon be the target of Athenian attacks. Perdikkas was, for the moment, an ally of Sparta and was footing the bill for a good proportion of Brasidas' army. In addition, some of his own forces served under Brasidas. Although this was a very inconvenient time for Brasidas, it may well be that Perdikkas insisted on his support in another attack on the Lynkestian Makedonians. Perdikkas may have perceived that Brasidas was going to have his hands full in the not too distant future and not be available for his plans for aggrandisement. While he was in a position to demand assistance from the Peloponnesians, he was never likely to have the same form of support from the Athenians if he were to revert to their side; which very soon was to become a political necessity.

The operation against the Lynkestians reveals more of Brasidas' tactical thinking. A sizeable force was gathered and the advance into enemy territory found opposing armies with their infantry drawn up on hills with a plain between. The engagement started with cavalry skirmishing in the plain below the two forces. There followed an advance by the Lynkestian phalanx supported by their cavalry, which was met by the forces of Perdikkas and Brasidas. The Lynkestians were routed, trophies set up, and the victorious army encamped to await the arrival of Illyrian forces hired by Perdikkas. It had been the latter's intention that on their arrival a further advance into enemy territory be made. However, during the days of waiting, Brasidas worried that the Athenians might arrive before he could be on hand to assist Mende and he wished to return. In the ensuing altercation it became clear that the Illyrians had changed sides and were now coming to the aid of Arrhabaios. The Makedonians are supposed to have feared the Illyrians (IV. 125. 1) and both Perdikkas and Brasidas decided that retreat at this point was the most sensible course. That fear may well have been prevalent among the Makedonian troops – but the agreement to withdraw suited Brasidas well. Once the Illyrians' change of allegiance became generally known panic took hold of the Makedonian and allied forces.

...when night came on the Makedonians and the mass of barbarians immediately took fright, as large armies are wont to be smitten with unaccountable panic, and thinking that the advancing enemy were many times more numerous than they really were and were all but on them, betook themselves to sudden flight and hastened home-wards. (IV. 125. 1)

The camps of Perdikkas and Brasidas were at a considerable distance from each other. Even Perdikkas himself is reported as not having been aware of the panic in his camp until it became essential for him to follow on after his men.

Dawn brought the realisation to Brasidas that not only had his ally gone, but that the combined forces of Arrhabaios and the Illyrians were advanc-ing against him. There was nothing left for him other than to attempt a withdrawal. His arrangements are interesting.

The hoplite heavy infantry was arranged into a square within which his peltasts and light-armed troops were placed.[20] The youngest and obviously the most fleet of foot were positioned at the outer perimeter of this square so that they could make sallies against the enemy should they attack any point of the formation. This appears to be the first recorded Spartan use of this tactic to repel missile throwing skirmishers. This per-mitted heavy infantry to ward off attacks by essentially light-armed forces and to protect their own light infantry. A special force of 300 picked men was selected under Brasidas' direct command to act as a rearguard. These too would have been hoplites. His speech to his men emphasised the lack of discipline and cohesion in those forces they were about to encounter.

At the beginning of the withdrawal the enemy thought that his army was in flight. But when successive attacks had been repulsed they divided their forces so that the harassment of Brasidas' army could be sustained, while the remainder pursued the Makedonians, killing the stragglers and occupying a pass through which Brasidas' forces must pass.

Brasidas was aware of the danger. Seeing the encirclement which was now being made by the enemy as he neared the border, he ordered his special force to advance as quickly as it could against one of the high points flanking the pass in an attempt to take it from the enemy. In secur-ing one flanking high point he threatened the other while the progress of the main body of his men continued. His plan worked and his army moved relatively unimpeded into Makedonia where his soldiers, enraged at being deserted by their allies, slaughtered any baggage animals left by the panic-stricken Makedonian forces and took their loads.

This more than anything persuaded Perdikkas that he should wash his hands of Brasidas and renegotiate terms with Athens. So the actions of this fickle monarch set the seal on the imaginative activities of one of the greatest commanders of this war.

When the Spartans eventually attempted to send Brasidas reinforcements, Perdikkas was again within the Athenian sphere of influence. His friends in Thessaly refused to allow the Peloponnesians to march through their territory.

The Spartans Ischagoras, Ameinias and Aristesteis, who had been sent out to evaluate the circumstances, managed to reach Brasidas with some young men whom they placed in cities as governors rather than as garrison commanders. Two are named as Klearidas and Pasitelidas, the former placed in control of Amphipolis and the latter of Torone.

Such arrangements were in direct contradiction to Brasidas' pledges that cities which came over to the Spartan side would be self-governing and free. He could do nothing because the commissioners were under direct instructions from the home government. To have refused to countenance such arrangements would have brought him into direct opposition to the wishes of his homeland with the inevitable outcome of exile or worse. This further weakened his position when it could be perceived by his hitherto enthusiastic allies that their so-called freedom was to be limited. The feasibility of holding on to the gains was much diminished. One can only wonder why the Spartan commissioners carried out the easier first part of their mission, namely to establish direct Spartan control of the cities, in the absence of the reinforcements that should have been with them and which would have made the appointments viable. Their actions can be further questioned when, prior to their arrival, Mende had fallen and Skione was under siege by the Athenians led by Nikias and Nikostratos. Perdikkas had rejoined the Athenian side and shown his support by ensuring that the Spartan army of reinforcement was unable to proceed through Thessaly. Under such circumstances a more intelligent and imaginative approach ought to have been forthcoming. By comparison their actions and that of the garrison commander of Mende (see below) show Brasidas to have been an exceptional personality among Spartans.

Mende had fallen within two days to the Athenian-led force of 1,000 Athenian hoplites, 600 archers and 1,000 Thrakian mercenaries who were most likely to be peltasts, together with other peltasts from regional allies. The Athenians had come with fifty ships and achieved this success just prior to Brasidas' return from his expedition with Perdikkas.

Polydamidas, the commander at Mende, had successfully rebutted the initial assault on his hill position outside the city walls and had come close to totally defeating the Athenian two-pronged attack. The following day half the Athenian force under Nikias sailed to the south side of the city and ravaged the territory up to the boundary with Skione. The other half, under Nikostratos, occupied a position not far from the northern gates on the road leading to their base at Poteidaia. Within the city near those gates the Mendaians had stacked their arms. Polydamidas was encouraging those under his command to prepare to make a sortie when a Mendaian citizen, a democrat – Thucydides describes him as being a member of the 'popular' party (IV. 130. 4) – rounded on him and declared that he had no intention of taking part in the sally. Polydamidas' reaction could be regarded as the typical Spartan commander's response to insubordination.[21] He took hold of the man and obviously, from the description, physically attacked him. This provoked the democrats among the populace to snatch up their arms and put to rout the Peloponnesians and those of their citizens who sympathised with them. The gates were opened to the Athenians (one must assume that they were the northern gates) and the Peloponnesians understandably assumed that the city had been betrayed to the enemy. Those surviving the onslaught took refuge on the acropolis. Meanwhile, Nikias had returned to the city and he too entered with his force, assuming that it had been taken by storm. It took some time to stop the killing of the inhabitants as a consequence of this misunderstanding. One thing in Thucydides' narrative is not wholly clear. He states (IV. 130. 5) that the gates were opened to the Athenians and here he is surely referring to the northern gates. At IV. 130. 6, mention is made of Nikias discovering that the gates had been opened. Whether the Mendaians had also opened the southern gates facing Skione is debatable but probable. However, the author prefers to assume that Nikias' intention was to rejoin that portion of the army posted outside the northern gates and it was through these that he and his men made entry.

Having cut off the enemy in the acropolis by a wall which went down to the sea on both sides, Nikias made no reprisals but advised the Mendaians to re-establish their former constitution and bring those who acted against it to trial.

The spontaneous action of Polydamidas had been disastrous. As mentioned earlier, Spartan commanders were severe on any sign of insubordination, but this occasion showed a clear lack of understanding of the people he was expected to lead. One could argue that it is the responsibility of command to place subordinates in positions in which they are most effective and therefore lay the blame for the fall of Mende at the door of Brasidas. However, that would be too simplistic. Polydamidas had proved himself a successful commander. He had very nearly defeated the Athenian forces on the first day. He was obviously an effective commander in the field and his decisions there had been sound. His fault lay in his personal relationships with those under his command away from the battlefield. While Brasidas appears to have recognised the individual needs and aspirations of those civilian populations he was so successful in bringing to his side, Polydamidas had not taken the lesson to heart. He was probably accustomed to orders once given being obeyed. It is here that we see the fundamental difference between Brasidas and the average Spartan commander. The recognition of personally held opinion and the need to take cognisance of this phenomenon in Greek politics shows his sensitivity to public opinion.

The Athenians then moved against Skione and had a little less trouble in forcing the Peloponnesians and Skionians from their position on a hill in front of the city and making them retreat into the city. The defensive procedures were similar, the manning of a strong position on a hill in close proximity to the city, which had to be taken before any possibility of siege operations. This suggests a method decided upon by the commander-in-chief, Brasidas, and which his subordinates at both locations followed. While Polydamidas had almost succeeded in thwarting the Athenian attack, the unknown commander at Skione was not so successful.

In the absence of anything to the contrary in the sources, one must presume that Polydamidas had survived and was in command of those who had been sealed off on the acropolis at Mende. Those entrapped fought their way through the forces guarding them and the majority infiltrated the men working on the circumvallation of Skione to join their fellows in that city. If Polydamidas was still alive this escape must reflect to his credit.

The late winter of 423/2 saw an abortive attempt by Brasidas to take Poteidaia. The approach to the walls was made without discovery. Here Thucydides alludes to the passing on of a bell from a patrol to successive guards around the perimeter. It would appear to have been a means of ensuring that each guard remained alert. The patrol was likely to have made a regular circuit of the walls. A scaling ladder was put in place against the wall just after the patrol had passed. Had the guard above not discovered it almost immediately, Brasidas' men would have successfully entered the perimeter. As it was, Brasidas was obliged to give up the attempt.[22]

In the summer of 422 BC, with Skione still under siege, Kleon managed to get himself elected commander of an expedition to Thrace. With him were thirty ships, 1,200 Athenian hoplites and 300 cavalry with an unspecified larger number of allied forces. Calling first at Skione he enlarged his army by taking a number of heavy infantry from the besiegers and sailed for the harbour of Kophos in the vicinity of Torone. This in itself was a speedy and imaginative tactical move and struck at a key area of Brasidas' support.

Intelligence from deserters informed him that Brasidas was not present and that the forces remaining were highly unlikely to present significant opposition. Ten ships were sent into the harbour while Kleon with his land forces advanced on the city. The impending attack from two sides was sufficient to persuade Pasitelidas, the Spartan commander, to retreat from the position he had taken up at the extended outer wall. Brasidas had caused this to be built to take into the city perimeter some of those dwellings which were outside the original walls. On his rapid return to the old city, he discovered that men from Kleon's fleet had already gained control. On his abandonment of the walls the land forces had broken through and followed hard upon him. After briefly resisting, those remaining alive, including Pasitelidas, were taken prisoner. On his way to bring relief, Brasidas was but a short distance away when he heard the news of the fall of Torone

Kleon's next objective proved to be Amphipolis itself. Sailing round the most easterly prong of the three peninsulas, he established his force in Eion. Before contemplating a direct assault upon Amphipolis he sought to secure his position further by neutralising the surrounding area support-ive of Brasidas. To the south Stagiros withstood his attack but he was more fortunate in the storming of Galepsos to the west. His campaign up to that point, particularly in securing his lines of communication and reducing the area which had hitherto been under the control of Brasidas, had been eminently successful. He had achieved much in a very short time.

Kleon showed himself to be a realist and was not swept into making a direct attack on Amphipolis. (See map, page xix.) He settled in Eion to await reinforcements. He called for Perdikkas to send an army as agreed in the terms of his renewed alliance with the Athenians. Envoys were also sent to the king of the Odomantians to the north of Amphipolis, request-ing Thrakian mercenaries.

Brasidas, now in Amphipolis, was not idle. He summoned the Edonian cavalry and light infantry from the area just north of Amphipolis and 1,500 Thrakian mercenaries. The hoplites and cavalry at his immediate disposal numbered 2,000 and 300 respectively, together with another 1,000 peltasts and the troops in Amphipolis itself. Taking 1,500 of these he estab-lished himself on high ground across the river at Kerdileon not far from Amphipolis. From this vantage point he could see in all directions so that any move made by Kleon would be immediately observed. The remainder stayed within the city under the command of Klearidas. Thucydides (V. 6. 3) surmises that Brasidas expected Kleon to make an attack on Amphipolis without the expected reinforcements, on the grounds that the forces of the city were derisory. Not for the first time do we see the low opinion in which Thucydides held Kleon, clouding his usually even-handed assessments.

What Brasidas was attempting was to provoke some action from Kleon prior to the arrival of reinforcements for the Athenians. The number he had with him was probably sufficient to defend his position but could not pose a serious threat should he come down to engage with Kleon. The latter's forces were much too strong.

However, Brasidas rightly guessed that prolonged inactivity has an adverse effect on morale. It was not long before the Athenians started complaining.

> For when the soldiers began to be annoyed at sitting still and to discuss the quality of his [Kleon's] leadership – what experience and daring there was on the other side and what incompetence and cowardice would be pitted against it, and how unwillingly they had

come with him from home – he [Kleon] became aware of their grum-
bling, and unwilling that they should be exasperated by remaining
inactive in the same place, marched out with them. (V. 7. 1)

So it was that Brasidas retained the initiative despite having inferior forces.
Kleon is described by Thucydides as not having any fear that an engagement would ensue and advanced towards the city to make reconnaissance
of the environs. He took up a position on a hill from which he could assess
the defences thinking that he could withdraw in safety. All gates were
closed and the city had every appearance of being undefended.

At the first sight of the Athenian advance Brasidas left his elevated position, recrossed the river and re-entered Amphipolis.

Kleon would have been reasonably confident that he would not be subject to any attack. Under most circumstances that supposition would have
been correct. However, this was to be his first, and only, encounter with
Brasidas and he did not appreciate the inventiveness or opportunism of the
military mind opposed to him. No one seemed to be manning the walls and
the gates were closed. Attack from that quarter seemed highly unlikely.

Thucydides makes the point (V. 8. 2–3) that Brasidas avoided a formal
engagement because he recognised the disparity between the quality of
his men and their equipment and of his opponent's forces. To plan to
defeat one's enemy by guile rather than by direct confrontation is a skill
possessed only by great commanders. Often by taking such an approach
losses to the winning side are greatly diminished; but the commander
must have the imagination and intellect to devise a plan that will work
within the limitations of the number and capabilities of his men.

He realised that an opportunity to attack Kleon before the Athenians
received reinforcements would be unlikely to present itself again. To that
end he organised 150 hoplites to be under his command with the remainder
of the forces under his fellow Spartiate and subordinate Klearidas. Those
selected by Brasidas were likely to be fleet of foot and from the best trained
element of his forces. Thucydides reports the speech Brasidas made to his
men after the division of the forces. There is no reason to think that this is
a wholly manufactured address. Thucydides was careful with his sources
and can be trusted to reflect accurately the substance of what was said. It
is worth setting that speech down here so that the quality of Brasidas as a
commander in the eyes of his contemporaries can be recognised.

Men of the Peloponnesos, let it suffice to remind you briefly from
what manner of country we have come, that it has ever been free
because of its courage, and that you are going to fight, Dorians
against Ionians, whom you have been accustomed to vanquish. I will,
however, explain to you in what way I intend to make the attack, in
order that my plan of fighting in detachments and not in a body may

not seem to anyone poor tactics and thus cause discouragement. For I imagine that the enemy ascended the hill in contempt of us and because they could not have expected that anybody would come out for battle against them, and now, with broken ranks and intent upon reconnoitring, are taking small account of us. Now when an assailant having most clearly observed such errors in the enemy also makes his attack in accordance with the force at his own disposal, not openly and in array of battle, but as may be advantageous under present circumstances, then he would be most likely to succeed. And those stratagems have won the highest credit by which a man most completely deceives the enemy and helps his friends. While, then, the Athenians, still unprepared, are full of confidence and are think-ing, so far as I can see, more of withdrawing than of staying where they are, while their tension of mind is relaxed and before they have got their thoughts together, I will take my own troops and if pos-sible surprise them by a dash upon the centre of their army. Then, Klearidas, the moment you see me pressing on and in all likelihood striking terror into them, do you suddenly throw open the gates and at the head of your own men and the Amphipolitans and the rest of our allies rush out upon them and make all haste to close with them at once. In this way there is the best hope to put them in a panic; for a force that comes up afterwards has always more terror for an enemy than that with which he is already engaged. As for yourself, show yourself a brave man, as becomes a Spartan [Σπαρτιατην – here meaning Spartiate or full citizen]; and do you, men of the allies, follow him bravely, and bear in mind that the three virtues of a good soldier are zeal, sense of honour, and obedience to his leaders; if you are brave, freedom and to be called allies of the Lakedaimonians – or else vassals of the Athenians (if you be so fortunate as to escape death or being sold into slavery) and that, too, in a harsher vassalage than you had before, while for the rest of the Hellenes you will prove a barrier to their liberation. Do not, then, seeing how much is at stake, on your part play the coward; and I, for my part, will show that I am not better able to exhort others than to carry out myself in action the advice I give to my fellows. (V. 9. 1–10)

The Athenians had seen him re-enter the city from their point of high vantage overlooking the city and it was reported to Kleon that Brasidas had been observed making sacrifice close to the temple of Athena. Further, at the bottom of the gates the feet of both men and horses were seen to be massing, giving every indication that a sally was imminent.

Here, the decision made by Kleon was crucial. Looking at the evidence he had two options. The first was to bring his forces into battle line and stand his ground against the likely attack. That they were not in good order is mentioned early in Brasidas' speech to his men. Second, was to bring his men into order for a carefully staged and covered withdrawal. The former would seem to have been the obvious course to follow if Thucydides' comments on Kleon's regard for the opposition forces are to be believed but, as Kleon was one of the likely instruments of Thucydides' exile, some of his arrogance as described may well have been exaggerated.

Kleon decided he had time to effect a withdrawal (V. 10. 3) and sounded the retreat, giving verbal orders that it should be made by the most obvious and easiest route, the road to Eion. Eion was due south. To move northwards in an advance towards and alongside Amphipolis was relatively safe in that a column would have its shielded side towards the city. However, when moving south, the unshielded side became exposed.

The withdrawal was compromised by Kleon's impatience or nervousness. Believing that the retreat was too tardy he wheeled his right wing, which should have been facing the city covering the moves of the left and centre, and thus had his whole force with its unshielded side towards the city. The very manoeuvre itself may have contributed further to the obvious disarray observed by Brasidas. 'These men will not stand before us; they show it by the wagging of their spears and of their heads; men who do that never await an attack.' (V. 10. 5).

His judgement was sound and as he and his 150 men issued out of the first gate in the long wall to launch an attack on the enemy's centre in the line of its march, Klearidas' force made their attack from the Thrakian gate.

It happened that the left wing of the Athenian army which had led off first had proceeded some distance down the road before the attack occurred. It was not in contact with the remainder of its forces and fled without attempting to engage.

The effect of an attack being made from two directions compounded the disorganisation of the Athenian forces. It is at such moments of uncertainty that a force as small as that of Brasidas is able to achieve a rout, here of the enemy centre. At the point of continuing his victorious advance, this time against the enemy's right, Brasidas was wounded and carried from the field unnoticed by the Athenians. The right wing was nearer to the higher ground from which the entire army had sought to make their retreat and, after regrouping, put up a fairly spirited defence of their position until such time as they became the object of missile attacks from both cavalry and javelineers. They too eventually broke and took to flight by any available route, often to be overtaken and killed by Chalkidian horse or peltasts. Kleon had taken to his heels at the first onslaught against the right and had been killed by a peltast.

Victory was complete. Klearidas set up a trophy and stripped the dead. When the time came for the Athenians to reclaim their dead in time-honoured fashion it was discovered that around 600 of their men had been killed as against seven of their opponents. Unluckily Brasidas was to be counted among these; but at least he had the satisfaction of surviving long enough to hear of the victory.

He was given a state funeral by the Amphipolitans who also revered him as the saviour of their city in place of their original Athenian founder, Hagnon. Annual sacrifices were made to him and games held in his honour thereafter.

It is ironic that at about the time of the battle a force of 900 hoplites under the command of the Spartans Ramphias, Autocharidas and Epikydidas were at the Spartan colony of Herakleia in Trachis close to Lamia, preparing to come as reinforcements to Brasidas.

The surviving Athenians took ship soon thereafter for Athens and peace negotiations began between Sparta and Athens.

Thucydides' comments (V. 11. 2) that the disparity in the numbers of dead between the two sides was the result of an action which did not follow the normal practices of engagement. In all his military actions, other than those conducted jointly with Perdikkas, which are not reported at length, Brasidas did not follow the orthodoxy of his times. The achievement of his objectives was always made with the safety of his own forces being of paramount importance. That being so, morale in his forces must have been high and the loyalty of the great majority of his men unquestionable. In his only set 'battle' – before Megara – he achieved the ultimate goal of any defending commander. To deploy for battle and in so doing dissuade the enemy from taking up the challenge. He thereby safeguarded the city without a single casualty.

He was obviously a highly intelligent and inventive commander. His planning was meticulous and his speed of manoeuvre remarkable. Activities at night were eminently well planned: his marches to Amphipolis and Torone, his night sea crossing to Skione and his near successful attempt on Poteidaia. His campaigning continued throughout the year and did not follow the usual season of activity of the Greeks, which avoided winter operations except for sieges.

Brasidas' superbly organised withdrawal after being abandoned by Perdikkas in enemy territory testifies to his memory and understanding of terrain and to his ability to choose a successful deployment. In assessing developing situations his suppositions were almost always productive of a successful outcome. On his obligatory second expedition with Perdikkas against the Lynkestians, Brasidas had made all possible preparations against the likely appearance of the Athenians in Chalkidike. He had been a reluctant partner in the enterprise from the outset and had been correct in wishing to return as quickly as possible to the region of the cities which had come over to him. The major problem for him at this time was that Perdikkas' influence on the Thessalians was his only guarantee that any reinforcements sent north would reach him; therefore mutual co-operation was a necessity. The pity was that Sparta was shamefully neglectful in this matter. One can only guess what Brasidas might have achieved had he been given the material support his successes so thoroughly deserved.

He shared the attributes recognised in and expected of the successful modern general with one exception. His was still an heroic world in which the commander was expected to lead by example. The idea that a commander should protect himself for the sake of those serving under him was just about to emerge and therefore his leadership in his last action should be seen as typical of expectations. In addition, capable subordinates in the field were in short supply, spread as they were as commanders of garrisons to the various cities. He and Klearidas appear to have been the only Spartiates who were present at Amphipolis. In leading the smaller group of 150 and being one of only seven fatalities, his leadership must have been literally from the front.

Thucydides' evaluation of Brasidas is probably the best encomium.

As for Brasidas himself, the Lakedaimonians sent him chiefly at his own desire, though the Chalkidians also were eager to have him. He was a man esteemed at Sparta as being energetic in everything he did, and indeed, after he had gone abroad, he proved invaluable to the Lakedaimonians. For, at the present crisis, by showing himself just and moderate in his dealings with the cities he caused most of the places to revolt, and secured possession of others by the treachery of their inhabitants, so that when the Lakedaimonians wished to make terms with Athens, as they did ultimately, they had places to offer in exchange for places they wished to recover and were able to secure for the Peloponnese a respite from the war; and in the later part of the war, after the events in Sicily, it was the virtue and tact which Brasidas had displayed at this time – qualities of which some had experience, while others knew of them by report – that did most to inspire in the allies of the Athenians a sentiment favourable to the Lakedaimonians. For since he was the first Lakedaimonian abroad who gained a reputation for being in all respects a good man, he left behind him a confident belief that other Lakedaimonians also were of the same stamp. (IV. 81)

Notes

1. For example, in his volume *The Archidamian War*, p.116, Donald Kagan suggests that Brasidas might have been outvoted by his fellow commanders when the condition of the vessels became known. This supports my view that the fact was considered earlier rather than later.

2. See Chapter I.

3. For the context of this action see Chapter IV.

4. See Chapter IV.

5. For an account of these activities see Chapter III.

6. The use of the word *peripoloi* (περίπολοι) here in this action at Megara is
   problematic. Its appearance refers to a unit of men, but of what designation
   and why the special designation? The later mention at VIII. 92 .2 is too
   obscure to derive much information, merely that Phrynichos was killed
   by one of the *peripoloi*. VI. 45. 1 describes the placing of garrisons by the
   Syracusans into places hitherto manned by the *peripoloi*, which indicates that
   the latter were either insufficient in number or experience for the coming
   problems. Finally, VIII. 92. 5 describes the commander of the *peripoloi*
   stationed in a high position, 'a hill in the Peiraeus', Mounychia, the acropolis
   of Peraeus with a clear view over the Saronic Gulf. The Loeb translation
   of the word as a 'frontier patrol' is slightly misleading in the context of
   the conduct of the war. Whereas it can be accepted that a 'home guard'
   of young Athenians between the ages of 18 and 20 could patrol and keep
   watch over the frontiers in times of relative peace, it is more likely that at
   this time they patrolled and manned the walls and fortifications of Athens,
   i.e. doing the 'rounds'. In the Siege of Syracuse we can also deduce that the
   Syracusans reinforced the positions previously held by their *peripoloi*. It is
   known that the defences of Athens were manned by the young and some
   of the older men. It is likely that other states followed the same procedures,
   not by imitation but by the same virtue of allowing all mature and able
   bodied men to be available for more aggressive operations. The *peripoloi* may
   well have been designated to man lookout points which in time of danger
   would need to be garrisoned by regular troops. The fact that Demosthenes
   had a detachment of Plataian light troops and another of the *peripoloi* lying
   in ambush ready for the taking of the walls from Megara to Nisaia implies
   that these were very mobile forces. This makes sense considering the dash
   they would have to make to secure the gates, the light-armed troops being
   supported by the *peripoloi* as agile heavy infantry. So it would appear that
   the *peripoloi* were the young men still in Athens and not normally taken
   on active service and as such their presence on this occasion was highly
   unusual.

7. With the surrender of the Spartans on the island of Sphakteria, it is possible
   that a precedent had been set whereby the time-honoured custom of
   Spartans never giving up their arms was undermined. In this case the
   only Spartiate likely to have been present was the garrison commander.
   Pasitelidas at Torone is a later example of another Spartan who did not fight
   to the death.

8. A hipparch was a commander of cavalry.

9. To reclaim under truce the bodies of those of one's side who had fallen in

battle signified the acceptance of defeat. It permitted the opposition to set up trophies signifying their victory at the location of the engagement. These trophies were usually in the form of captured arms and armour stripped from the fallen set up on a pole. In exceptional circumstances, such as those which were seen to have significantly changed the balance of power, monuments were set up. Two examples can still be seen: at Leuktra commemorating the victory of the Thebans over the Spartans; and at Chaironeia where Philip II of Macedon set up the Lion over the bodies of the Theban Sacred Band after his victory over the Greek forces.

10. Where there were sufficient forces among the defenders this was a usual ploy whenever an attacking force threatened siege operations or an assault on a city. Taking up a position on high ground near a city posed a threat to the invader and had to be dealt with before any attention to the city itself could be paid. The attacking commander could not allow his men to forage or to follow any procedure which led to a break in formation until he had dislodged his enemy from its position. Skione is a good example of this defensive tactic against Athenian forces. The Athenian hoplite not only fought but also built the circumvallation in any siege, so to keep them under arms delayed the construction.

11. Sun Tzu, *The Art of War*: 'Thus the highest form of generalship is to baulk the enemy's plans.' (III. 3); and, 'Therefore the skilled leader subdues the enemy's troops without any fighting' (III. 6).

12. The helots of Lakonia and Messenia provided the economic basis for the continued existence of the ruling military caste, the Spartiates. They massively outnumbered their masters, coming from those who farmed Lakonia and Messenia alongside the *perioikoi*, i.e, 'those who dwelt around' and who were freemen with little or no influence on Spartan policy. Unlike those in servitude in other states there were no opportunities to buy freedom, nor could a grateful master free a loyal slave, for all helots were the property of the state. The Messenians were particularly volatile in times of Spartan duress, such as the revolt at Ithome, leading to the rebels being resettled by the Athenians at Naupaktos, their aid to Demosthenes in Akarnania, Aitolia and at Pylos, and their service with the Athenians in Sicily. Although they had been in servitude for some generations, it is reasonable to think the hope of liberty and regained statehood kept them in ferment. Keeping the lid on this cauldron of discontent brought about a form of paranoia among the Spartans leading to extreme measures. Within the system of education for youths it had become the custom for the *ephors* (the five chief magistrates) to declare a war against the helots on taking office. Those under training who, thereafter, by this ruling, murdered a helot, were not held guilty of any crime in the eyes of the gods.

   An extreme example of the paranoia is described at IV. 80. 3–4 where, around 424 BC, Thucydides reports that a proclamation was issued whereby helots were asked to select from their own kind those who had done good service in war in the Spartan cause. All indications were that they were to be given their freedom. The chosen 2,000 were secretly done away with, this after processions and temple ceremonials. The Spartans thought that in this way they would eliminate the most courageous and vociferous of their serfs. It is now thought that this event might well have taken place earlier in the 460s. Some question the truth of the story, e.g., R J A Talbot, *Historia* 38 (1989), 22–40, and M Whitby 'Two shadows: images of Sparta and the helots', in *The Shadow of Sparta* (eds, A Powell and S Hodkinson, 1994).

A change of policy emerges and this may have a great deal to do with the conduct of the helots serving under Brasidas in his northern campaign. They were given their freedom and joined others who had already received theirs, the Neodamodeis. At the time of their commitment to Brasidas' campaign Spartans would regard this as reducing the likelihood of problems at home. For later problems with helots and further information on the Neodamodeis see Hutchinson, Godfrey, *Xenophon and the Art of Command*, (2000).

13. The possible remains of the citadel of Herakleia in Trachis are situated not far from Thermopylai but up in the mountains, just off the alpine plain in which Sparta's mother city, Doris, lay. Its location overlooks modern Lamia and the Malian Gulf. The city itself was on the river plain below on the north side of the massif, possibly near the emergence of the river from the gorge. It was founded in 426 BC. It acted not only as protection for Doris but also as a point from which expeditions could be launched against the nearby island of Euboia and even as far as Chalkidike and Thrace. Dockyards were started at the coast but not completed. A new wall was built at the pass of Thermopylai. At its founding some 10,000 settlers are said to have made their homes there. Although this figure seems rather improbable, the fact that Spartan citizens and *perioikoi* ('dwellers around' from cities and villages in Lakonia) were among them shows this to have been an important and aggressively pursued strategic decision by the ruling caste at Sparta. No doubt Brasidas would have been among the strongest supporters of the foundation.

14. As reported by Thucydides (IV. 79. 2), Perdikkas had reason to fear the intentions of the Athenians. He also wished to subdue the neighbouring kingdom of Lynkestis. Together with those of the Thrakian cities in revolt or considering revolt against Athens, the offer to maintain any forces sent north by the Spartans was a ready inducement. Beset by the problem of Pylos and the attacks on the Lakonian coastline, the Spartans sought to divert the attention of Athens to areas anew.

15. See II. 97. 3. Greek cities on the Thrakian littoral were obliged to pay tribute to both Athens and the successive Odrysian kings certainly down to 423 BC. Amphipolis had been founded in 437/6 BC to counter Thrakian expansion and was exempt from the payment of Athenian tribute. Its strategic location and resources of timber for ship building made it a valuable outpost of the Athenian empire. See J M F May, *Coinage of Abdera*, (OUP Special Publication No. 3, London, 1966).

16. An attack during winter would not be expected. Not only would the conditions make the march arduous, but there would be little forage available. To march at night during winter required careful planning and good intelligence of the area to be approached. One reason for undertaking the operation at this time of the year may have been the knowledge that winter conditions could well delay any seaborne support for the city from the Athenians.

17. Kagan in *The Archidamian War,* pp.302–3, rightly suggests that after the taking of Amphipolis, the jewel in the Athenian empire in the north, Brasidas would expect reinforcements. His immediate building of ships would not only give him greater mobility but also better coastal protection. But without those reinforcements it is hard to see how he could man a fleet from the forces at his disposal. Had those reinforcements arrived, it is possible that after consolidating his hold over Chalkidike, he might have pursued a campaign eastwards by both land and sea, picking off the coastal cities of Athens' north Aegean empire until he arrived to possess the Hellespont. There he could have disrupted the grain supplies from the Black Sea region on which Athens relied. Had this been the case, Lysander's later strategy would have been forestalled.

18. Those whose duty it was to secure the city placed a bolt or wooden peg through the bar which could only be removed by a tool which fitted its head. With this key in the possession of the duty guard, extraction was nigh on impossible and those wishing to open gates had to resort to cutting through the bar.

19. This flame thrower was a device similar to the engine used by the Thebans after the battle of Delion. See Chapter III.

20. A similar defensive formation was used by Agesilaos early in the next century marching through Thessaly, when his cavalry defeated the supposedly superior Thessalian cavalry. Although no cavalry is mentioned as being with Brasidas it is likely that he had some Chalkidian horse. The notion of placing the more vulnerable within a protective square seems to be not only commonsense but intuitive. American wild horses are known to place their young within a defensive screen of mature animals as a protection against predatory mountain lions.
    More detail of Brasidas' and Agesilaos' formations would be helpful. The right flank would have had the unshielded side facing the enemy and full protection could only be afforded if the shield was held on the right arm. That this was not done can be assumed because Xenophon changed from a hollow square protecting slaves, booty and animals to a line which was curved to gain protection from missiles. 'And Xenophon and his men, by this time sorely distressed by the arrows and sling-stones, and marching in a curved line in order to keep their shields facing the arrows…' (Xenophon, *Anabasis* VII. 8. 18.) It is highly likely that the younger hoplites on Brasidas'right flank were very much more active than those on the left where the protection of the shield was greatest.

98

21. Later descriptions of the reactions of Spartan commanders to what they took to be insubordination can be found in the case of the extreme behaviour of Mnasippos (Xenophon, *Hellenica*, VI. 2. 18–19), who physically strikes his men personally – they then follow him, but 'without courage and with hatred in the heart'; and in the more conventional meting out of punishment by Klearchos (Xenophon, *Anabasis*, II. 3. 11). J K Anderson in *Xenophon*, p.123, suggests that corporal punishment was used as a last resort to maintain discipline.

22. Potidaia was founded around 600 BC by Corinth and became a member of the Delian League after the Persian invasion of Greece. It held a highly strategic position at the isthmus which connects the Kassandreia peninsula to Chalkidike. As one of the disaffected cities within what became the Athenian empire its revolt in 432 BC and the subsequent two-year siege proved to be one of the causes for the Peloponnesian War. Socrates is reputed to have saved the life of the young Alkibiades while serving in the campaign there.

VI

The Battle of Mantineia 418 BC

Full scale land battles were few in this war. It had been a matter of strategy for Athens to avoid any such trial of strength against Sparta. In the period of shifting alliances during the so-called Peace of Nikias it may have been the opportune seceding of allies from the Peloponnesian League which persuaded those opposed to Sparta finally to undertake a trial of strength. Certainly, Sparta's reputation as an invincible war machine had been dented by the surrender at Sphakteria (425 BC). Thereafter, it is no exaggeration to suggest that Sparta was obsessed with the notion of securing the return of their citizens and, thanks largely to the successes of Brasidas, it found itself in a position to negotiate a peace settlement with Athens. Circumstances were helped by the deaths of both Brasidas and Kleon at Amphipolis, thereby removing from each side the most vociferous supporters of the war's continuation. While Sparta feared a helot revolt, Athens feared the revolt of allies. Both states had lost confidence and Athens in particular was mindful of the setbacks she had sustained at Delion and Amphipolis.

The Peace of Nikias (421 BC) as it came to be called, did not see an end to hostilities in the long run. It did not receive the agreement of Sparta's allies. Corinth in particular had suffered considerable losses in the northwest. The Megaran harbour of Nisaea still had an Athenian garrison and Boiotia saw no reason to suspend hostilities after its triumph over the Athenians three years earlier at Delion or to return the border fortification of Panakton to Athens. The thirty-year truce between Sparta and Argos was now at an end and the latter, probably seeing an opportunity emerging for it to attempt to regain its ancient hegemony in the Peloponnese, refused to renew the agreement.

Members of the Peloponnesian League refused to accept the Peace of Nikias and Sparta entered into an alliance with Athens. Realignments occurred to the benefit of Argos, with Mantineia and Elis joining her. Sparta made copious diplomatic moves to regain her old allies and, although unsuccessful in the main, managed to forge an alliance with the Boiotians. At this time Alkibiades perversely swayed public opinion in Athens to the support of Argos and her new allies and was active in promoting an anti-Spartan alliance of democracies in the Peloponnese. He was able to do this largely on the grounds that little had been achieved in the detail of the peace agreement other than an exchange of prisoners. Amphipolis remained beyond Athens' control and Pylos was not given back to Sparta.

Alkibiades – with greater subtlety than Kleon had ever been capable of showing – was seeking a continuation of hostilities with Sparta even within the limits of the Spartan Athenian alliance.[1] His efforts brought Argos, Elis and Mantineia into a pact with Athens while Megara returned to the diminished Peloponnesian League along with Corinth. It is against this background that the following events were played out.

In scrutinising Thucydides' text, much can be learned of the relationship between the commander and those serving under him, the restrictions governing the conduct and remit of a commander and the consequences following on from his actions. These will be discussed within the framework of the evidence which Thucydides offers with particular reference to the command of Agis, king of Sparta.

As a prelude to the battle itself, the activities of the preceding months need consideration. Epidauros, a constant irritant to the Argives, was attacked again by Argive forces, under a religious pretext. The true reason was that Alkibiades and the leading Argives wished to coerce the Epidaurians into joining their alliance, thereby making it easier for naval-borne help to reach the Argolid rather than having to sail much farther around Cape Skillaeon into the Gulf of Nauplio. Another outcome would have been the neutrality of Corinth in future conflict.

During the following winter the Spartans had cleverly eluded detection by the Athenian patrol vessels to establish a garrison of 300 men in the city of their ally, Epidauros. The Argives felt that they had the right to complain to Athens that, in accordance with their treaty, this should not have happened. If the sea surrounding the area was under Athenian control, the sea itself could be regarded as Athenian territory. The agreement that allies should not permit passage of forces of the opposition through their own territory was obviously breached. The Argives continued their attempts on Epidauros until the coming of spring.

Thereafter the Spartans decided to take action against Argos to relieve the Epidaurians and also to put a stop to the growing disaffection within the Peloponnese caused by the Argive-Athenian alliance. The meeting point for the Spartan allies was Phleious and these included 2,000 hoplites from Corinth, contingents from all the Arkadian allies, the Tegeates, the full muster from Phleious itself, and 5,000 hoplites and 5,000 light-armed men from Boiotia together with 500 of their cavalry. With the cavalry came the ἄμιπποι (amippoi), a further 500 light armed troops who often rode behind their partner cavalrymen, ran alongside, or were pulled along by holding onto the horse's tail. Their commander was King Agis, son of Archidamos, who brought with him the whole Spartan army together with helots. Later, at V. 60. 3, mention is made of Sikyonians and Pellenians as also being in the muster.

Argos was not unprepared for the invasion. Mantineia with its own forces and those of its own allies, together with 3,000 hoplites from Elis, joined them. In an attempt to forestall the joining of the Spartans with the rest of their allies at Phleious, the Argives made contact with the Spartans at Methidrion in Arkadia intending to give battle. Although Thucydides does not say so, it can be presumed that the Spartan forces were inferior in numbers, particularly if the Argives were going to take the offensive. The Spartan line of march was planned to skirt Mantineian-held areas. Both sides encamped on hills but during the night Agis led his forces quietly away. That he was able to do so undetected shows both the discipline of the Spartan forces and the inadequate surveillance measures taken by the opposing commanders.

At dawn the following day the duped Argives started their march back to Argos from where they moved north towards Nemea, the expected line of the enemy advance. Knowledge of the terrain makes this supposition a reasonable one. With mountains farther to the west, the route comes out through low-lying hills in rolling countryside towards a plain in which the huge rocky outcrop of the acropolis of Argos sits. They were therefore surely right about the muster location.

At Phleious, however, Agis had different ideas. Dividing the forces gathered there into three bodies, each advanced upon Argos by separate routes. At V. 58. 4 more information is given on the identities of the Spartan allies. The Epidaurians were with the Spartans and the Arkadians in one force, the Pellenians were with the Corinthians and Phleiasions in another, and in the third assemblage the Megarans and Sicyonians were with the Boiotians. The first two groups approached the plain of Argos by difficult and unexpected routes, the last made their approach down the expected route towards Nemea. The last group was to use its Boiotian cavalry to harass the rear of the enemy if it should attack the main force, which was led by Agis. This implies that Agis anticipated being to the south of the Argive army as he entered the plain of Argos. Unfortunately, the routes of other marches are not given by Thucydides, but there are one or two clues.

The three-pronged approach to the plain of Argos appears at first to be a clever plan devised by Agis to outwit and outflank the forces opposing him.[2] If this is the case he is to be applauded. However, considering the outcome of this invasion, doubts surface. It is possible that Agis was seeking to strike at the environs of Argos itself with the Argive army to his north.

The march of Agis' force must have been made during the night because Thucydides states that the Argives became aware that the main Spartan

1 A Corinthian style helmet of the last half of the 5th century BC.

2 and 3 *Opposite and above:* Far above the Spartan colony of Herakleia in Trachis set up during the war are the scattered remains of the sanctuary at Herakles' place of death. At 6,000 feet near the summit of Mt Oiti, this is the highest sanctuary in Greece.

4 A 5th-century vase depicting two hoplites in combat, found at Domokos north-north-west of Lamia.

5 View from the Acrocorinth over Corinth towards the Gulf.

6 Typical cisterns used to store and supply water for a city, this one at Pleuron. These proved essential in times when access to springs or rivers were restricted by invading forces or during a siege.

7 Area of Phormio's first naval action immediately outside the Gulf of Corinth.

8 The narrow northern entrance to the bay between Sphakteria and the mainland.

9 At the end of the first decade of the Peloponnesian War the strategically vital Amphipolis broke away from Athens and remained independent until its incorporation into the kingdom of Macedonia by Philip II in 357. Thucydides' failure to retake the city led to his exile. The city's bridge over the Strymon river was made of wooden beams.

10 From Amphipolis to the North over the area formerly covered by Lake Kerkinitis.

11 From Amphipolis to the South and the position of Eion.

12 The view from the area controlled by the Spartan colony Irakleia in Trachis toward Themopylai where the Spartans started building dockyards. The island of Euboia, the target of their proposed assaults, is in the background. The mainland coast shows the considerable deposition of silt that has built up over the last 2,500 years.

13 The Diolchos, the paved way over which mercantile vessels were hauled by wheeled vehicles between the Gulf of Corinth and the Saronic Gulf. The Spartans started building larger vehicles for the purpose of moving warships between the gulfs but the effort came to nothing.

14 A small section of the fine coastal defences of Aigosthena near Syphai in the Gulf of Corinth, started in the 5th century BC.

15 *Opposite:* Perikles had unofficially assumed the leadership of the Athenian democracy by 443 BC, although he continued to run for office every year. The few years of peace before the Peloponnesian Wars he devoted to making visible the glory of Athens by construction work on the Acropolis.

16 *Above:* A frieze fragment from the Parthenon. Perikles oversaw the building of the Parthenon personally. Costing 5000 talents in the first year alone – a figure equivalent to some £2 billion – the building was completed in less than 15 years, despite attempts to derail the projects by Perikles' political opponents. Made from 20 thousand tons of marble quarried from nearby Mount Pentelicus, the huge cost of the building was partly financed from the treasury of the Delian League, which caused great resentment. (LOC: LC-USZ62-108948)

18 An early 20th-century image of the remains of the castle tower later rebuilt at Plataia, after the Thebans had razed the city.

17 *Opposite:* Perikles orates before the Athenian assembly, a 'classic' Victorian take on the scene, the Parthenon in the background, naturally.

19 *Above:* Athenian decree (409/8 BC) honouring Polykles, Peiraieus and M[andr]oboulos for their assistance in the Peloponnesian War and providing for their escort to the Hellespont to assist in Athenian operations there. (Centre for the Study of Ancient Documents, Oxford)

20 *Above right:* Mosaic of Thucydides in the Altes Museum, Berlin.

21 The bronze outer skin of a Spartan shield captured at Pylos and brought back to Athens as a trophy. Housed in the Agora Museum, the shield is almost inevitably tenuously linked to the one lost by Brasidas in his assault.

22 Coin with representation of Tissaphernes, Satrap of Lydia and Caria and commander of the Persian army in Asia Minor. Alkibiades persuaded him to stay out of the fight. When the Persians finally supported the Spartans with intent in 408 he lost the generalship and was limited to the satrapy of Caria only.

23 The remains of the ancient harbour mole at Thasos can just be made out under the surface. This is where Thucydides commanded the Athenian naval squadron.

24 This vase painting of a hoplite engagement dates from about a century before the War, but it would not look so anachronistic to those engaged in the conflict. The hoplite had dominated Greek warfare for even longer; but the Peloponnesian War would see the beginning of the end for these heavily armed and relatively immobile troops as the key element on the battlefield.

25 Bronze head of a warrior from the beginning of the 5th century BC. Bronzes like this found at the Acropolis are of a high standard of workmanship and artistry, dedicated to Athena. This bronze head was probably dedicated by an Athenian general or by a winner of the hoplite race.

force was to their south when day came (V. 59.1). The Argive coalition therefore left Nemea to come to the rescue and, in so doing, made contact with and fought the second army. This too must have started its march at night. Some Phleiasion casualties are recorded, but the Argives were worsted by the Corinthians before contact was lost. No other details of this action are given by Thucydides. In the meantime, the Boiotian forces had advanced on Nemea and found no opposition awaiting their arrival. They obviously started their march later than the two other contingents, possibly at daybreak. The position as described by Thucydides (V. 59. 2–3) was a disastrous one for the Argives. The Spartans to the south had cut them off from Argos, the second force of Phleiasions, Corinthians and Pellenians were now coming *down from above* (καθύπερθεν) and the army of the Boiotians, Sicyonians and Megarans were advancing directly south from Nemea and could take the Argives in the rear if they engaged the Spartans.

Apart from that taken by the Boiotians, as previously mentioned, the exact routes of the other two forces can only be guessed at. However, as that taken by Agis is described as being 'unexpected' and 'more difficult' than the approach from Nemea, and that of the Corinthians 'by another steep road', it seems likely that Agis entered the plain of Argos from the west and the Corinthians, Phleiasions and Pellenians from the north-east. The latter were encountered by the Argive army returning southward from Nemea and had probably come down from the foothills into the north of the plain before the brief action alluded to above. It can be assumed that they had broken contact with the larger force after the brief action and continued their march more indirectly through the rolling hills a little to the east.

Agis is described as ravaging 'Saminthos and other places'. Unfortunately Saminthos is not identifiable; otherwise we would be more certain of the direction of the king's entry into the plain. A possible route for an army in column is over the rolling upland from the western end of the Nemean plain south-west and then turning eastward at modern Malendreni or, a little farther south, at Sterna. From these points the country becomes gentler moving east, allowing for full deployment in battle order relatively soon thereafter. One advantage of this approach is the Inachos river, which would have shielded the right wing of the Spartan advance.

The Argives appeared happily unaware of their disastrous position. The main body of soldiery was probably also unaware that they were surrounded and thought that a battle now could be fought under very favourable conditions, with the Spartans close to their city and apparently cut off from a safe retreat or support from their allies. From the possible direction of Agis's' incursion many may have thought that a planned junction of forces had not been made and that here was a unique opportunity to worst the Spartans. No report is given by Thucydides of the intelligence received by the Argives prior to the position in which they now found themselves. If it came as a surprise to them that Agis was ravaging their lands to the south of their position, they may have concluded that the junction at Phleious had not been made and that the Spartans had unilaterally invaded their lands after their overnight withdrawal much farther to the west near Methydrion. They may have believed that their skirmish with the Phleiasions and Corinthians had nullified immediate danger from that quarter and, while it is difficult to believe that they could have been unaware of the large Boiotian and Megaran forces which had gathered at Phleios, they may have thought them a little too distant to be a cause for immediate concern in their present undertaking. All this is conjecture, but whatever the case, the main body of Argives appeared bent on a trial of strength despite the fact that they were without any cavalry. For this arm they were relying on their Athenian ally and, as yet, the Athenians had not arrived. However, Argive forces outnumbered those directly under the command of Agis.

What followed is given no explanation by Thucydides, only the facts are reported. He tells us that one of the five generals, Thrasyllos, of the army opposing Agis and an Argive *proxenos* to the Spartans, Alkiphron (one who represented the views of Sparta in Argos because of guest friendship or family ties), went to the king just prior to the engagement of both sides to plead the case for arbitration in the dispute. The fact that Thrasillos was one of five generals indicates that he may have been acting as spokesman for the command structure rather than entirely on his own account. Had this not been the case, the battle would have taken its course, the Argive and allied army being led by the majority against Agis. A further question arises. Were the five generals referred to all Argives or were some of them Mantineians, Eleans or from another of the allies, for they too would have had their generals? Needless to say, precedence was always given to the commanders in whose territory an action was to take place. The exception to this was that the Spartans always had primacy in the command structure wherever hostilities were entered into. This was to be the rule until the Second Battle of Mantineia in the next century, at a time when Sparta no longer could be considered a great power.[3] However, the number of five generals would seem to indicate those of the Argive contingent only. The approach of the two Argive representatives, Thrasyllos and Alkiphron, must have been under some form of signal for a parley not identified by Thucydides.

Their plea for non-engagement and for arbitration in the dispute is described as being wholly personal, however. What is significant is that Agis heard their proposals alone and informed only one of the leading men accompanying his expedition. His talks were conducted in secret with the two Argives. This must bring into question Agis' judgement. Admittedly, the king had always been in a position of supreme power when in the field but the outcome of his decision was to have later repercussions (see below).

A truce was made, no battle ensuing, and the Spartan army left the territory of Argos forthwith.

Several aspects of this outcome must be questioned from the point of view of both Agis and Thrasyllos as commanders. Had the latter recognised, appreciating the wider tactical issues, that the Argives were going to suffer an ignominious defeat? Was the Argive command structure more aware than the men of the true nature of their situation? This seems likely, otherwise such overtures made would make little sense. However, if the Argive commanders *were* aware of the danger, why did they not communicate the facts to their men?

What is particularly intriguing is that Agis conducted his talks with the Argive representatives *in camera*. Perhaps Agis was not secure in his own mind that the allies were close enough to give him the support he might need if he came to battle. If true, this would suggest that his own communications were not all they should have been. A truce for four months was agreed and the Argives were to use this time to fulfil their part of the agreement. It would seem at first sight that an alliance might be made between Argos and Sparta. This would have been a diplomatic coup had it been the case. We can excuse Agis, in part, for wishing to achieve an alliance with brother Dorians such as the Argives. But the secrecy surrounding the talks, with only one other on the Spartan side being informed, suggests that there may have been more to the agreement than we know. To have abandoned a well laid plan which had almost come to fruition – with the Spartans, had battle been joined, holding the Argives and their allies until such time as they would have been taken in flank and rear by the Corinthians and the Boiotians – remains inexplicable.

It is not surprising, therefore, that Sparta's allies did not take kindly to Agis' decision. They had achieved nothing in return for their preparations. His own Spartan followers were aggrieved, but they and the allies had to follow the edict of the commander-in-chief.

So, with the forces on both sides feeling that an opportune time for dealing with their enemy had slipped by, recriminations were soon to follow. In the case of the Argives their reaction was immediate. Thrasyllos was stoned at the walls of Argos and only managed to escape death by seeking sanctuary. His property was confiscated. Shortly after, the expected Athenian forces arrived, a force consisting of 1,000 hoplites and 300 cavalry. Their commanders were Laches and Nikostratos and they were accompanied by Alkibiades as ambassador from Athens. Their arrival put the Argives in a quandary. Whereas they condemned the action of Thrasyllos, they baulked at the idea of breaking the truce engineered by him with Sparta. It may well be that others of the command complement spoke in support of honouring his agreement in assembly for, initially, the Athenians were not allowed to make the case that the Argives should not have agreed to a truce without the consent of their allies. It was only by virtue of Mantineian and Elean arguments that the Athenians were allowed to give voice to their objections. Thereafter, all but the Argives advanced against Orchomenos in the Peloponnese which went over to their side to avoid destruction. Though late, the Argives followed their lead, technically breaking the truce.

The settlement of Orchomenos left the allies to deliberate what they should next undertake. The Elians argued that Lepreon, a small city which had come under Spartan control, should be the next target. The majority voted for an expedition against Tegea and as a result the Elians, in a fit of pique, left the allied forces and returned home.

At Sparta, news of the fall of Orchomenos further fuelled the resentment felt against Agis, for here was the old adversary, with her allies, totally disregarding what Agis had claimed had been agreed. They had kept their resentment in check up to the time of the news of Orchomenos, but at that point, so soon after the return of the army, their normal self-disciplined demeanour left them. Agis was threatened with the destruction of his house and a hefty fine, in Spartan terms, of ten thousand drachmas. He pleaded that he would make good his error by some act in the field. Persuaded by his arguments the Spartans did not do as they had originally planned but passed a law by which Agis could not lead out an army from their territory unless it was agreed by ten Spartiates, who were assigned as counsellors to him.

News from Tegea indicated that if help did not arrive soon a faction in the city would surrender it to the Argives and their allies.[4] Agis quickly led the army north. Thucydides states at V. 64. 2 that the Spartans had mobilised '...the Lakedaimonians themselves and...the helots, in full force, promptly and on such a scale as never before.' Messages had been sent to Sparta's allies in Corinth, Boiotia, Phokis and Lokris to make all haste to Mantineia. To do this they had to come through enemy territory and therefore for their own security had to muster in force before making the journey. One can imagine that, having only recently returned to their homes after what they must have considered a wasted effort, they were not a little aggrieved to be setting off once more to engage the same enemy. Time was of the essence if Tegea was to be saved, and that was probably the reason for sending out the whole Spartan complement. In the event of a battle taking place before any of the allies appeared, Agis would still have a powerful army. The closer Arkadian allies had been summoned. Possibly when they were near the Spartan army Agis sent home a sixth of his forces, namely the youngest and oldest of the ban or call-up. This occurred when Agis had reached the Oresteion of Maenalia which was some fifty kilometres NNW of Sparta (see Pausanias VIII. 3. 1) just beyond the frontier of Spartan-held Messenia. After the Arkadians had joined Agis, he led the army into Mantineian territory making camp at a sanctuary of Herakles.

The Argives reacted by forming for battle at a place whose approach was steep, thus giving them an immediate advantage. Agis made his advance and must have started the ascent when one of the older men shouted out to him that he was trying to make amends for one error (his retreat from Argos) by making another (attacking such a strong position).[5] Thucydides puts the distance between the two armies at that time as being a javelin throw (V. 65. 2). Whether as a reaction to this call or because he realised his foolhardiness anyway, Agis quickly withdrew his army and marched back into Tegeate territory where he started the work of diverting a small river into Mantineian lands. This he did to induce the opposition to come down into the plain to attempt to put a stop to the damage the water would cause.

The withdrawal was no doubt in good order, but what is surprising is that there was no attack made upon the Spartans by the Argives at this time. The Argives and allies are described as being amazed by the turn of events (V. 65. 5). Clearly the generals of the Argive coalition were no clearer in their intentions at this time than Agis. When the Spartans were no longer to be seen, these generals were harangued by their men, who accused them of letting the Spartans escape a second time. It was probably more for this reason that the generals at last ordered a move forward into the plain where they encamped.

The following day the Spartans, returning from the river to their old camp at the Herakleion, were confronted by the Argive army in full battle order. Thucydides records their surprise: '...never had the Lakedaimonians, as far back as they remembered, been in such consternation as on this occasion.'

At first sight this may appear a surprising comment. Not to be aware of several thousand men in close proximity until virtually the last moment is unusual. The suggestion that they were masked from view by an ancient woodland has merit.[6] However, the text suggests that the Argives and their allies had only moved out of camp and deployed in line of battle. There is no suggestion that they were actually on the move and advancing in battle order. Certainly this would have been their intention but the words 'occupying an advanced position away from the hill' do not imply the forward movement of an advance. To have done so would have caused considerable dust clouds which even an intervening stretch of woodland would not have entirely obscured.

It suggests that Agis had no scouts operating in advance of his main body, obviously in column, and this would have been a notable act of negligence. Nor would it appear that he had left any to observe the enemy. If, as Thucydides states at V. 65. 4–5, he had returned to Tegean territory on his stream-diverting mission, ' to make the enemy on the hill come down to prevent the diversion of the water', it would seem appropriate to have left observers who could have forewarned him of any movement made by the Argives and to report that his ploy had achieved the response he desired. The ten Spartiate counsellors appointed to him would surely have made suggestions for such arrangements even if he himself had been remiss. (It may well have been one of these men who had had made him aware of his foolhardiness in ordering the uphill advance.) Lack of evidence is not proof that Agis did not make these dispositions.[7]

There are several possibilities which could explain the 'surprise' registered at the unexpected sight of the Argive army in full battle array. Observers could have had their positions overrun prior to the Argive change of camp. Scouts or reconnaisance groups well ahead of the returning main body of the Spartan army could have fallen in with the enemy, now in an unexpectedly advanced position. The fact that the Argives were not 'surprised' would indicate that they were aware of the impending return of the Lakedaimonians.

The hurried deployments were all made, as usual, according to the orders of the king. Thucydides outlines the method by saying that 'the responsibility for the execution of orders devolves upon many' (V. 66. 4), i.e. from the king to the polemarch, and from the polemarch to the lochargos, then to the commanders of fifty men and on to the subcommanders of smaller units.

The battle line for the Spartans and their allies was ordered as follows. On the left wing the *Skiritai* took up their traditional position. Adjacent to them were the newly freed helots, the *Brasideioi*, who had served with Brasidas in the north, together with the *Neodamodeis*, other formerly freed helots settled at Lepreon on the border of Elis. Then came the Lakedaimonian battalions, then the Heraions, the Maenalaions, with the right wing taken by the force from Tegea and a small number of Lakedaimonians. This last group is puzzling because it is not described as being in any identifiable unit, for example a designated small number of *enomotia*. They may have been Spartans taken from a battalion, the remainder of which was posted to guard the baggage train (V. 72. 3). A few proven and loyal *perioikoi* volunteers, gathered from towns near Sparta, such as Geronthrai a few miles to the south-east, may also have been present. Certainly one such person from that town is commemorated in an inscription as having fought at Mantineia.[8] Each wing was covered by cavalry. (See maps pp xxi-xxii.)

The Argive dispositions recognised that the territory they were fighting within was Mantineian and therefore this group of allies occupied the right wing. To their left were their Arkadian allies, then the 1,000-strong special force of the Argives who were supported at public expense, and then the mass of the Argives. The left wing was taken up by the Kleonians and the Orneates with the Athenian force at the outermost point of the left wing supported by their cavalry. No cavalry force is reported to have been stationed on the right wing.

It is regrettable that Thucydides is not so explicit about the numbers and details of the Spartan forces as usual. In his description no mention is made of *perioikoi* (dwellers around). While these could well be described as Lakedaimonians, the following will hopefully suggest that this omission is not accidental; except for possible trusted volunteers and of course the *Skiritai*, (those men with a similar standing to the *perioikoi* who traditionally fought as an elite force of light infantry).

Thucydides suggests that the Lakedaimonian army appeared the larger (V. 68. 1). Here he is referring to the totality of the army including the allies. His computation of the Lakedaimonians present (V. 68. 2–3) surely refers *only* to the Spartans and obviously not to the numbers of the allies. The mobilisation had been speedier than usual and some or all of the *perioikoi* are likely to have been absent for one of two reasons. First, through not having had sufficient time to reach the muster point living as they did in many townships throughout Lakedaimon. That they were slow to join a main force can be seen in the example of the Battle of Plataia 479 BC, when 5,000 *perioikoi* followed some days after the main force of 5,000 Spartans and 35,000 helots had marched north (Herod, IX. 10. 1).[9]

The second and more likely reason for their absence is that they were not included in the ban or call-up. The *perioikoi* appear to have been rarely used at this time in action against other Peloponnesian states. It may be a reflection of Sparta's psychological insecurity following on from Sphakteria, their continued worry regarding the helots and the vacillations of their former Peloponnesian allies, against some of whom they were now to fight.

Thucydides is reasonably specific in naming the other components of the army. Adding to his computation of 4,184 Lakedaimonians, the known 600 *Skiritai* (V. 67. 1) and the likely numbers of the other contingents, e.g. 2,500–3,000 Tegeates, no more than 1,000 Heraians and Mainalians, 1,200 in the joint forces of the Neadamodeis and Brasideioi and at least 250 cavalry, the whole army would have numbered 9,500 men or more.

However, Thucydides leaves us to guess at the numbers of the Argive coalition force. Possibly there were at least 4,000 Argives present, including the 1,000 hoplites trained at public expense with 2,500–3,000 Mantineians. He informs us that the Athenian reinforcements numbered 1,000 hoplites and 300 cavalry. The Arkadian allies of the Mantineians may have added a further 1,000, with the Kleonaians and Orneaians adding a lesser number. This being so, the numbers on each side appear balanced. The fact that the Lakedaimonian army *appeared* the larger was either as a consequence of their deployment or because they were indeed fielding more men.

If the Spartans had appeared for the battle with numerical superiority (see below) and the Argives and their allies were not deterred from taking the offensive, then this indicates the waning of Greek belief in the invincibility of the Spartans since Sphakteria. Their apparent indecisiveness, when recently in such an advantageous position in the Argolid, must have helped.

A further problem requiring resolution is Thucydides' references to the largest section of the Spartan army as a *lochos*, and the absence of the term *mora*. Indeed, he describes Agis's army as having had seven *lochoi* and extrapolates his total numbers from these. It seems unlikely that Thucydides would be unaware of the military organisation of the Spartans, despite the differences between it and that of Athens. Nor would the fact that prior to his exile he was a *navarch* (admiral) have led to any confusion, particularly when he shows himself to be fully conversant with other descriptive labels such as *pentekostys* (a corps of 150–160 men), *enomotia* (a subdivision of up to forty men) and *Hippeis* (300 young men making up the Royal Guard). Although the term *mora* is first encountered in sources in Xenophon's *Hellenika* (II. iv. 31) referring to activity in 403 BC, there is no reason to assume that it had not been in currency for many years prior to that date. As a *mora* was commanded by a polemarch and was made up of two *lochoi*, each commanded by a lochargos, convincing arguments have been made to suggest that the numbers in Agis's army were much greater.[10] The idea is leant added weight in the details of the dangerous order given to fill the space in the line caused by Agis' order for the *Skiritai* and *Brasideioi* of the left wing to move even farther left to match the line of the opposing Mantineians and Argives (V. 71. 3, see later in the description of the battle).

The conflict between evidence spanning a matter of a few years leads us to give more weight to Xenophon, who for much of his life lived in Spartan-held territory. He was an intimate of King Agesilaos and the leading Spartiates, fighting alongside them.[11] In consequence, further consideration should be given to the likely numbers of Lakedaimonians present at the battle.

Had they been present it is almost unthinkable that the *perioikoi* would have been brigaded with the *Spartiatai*, thus leading to the notion that half a *mora*, or the equivalent of a *lochos* in Xenophon's reckoning, was made up of such men. Such would be a convenient solution to the problem which Thucydides presents, but would have been unworkable in practice. Rather, the *perioikoi* would have been organised on a regional basis quite separately from the professional soldiery of the Spartans. Again, the argument that in the absence of the *perioikoi* the numbers of Lakedaimonians would be as Thucydides suggests due to a fall in manpower can be countered. We are now in the period when the decline in the number of Spartiates (*Spartiatai* or 'peers') is beginning to show itself. It is suggested that by the time of Leuktra in 371 BC their numbers had dwindled to around 1,000. However, those of the 'peers' who were disenfranchised because of their inability to pay their 'mess' (syssition) bills would have been Spartans who may have been through the *agoge* and would have been considered as being suitable to serve in the *morai* with the more fortunate full citizens. These *hypomeiones,* were one of several groups within Spartan society. *Mothakes* or *mothones* are defined as the sons of Spartiates by non-Spartan women of the *perioikoi* and were sometimes called *partheniai.* They were usually put through the *agoge* by their fathers or guardians. There were also *tresantes,* those of the peers who had been labelled cowards and had lost their citizenship until such time as they might redeem it. Thucydides makes clear what this last group might expect of any loss of franchise in his description of the returned prisoners from Sphakteria (V. 34.2). All the above groups would have been ideal members of the Spartan army, being very local and easily available for regular training. After all, they all at least had a Spartiate father. The number of Spartiates may have begun to decline but the Spartan population was little changed.[12]

In accepting Thucydides' numbers based on the questionable *lochoi,* we must agree that there were 4,184 Spartans present in the battle line, the *lochos,* being the largest group in Thucydides' account, containing just under 600 men. However, if we accept Xenophon's statement (Lak. X. 11. 4) that the army was divided into six regiments (*morai*), by his enumeration this would suggest twelve *lochoi,* each *mora* having around 1,200 men.

Although evidence is limited, it can be fairly confidently claimed that the organisation of the Spartan army at this time was as follows. Six *morai* each commanded by a *polemarch,* having two subordinate commanders or *lochargoi.* This does not mean necessarily that a *lochos* was exactly half a *mora.* The seven *lochoi* become three and a half *morai.* This may suggest that Thucydides mistook the nomenclature for the largest unit but did not miscalculate the total numbers within the battle and that there were indeed seven *lochoi.* Accepting that Thucydides is correct in the number of *lochoi* present thereby representing a force of three and half *mora* deployed in the battle line, we reach a figure which closely agrees with the computation of 4,184.

A further objection to the direct substitution of *mora* for *lochos* is the number seven given by Thucydides as the total number of *lochoi* present at Mantineia. If Xenophon's later evidence is to be accepted as the norm even for some years earlier than the period of which he was to write, it must be accepted that the Spartan army was made up of six *morai* i.e. at Xen *Hell* VI. 1. 1. we are informed that Kleombrotos went to Phokis with four *morai,* and at *Hell.* VI. 4. 17, after the disaster at Leuktra, the two remaining *morai* were called up.

Accepting this organisation and practice, it can be suggested that Agis had four *morai* (eight *lochoi*) with him. Then the few Lakedaimonians on the important extreme right (V. 67. 1) come from a half *mora* or *lochos* the remainder of which was set to guard the baggage train along with the other half mora or *lochos.*

Given that the depth of the line was on average eight men, a front of fifteen or twenty or even twenty-five men for the few on the right would have totals of 120, 160, or 200. In the case of the largest total of 200 the extension of the line of battle would only be about twenty-five yards or less. These would be men in their prime, with the balance of about 360 or so making up a *lochos or* half *mora* set to guard the camp, made up the older age groups.

Thucydides' totals and seven *lochoi* can therefore be accepted as being those deployed for the battle, without ignoring the slightly later evidence of Xenophon.

It is clear at V. 64. 3 that the Spartans had given orders for their Arkadian allies to muster quickly and follow on after them to Tegea. The closest would obviously be the first to join the Spartans and it may well be that a sufficient force of Arkadians was already gathered at, or were known to be very near, the Orestheion for the Spartans to send home one sixth of the overall total of Lakedaimonians. The Heraians had but a short distance to travel and the Mainalians lived in the district around the Orestheion itself. Although not as clear cut an argument as would be desired, the force would have been large enough to permit the notion of the customary two *morai* of Lakedaimonians containing the oldest and youngest age groups to return home.

To the battle itself. Enlightening comments are made by Thucydides about the preparations for the conflict. The various commanders of the Argives and their allies exhorted their men on issues which were directly pertinent to their own condition and desires. The Mantineians, for example, let it be a clear choice between freedom or servitude. The Argives wished for a return to their old hegemony within the area, although this was far back in the mists of time. The Athenians, thought that a victory in the Peloponnese would render their own territory inviolable. By contrast, the Lakedaimonians dispensed with the commander's address and put their trust as usual in discipline and training, singing war songs to raise their spirits.

The advance of the two armies is described, and herein one can see a difference of approach. The Argives and their allies moved eagerly to the fray, the Lakedaimonians to the measured strains of the aulos. This instrument has long been described by scholars in translation as a flute. Although a convenient term it is misleading. The aulos was a double reed instrument with a loud, penetrating sound, more akin to a cross between an oboe and a shawm. This allowed the Spartan advance to be measured and in consequence maintained the integrity of the line.

Just prior to the point of engagement, Agis noticed that the Mantineians on the right wing had achieved an extension of their line well beyond the Skiritae. Thucydides mentions (V. 71. 1) the habit of men in the line, fearful of danger to their unshielded and unprotected side, of moving to their right. They did so to gain the protection of their neighbour's shield. The man at the extreme position of the right wing who was without any neighbour to his right started the sideways readjustment, being the most eager to keep his own unprotected side well away from the enemy. Thucydides states that both sides had effected an overlap on their right wing. He implies that because of this 'natural drift to the right' the Mantineians were well beyond the Skiritae, and the Spartans and Tegeates considerably overlapped the Athenians because their numbers were thought to be greater.[13]

Agis came to the conclusion (or perhaps it was drawn to his attention) that while he could encircle his enemy's left, his own left was in danger of the same by the Mantineians. His decision to take action to remedy the problem was taken, as Thucydides puts it, 'while they were still closing' (V. 71. 1). So the time available from the point of decision to the receipt of a command that could be followed was minimal. He sent orders to the Neodamodes and the Skiritae to distance themselves from the main body to a point where the Mantineian overlap would be nullified. At the same time he ordered the polemarchs, Hipponoidas and Aristokles, to leave the right wing of the Spartan section of the army with their men and move left behind the advancing line to make good the gap newly created in it. Spartan discipline was certainly up to such manoeuvres and his right wing may still have been in a superior position. Here the problem of *mora* and *lochos* looms large. If Thucydides mistakenly meant the former, Agis was ordering a huge single body of his forces to change position, i.e.two *morai* or half the Lakedaimonians present. We must therefore assume he is using the correct nomenclature on this occasion and he was asking for two *lochoi* to be moved from the line under the command of their polemarchs. Although two *lochoi* is the equivalent of one *mora* the fact that two polemarchs received the order suggests that each was being ordered to move half of those under his command rather than the whole of his force. This would initially have caused two gaps in the line each of about seventy yards which, though large in themselves, would have been easier to close than a gap of about 140 yards had a single *mora* been ordered to make the manoeuvre.

At V. 72. 1, Thucydides makes it clear that Agis's commands were made just as the two armies closed and because of this, the two subcommanders refused to move from their places in the line. A further order to the Skiritae and Neomadodes to close up the line once more found them unable to do so, clearly indicating the proximity of the enemy.

Although Agis had eventually recognised his problem and had seen how it might be rectified, he had insufficient time for the completion of his orders and therefore should not have given them. The order for the left wing to move away from the main body would have had an immediate effect, an initial break in the line would have occurred, thereafter widening to become a considerable gap. The order to the polemarchs required them to move from the right to the left wing to begin to fill the space in the line left by the Skiritae and Neomadodes. If Thucydides' number of Lakedaimonians present is accepted, a total front for this part of the army would have been 448 shields (V. 68. 3). This assumes the usual depth of eight men. Agis' order required the polemarchs to march their men almost quarter of a mile to their left behind their own advancing front. As they marched, that very front itself would have been moving away from them to their right towards the enemy. They would then have to wheel right to come up to their proposed new position. What was wrong with Agis' calculation? Obviously the distance between the two armies would have had to be greater for the polemarchs to complete their move. 'It turned out, then, as he gave this order at the very moment of the attack and on a sudden that Aristokles and Hipponoindas refused to move over' (V. 72. 1).

The Mantineians, their allies and the crack force of 1,000 Argive hoplites routed the left wing and exploited the gap to attack the left of the Lakedaimonian section of the line, and drove them back upon their own transport wagons. Thucydides notes it was mainly the older men there who were casualties. In the rest of the field fortunes were very different.

Agis, near the centre, surrounded by the specially chosen royal bodyguard of 300 young hoplites (*Hippeis*), was overwhelmingly successful in the attack. Not only was the enemy routed but many chose not even to engage but fled, several falling and being trodden underfoot in the scramble to escape. The right wing of the Lakedaimonians and Tegeates, which had enjoyed an overlap, now threatened to encircle the Athenians. Thucydides makes it clear that casualties on the Athenian side would have been greater had not their cavalry been present. It is pity that we do not have any details of the tactics employed by this arm during the battle. One can only assume that hit and run tactics were employed in which the discharge of javelins blunted the onset of the enemy attack. Nonetheless, the Athenians were saved from total encirclement and possible annihilation by what followed.

Now Agis ordered the army to go to the assistance of his beleaguered left, which allowed the Athenians and those Argives with them to escape. The hitherto successful Mantineian and Argive right wing was now faced with a successful Lakedaimonian centre and right wing crossing the field of battle towards them. Their reaction was to take to flight. The Mantineians suffered the most casualties, the majority of the picked men of the Argives surviving. The pursuit was short as was the custom of the Spartans (V. 73. 4 see also Plut. *Lycurgus* 22). By maintaining good order the likelihood of a counter-attack was minimised. Knowledge of this habit may have persuaded many reluctant opponents before and after Mantineia to take to their heels even before engaging.

The immediate outcome was the setting up of a trophy by the Spartans and the taking up of their dead. Thereafter, as was the custom, their enemy, under truce, reclaimed their own dead. Thucydides observes that this was the greatest battle between Hellenic states for a very long time. The casualties he gives in round figures are significant for a hoplite engagement: 700 Argives, Keonions and Orneates, 200 Mantineians, and Athenian and Aeginetan losses of 200, including two generals. Thucydides makes the point that while the allies of the Spartans suffered little, it is difficult to ascertain the number of casualties suffered by the Lakedaimonians. He puts the number at around 300, presumably on their left wing and within their camp.

The other Spartan king, Pleistoanax, had come in support of his royal colleague with the older and younger age groups.[14] On his arrival at Tegea he received the news of the victory. Those allies to the north who had marched in response to the original summons were turned back by messengers. The outcome of this successful action was the restoration of Spartan reputation in the Greek world.

The aftermath of the battle saw the two polemarchs exiled from Sparta on the charge of cowardice. Insubordination would have been closer to the mark; but a Spartan king was pre-eminent in battle and his orders were sacrosanct. The question remains, however, whether or not the success enjoyed by the centre and right of the Lakedainonian army rested on the refusal of the two to obey Agis' order. Had they taken their men from the line at the moment of contact or near contact, the integrity of that part of the line might well have been compromised, creating further gaps in the line which could have been exploited by the enemy.

So it was that Agis redeemed himself in the eyes of his compatriots and, as a result of this battle, went some way to repairing the damage done to Spartan reputation at Sphakteria. In the Greek world Sparta was once again regarded as invincible on land. In a very short time her leadership of the Peloponnesian League was as strong as it had ever been.

However, it can be seen that Agis was a commander of suspect judgement and prone to impetuous and wrong-headed decisions that sometimes endangered those he led. He was tactically inept and saved only by the outstanding qualities of his fighting force.

Notes

1. Alkibiades had commanded a force of 1,000 Athenian hoplites in support of Argive activities against the Epidaurians in 419 BC. (V. 55. 4).

2. The three-pronged approach to the Argive plain may well have been planned to speed the invasion and to minimise the bottlenecks which occur in ever-changing terrain. A column of a few thousand men could stretch several miles in restrictive terrain and on issuing into a plain usually advanced in line of battle if the enemy was known to be in the vicinity. A vanguard being

caught entering a plain would receive little or no support from the main body and rearguard.

3. After the battle of Leuktra in 371 BC Sparta was beset by the annual invasion of her territories by the Thebans and their allies. Helots deserted and Messenia was lost. Sparta found herself economically hard pressed and encircled by hostile states. With the later disenchantment of some of Thebes' Peloponnesian allies, a realignment brought on the second battle of Mantineia (462 BC) at which, because of its reduced position, Sparta no longer held overall command.

4. There were obvious differences of political opinion. Factions existed in most cities and democracy proved an increasing threat to the power base of governing bodies made up of restricted groups of leading men or aristocrats. Throughout the Peloponnesian War constant allusion is made to such factionalism.

5. Sun Tzu, *The Art of War*, VII. 33. 'It is a military axiom not to advance uphill against the enemy, nor to oppose him when he comes downhill'. The Chinese general wrote his manual of practice at about the time of the Persian invasion of Greece (490–486 BC). In all but religious practices his view of the conduct of war is mirrored in the writings of Xenophon who lived c.430–354 BC.

6. The Pelagos woodland. See J F Lazenby *The Spartan Army*, p.126.

7. It is unlikely that there would have been an abandonment of practices which had been current nearly seventy years before. Rather it would be expected that they would be further developed and refined until they were so commonplace that omitting full and detailed reference to them is not unexpected. For references to observers, lookouts, signals, guides etc., in the Persian War see Herodotos VII. 183, VII. 194, VII, 208, VII. 220, VIII. 22, VIII. 34, VIII. 35. J F Lazenby *The Spartan Army*, pp.126-7 is even handed and is not wholly persuaded that Agis had set up observers. He also refers to Thuc. IV. 14. 1 and IV. 32. 1, Xen. *Hell*. VI. 5. 17 and VII. 1. 16 concerning scouting failures by Spartans. However, W K Pritchett argues that such a conclusion reached by the present author and other historians is misconceived. See *The Greek State at War, Part II*, pp.156 et seq.

8. *Inscriptiones Graecae*, V. i. 1124.

9. Other examples of Spartan forces having to wait for the *perioikoi* to join them can be found in Xenophon's *Hellenika* at III. 5. 7 and V. 1. 33.

10. See Lazenby *The Spartan Army*, pp. 5–11 and 42–43 for convincing arguments that Thucydides misapplied the term *lochos* for *mora*. Although there is no disagreement on the relative strengths of a *lochos* or *mora* Lazenby approaches his proposed solution from a differing standpoint from this

author's. Both seek to clarify a statement within the source which must be in error. Michael Sage, *Warfare in Ancient Greece*, p.39, supports the view of doubling the numbers within a *mora* bringing its total to around 1,200. Donald Kagan, *The Peace of Nicias and the Sicilian Expedition*, pp.122–5 does not persuade and G L Cawkwell, *Classical Quarterly* 33 , 1983 is in the author's opinion incorrect. However, the arguments of W G Forrest, *A History of Sparta*, pp.133-4, still have resonance and his caveat concerning the positive assertion of the number of men in a *mora* needs consideration.

11. Xenophon served with Agesilaos in Asia Minor and at the battle of Koroneia.

12. The constitution required the Spartan citizen to pay his mess dues. The growing concentration into fewer hands of the lands producing the necessary wealth was accompanied by an inevitable reduction in the number of Spartans who could afford full citizen status. It is estimated that by the first quarter of the 4th century Spartan women owned the property rights of approximately a third of available land.

13. This 'natural drift to the right' was developed into a tactical outflanking movement by the Spartans at the battles of the Nemea and Koroneia (both in 394 BC). Kleombrotos was obviously attempting the same at Leuktra (371 BC) when caught in mid-manoeuvre by Epaminondas. For treatments of these battles see Lazenby, *The Spartan Army* and Hutchinson, *Xenophon and the Art of Command.*

14. According to Herodotos V, 75, a law was enacted around 507 BC which allowed only one of the two Spartan kings to lead an army out on campaign, the other being required to remain in Sparta. The fact that Pleistoanax was sent out with the oldest and youngest age groups (the remaining equivalent of two *morai*) before the result of the battle was known indicates how seriously the crisis was being taken. Contrast this with the two *morai* and the gathering of allies by Archidamus, son of the remaining king, Agesilaos, to go to the support of the undefeated part of the Spartan army at Leuktra after the death of Kleombrotos. This army set out at least two days after the initial action.

VII

The Great Sicilian Expedition 415–413 BC

The term 'Great' applies to the third Athenian expedition to Sicily. It provides an opportunity to scrutinise a complete campaign rather a single action.[1] Opinion is divided on whether or not the three expeditions to Sicily which took place during the Peloponnesian War were a departure from the Periklean strategy laid down for Athens at the opening of hostilities, namely that they should avoid further conquest during the conflict.

> For he [Perikles] had told the Athenians that if they would maintain a defensive policy, attend to their navy, and not seek to extend their sway during the war, or do anything to imperil the existence of the state, they would prove superior. (II. 65. 7)

Such was the policy advocated by Perikles for the conduct of the war. With great perception Thucydides takes this defensive policy and extrapolates from it to explain Athens' failure in the war following Perikles' death from the plague.

> But they not only acted contrary to his advice in all these things, but also in matters that apparently had no connection with the war they were led by private ambitions and private greed to adopt policies which proved injurious both as to themselves and their allies; for these policies, so long as they were successful, merely brought honour or profit to individual citizens, but when they failed proved detrimental to the state in the conduct of the war. (II. 65. 7)

Here, Thucydides is drawing specific attention to the disaster of the last expedition to Sicily. Athens had made at least two expeditions to Sicily before this.[2]

This author is of the opinion that Sicily was considered of paramount importance to Athens and that the last expedition was merely a natural development of a policy which had been sustained for years, well before Perikles' death.[3] At the time of its commission that policy had become pivotal to Athens. She had to regain the initiative with the resurgence of

Spartan fortunes following the Battle of Mantineia and to deny Sparta direct help from her Dorian cousins in Syracuse and other cities in Sicily, which up to that point she had not yet received. While the technicality of Nikias' peace still existed, pre-emptive measures had to be taken against possible future combatants. Further, the Athenians were in need of manpower and those disaffected with Syracuse could well have been the source.

Thucydides shows in the first part of Book Six that the Athenians were well aware of the conditions and composition of the peoples in Sicily. Diodoros gives more detail in Books XI and XIII. As early as 479 BC Themistokles had warned the remaining Greeks opposed to the Persian invasion that the Athenians would move to Siris rather than stay in their homeland (Herod. VIII. 62). This he claimed was foretold by the oracles. His interest in the west is further indicated by the fact that he called his daughter Italia. Inscriptions show that Athens had diplomatic relations with several cities in southern Italy and Sicily.[4] Alliances were made in the fifties and forties of the 5th century with Halykiai and Rhegion. Those with Leontini and Egesta were renewed in part in 433 BC. The Athenian colony of Thouria was founded in 446 BC. This shows considerable interest in, and knowledge of, the area on the part of Athens.

So we must question Thucydides' interpretation of Perikles' speech. Did his 'strategy' mean a cessation of involvement in Sicilian matters?[5] He defines a defensive policy, but it is in Athens' interest to keep the Dorian Sicilians preoccupied with their own island. Before his death he had overseen the alliance with Kerkyra and the establishment of a naval squadron at Naupaktos that threatened any traffic from either Sicily or the Peloponnese. This is evidence of sound strategic planning, aiming to seal off the Peloponnese from grain supplies or military support from the Syracusans or other Dorian settlements coming via the safe sea route.

In examining further the deeds of Perikles as measured against his words, we see that Perikles himself led an expedition early in the war against Epidauros with forces not dissimilar in size to those sent to Sicily on the last expedition.[6] In the same year Hagnon was operating in Chalkidike with an army only a little smaller than the two already mentioned, and this at a time when the plague was at its height in Athens. Admittedly both were shorter distances from home than Sicily and in waters much better known to the Athenians; and there may have been some unreported policy of removing the able-bodied from the area of infection which was taking its toll in the city.

The development of trade with the western Mediterranean had long been of interest to Athens. In 444 BC she had set up a colony in Southern Italy at Thouria and about a year later had concluded alliances, first with Rhegion at the toe of the Italian peninsula, and then with Leontini, an inland city not far from Syracuse. Up to that time trading in the region had been dominated by Corinth, and Athens' growing influence in that area caused resentment. With the establishment of a naval base at Naupaktos and the alliance with one of Corinth's earlier colonies, Kerkyra, Corinth had reason to feel aggrieved. (See Chapter I.) Her route to the west was now compromised and this was certainly one of the main causes of the Peloponnesian War. Athens was most definitely pursuing a policy to increase her influence in the west prior to Perikles' death. The alliances were made no doubt in the hope that they might afford Athens an opportunity to interfere in Sicilian matters and the expeditions thereafter were merely a logical continuation of that policy.

Such a policy was followed primarily to restrict the growing power of Syracuse. To have dropped it would have been to give Syracuse the opportunity to extend its dominion over most, if not all, of the island. The expeditions of 427 and 425 BC were not so much the product of a more aggressive policy on the part of the Athenians as a defensive policy, serving to distract and deflect what could have been more positive help to the Peloponnesian alliance and always with an opportunist eye to increasing Athens' influence and control on the island. At the conference at Gela in 424 BC the great Sicilian leader Hermokrates persuaded the warring cities in Sicily to bring an end to the hostilities that had largely been encouraged by Athens.

Other factors played a part. While the Syracusans, originally a Corinthian colony, were Dorians, there were other Greek colonies, such as Leontini, which were Ionian. Fundamental cultural differences existed between these Greek speaking peoples and this influenced the course of the conflict in ways not usually fully appreciated today.

Syracuse was a city similar in size and resources to Athens and this must have exercised Athenian minds. Some form of brake on Syracusan expansion was essential if Athenian control of trade in the west was to be established. Eventually, they would have had to deal with Carthage also. To have left Syracuse to her own devices at the start of the Peloponnesian War would have been to miss an opportunity and leave a hostage to fortune. Therefore, it was important that Athens continued to be engaged in Sicilian affairs.

Syracusan support for the Peloponnesian cause was slow to mature. One can assume that shipments of grain continued to arrive in the Peloponnese as a matter of course. Syracuse did not offer direct help in the hostilities away from home until Athenian interference and influence in Sicily had been wholly blunted by the disastrous outcome of the third expedition, which is the subject of this chapter.

The first expedition had followed the visit of an embassy from Leontini. This provided a convenient excuse for Athenian interference in Sicilian affairs. Laches was the commander of twenty ships that secured the straits between Italy and Sicily and affirmed the alliance with Egesta on the north-western coast of Sicily.

The second expedition, led by Pythodoros, Sophokles and Eurymedon, was a muted affair largely due to the diplomacy of Hermokrates at Gela referred to above.

It was not until 416 BC that Athens became directly involved with Sicily once more. The intervening years had seen Sphakteria, the northern exploits of Brasidas, and the battles of Delion and Mantineia.[7] An uneasy interlude had ensued, with some states of the Peloponnesian League refusing to accept the tenuous peace brokered between Athens and Sparta. In that year of 416 BC Egesta asked for Athens' help as an ally in its dispute with Selinous. The latter city was being helped by Syracuse and the Egestan envoys to Athens bolstered their request with a claim that the Syracusans were intent on gaining overall control of Sicily, whereafter, as Dorians, they could directly assist the Peloponnesians to bring Athens into subjection (VI. 6. 2–3). As an inducement, the Egestan envoys were authorised to offer to pay for the expedition. On this matter being investigated by Athenian envoys to Egesta, they succeeded in duping the Athenians as to the extent of their financial resources.

The Athenians voted that a fleet of sixty ships be sent under the command of Nikias, Alkibiades and Lamachos. The two main speakers, as reported by Thucydides, at the meetings of the Athenian Assembly were Alkibiades and Nikias.

Alkibiades was the coming young man in politics who had used the time of the truce to forge anti-Spartan coalitions within the Peloponnese, culminating in the Battle of Mantineia, and Nikias was the architect of that truce, a commander of unblemished record, though one whose achievements were accomplished with caution. The animosity between the two in the reported speeches represented the opposing opinions on Sicilian matters.[8]

The main points on each side were as follows. Nikias stressed the danger of leaving home waters at a time when states such as Corinth had not accepted the peace and many subject 'allies' within the empire were restive. He stressed the necessity of making a financial recovery from the war; the probable problems arising from the control of Sicily if their expedition were to be successful; and on a personal note, the dangers of heeding such a personally ambitious young fellow as Alkibiades, whose waste of his own personal property did not augur well for his attention to the care of the state.

Alkibiades' reply was that Athens was safe from the Peloponnesians because she had a reserve fleet; they must honour obligations to allies; the disunity among the Sicilians would work in Athens' favour; when successful in Sicily Athens would be stronger than ever; and that inactivity and Nikias' attempt to set young against old was a dangerous policy.

Thucydides (VI. 15. 2) claims that Alkibiades was pleased to have been voted as general for the Sicilian expedition because he saw this as an opportunity to subdue not only Sicily but also Carthage. Alkibiades' later speech at Sparta reiterates the point (VI. 90. 1–4). He sought safe refuge there for a time after he had eluded the Athenian state trireme which had come to take him back to Athens for trial (see below). There he set out the supposed aims of the Athenians in his desire to stir the Spartans into activity. He claimed Sicily, Italy and Carthage had been the targets for Athenian domination so that an overwhelming attack could then be made on the Peloponnese using the resources of the enlarged empire.

We thus have the diametrically opposed views expressed within the Assembly, the party for the aggressive prosecution of the war pitted against the party ready to seek a peaceable agreement. It may well have been that the 'war faction' had the aims stated by Alkibiades.[9] The continuation of the tenuous truce between Sparta and Athens would have been dear to the heart of Nikias, who could take some credit for its making. The activities of Alkibiades in fomenting trouble in the Peloponnese during this time of peace underlined his opposition to Nikias' position.

Alkibiades recognised that while the Periklean strategy of avoiding land engagements with the Spartan led-coalition was sensible at the time of its making, there were now opportunities which could be taken to bring about circumstances in which Athens could challenge Sparta on land. After all, he had brought Sparta to a position where she risked all at the battle of Mantineia. He may have firmly believed in what he claimed later at Sparta to be the Athenian policy underlying its expedition to Sicily. If Periklean strategy was designed to bring a kind of victory by default, Alkibiades saw possibilities of bringing about total victory by force of arms. His approach meant taking risks which Perikles would never have countenanced, seeing them as threats to the security of the state.

It is interesting to review the Athenian decision to send out two of the three commanders with such opposed views. The first and major error of the Assembly was not to lay down a clear strategic and limited objective for the expedition. Both commanders would seek to promote and follow their own agenda.

What of the third commander, Lamachos? He was an ordinary citizen lacking the wealth and influence of his two colleagues; but very competent nonetheless. Possibly the Assembly thought that Nikias and Alkibiades would act as a counter-balance, one to the other, with Lamachos providing the unbiased viewpoint in any dispute between the two.

In a last attempt to dissuade the Assembly from what he saw as a reckless decision, Nikias described the requirements for the expedition as greater than those which had already been voted for the enterprise. The effect of his speech was contrary to his expectation. The great majority of the Assembly became even more enthusiastic, thinking that a larger force would have greater security and that the financial rewards of increased empire could not then be lost. Rather than vote in opposition to the enterprise and appear disloyal, Nikias acquiesced. The Assembly voted full powers to the three commanders to decide their requirements. This is the second major error, the presumption that such a large force would indeed be safe. The forces at a tactical level should have been in line with the strategic objective. The strategy was not clear. The commitment of a force that, if lost, would put Athens at risk was, indeed, against the Periklean idea for the conduct of the war against the Peloponnesian League. It is this muddled thinking of the Assembly that put the outcome at risk.

Shortly thereafter responsibility for the mutilation of the hermai throughout Athens was debated and accusations of similar destruction of statues and blasphemy were laid at the feet of Alkibiades.[10] His political enemies, fearful that the army might support him if they arraigned him, allowed him to sail with the expedition before recalling him to face charges.

It is only in Chapter 43 of Book Six that Thucydides finally gives the figures for the expeditionary force of Athenian ships. There were 134 triremes of which forty were troop transports and an unspecified number of allied vessels. The roll of hoplites numbered 5,100, including Argives, Mantineians, Eleians and mercenaries, 480 archers, of whom eighty were Cretan, together with 700 Rhodian slingers and 120 Megaran light infantry.[11] These figures do not include carpenters, stonemasons, cooks, baggage carriers and camp followers, not to mention all those entrepreneurs who accompanied the expedition in search of profit. Well over 30,000 men sailed to Sicily after gathering at Kerkyra. However, only one horse transport carrying thirty animals accompanied the fleet. This is quite astonishing. Either the Athenian commanders, who after all had the freedom to garner whatever forces they wished, thought that they would acquire sufficient cavalry from their supposed allies, or they chose to ignore the well known fact that the cavalry arm of Syracuse was strong. Unless some unreported arrangement had been made with Sicilian allies on this matter, such a deficiency was folly. The cautious Nikias could have been expected to have made better preparation. A serious error of omission had been made.

Obviously, preparations took time and news of them filtered through to Sicily. There some expressed concern while others dismissed the reports as false and alarmist. Hermokrates, a leading man of Syracuse, recognised the danger and urged preparedness (VI. 34 – 35).[12] Tactically he proposed a course of action that would have caused great problems for the Athenian fleet: to send out the Syracusan fleet with two months provisions in order to waylay the Athenians at Taras (modern Taranto) and Iapygia. He emphasised the surprise that the Athenians would have to discover that Tarenton was a city not only friendly to the Syracusans, but willing to lend it its support. Using that area as a base, they would dissuade the Athenian fleet from hugging the safer coastline route and force them to use the more dangerous open waters. There, with the difficulty of maintaining formation, they could be attacked at will, retaining the Syracusan initiative against superior Athenian techniques of sea warfare. If the Athenians chose to lighten their ships and use rowing power, attacks could be made when the oarsmen were tired. Denied access to re-supply points along the coast, segments of the Athenian fleet could be blockaded or made to leave essential parts of their equipment ashore.

Hermokrates also suggested that they send the news to Carthage in the hope that Syracuse might elicit some support. Thucydides goes on to say that Hermokrates suggested the Carthaginians were fearful that Athens would eventually make an attack upon her. This appears to be the exercise of hindsight by the historian. It is unlikely that at this time Carthage had anything to fear from Athens.

Few heeded or gave credibility to the words of Hermokrates, but chose to be persuaded by the argument of the popular leader, Athenagoras, who labelled the words of Hermokrates as mere fabrications.

So it was that the Athenian fleet sailed without due preparations being made at Syracuse to meet it. All was going in Athens' favour and at Kerkyra, while the Syracusans were wrangling over the credibility of the rumours of invasion, the Athenians decided, wisely, to proceed in three flotillas, each under one of the appointed commanders. By splitting the fleet, at landing points there would be enough water and provisions available.

In advance of the three main groups three ships were sent ahead to negotiate friendly landfalls which could offer them a market for supplies. A mixed reception awaited them. Some cities refused to accept their presence, such as Taras and Lokri, and others offered no more than anchorage and water. It was only at Rhegion that a camping place and market was granted. There they stayed until the ships which had preceded them to Egesta arrived to inform them that the Egestans did not have the funds which had been promised to the Athenians as an inducement to come to their aid. Rhegion had declared itself neutral in the coming conflict.

By this time news had filtered through to Syracuse of the Athenian arrival and belatedly the citizens began making preparations for its defence. Here we are given further insight into the commissioned objectives of the expedition. 'It was the judgement of Nikias that they should sail with their whole armament against Selinous, which was the object for which they had *chiefly* been sent out…' (Author's italics, VI. 47.)

So to move against Selinous was the priority in Nikias' eyes. With the discovery of the shortfall in funding promised by the Egestaians, he proposed that they should give coastal cities a sight of the power of Athens and sail home, unless cities came to their support. This would safeguard the finances of the mother city.

Alkibiades, however, expressed the opinion that, having made the journey with such a significant force, they should send heralds to cities, with the exception of Selinous and Syracuse, in the hope that they would ally themselves to the Athenians. The generals would be disgraced if they were not to achieve anything before returning home. He further suggested attempting to turn some of the Sikel allies of the Syracusans, from whom the Athenians might also receive supplies. Messene, he said, should be persuaded to give anchorage for a naval squadron to guard the waters through which the fleet would move. Thereafter, if all fell as planned, attacks could be launched against Selinous and Syracuse. The caveat of calling off the attacks if an agreement was reached between Egesta and Selinous was most probably made to mollify Nikias and leave open the possibility of an attack on Syracuse.

Under the circumstances, the proposal of Lamachos to sail directly to Syracuse and attack while the Syracusans were still in a state of unpreparedness and consternation had merit. The flow of people moving with their possessions from the countryside around to the greater safety of Syracuse would still be taking place. Supplies would therefore be ready to hand, the population split, and any army sent to meet them would be unsure of the size of the Athenian forces and most probably make an over-estimate, further lowering morale. With an initial success born out of surprise they would be more likely to garner allies. He was, however, persuaded by Alkibiades' proposals.

Shortly after, Alkibiades travelled in his own vessel to Messene and attempted unsuccessfully to bring the city into alliance. What followed seemed equally ineffectual, or at least uncommitted, and one has to wonder whether the opinion of Nikias was now in the ascendancy. Leaving part of the army at Rhegion, sixty ships, fully provisioned, sailed south, first to Naxos where they were welcomed, and then to Katana. There the divided opinion of the populace led to the Katanians refusing the Athenians entry, so that the entire force moved on to make camp near the Terias river a little to the north of Syracuse. The following day an advance squadron of ten ships was sent into the Great Harbour at Syracuse ostensibly to make a proclamation that the Athenian mission was for the restitution of the Leontines to their own city, in accordance with their existing alliance.
The true reason was reconnaissance. The ten were followed by the rest of the fleet in single file, but as no activity or opposing fleet was in evidence, the entire force returned to Katana.

There, fortune worked in their favour. The Assembly was in session on their arrival, still refusing to receive the army in its environs. However, the Katanians agreed to allow the generals to address the Assembly. During Alkibiades' speech, Athenian soldiers discovered a poorly maintained postern gate and, having broken through, were seen openly walking about the city. A number of the pro-Syracusan faction took fright and left the city, whereupon the Assembly voted for an alliance with the Athenians.

This last episode had clearly been the subject of bold planning on the part of the Athenians. It had borne fruit, and the covert means of occupation was probably the suggestion of the imaginative Alkibiades. The Athenians now had a base from which to operate against the Syracusans and forthwith brought their forces still at Rhegion to establish a unified encampment at Katana.

While there, a message came from Kamarina to the effect that the city would join them in operations against Syracuse. Kamarina is on the southern coast of Sicily and a significant distance from Syracuse. The army first marched to the environs of Syracuse where intelligence had been received that a fleet was about to sail against them, then re-embarked in the absence of any opposing naval activity, and proceeded to Kamarina. There they must have been surprised that the city would not countenance anything more than a single ship being received. Disappointed, they returned, first to Syracuse where they pillaged the countryside, and then to Katana. It is significant that the Syracusan cavalry wreaked damage on their stragglers.

Awaiting them was the state ship, *Salaminia*. It had come to take Alkibiades back for trial in Athens. Quite apart from the accusations made against him concerning the mutilation of the hermai and the suggested profanation of the Eleusinian mysteries, there was a charge of conspiracy levelled against him suggesting that he planned to overthrow the democracy. This was based on the coincidental fact that, at the time of the initial charges, a small Spartan army had arrived at the Isthmus in accordance with some agreement with the Boiotians. Athenian opinion was swayed to believe that this army was on its way in the expectation that the city was to be betrayed to them. Whatever the truth of the matter, the citizens were sufficiently alarmed to spend the night at the ready for combat and to deliver back to Argos for execution those Argive hostages thought to be implicated.

Under such circumstances it comes as no surprise that Alkibiades, and those other companions who were recalled, slipped away when they reached Thouria in southern Italy.

This left only the cautious Nikias and Lamachos in command. The latter – though obviously a bolder spirit – being of humbler status deferred to Nikias. So, right at the point of the opening moves of the campaign, the command structure was compromised.

Each commander took half of the army and sailed to Egesta and Selinous. The route was along the northern coast of the island. Stopping at Himera where they were refused entry, they continued on, taking a small Sikanian township. They were helped in this by some Egestaian cavalry, who, when later joined by their infantry, proceeded overland to the Athenian base at Katana just north of Syracuse. Nikias, with his forces, sailed around the southern coastline of Sicily, then went against Hybla Geleatis, a small inland township NNW of Syracuse, but failed in his attempt to take it. Arrangements to ensure military support from the Sikel population opposed to Syracuse were made.

All this smacks of Nikias' total control of planning. He had wanted to sail along the coast in a show of strength: the result was a rebuttal from Himera, failure at Hybla and a paltry success in the taking of the Sikel township. Admittedly, the Egestaians were in place at Katana and the Sikels were mobilising for the spring offensive, but, by this time, the Syracusan trepidation at the initial appearance of the Athenians was fast evaoporating. They had had their own small successes against stragglers and now, wishing to demonstrate their contempt for the Athenians' inactivity, rode up to their lines at Katana in order to taunt them. Had Lamachos' proposal been adopted, Syracusan morale would have had no time to recover as it did.[13]

Nikias had lost the initiative: his original plan had been to significantly increase his power prior to his main offensive by gathering new allied forces. However, the strategy proved to be difficult to implement because Syracuse was not under the pressure of attack. The hopes of its people were actually fuelled by news of Nikias' lack of success at recruiting support.

Such was the restitution of their morale that the Syracusans planned to engage in battle. The Athenian command knew of their intentions and planned to lure the Syracusan forces towards Katana while themselves sailing away and setting up camp by the city of Syracuse itself.[14] This was preferred to attempting to beach their ships and face the enemy, or to making an overland advance on the city; a good ploy, but some months too late. The commanders were in part obliged to take this course because of the dangers to their light-armed troops and camp followers, who would have suffered greatly under attack from the Syracusan cavalry. This vulnerability stemmed from the original planning of the expedition when the size of the cavalry contingent embarked was totally insufficient.

Some largely irrelevant Athenian scheming now follows (VI. 64. 2 et seq). Using a Katanian loyal to the Athenian cause but known and trusted by the Syracusan generals, Nikias passed on to the enemy the disinformation that the Athenians spent their nights in Katana, leaving their arms in the camp. If the Syracusans were to come to make an attack on an appointed day, those within the city who were loyal to Syracuse would fire the Athenian ships, close the city gates on the Athenians and thus render both them and their camp susceptible to capture. Thucydides notes that the Syracusans had already decided to attack Katana (VI. 65. 1) so that this news merely fortified their intention.

Near the agreed time the whole Syracusan army advanced and encamped near the Symaithon river; whereupon the Athenians embarked their whole force and sailed by night to a place not far from the Olympeion, a shrine near Syracuse. Having landed all their troops, the Athenians took up a position flanked by walls, houses and swampland on one side and cliffs on the other in order to offer themselves more protection and negate the Syracusan superiority in cavalry. The Syracusan cavalry had discovered by then what the Athenians had done, and when they informed the infantry, the return march was made.

In the time it took for the Syracusans to return, the Athenians had built a stockade near their ships from timber which was cut down in the locality. To their south at Daskon they had set up a barrier of stone and timber, meanwhile destroying the bridge over the Anapos river to their north.

Ignoring the outcome it is difficult to fault Nikias in his preparations for any coming hostilities, but it is equally difficult to see what he thought he was going to gain by acting so late in the year. The Syracusans had willingly gone in search of the Athenians at Katana in the hope of destroying them. They were not the same men who had been cowed by the first appearance of the Athenians. They were now more confident and were actively promoting hostilities by their current action.

One can only conclude that Nikias thought that by meeting the enemy at a place where the approach to his position was restricted, he would have a better chance of destroying their forces, thus making investment easier. If that was his intention, his position was a little too far to the south to have the desired effect.

A look at the map of Syracuse and its surroundings will clarify the Athenian position. The fact that they placed themselves at that specific location – made known to them by Syracusan exiles at Katana (VI. 64. 1) – demonstrates their acute awareness that the Syracusan cavalry was a prime threat.

With the arrival of the Syracusan infantry, their whole force approached the Athenian camp, obviously eager for combat. When no move was made from the camp the Syracusans withdrew to encamp beyond the Elorine road.

Some of the Syracusans must have decided to go back to the city for the night because when the Athenians made ready for battle the following day, many had to come at a run to join their comrades as best they could. Some did not even arrive at their appointed place and had to enter the ranks wherever they could (VI. 69. 1). Perhaps Nikias was aware that a significant number of the enemy had gone to their homes the night before and sought to take advantage of this.

In selecting a position in order to counter the threat from Syracusan cavalry, the location put limits on the length of the battle-front. Half of the invading army was drawn up with the Athenians in the centre, the Argives and Mantineians on the right and the other allies on the left, to a depth of eight men. The other half was placed to their rear, also to a depth of eight, in the formation of a hollow square for the protection of the camp followers, artisans and the like. Although confident of the outcome, the Athenian commanders had rightly seen to it that they would be able to make an ordered withdrawal from their position so that the force could re-embark in relative safety. They were given orders to assist any section of the line which might come under pressure.

Some further detail of those orders would have been informative. As it is, questions arise. Was the integrity of the square to be maintained come what may? In coming to the aid of their fellows should the occasion arise, how many ranks were to be committed? It must be assumed that the left and right sides of the square would help the respective wings of the combatants, with the front of the square being committed to the centre, but what of the rear? What were its suggested duties should the need arise? This remains an unresolved question, along with others. For example, why bring so many camp followers in the first place, necessitating their protection, if there was no intention to stay? Did they hope for outright success from the start and almost immediate Syracusan capitulation? It would appear that these hoplites were a form of reserve, but this would be to stretch the meaning of the word. Their placement in a hollow square formation near the camp was technically defensive. Their prime duty was to protect the non-combatants. Had the topography been different and had the Athenians possessed a reasonable cavalry corps, these men would have been in the battle-line. The chosen location and the makeup of the invading force defined their role. Their secondary duties of support to the line, when and if necessary, were not the outcome of aggressive planning but rather an accidental afterthought suggested by the location itself and the result of bringing that unbalanced invasion force.

The Athenian ships were beached in the Great Harbour. No Syracusan fleet had come against them. It appeared to augur well for the Athenians. Looking at the Syracusan dispositions we find from Thucydides (VI. 67. 2), that their hoplites were arranged to a depth of sixteen ranks. This would probably not be with any preconceived intent to add weight to their phalanx in the manner of Theban deployments but was dictated by the confines of the location. Some Selinountines were present and seem to have been to the Syracusan left, beside whom was a mixture of about 220 cavalry with fifty archers at the flank. The 1,200 Syracusan cavalry were stationed on the right wing along with some light infantry whose main offensive weapon was the javelin. It is obvious that the Syracusans wished to exploit their cavalry superiority if possible. There were stone throwers and slingers on both sides (VI. 69. 2).These had their own customary skirmishes against each other while the preliminaries of sacrifices were completed.

The two lines of hoplites charged upon one another at the signal of the *salpinx*, a loud and piercing instrument capable of being heard over large distances and in the tumult of the battle.[15]

The battle appeared evenly matched for some time. It was with the coming of a thunderstorm that the less battle-hardened Syracusans became disconcerted. Doubts as to which side the gods favoured arose within the Syracusan ranks and it was at that moment of uncertainty that the Argives gained the upper hand on their right wing. No doubt this success further dismayed the Syracusans and confirmed their worst fears. Their centre buckled against the Athenians and the rest of their line disintegrated. On a relatively short front, news of adversity travelled fast, or a deteriorating position could be seen; unlike those engagements which took place on a much longer front where one wing on either side could be victorious without a calamity for their other wing becoming known to it until much later.

The Syracusan flight could not be exploited and no rout ensued. The Athenian pursuit had to be circumspect. The overwhelming and unde-feated cavalry superiority of the Syracusans made the retreat tolerable for their fellows. They attacked any Athenian hoplites foolish enough to lose contact with their main body.

The proof that the Syracusans were not demoralised lies in the fact that, once they had reached the Elorine road, they reformed in battle-line and sent a force to guard the sacred treasures of the Olympeion before retiring in good order to the city. The Athenians set up their victory trophy, gave funeral rites to their fallen and on the following day, under truce, gave back the Syracusan dead. The fatalities were about fifty for the victors and 260 for the Syracusans.

The Athenian command had come to the conclusion that the army could not remain in its present position for the winter. The logistics were too daunting. The Athenians would have had to rely on being provisioned by sea. While they would feel confident in their naval strength they would have been subject to the vagaries of the weather, not to mention possible attacks from the, as yet, uncommitted Syracusan fleet. The Athenians therefore re-embarked and returned to Katana.

In reality, little had been gained by the Athenians, and perhaps much lost, by this foray. Nikias had given his enemy direct contact with his forces and the fear of the unknown was not now an issue for the Syracusans The latter had not acquitted themselves too badly in the contest. The Athenians had no way to capitalise on the victory. The position was technically unchanged, except that Nikias and Lamachos had had the opportunity to reconnoitre the area for future operations.

Hermokrates, described by Thucydides as 'a man who was in general sec-ond to none in point of intelligence, and had shown himself in this war both competent by reason of experience and conspicuous for courage' (VI. 72. 2) now exhorted his fellow citizens in the Assembly to continue the struggle. His analysis was straightforward and positive. The Syracusans were not so practised in war as their enemy, but their lack of discipline was a problem that could be corrected; they had no less courage than the Athenians; and fifteen generals were too many and had led to some confusion. He proposed that fewer commanders be elected and given full powers so that better preparations could be made and secrecy more easily maintained.

The outcome of this meeting was that Hermokrates was elected general along with two others, Herakleides and Sikanos. Emissaries were sent to the mother city Corinth and to Sparta requesting military support for Syracuse, hoping that more open hostilities would be undertaken on the mainland by the Spartans to force the withdrawal of Athenian forces from Sicily.

On arriving at Katana, Nikias next moved against Messene, hoping that it might be captured by guile as had been arranged earlier. He failed in this enterprise largely because the Messenians, who supported Syracuse, had been forewarned by Alkibiades at the time of his recall. Those Messenians had executed the members of the pro-Athenian party and were under arms and ready to repel any attempted incursion. After spending thirteen days there, under adverse weather conditions and with diminishing provisions, the Athenians eventually withdrew to set up a stockaded camp and docks at Naxos. From there a report was sent to Athens requesting funds and cavalry.

Preparations for the coming season's conflict went on apace at Syracuse. With their enemy in camp at Naxos they could enjoy some time unmolested. The first requirement was to make the land around the city safer. They could only be besieged if they lost control of the surrounding countryside. If that should happen following some future engagement, it was prudent to make it as difficult as possible for the Athenians to erect a circumvallation. With this in mind, and in order to bring in those properties that had been built outside the city wall near a temple of Apollo Temenites, a new wall was built facing the plateau called Epipolai, from where an enemy attack might come. This made the problem of encirclement more difficult for the Athenians. Farther north a garrison was placed in the town of Megara Hyblaia and a permanent garrison established at the Olympeion. With the additional wall enclosing the Temenites the city precincts had been enlarged by about a third. (See map, page xx.)

A sortie was made into the territory of Katana by the whole Syracusan army, which caused great damage and destroyed the Athenian camp there. While this would cause the Athenians a delay to operations in the spring, the main reason for this short expedition was more likely to have been to improve the morale and discipline of the Syracusan forces, which were undergoing training in this period.

It is difficult to see what better preparations could have been made by Hermokrates and his two colleagues. Hermokrates led an embassy to Kamarina, a city on the south coast of Sicily whose territory abutted that of Syracuse. He tried to persuade them to join against the Athenians for the common good. Present also was an Athenian delegation wishing to renew the alliance they had had with the city. Kamarina had played a safety-first game in the initial hostilities by sending a small number of cavalry to the Syracusans. However, as near neighbours, there had often been conflict between Syracuse and Kamarina in the past. Despite Hermokrates' call that they, as fellow Dorians, unite against the Ionian invader, those at Kamarina publicly announced that, as allies to both the Syracusans and the Athenians, they should remain neutral. Secretly, however, they decided to continue giving a modicum of support to the Syracusans.

The Athenians used the early part of the winter to try to bring over to their side as many Sikel communities as possible. Most of those under the control of Syracuse stayed loyal, but those independent settlements towards the centre of the island came over to the Athenians. These new allies supplied the Athenian army with funds and grain. Those Sikel communities that decided against joining the Athenians were subjected to attacks in order to bring them to the Athenian side by compulsion. Some were protected by the Syracusans, who placed garrisons in the towns.

Returning to Katana the Athenians rebuilt their camp and went into winter quarters. From there they sent envoys to Carthage and Etruria requesting assistance. Some cities in Etruria proved ready to join in the hostilities against Syracuse. Further building of the allied forces went on among the Sikel population, and Egesta was asked to supply horses for the Athenians. Meantime, along with other preparations, materials were prepared for the building of the proposed circumvallation.

While all this was happening, Alkibiades had reached Elis in the Peloponnese from where he went to Sparta under a guarantee of safe-conduct. He was present when the Syracusan envoys arrived from Corinth to plead for help from Sparta. On their journey to Corinth these envoys had made it their business to attempt to persuade the Greek cities on the coast of southern Italy not to give any support to the Athenians. Once arrived at Corinth they had little difficulty in gaining active support from their mother city. Accompanied by Corinthian envoys they then proceeded to Sparta where, after initial reluctance, the Spartans were persuaded to the cause by a speech made by none other than Alkibiades, who for some time to come was to stay with the Spartans, adopting many of their customs. He urged them to send a Spartiate as general to Syracuse and to fortify Dekeleia in northern Attika. By placing a large permanent garrison there they would deny the Athenians access to their land, their silver mines and most probably a sizeable amount of tribute from subject allies. These would see a more vigorous Spartan prosecution of the war and be the more disinclined to make their payments.[16]

It was in this speech (VI. 90.1–4) that Alkibiades set out the objectives of the Athenian expedition to Sicily as previously mentioned, in such a way as was bound to provoke a Spartan reaction. These were the subjugation of Sicily and the Greek cities in Magna Graecia, an attempt on Carthage and her possessions, the hiring of mercenaries from as far afield as Spain, the building of a huge fleet with timber from southern Italy (Magna Graecia), and with this immense armament augmenting their own, a blockade of the Peloponnese, meantime invading it with the additional forces from Sicily and those mercenaries they had gathered.

Whether Nikias would have concurred that *any* of these were an objective of the expedition is doubtful, but the speech had its desired effect and the Spartans appointed Gylippos supreme commander. He asked the Corinthians to send two ships to Asine (modern-day Koroni) immediately, and to make preparations for the remainder of the expedition to sail as soon as it was ready.

The Athenians had by this time received the request from Nikias and agreed to send additional funds and cavalry to Sicily. Perhaps the request had not been specific enough for the 'cavalry' consisted of 250 cavalrymen with equipment but no horses.[17] The Assembly had assumed that the animals would be procured in Sicily. Therefore this reinforcement, arriving in late spring of 414 BC, was of no immediate help to the Athenian commanders. Before its arrival the Athenians had gone south to despoil the land around Megara and make an unsuccessful attempt on a Syracusan fortress in the area, returning a little to the north, inland near the Terias river, pillaging as they went. In the course of this activity they had defeated a small Syracusan detachment and duly set up a trophy to celebrate this triumph.

Having returned to Katana, the whole Athenian army was mobilised to move west against the Sikels of Kentoripa, bring it over to their side by force, and then to return to Katana ravaging the crops of the cities of Inessa and Hybla Geleatis. The intention, no doubt, was to reduce the immediately available crops in the area in preparation for the investment of Syracuse, but the outcome was small beer and would not have unduly worried the Syracusans.

In early summer news came to Syracuse that, with the 250 additional cavalry and thirty mounted archers sent from Athens, Nikias was making preparations to move against them. The whole Syracusan army was paraded alongside the Anapos river at daybreak and Hermokrates and his fellow generals selected 600 men to guard the steep approaches to the Epipolai, the large plateau overlooking the city. However, they were not to know that the Athenians had left Katana and had sailed during the night to Leon, some three-quarters of a mile from the Epipolai. There they disembarked the land forces. The fleet retired a little farther north, to the peninsula of Thapsos, where they built a defensive palisade across its narrowest point. In the meantime the army had set off post haste towards the Epipolai and managed to gain the heights by way of Euryelos before the Syracusans were aware of their presence. In some consternation therefore the Syracusan army made a hurried advance to the plateau. Unlike the short distance the Athenians had had to cover, the Syracusans were faced with a distance of a little over three miles. The result of making approaches to the heights by steeper routes and being given no time to come into some form of order was that they were defeated, losing the commander of the 600, Diomilos, and about 300 men, before retreating to the city (VI. 97. 4–5).

With the formalities of the truce, the setting up of the trophy, and the return of the bodies of the fallen to the Syracusans completed, the Athenians advanced on the following day directly against the city. No Syracusan army came out to oppose them so the Athenians set to and built a fort at Labdalon to house their stores and equipment. This was to serve as a base from which they could service the building of a wall or go against any enemy force. Reinforcements came from the Egestans, Sikels and Naxians together with horses from Egesta and Katana. They now had a cavalry force of 650, a not insignificant number but still not a match for the expertise and number of Syracusan horsemen.

For the first time in the expedition Nikias and his colleague had carried out a meticulously planned operation with significant success. The night advance had been undetected up to the point of the occupation of the plateau. This may well have been made possible by the information gained on their otherwise inexplicable move against Syracuse some months earlier. Nonetheless, the Athenians had been abetted in the operation by the failure of the Syracusan commanders to set up adequate measures for reconnaissance by land and sea. The Syracusan fleet should have been employed to watch for any signs of naval movement by the Athenians. Cavalry patrols and surveillance points should have been active to the north of the city to signal any impending approach by the enemy.

Thereafter, the circumvallation was begun and proceeded at such a pace that the Syracusans were alarmed enough to offer battle.[18] However, as their hoplites still showed a lack of discipline, they retired again to the city leaving some cavalry to harass the Athenians while they were bringing up materials for the wall and to pick off any who strayed from their main force. To combat this threat one division from the ten Athenian tribes, together with the whole of the cavalry, went against them and drove them off, killing several of their number: a clear and early example of interdependent forces of different arms being superior to that of a single arm. It would have been illuminating to have had more detail of the engagement to fully understand the tactics employed. One can hazard a guess, however, in the knowledge of tactics explained in the writings of Xenophon a few years later (e.g. Xen. *Hell*, III. 4. 22.–24 and IV. 6. 10–11). As the Syracusans had committed only part of their cavalry to the task of harassment it may well have been that the Athenian allied horse outnumbered them. This in itself would not have been an insuperable problem for the Syracusans, who were more skilled in this arm. It is likely, however, that the Athenian cavalry engaged and, in so doing, pinned the Syracusan cavalry down long enough for the supporting infantry to arrive on the scene and decisively defeat the now less mobile force.

From the large circular fortress in the middle of the plateau which had been quickly constructed, the Athenians laid out building supplies along a line to the north towards Trogilos and proceeded with the construction of a wall towards the coast.

Hermokrates and his colleagues were reluctant to risk their whole army in battle and decided instead to build a counter-wall across the line of the proposed Athenian wall to the south of the circular fortress. This plan had certain advantages. If the Athenians decided to attack their building parties, they would have to commit part of their army to this action while their own building continued. That would mean withdrawing their own builders to ensure sufficient numbers in their force, thereby slowing down their own building operations. The ploy worked insofar as the Syracusans completed their building work and placed guards in the towers along their stockade before the main body returned to the city. Hermokrates had rightly guessed that the Athenians would be unwilling to divide their forces to come against the Syracusans (VI. 100. 1).

Thucydides notes at VI. 99.4 that the Athenian fleet had not as yet sailed into the Great Harbour and that the Syracusan fleet was still technically in control of the immediate sea area.

Obviously, some action had to be taken by the Athenians if their circumvallation was to continue. First, the underground pipes supplying Syracuse with drinking water were destroyed and an assault made on the Syracusan cross-wall. Dividing their forces, one to engage any Syracusan advance from the city and the other to make the attack on the stockade, the Athenian generals arranged that a special force of 300 hoplites and light-armed troops make a sudden attack on the counter-wall. These light-armed troops are described as being in 'heavy armour'. This is a contradiction in terms but the armour would be for the increased protection of the missile throwers who were to be closer to their opposition than would be their normal practice.

The attack was made in the heat of the day when the Syracusans were in their tents or had even gone to their homes in the city. This proves that the Athenian generals had arranged for continuous observation to be made of the defence force. Having perceived a regular pattern of behaviour, Nikias and Lamachos tried to turn this to their advantage.

As the special force made its attack, the rest of the divided army made its advance in column towards the two objectives, the stockade and the city. Thucydides does not identify the general leading each column. The initial attack was successful and the Syracusans hastily retreated to the safety of the new wall which had enlarged the city area and enclosed the Temenites district. The pursuers did manage to follow them through this wall but the Syracusans regrouped and forced them out. The main body of one of the columns had been involved at this stage because Thucydides notes (VI. 100. 2) that some Argives were among the casualties, whereas the composition of the special force was 300 Athenians together with light infantry. The Argive contingent in the expedition were hoplites.

Having set up a trophy, the Athenians destroyed the cross-wall and took the building materials for their own use.

Construction by both sides now continued apace. The Athenians resumed their circumvallation to the south of the circular fort towards the southern slope of the Epipolai, and the Syracusans, still farther south, through the marshland, began another cross-defence.

Again, the Athenians attacked and destroyed the Syracusan construction, this time at first light, having come down from the Epipolai to the plain and made their approach through the marsh on planks laid to make the way firmer. The Syracusans obviously put up a spirited resistance for Thucydides reports that a battle followed. In its first phase the Athenians were victorious. Thucydides makes mention of the right and left wings but not of the centre of the Syracusan army. The right wing fled to the city and the left wing towards the river, presumably the Anapos to the south. Reference is again made to the special force of 300 picked Athenians (VI. 101. 4). They were ordered to take the bridge over the river so that the Syracusan left wing could be cut off. The greater part of the Syracusan cavalry were with this wing, having been positioned there because of the difficulties of movement for them in the marshy areas outside their right wing. The 300 were destroyed, however, and an attack launched on the Athenian right caused great consternation. Lamachos himself came up in support with some archers and Argive hoplites. In crossing a ditch he and a portion of his followers were cut off and killed, their bodies being taken up by the Syracusans who retreated with them over the river to safety as the Athenian army advanced against them.

Within the very brief description of the clash and what follows immediately thereafter, some interesting facts emerge. Lamachos was the only general to be present for the taking of the counter-wall and for the ensuing battle. Nikias stayed behind at the circular fort. His worsening kidney disease prevented him from taking any part in the action. This being the case, Lamachos' position on the left wing was unusual for the period. He may have taken this place in the hope that, as it was nearer the city, an opportunity might have arisen whereby he could launch an attack upon it. Significantly, the hoplites with him were Argives and one must assume that the Athenian portion of the army had able subcommanders who, on his death, continued to exercise control and ordered the advance on the retreating left of the Syracusans.

In this later phase of the battle the Athenian army had become divided. The victorious Athenian left had continued to face the city as the Syracusan right had fled. They would have been ordered to do so by Lamachos when he left them to go in support of the Athenian special forces. Who his deputy was is not known. On Lamachos' death the Athenian right wing had pursued the Syracusan left. It is at this point that the Syracusans who had fled the field to the safety of the city now reassembled. Their morale had been bolstered by the emerging success of their left wing. They now divided their own forces with one part making ready to engage the Athenian left wing and the other going up onto Epipolai against the circular fort. This last group destroyed 300 yards of the newly constructed wall but were prevented by Nikias from taking the fort itself. He did this – in the absence of a sufficient number of defenders – by ordering non-combatants to set fire to the wood and siege engines deposited outside the walls. The conflagration was too fierce for the Syracusans to approach and they withdrew when support was on its way from the Athenians on the plain below who had, once again, worsted the opposition.

The Syracusan retreat to the city coincided with the arrival from Thapsos of the Athenian fleet. No resistance to it by the Syracusan fleet is reported by Thucydides. The Athenians sailing into the Great Harbour at this juncture caused great consternation among the Syracusans and they concluded that they were not strong enough to stop the circumvallation being completed.

From the taking of the Epipolai to this last action a particular vigour is shown which had been notably absent in previous operations. We have from Thucydides no evidence to show the degree of the incapacity suffered by Nikias or its duration. It could well be that Lamachos had been obliged to assume full control of the allied forces. If this is so, and the present author believes it is, Lamachos must be credited with the successes achieved. The expeditionary force had moved from relative passivity and seemingly never-ending preparations to committed and forceful aggression, leaving no doubt in the minds of the Syracusans that their enemy was not to be easily denied his objective. Admittedly the Athenians now possessed a reasonable force of cavalry and this made land operations easier. However, the manner in which the war was now being prosecuted had markedly changed. The tempo of activity had suddenly quickened and the initiative had passed into the hands of the Athenians. For this we must give credit to Lamachos who may well have also been solely responsible for the timely arrival of the fleet in the Great Harbour, an immense psychological blow to the Syracusans.

Lamachos was the kind of commander who led from the front and quickly evaluated a situation. In the action in which he lost his life he could well have sent the relieving force under a subordinate. If anything he underestimated the number of men required for the task. To his credit the composition of that force was mixed, archers and hoplites. The addition of some cavalry might have made all the difference, not least in defending his flanks or dispersing any of the opposition not wholly in good order.

Perhaps the whole operation had been jointly planned between Nikias and Lamachos with the latter following through the various stages in turn. But those who are ill are usually in no condition to protest their point vehemently and are quick to acquiesce to another's opinion, if only to be relieved of the necessity to think or make decisions. They are only likely to show obstinacy when holding out for a goal that they strongly desire or believe in, as will be seen below.

Looking at what followed and how Nikias, now in sole command, built on this success (or rather, did not) gives us some evidence of his passivity. News of the Athenian successes brought to their side those of the Sikels who, up to that point, had made no commitment. Supplies and provisions poured in from Italy and three Etruscan ships were sent to join them. Work on the building of a double wall was completed from Epipolai southward to the sea. Despite all this Nikias chose to negotiate conditions with the Syracusans, whose morale was extremely low and who might have soon capitulated if more pressure had been constantly applied. No report is given of any raids on Syracusan outworks or activities other than the continued building of the circumvallation. The Syracusans replaced Hermokrates and his colleagues with Herakleides, Eukles and Tellias as commanders.

Returning to the progress of the Peloponnesian relief mission we find that Gylippos received news at Leukas that Syracuse was now totally sealed off. Although this was untrue he left the assembled fleet and crossed to Italy to attempt to dissuade the cities there from going over to the Athenians. With him went a Corinthian commander named Pythen, plus two Spartan and two Corinthian ships. He had no success at Thouria and after being caught in a storm at sea managed to return to Taras where he beached the ships for repair. Thucydides notes (VI. 103. 4) that Nikias '...although he heard that he [Gylippos] was sailing up, despised the small number of his ships...he took as yet no precautions'. Meantime the Peloponnesian ships still at Leukas, namely ten Corinthian, two Leukadian and three Ambrakian vessels, set sail.

In that same summer the Spartans invaded and pillaged the territories of Argos. Athens, in sending thirty ships to support the Argives violated the terms of the truce with Sparta within the 'Peace of Nikias' by making direct attacks on Lakedaimonian territory. This breach hardened the resolve of the Spartans. They had carried a sense of guilt since the very opening of the war. Their involvement at the Siege of Plataea they acknowledged to be contrary to divine ordinance and to this act they had ascribed the misfortune of Sphakteria and their general lack of success. Now with the contravention of an agreement made under oath by the Athenians, the Spartans felt piously justified in resuming open hostilities. The Spartans were probably the most conservative and meticulous in the observation of matters concerning the divine. It is difficult for us today to appreciate how important it was that the actions of the Athenians at this time gave the Spartans a sense of justification before the gods for their own aggression.

Gylippos, having reached Lokroi, now heard that the investment of Syracuse was incomplete and that a fighting entry to the city could still be made over the Epipolai where the remaining part of the circumvallation was to be built. He and his colleague Pythen had to decide which of two options to take. The first was to go directly to Syracuse and attempt entry by the harbours. Syracuse had two harbours, the Great Harbour and the Lesser Harbour. Coming in this way it is highly likely that the choice would have been the latter, still under Syracusan control and between the main city and the heavily fortified Ortygia or Inner City, which lay on the prom-ontory dividing the two harbours. The second option was to sail through the Straits of Messene and along the north coast to Himera from where they could march overland to Syracuse, raising forces as they went.

The first option was discarded possibly because of the risk of being waylaid by part of the Athenian fleet. Gylippos' intelligence collection was superb. Thucydides implies at VII. 1. 2, that their decision not to try for the harbour was confirmed by the news that the four ships Nikias had eventually sent to intercept them had not arrived at Rhegion. This change of mind by Nikias was all too typical of his judgements whereas those of Gylippos were prompt and astute. He had chosen correctly. To have risked death or capture at sea would have done nothing to help the Syracusans. As a prospective commander-in-chief it was more important that he safeguard his own life so that his skills could be put to use in the saving of Syracuse. He had risked enough by sailing ahead of the main expedition.

They managed to evade the Athenian ships and, reaching Himera, derived forces from that city and arms for their ships' crews, meantime sending instructions to the Selinountines to rendezvous with them with their entire forces. Geloans and Sikels also joined the coalition and the army that marched towards Syracuse was composed of around 4,000 men, of which possibly 200 were cavalry.

The main expedition now left Leukas and a Corinthian navarch managed to reach Syracuse well ahead of the fleet, braving capture by the Athenians. He arrived shortly before Gylippos (VII. 2. 1). It was just as well that the navarch had taken steps to hurry to Syracuse for, on his arrival, he discovered that an Assembly was being called to debate coming to terms with the enemy.

For all the Athenian claims to be in possession of the sea, this arrival demonstrates that the Athenian blockade of Syracuse was not really effective and continued to be breached throughout the conflict.

Morale rose immediately in the city at his news and, on learning that Gylippos was very near, the Syracusans sent out their entire forces to meet him. Gylippos' approach to the Epipolai was made by the same route as the one taken earlier by the Athenians. The two armies met without incident and advanced against the Athenian wall. Thucydides makes no mention of any opposition to Gylippos' move to the Epipolai.

It is hard to believe that Nikias had not placed a substantial guard at Euryelos. Surely his intelligence had kept him informed of Gylippos' movements and he had made due preparations? The clue to the fact that he did not lies at VII. 3. 1: 'The Athenians were at first thrown into a tumult by the sudden *attack* of Gylippos and the Syracusans...'

The *attack*, which comes in the narrative before the description of the Athenian army coming to battle order, may well have been made upon the guard to the Euryelos approach to Epipolai. It could well have been made by Gylippos from below and the Syracusans from above.

With the two armies facing each other, Gylippos dispatched a herald to demand that the Athenians quit Sicily within five days. No answer was given and, during the preparations for battle, Gylippos observed that the Syracusans were having difficulty in ordering their line. To give them more space to do so he led them a little distance away from the Athenian wall and awaited the Athenian response. None came and Nikias remained with his own army near the fortifications. At this Gylippos withdrew his forces to that section of the Epipolai which the Syracusans had walled off in the winter of 415/4 and which now enclosed the Temenites district. There he made camp overnight. On the following day, while the main army was led out to face the wall, thereby denying the Athenians the option of sending reinforcements to any specific point, Gylippos sent a unit to take the fort at Labdalon.[19] This is described as being out of sight from the Athenian position. Further success on the same day came with the capture of an Athenian trireme by the Syracusans at the entry to the Great Harbour, presumably placed there to watch for the coming of the Peloponnesian relieving fleet.

A third counter-wall was now quickly built by the Syracusans across the line of the unfinished part of the Athenian circumvallation. That Gylippos had arrived literally within days of the completion of that circumvallation was opportune. He continued to threaten the weaker completed parts of the Athenian wall, particularly at night. This caused the Athenians to build one section higher and to guard that area. The besiegers were now in a reactive mode and Gylippos was gradually wresting the initiative from the passive Nikias.

Nikias turned his attention to the fortification of Plemmyrion, a large promontory to the south of the Great Harbour. This, he considered, would allow him to receive supplies more easily and give him a better view of any Syracusan naval activity. Three forts were built in which equipment and other stores were lodged and the fleet was moored there. A significant comment by Thucydides shows us how far he had allowed the initiative to be stolen from him. 'And in general from now on he gave his attention more to naval warfare, seeing that matters on land were less hopeful for themselves, now that Gylippos had come.' (VII. 4. 4.)

Even this fortification was badly thought through. The water supply was insufficient for the crews stationed there and they were attacked by Syracusan cavalry every time they went out to gather firewood. Such was the turnaround of fortunes that Syracusan troop movements appear to have been made without hindrance. Apart from the Athenian walls and other fortifications, Gylippos' forces had the countryside firmly under their control. A semi-permanent base was made for a third of the Syracusan cavalry near the Olympieon to counter any moves being made by the Athenian troops at Plemmyrion.

Gylippos continued to threaten the Athenian wall. In so doing he kept substantial enemy forces in that location while his counterwall was completed using the building materials which had been brought up by the Athenians for their own wall. The ritual of the two forces lining up one against the other must have gone on for several days without any action taking place. This allowed the counterwall to approach the point where it would cross the line of the Athenian wall. Gylippos then made an attack on the Athenian line and was defeated, though obviously not decisively.

Here is a rare example of a commander who takes upon himself the full responsibility for the defeat of his forces. Gylippos addressed his troops and claimed that the blame for the defeat should be levelled at him. He admitted having undertaken the battle in an area which was too confined to allow the cavalry and light infantry to be deployed successfully. He pointed out to them that they were as well equipped as their opposition and that, in spirit, as Dorians going against Ionians, they were the superior.

This admission must have raised morale and it proved to be a wise move on Gylippos' part for, at the first opportunity thereafter to engage, his men proved successful.

This battle too was provoked by the Syracusans not by their army but by the fact that the Athenians had to take some action to delay or stop the building of the counterwall. Again the Athenians were reacting to events and the tempo of activity lay with the decisions of their enemy.

The part of the Athenian army which advanced against the Syracusans was met by Gylippos' men at the open area at the ends of the incomplete walls. Gylippos saw to it that his army had sufficient room away from the walls to manoeuvre. The Syracusan cavalry defeated the Athenian left wing. This led to the rest of the line breaking and seeking refuge within their fortifications; a complete victory and the first significant success in battle for the Syracusans. It should be noted that Gylippos had obviously recognised the quality of the Syracusan cavalry. It was not usual for a Spartan commander to put such trust in this arm. The aversion to the use of cavalry other than for screening flanks and skirmishing was an attitude that remained a characteristic of Spartan warfare for many years to come.

It would be useful to know in what ways the Syracusan cavalry were more efficient than similar corps from other cities. That their tactics varied can be seen from the example of the fifty cavalry which were sent to the Peloponnese to aid Sparta against Thebes more than forty years later (Xen. *Hell.* VII. 1. 21). There in 369 BC they charged the Theban lines letting loose a barrage of javelins, retiring and dismounting to rest, only to remount and retire farther when pursued. These tactics lured the enemy away from the relative safety of their lines, at which point the cavalry would turn to counter-attack. This was a large Theban army and Xenophon says that these few Syracusans were able to cause it to move to and fro pretty much according to their will.

The following night the Syracusan counterwall passed the Athenian wall and the danger of investment was over. Much had been achieved by Gylippos. He had raised the morale of the Syracusans, taken the initiative away from the enemy, blocked the possibility of a circumvallation of the city, given the Syracusans a taste of victory, and generally put Nikias on the defensive in matters pertaining to land warfare.

Nikias had heard that the Peloponnesian-led fleet was on its way and had dispatched twenty ships with orders to prevent their crossing to Sicily. This they were unable to do and the twelve vessels reached Syracuse without any contact with the Athenians. This suggests that Nikias had no other vessels on patrol in that part of the Sicilian coast close to Syracuse. It would appear to be a strange omission. What had he to fear from the Syracusan fleet? They had not yet been seen to threaten either the incoming supply vessels or indeed even appear at sea.

Following their arrival, the crews from the ships assisted in extending the counterwall while Gylippos set out to gather more land and sea forces from Sicily. He must have been a charismatic character for one senses in Thucydides' narrative that since his arrival self-belief had returned to the Syracusans. Their fleet, hitherto passive, now began to practise sea manoeuvres and it became evident to Nikias that they meant to try their strength against him. He may well have welcomed the prospect of a naval engagement. He would have had confidence in the notion of Athenian naval superiority. However, with the disadvantages of his base at Plemmyrion becoming daily more apparent, the evidence that his opposition was now prepared to test itself against what he perceived as being his primary strength must have given him pause for thought; particularly when there appeared to be no pressing reason for his enemy to take to the sea when they had achieved supremacy on land.

In the knowledge that Nikias was sending frequent reports to Athens together with requests either to supply more troops or recall the expedition, the Syracusans despatched envoys to Corinth and Sparta to exhort them to commit additional troops by whatever means possible.

Finally, Nikias, now wholly on the defensive, sent a letter with the express intention of ensuring there could be no doubt in the minds of the Athenians about the situation. Thucydides gives us the full content of the letter (VII. 11–15). In it Nikias described what had happened in recent times and warns of the preparations being made by the Syracusans to contest control of the seas when his own ships were becoming less and less seaworthy.[20] In maintaining the blockade he was unable to have them dried out ashore and more and more were becoming water-logged. That he pursued this blockade is perplexing. The Syracusans could easily receive provisions overland through the corridor behind their cross-wall. Losses of crewmen to Syracusan cavalry while foraging were having an impact. Servants and mercenaries were deserting, some of the latter persuading the trierarchs to accept Hyccarian slaves in their place. The enemy had sent for reinforcements from the Peloponnese and was gathering further resources and allies from the rest of Sicily. The two cities in Sicily still notionally giving support to the Athenians, Naxos and Katana, could give them no further assistance. He admitted that he was more the besieged than the besieger and stated that Athens had two options: either to send another force equal to that of the current expedition or to recall the present one. He admitted his illness and asked to be relieved of his command.

For some unaccountable reason the Athenians did not accede to the last of his requests but immediately appointed two temporary commanders, Menander and Euthydemos, who were already in Sicily, to help him until the arrival of the elected commanders. These were Eurymedon and Demosthenes. Eurymedon had been on the expedition of 424 BC and was no doubt elected for his knowledge of the island. He was sent post haste to Sicily with ten ships and twenty talents of silver, reassuring the forces there of their coming relief. Demosthenes stayed to prepare the armament. As a precautionary measure the Athenians sent a squadron of twenty ships around the Peloponnese to waylay any attempt by Corinth and Sparta to send reinforcements to Syracuse. Those two cities were recruiting fast and arranging for troops to be sent on merchantmen. The Corinthians also manned twenty-five vessels to challenge the Athenian naval squadron of twenty ships stationed at Naupaktos, thus allowing their troop-carrying merchantmen to slip past the danger. With Alkibiades urging them on, the Spartans prepared to invade Attika and to fortify Dekeleia. In the spring of 413 BC Agis led the Spartan forces to Attika and started work on the fortifications. At a distance of some twelve miles and in clear sight of Athens, this fortress now controlled the most fertile area in Attika and endangered any movement by land the Athenians might wish to make. The overland transport of food supplies from Euboia could not now be made safely via Oropos, but had to be carried by ship around Sounion to the Peiraeus.

The Corinthian squadron opposite Naupaktos remained there until the merchant vessels carrying the troops had distanced themselves sufficiently from any possible pursuit. The first group to go left Tainaron, the most southerly point of the middle prong of the Peloponnese. It held 600 hoplites picked by the Spartans from their helots and the Neodamodeis under the command of a Spartiate, Ekkritos.[21] With them went 300 Boiotian hoplites commanded by the Thebans Nikon and Xenon and the Thespian Hegesander.

A little later the second group sailed from Corinth. In their number were 500 hoplites from Corinth and mercenaries from Arkadia commanded by the Corinthian, Alexarchos. The Sikyonians sent 200 hoplites under Sargaos with this force.

The Athenians had also been busy gathering supplies and forces from the islands during the spring of 413 BC. Demosthenes went to Aigina where the disparate parts of the expedition gathered. On his way to Syracuse he had been ordered to assist Charikles, who with thirty ships was to make raids on the coast of Lakedaimon. Charikles had been instructed to bring over to Demosthenes the Argive hoplites who were to serve with the 1,200 Athenian heavy infantry and the other Athenian allied forces.

The Athenian mobilisation was a little slower than that of the Peloponnesians. They had to try any means by which they might force the

Spartans to withdraw from Attika. However, the raids in strength on the enemy coast of early summer did not achieve the desired outcome.

In the spring of that year, Gylippos had been successful in raising additional troops from the rest of Sicily. On his return with them to Syracuse he exhorted the Syracusans to prepare to test their strength against the Athenian fleet. He was supported in this enterprise by Hermokrates. They must have been aware of the increasing difficulties facing the Athenians in keeping their ships fully seaworthy and their crews up to strength.

A plan was made by which a combined sea and land operation would be launched against the enemy. The Syracusan land forces under Gylippos were to attack the forts at Plemmyrion at the same time that the Syracusan fleet engaged the Athenian fleet. VII. 22. 1 gives us the dispositions of the Syracusan navy and their points of anchorage. In the Great Harbour were thirty-five Syracusan vessels. These were to be joined by the remaining forty-five, which would sail round from the Lesser Harbour.

At the sight of the Syracusan naval activity the Athenians manned sixty ships, sending twenty-five in an attack on the vessels within the Great Harbour and the remaining thirty-five to impede the entry of the Syracusan fleet coming round from the Lesser Harbour. The main concern of the Athenians was to stop the two Syracusan fleets from joining one another. Thucydides makes no mention of the commander who ordered this answer to the Syracusan threat. It may or may not have been Nikias. Whoever it was, the tactic was sound and was aimed at preventing a large number of vessels occupying the limited sea space of the Great Harbour. The Athenians needed to give their ships within that harbour enough room to manoeuvre so that their superior seamanship would offset the disparity in numbers.

Gylippos had made his landward approach to Plemmyrion during the night and launched his surprise attack at dawn when the bulk of the Athenians there were down at the shoreline viewing the naval engagements. All three forts were quickly taken. Those fleeing from the first and largest fort to be captured took to a merchantman and other small boats in order to reach the safety of the Athenian camp. They were hampered in this by a Syracusan trireme which was sent specifically to run them down. At that point the Syracusans held the upper hand in the sea battle within the Great Harbour. Later, when the initiative passed to the Athenian fleet, the garrisons of the other two forts were able to reach safety more easily.

The sea battle was not so much won by the Athenians as given to them by the Syracusans:

> For the Syracusan ships that were fighting in front of the entrance, after they had forced back the Athenian ships, sailed into the harbour in disorder, and falling foul of one another made a present of their victory to the Athenians, who routed not only this squadron but also the ships by which they were at first being beaten inside the harbour. (VII. 23. 3)

Each side set up trophies for their respective victories, the Syracusans for their land success and the Athenians at sea. The Syracusan fleet had lost eleven ships to the Athenian three. The captured forts, however, served as storehouses for food, naval equipment and the property of the merchants who had accompanied the Athenian expedition. Sails and equipment for forty triremes were found there and these and the capture of three triremes which had been beached nearby heavily tipped the balance in favour of the Syracusans. Plemmyrion was now lost to the Athenians and it could no longer serve its purpose in protecting incoming supplies. Ships carrying these now had to face the prospect of fighting their way into the harbour.

The fighting had been particularly bitter. Of the eleven ships lost by the Syracusans the crews of only three were saved from slaughter. Many Athenians had been killed in the attack on Plemmyrion and a significant number of prisoners taken.

In a relatively short time the energy and expertise of Gylippos, with the wholehearted support of Hermokrates, had turned a position of near desperation for the Syracusans to one of realistic hope that the invaders could be defeated.

Now that the Syracusans had engaged the Athenians on water, their earlier fear of naval action was much diminished. In their first battle, success could well have been theirs. Although the Athenians could still claim superiority, the Syracusans were now less diffident in initiating sea operations.

A squadron of twelve ships was sent to southern Italy. One of the twelve went on to the Peloponnese to report on the recent events at Syracuse and to request that the war on the mainland be stepped up. The remaining eleven waylaid and destroyed a fleet of supply ships bound for the Athenians at Syracuse before going to Kaulonia to burn a store of timber lying ready for the building of additional Athenian triremes. Proceeding south to Lokroi they took on board the Thespian hoplites who had arrived on a merchant ship. Making for Syracuse, all but one of the ships managed to evade capture by the Athenian squadron of twenty ships lying in wait for them at Megara to the north.

For a time hostilities were sporadic as each side jockeyed to strengthen its position. The Athenians on the one hand did not wish to be involved in any significant engagement before the arrival of their expected reinforcements, and the Syracusans on the other sought to strengthen both sea and land forces in an effort to force an end to the war.

During this period the Athenians attempted to attack the Syracusan ships at anchor. They were prevented from doing so by a defensive barrier of wooden poles and logs which had been driven down into the seabed and behind which the Syracusan fleet could shelter, safe in the knowledge that they could not be rammed. The Athenians contrived to remove these from the relative safety of a very large fortified vessel. Under missile fire from the Syracusans, they pulled the piles out of the water by hoists or sent divers below the surface to saw them down. Thucydides notes that there were some submerged posts which endangered approaching vessels just like concealed rocks. As these were removed by the Athenians more were put in place by the Syracusans. These activities, together with skirmishes between land forces, characterised much of the early summer.

Further east in Greece, Demosthenes and Charikles joined forces and with their armada ravaged Epidauros Limera on the south-east coast of Lakedaimon before attacking the area opposite the island of Kythera. There Thucydides reports that Demosthenes, 'fortified a place shaped like an isthmus, in order that the helots of the Lakedaimonians might desert thither and that at the same time marauders might make it, as they had made Pylos, a base for their operations'(VII. 26, 2).

The location was what is now the small island of Elafonisos, formerly known as Onugnathos. In ancient times it was a promontory of the mainland but is now separated by a short stretch of water of about 350 yards.

Leaving Charikles to complete the fortifications and to man a garrison there, Demosthenes sailed to Kerkyra. On his way he opportunistically destroyed a merchantman which was about to carry Corinthian hoplites to Syracuse. This he found at anchor at Pheia on the coast of Elis opposite the island of Zakynthos. He was unable to capture its crew or the hoplites, who escaped and found another ship to take them to Syracuse. Moving on first to Zakynthos and then to Kephallenia, Demosthenes gathered more heavy infantry and sent to Naupaktos for a contingent of Messenian hoplites. These would likely march overland to Alyzia in Akarnania where Demosthenes' next port of call was made before going north to Anaktorion for more allies to embark. There he met Eurymedon on his return from Syracuse and heard the news of the fall of Plemmyrion.

At Anaktorion, the commander in charge of the squadron at Naupaktos arrived to beg for assistance against the Corinthian blockade of twenty-five ships. He was given ten additional vessels manned by the best sailors of the fleet. This changed the numbers in favour of the Athenians to twenty-eight against twenty-five.

More vessels were added to each side. The Peloponnesian fleet had taken up a position in a bay to the east of modern day Rhion. The supporting land forces of the Corinthians and their allies were arrayed on the headlands to the left and right of the bay with the Peloponnesian fleet in line across the bay itself. There seems to have been a change in command on the Athenian side. Diphilos had evidently replaced Konon and his presence probably accounted for even more ships being available to the Athenians.[22] Thirty-three vessels made the approach towards the Peloponnesians. In the following engagement three Corinthian ships were sunk but seven Athenian ships had their bows destroyed in direct frontal attacks. The Corinthians had considerably strengthened their bows and a new tactic had become available to sea-warfare, prow to prow attacks. The Corinthians had obviously come off best in this meeting but because the unseaworthy Athenian wrecks had floated out to sea and were recovered by the Athenians, this was deemed to be a draw in ancient terms.

The buildup of forces continued with Eurymedon in his capacity as joint commander going to Kerkyra to organise the manning of fifteen additional ships and a force of hoplites from that island, while Demosthenes recruited light infantry, slingers and javelineers.

Back in Sicily the envoys who had been sent to raise more troops had been successful and were marching to Syracuse when they were ambushed at Nikias' request by Sikels allied to the Athenians. Some 800 are reported to have fallen in this action but the one surviving envoy managed to bring the remaining 1,500 safely to Syracuse. The fall of Plemmyrion and the partial success of the Syracusan fleet had done much to sway opinion to the side of the Syracusans. Now those who had held back their support committed themselves to their side with the exception of the Agrigentines who chose to remain neutral. The Kamarinians on the south coast of Sicily sent 500 hoplites, and 300 each of archers and javelineers and the Gelans, farther west of Kamarina, sent five ships, 200 cavalry and 400 javelineers.

The aim had been to make an attack on the Athenian forces before the relief expedition arrived. It is not clear why this was not carried out. Thucydides claims (VII. 33. 3) that they did not carry out their plan because of the disaster that had befallen the reinforcements ambushed by the Sikels. There must have been a more cogent reason. To hazard a guess, it may well have been their fear that these victorious Sikels would now march to reinforce the Athenians. To make an attack before the intentions of the Sikels became known was to risk being caught between two armies. Another reason may have been the time taken to complete the modifications to the prows of the Syracusan ships. In view of the success of the Corinthian modifications to their ships in the battle opposite Naupaktos, they decided to adopt the same design for their own. Prows were shortened and made much stronger with the intention of adopting the tactic of an attack on the prows of the opposition (See Chapter I). Whatever the reason the plan was delayed and precious time was lost as will be seen below.

Meanwhile Demosthenes and Eurymedon reached Iapygia in Italy and took on board 150 more javelineers. Proceeding on to Metapontion a further 300 javelineers and two triremes were added to their forces. Arriving at Thouria they found that the pro-Athenian party was again in the ascendancy. In a relatively short time the Thourians were persuaded to add 700 hoplites and 300 javelineers to the considerable Athenian armament.

The fleet now sailed to the territory under the control of Kroton. The land forces, after a review had been held, marched southward through Thourian territory. The Krotonites refused to allow the army passage through their country and, having re-embarked, the whole expedition sailed on to Petra in Rhegion territory, making landfalls at cities on their route.

Their preparations complete, and with the news that the Athenian expeditionary force was now near, the Syracusans decided to make a concerted attack before its arrival. The plan was based on the premise that a sea fight in the Great Harbour would be within restricted waters. The Athenian vessels would have less room to manoeuvre and being lighter in construction were unsuited to resist the prow attacks of the newly modified Syracusan vessels. The accidental prow collisions of inexperienced pilots had now been turned into an aggressive tactic, with the Syracusan vessels built for such a purpose. As the attack would be made from the entrance to the harbour, the only way the Athenians could back water was shorewards into an ever-decreasing area, thus risking eventually falling foul of one another. As Plemmyrion was now in Syracusan hands, the Athenians would be unable to reach open waters.

A two-pronged attack was launched by Gylippos who led the army from the city against the Athenian walls while the Syracusan cavalry and light infantry and hoplites, who had been stationed at the Olympieion, assailed the other side. The Syracusan fleet now made its appearance. The Athenian land forces were of necessity fragmented: one group to man the walls to meet the onslaught of Gylippos, another moving from the walls to meet the advancing forces from the Olympieion, and still another to man the ships and to give such help as they could at the shore. Again, the Athenians were on the defensive.

Seventy-five Athenian vessels were launched to meet the Syracusan eighty. The hostilities went on for most of the day with nothing obvious being achieved by either side, other than the sinking of two Athenian vessels, before the Syracusans withdrew both land and sea forces. The following day saw no activity by the Syracusans and Nikias used the breathing space to see that repairs were carried out on damaged vessels and to anchor merchant ships at intervals in front of the sea stockade that served to protect the Athenian fleet. The gaps between the merchantmen were set at δυο πλεθρα, about 200 feet, allowing ships to find sufficient safety in retreat so that, having gathered themselves again, they could rejoin the fight.

The following day the Syracusans recommenced land and sea attacks at an earlier hour. The combat was similar to the first day with no real commitment being made on water by either side. Thucydides (VII. 39. 2) tells of a Corinthian, Ariston, described as being the best pilot in the Syracusan fleet, persuading the Syracusan commanders to ask those in the city to set up a market on the shoreline. By doing so the men could take a meal and attempt a second unexpected attack on the same day.

That he did this in the midst of hostilities, light though they may have been, is extremely unlikely. As one who had been a navarch himself, Thucydides should have been alert to the difficulties of hatching a plan and having a conference with the naval commanders while involved in tactical manoeuvring. It is more likely that the plan was formed during the previous day's inactivity, if not before. With hindsight one can see that the operations of the first day in which the Syracusans risked little in the way of casualties served to unnerve the Athenians. With the Syracusans holding the initiative, their inactivity on the second day did not allow the Athenians to relax their guard. It was only on the third day when the Syracusans suddenly backed water and returned to the city that the Athenians allowed themselves to imagine that their enemy recognised their opposition's naval superiority. The fact that hostilities had started earlier that day is another pointer to the fact that the ploy was part of a larger plan, to launch an attack at a time when the Athenians were weary and unprepared for confrontation. It is always the case that the side which holds the initiative is the better rested, confident and prepared for the next phase of an operation which is, after all, only known to their side and can only be guessed at by the opposition. In that very uncertainty lies one of the keys to success.

It seems likely that with the newly modified bows on their ships the Syracusans held a specific meeting to discuss the tactics to be employed in the coming engagement. Obviously, the commanders would lean on the advice of someone of the pedigree of Ariston. That advice would seem, in the light of what transpired, to suggest a sapping of the strength of the Athenian rowers leading, ideally, to a desperate assault by the Athenian fleet before their ability to do so left them. Their forward movement would give the impetus by which the Syracusan prow-to-prow response would be the more effective. The ruse of keeping their own men in the best of trim in preparation for such an event is much to Ariston's credit.

So with the Athenians thinking that hostilities were over for the day, the Syracusans, refreshed and well nourished, took to the sea again. The Athenians were not in good order when they re-embarked, many of them not having had the chance to take a meal. The Syracusan ships again merely threatened without full commitment and the Athenians, thinking that by continuing the sparring their men would become more and more exhausted by the need to hold their positions, decided to attack. This was the moment for which the Syracusans had waited. With prow-to-prow collisions the Syracusans inflicted great damage on the Athenian vessels, which could not back away from their enemy. The combined speeds of the ships on either side closing with one another in confined waters was wholly to the advantage of the Syracusans. The javelineers on the Syracusan decks killed many among those trapped on the Athenian ships. Their plight was made even worse by smaller vessels moving in close to the stricken vessels from where volleys of missiles were poured into the decks of the rowers. The Athenian vessels retreated, seeking sanctuary through the merchant-men. These deterred the pursuing Syracusan vessels. They were equipped with 'dolphins', weights suspended on cranes to drop on enemy ships and hole them. Two Syracusan vessels are reported to have been over-enthusiastic in the pursuit and were damaged by this device.

Seven Athenian ships were sunk in what was a clear Syracusan victory. They now firmly believed that, with a further concerted attack by both land and sea, the war would be at an end.

However, their moment of confidence passed with the arrival of Demosthenes and Eurymedon. A fleet of seventy-three ships carrying 5,000 hoplites and un-numbered light infantry suddenly changed the balance of power. The prosecution of the war on the mainland had done little to diminish the Athenian desire to crush Syracuse.[23] Thucydides analyses what had gone before:

> For Nikias when he first came inspired terror; but as he did not immediately attack Syracuse but spent the winter at Katana, he came to be despised, and Gylippos forestalled him by coming from the Peloponnesos with an army. This force the Syracusans would not even have sent for if he [Nikias] had attacked without delay; for they would have supposed that they could cope with him unaided, and would not, therefore, have discovered that they were too weak until they had been completely walled in... (VII. 42. 3)

In this passage Thucydides illuminates what he sees as the basic problem of Nikias' command. To be fair however, one must place the siege of Syracuse in the context of Greek siege warfare up to that time. Assaults on fortified positions were rare. Accepted practice was that of investiture, blockade and the hope that some trick or sympathetic element within those besieged would allow entry to be achieved. What the Athenians experienced in Sicily was quite unusual. This was not the expected passive defence. The Syracusans mounted an aggressive defence and their series of counterwalls and large garrison at the Olympieion threatened the building operations of the Athenians, the security of their flanks and their supply routes. The capture of Plemmyrion caused supply problems by sea for the Athenians. In no way was this the usual relatively comfortable and straightforward siege anticipated. Nikias clung, almost to the end, to the notion that some within the city would come to an accommodation with him. But Syracuse, like Athens, was a democracy. There was no obvious and exploitable division between political elements within the population. There was no truly pro-Athenian party, only those who wished to see an end to the privations and to the expenditure incurred by having to maintain a large number of mercenaries. It was difficult enough to maintain an army in the field during a 'normal' siege. The problems for the commissariat were formidable and here in Sicily they proved more or less unsustainable.

With hindsight it is easy to suggest that the Athenians should have made an immediate start to an investment of Syracuse on their arrival in Sicily; and that the first stage should have been the completion of a single wall cutting off the Syracusans from the hinterland. The double wall could have been completed later at leisure. A full naval blockade should have been instituted at a time when the Syracusan naval resources were very modest. Not doing all or any of these things led to the besieging Athenians suffering more than the besieged. At no point does Thucydides mention any lack of provisions within Syracuse, the one sure measure by which the success of a siege can be assessed. But reports of privation are given for the Athenians when they occupied Plemmyrion. The whole operation up to the arrival of Demosthenes represents a very cautious unfolding of events predicated upon the usual passive defence by the besieged. That such a passive attitude was not struck for much of the time created problems which Nikias was unfitted to solve.

Now that Demosthenes had arrived one could expect a more aggressive Athenian approach to the prosecution of the war. He saw that the third cross-wall of the Syracusans was a single rather than a double one and judged that if he could take control of the ascent to the Epipolai and the enemy camp there, he would have little difficulty in overwhelming the wall defences. Demosthenes considered that if he were to be successful the city would fall, and if not, he could take the expedition home, thus sparing the Athenian state further expenditure.

His first actions were to make raids upon the Syracusan possessions near the Anapos river, the only response coming from his enemy's cavalry and light infantry from the Olympieion. No other aggressive response came from the Syracusan land or sea forces. When Demosthenes moved against their cross-wall it was vigorously defended, and any battering rams and other engines deployed were burned. At no point of attack was he successful. Gylippos had moved easily from offence to defence and was rightly taking no risks until he had had the opportunity to assess his opposition.

With the agreement of Nikias, Demosthenes planned a night attack on the Epipolai. Nikias was not part of this operation, being too unwell. He stayed behind in charge of the camp. In anticipation of success in the attacks, Demosthenes arranged that carpenters and masons should accompany the army with building materials so that work could immediately start on the unfinished stretch of wall down to Trogilos. Five days' provisions were taken and the army under Demosthenes, Eurymedon and Menander marched under darkness to make the approach to Epipolai via Euryelos. A daylight approach would have been observed by the enemy. They succeeded in passing the Syracusan guard to the approach of the first fortress, which was easily taken. There were three such forts on the cross-wall (VII. 43. 4), the first manned by Syracusans, the second garrisoned by

Sikeliots and the third and nearest to the city, by allied forces. Those who escaped the initial onslaught fled eastward and informed those in the two remaining forts of the attack.

The special force of 600 Syracusans stationed on the Epipolai advanced to meet the enemy but were inevitably routed by superior numbers. The van of the Athenians and allies were in two divisions (VII. 43. 5). Demosthenes, after defeating the special force, quickly advanced over the plateau while the other part of the army proceeded to demolish as much as they could of that part of the Syracusan counter-wall now in their possession and also to attack that part which was not yet under their control. Being behind the Syracusan fortification made it easier to dislodge defenders and they would be secure in the knowledge that Demosthenes was sweeping across the plateau to their rear.

Meantime Gylippos with the Syracusans and allies hastily launched an attack on the Athenians. They were likely to have been in some disorder as they did so, for the Athenians had caught them completely by surprise. Inevitably while in this condition, they were unable to stop the Athenian advance. That advance, however, was obviously not as controlled as it should have been. With some Athenians breaching the enemy line they pushed on too far in their attempt to prevent any recovery of their adversary; a laudable tactic which in daylight would have brought reward, but it brought their own line into disorder as various pockets of resistance impeded an even advance. The Boiotians are credited by Thucydides with having made the first successful counter-attack on the Athenians (VII. 43. 7). Others too were obviously having success. In the confined space within which the skirmishes were taking place confusion reigned.

> ...how could anyone know anything clearly? For though there was a bright moon, they could only see one another, as it is natural to do in moonlight – seeing before them the vision of a person but mistrusting their recognition of their own friends. There were, besides, large numbers of hoplites belonging to both sides moving about in a narrow space. And on the Athenian side, some were already being defeated. Others, still in their first onset, were advancing unchecked; but of the rest of the army a large portion had only just finished the ascent and others were still coming up, so that they did not know which body to join. For the front lines were already all in confusion in consequence of the rout that had taken place, and the two sides were difficult to distinguish by reason of the outcries. (VII. 54. 2-3)

In this passage and what follows Thucydides indicates the problems facing the Athenians and one has to consider how those problems might have been avoided. The objective of capturing the Syracusan cross-wall had initially been achieved in part by the van of the Athenian army. The advance

152

under Demosthenes over the plateau was a little too precipitate. To have defeated the special force of 600 with his men while the other section of the van was busy dismantling the fortifications was an excellent start. With the area available for manoeuvre limited, he could then have met the expected counter-attack by Gylippos in good order and maintained this until the remainder of the army came up in support. At that point he could have firmly gone onto the offensive in a pitched battle with good communication within his forces. As it was, he had gone too far, desiring no doubt to capitalise on the surprise of his attack and the initial confusion of the enemy. His line of communication became too tenuous and his own force was broken up by success and failure in the ensuing mêlée. Those elements of the Athenian army who reached the plateau thereafter were unsure to which groups they should offer support. They could not easily distinguish friend from foe. The Syracusans had maintained their cohesion to a far greater extent than the Athenians and had, besides, discovered the recognition password of the Athenians. Armed with this information:

> ...if a body of Athenians, even though superior in number, fell in with a party of the enemy, these would make their escape, inasmuch as they knew the Athenian watchword, whereas if they on their part could not give the answer [i.e. give the Syracusan password] they were put to the sword. (VII. 44. 5)

To have achieved his objective Demosthenes need not have taken the whole army on this enterprise (VII. 43. 2). It would have been far safer on a night mission to take a smaller force, preferably only Ionians, requisite for the task. These could have held their position until daybreak, at which time the remainder of his army could have come up in support to contest the untaken section of the counter-wall. Demosthenes' first and only objective of that night attack should have been to secure a position on the Epipolai from which subsequent attacks could be mounted. In going for a complete victory the very size and composition of his forces produced the scenario for failure.

> But that which put the Athenians at the greatest disadvantage and did them most harm was the singing of the paean; for the song of both armies was very similar and caused perplexity.[24] Whenever, that is, the Argives or the Kerkyrans or any Dorian contingent of the Athenian army would raise the paean, the Athenians were just as much terrified thereby as when the enemy sang. And so finally, when once they had been thrown into confusion, coming into collision with their own comrades in many different parts of the army, friends with friends and citizens with fellow-citizens, they not only became

panic-stricken but came to blows with one another and were with difficulty separated. And as they were being pursued by the enemy many hurled themselves down from the bluffs and perished… (VII. 44. 6–8)

Thucydides' words graphically describe the utter rout which ensued. Those who managed to escape and reach camp were mostly those who had come with the first expedition and had knowledge of the terrain. Others lost their way once down from Epipolai and at daybreak were run down by Syracusan cavalry.

Demosthenes of all people should have considered the problems of a night action involving both Ionian and Dorian forces. He had had experience of overnight marches and, indeed, had used Dorians (in that case Messenians) to fool Dorians in his dawn attack on the Ambrakiots (see Chapter III). This, together with the fact that he led considerable numbers of men over terrain which was unknown to them, through a confined approach to Epipolai, and that at night, is much to his discredit as a commander. Too much, too early, had been committed to the enterprise and with its complete failure the initiative passed once more to the Syracusans.

Gylippos made no immediate moves against the Athenians but sent Sikanos with fifteen ships to Akragas (Agrigentum) to try to bring over to his side this south-western Sicilian city, now in the throes of a revolution.[25] Gylippos himself, once again, went overland to raise additional troops with the aim of carrying the Athenian camp by storm.

He was a realist and had thus far made no move against the enemy unless he had a good chance of success and a safe avenue for withdrawal in the event of failure. The Athenians by contrast had no hopes of further reinforcements. It was in Gylippos' interest to let the failure of Demosthenes' attempt on the Epipolai prey on the minds of the opposing forces He was in no hurry. He wanted to build an army of a size and composition suitable for the annihilation of the Athenian expeditionary forces.

This intermission in hostilities allowed many of the Athenians time to come to the conclusion that success for their enterprise was far more elusive than they had imagined it would be. Morale dropped. Their camp was near a marsh and presumably malaria was taking its toll: another example of the limitations placed on Nikias' choices by his opposing commander. In this period of inactivity a sense of hopelessness grew to such an extent that Demosthenes proposed an abandonment of the siege. He wished to sail back to Athens with his forces while they still had superiority at sea and thereby reduce the cost to the state.

Nikias opposed this suggestion on the grounds that with the increased number of vessels at their disposal they could effect a blockade denying Syracuse supplies. But the argument carried no weight. The Syracusans had an avenue for supply over the Epipolai or from the coast to its north, and their cavalry were masters of the hinterland. As previously mentioned, nowhere in Thucydides' report does there appear any hint that Syracuse was suffering from lack of food or any of the expected privations of a city under siege. Nikias added that, according to information he had from sources within the city, the Syracusans' condition was worse than their own. His more cogent reason for continuing the struggle was that the enormous cost to the Syracusans in maintaining large numbers of mercenaries and a fleet would inevitably lead them to surrender. He declared that there was a party within the city which favoured surrendering to the Athenians and was urging him not to withdraw.

Here, arguably, lies the reason for the eventual Athenian defeat, revealed in Nikias' belief that the Syracusans were suffering and that betrayal of the city was imminent. Although not directly expressed, there is sufficient evidence to suggest that Nikias was the subject of disinformation and that the disinformation had been engineered by Hermokrates. In the final stages of the conflict Hermokrates used men to pass on messages to Nikias to delay withdrawal (VII. 73. 3). Responding to this advice led to the annihilation of most of the expeditionary force and the capture of the remnant. It is highly likely that Hermokrates maintained an organised disinformation service to disrupt Athenian intelligence. It also implies that Nikias did not double-check the credibility of his sources, a serious failing in any commander.

What we have in Nikias is a commander who had done sterling service to the state. He was on an expedition that initially he had opposed and was not comfortable to be commanding. He had been successful in almost all enterprises that he had undertaken up to that point. It is significant that these were almost all straightforward actions requiring nothing beyond conventional military reaction to circumstances. With the aggressive defence of Syracuse he was out of his depth.[26] Had he been in better health it is doubtful that his decisions would have been any different. His success in arguing against the plans of Lamachos and more importantly Demosthenes after the battle on the Epipolai says much for his standing in Athenian society. At the heart of the problem lay the fear of disgrace.

Demosthenes refused to let the current situation continue. What he proposed had merit considering the circumstances, abandonment of their present unsuitable base and the setting up of a new one farther north at either Thapsos or Katana. From either of these more comfortable locations they could wreak havoc on the Syracusan hinterland with their land forces and their fleet would be able to operate in open waters, allowing their superior naval skills to be used to advantage. Eurymedon was of the same opinion. Nikias' reluctance to go along with the plan led both of them to believe that he was party to knowledge of the enemy – perhaps its situation, disposition or plans – they did not have. This led to delay and in that time Gylippos returned to Syracuse with not only large numbers of Sicilian reinforcements but also Peloponnesian hoplites who had lately arrived at Selinous. These last had been blown off course and had arrived late by way of Libya. As for Sikanos, he had discovered that the party favouring Syracuse had been ejected from Akragas.

With the prospect of an impending attack upon their camp, even Nikias reluctantly agreed that a move from their position should be made. He was still of the opinion that the men should not be permitted to vote on the matter and only the officers be told to prepare for evacuation by sea. Sickness was rife within the Athenian camp and morale understandably low. With all made ready, as luck would have it, an eclipse of the full moon occurred. Omens and portents were taken very seriously by the vast majority of Greeks and on the advice of the seers and soothsayers it was decided that no move should be made until three times nine days had passed, a moon cycle. This had to pass so that any malign influences might be expunged by the next cycle. Nikias was adamant on the observance of this period and in a phrase which tells the reader as much about Thucydides as about Nikias we have:

> Nikias also, who was somewhat *too much given to divination and the like*, refused even to discuss further the question of their removal... (Author's italics, VII. 50. 4)

Considering how matters stood for the Athenians, this will appear almost incomprehensible to some modern readers. But at the time, such a position was not unusual. Examples abound of natural phenomena causing a change of action. To cite only two such examples: in 426 BC an earthquake caused the abandonment of a Peloponnesian invasion of Attika. While this might be explained as a sensible course of action to take in the interests of self-preservation, it was actually a response to a sign from the deities. Even in the next century the Spartan army invading Argos expected to abandon their project in the wake of an earthquake. Indeed their whole camp raised chants of supplication to Poseidon. Their leader Agesipolis continued the invasion on the grounds that the god had been showing his approval of their action. He only acceded to a withdrawal later when lightning killed several men in camp (Xenophon *Hell.* IV. vii. 4). Other eclipses of both moon and sun reported by Thucydides occur at I. 23. 3; II. 28. 1 and IV. 52. 1; and earthquakes at I. 23. 3; I. 101. 2; II. 72. 2; III. 87. 4; III. 89. 1–5; IV. 52. 1; V. 45. 4; V. 50. 5; VI. 95. 1; VIII. 6. 5; and VIII. 41. 2.

Divination, sacrifices, the examination of entrails and bird flight were daily occurrences in any Greek army. Though reports of them are few in the writings of Thucydides, numerous examples can be found in the works of Herodotos, Xenophon and others.[27]

Needless to say, this delay was to prove disastrous. News of the proposed Athenian withdrawal inevitably reached Syracuse. This further raised morale there. It seemed to the Syracusans that the Athenians were admitting that they were not a match for them on land or at sea. The Syracusans decided that come what may the Athenians would not be permitted to leave their present location. To let them regroup elsewhere in Sicily would merely prolong the conflict: better that they should be dealt with in their present declining condition, in circumstances favourable to the Syracusans. They prepared to test the issue at sea. Regular training was undertaken by the Syracusan fleet. Such preparations would have been carried out in the knowledge that they had a month's grace. When they felt themselves to be ready, a land attack was made on the Athenian fortifications. In this a sortie made by Athenian cavalry and hoplites was cut off and severely mauled with the loss of seventy horses and a few hoplites. The following day the Syracusan fleet of seventy-six vessels deployed with a simultaneous land attack being made on the Athenian walls.

This predilection for attacks to be launched by both land and sea, which characterised the Syracusan approach, was imaginative. The joint operations divided the command structure opposing them and multiplied the possibility of mistakes occurring. It sustained pressure on all sections of the enemy forces and kept them wholly in reactive mode. The Athenians and their allies were merely waiting to see what they had to face next. Such an attitude would not have suited Demosthenes and it is surprising that we see nothing in the evidence available for this time to suggest that he was active in any of the planning or indeed the actions. It is some eight chapters later in Thucydides' account that his name resurfaces. He must have been active during this time and it is regrettable that we lose him now.

Against the seventy-six Syracusan vessels the Athenians manned eighty-six ships, with their land forces moving in defence of their walls. From their naval base near the marshland, the Athenians spread across the harbour with Eurymedon on the right wing attempting to outflank the Syracusan left. His manoeuvre, an attempted *periplous* (see Chapter I) took him too close to the shoreline and created a gap in the Athenian line by which the Syracusans quickly defeated the Athenian centre. The speed of their success allowed the Syracusans to turn their attention to the Athenian right wing before the *periplous* developed. Their victorious ships now turned on Eurymedon and cut him off from the remainder of the Athenian fleet, possibly in the bay west of Plemmyrion. Eurymedon's ships were destroyed there and the remainder of the Athenian fleet was pursued to the shore-line.

The point at which the Athenians sought refuge was beyond the safety of the stockades and their own camp and nearer the Ortygia, or inner city of Syracuse, such had been the success of the Syracusan naval attack. Part of the Syracusan land forces under Gylippos now moved from near the Temenite wall towards this position in order to attack those disembarking and make easier the towing away any captured ships. The advance was made hurriedly and in some disorder so that the Etruscans who were guarding the approach had little difficulty in disrupting this attack. Other Syracusan troops joined them, as did Athenians from the camp and on this occasion the Athenians won the day. They did not, however, prevent eighteen of their ships from being captured by the enemy and their entire crews killed.[28] Following up their successful sea engagement, the Syracusans sent a fire ship towards the surviving Athenian fleet. This was unsuccessful and Thucydides gives no explanation as to how the Athenians avoided the potential calamity. Trophies were set up by both sides commemorating the Syracusan naval victory and the Athenian land success.

For the Athenians their land victory was a hollow one. They had again been defeated at sea, and this time most emphatically. For them the naval arm had been their strongest asset. To see it beaten was a cause for despair. The fleet had been their eventual route of escape. In a relatively short time the Athenian position of strength on the arrival of their reinforcements had been eroded.

It would be too easy to lay the blame for their misfortunes wholly at the feet of Nikias. Much of it must be shared between Nikias and Demosthenes. As has been discussed above, the latter had been much too ambitious in his attack on the Epipolai. Having taken the whole army on this mission he had suffered losses which had given the enemy superiority in morale if not in numbers on land. The role of the army could not now be anything other than defensive. Apart from the numerous questionable actions or indeed inaction on the part of Nikias, which have been a relatively constant theme, his insistence on piously observing the recommendations of the seers had given the Syracusan fleet more than adequate time to prepare for a trial of strength. That they did so with an inferior number of vessels is a measure of their new-found confidence at sea.

Thucydides now describes the realisation by the Syracusans that in totally defeating the Athenians, they would go down in history as the liberators of Hellas. Be that as it may, one can be sure that their concerns were more immediate. By following up their recent successes and inflicting a crippling defeat on the Athenians they could be assured that no repetition of the invasion they had suffered would occur. To achieve this end they set about the business of cutting off any means by which the Athenians could make their escape.

Their first priority was to close the entrance to the Great Harbour, thus confining the Athenian fleet within it. The entrance was just under a mile wide and was blocked by triremes and smaller vessels anchored broadside in a line. This meant that no supplies could reach the Athenians even if any ally were brave enough to take the risk. Another tantalising observation occurs at this point which, had its subject actually featured in the conflict later, would have been fascinating:

... and they made other preparations in case the Athenians should still venture to fight at sea, and there was nothing small about any of the designs they formed. (VII. 59. 3)

Had the Athenian commanders taken Demosthenes' advice and agreed to remove immediately after the battle on the Epipolai to a position north of Syracuse, they would not have been in their current plight. The question of seniority does not explain the demurral and the error. Demosthenes was a joint commander, a position he had not been appointed to hitherto, unless we look at his activities at Megara and at Sphakteria. He had been eminently successful in the north-west following the debacle in Aitolia and was used to acting on his own initiative. His failure on the Epipolai may have diminished his confidence somewhat and this may be the reason why he fatally deferred to the opinions of Nikias at this time.[29] The continued primacy of Nikias, despite his debilitating illness, is nevertheless hard to account for.

Too late, the Athenians decided to put all able-bodied men on board their ships and try to effect a breakout from the naval blockade. In preparation for this they abandoned their walls leading up to the heights of the Epipolai and built a cross-wall near their naval base into which they placed the remaining stores, the sick and a garrison. Their purpose was to attempt to reach Katana. The secondary plan, if this attempt failed, was to burn their fleet and make a retreat in battle line by land. Thucydides states that their destination would be to any friendly place, but realistically we must assume that their eventual goal was Katana.

Preparations for this eventuality seem to have gone well and initially without any intelligence breaches. This was one of the few occasions in the struggle when Nikias appeared to be taking the initiative. However, such preparations could not be made under the scrutiny of the enemy without conclusions being reached as to their implications. Gylippos and his fellow un-named Syracusan commanders concluded that the Athenians were going to attempt another sea battle and made their own preparations. Their intelligence had made them aware of the Athenian plan to use grappling hooks to stop the Syracusan ships from backing away after they had rammed the Athenian vessels. The knowledge of this plan to allow the Athenian marines to contest the decks of the Syracusan vessels while they were thus impeded from backing water led the Syracusans to screen their ships with hides placed over their prows and on much of the upper decks. This would cause the irons to slip off.

The Athenian fleet of 110 ships set sail against the blockade. Thucydides remarks that the Syracusans sailed out with 'the same number of ships as before' (VII. 70. 1), i.e. seventy-six, positioned at various points within the harbour area. Those of the Athenian army who were not aboard were arrayed along the shore-line in support of their maritime colleagues.

Demosthenes, Menander and Euthydemos were the Athenian commanders and Agatharchos and Sikanos were the wing commanders of the Syracusan fleet, with Pythen and the Corinthian contingent at their centre. This left Nikias and Eurymedon ashore on the Athenian side and Gylippos with the Syracusan land forces. The latter's role was to prevent the Athenian vessels from coming ashore at any point within the harbour, so that the Syracusan ships could, hopefully, effect their destruction.

In the first part of the engagement the Athenians would seem to have held the upper hand. They had charged the barrier and were sufficiently successful to be in the process of attempting to break through the chains in place, before they were assailed on all sides. The area of the harbour is described as being so crowded that attack by *diekplous* (see Chapter I) was very difficult (VII. 70. 4). Because of the confined space collisions were commonplace and fighting from the decks became the norm. Obviously in such conditions the Athenian naval skills were frustrated and the Syracusan tactic of ramming the prow of an opposition vessel once again proved successful.

Having indicated that the Syracusans had gone to sea with seventy-six ships, Thucydides states (VII. 70. 4) that the total of the combined fleets fell little short of 200. The remainder of Thucydides' description is confused. One can assume that the sea battle came to resemble a land engagement, with ships immobile and the antagonists contesting deck areas. Thucydides waxes lyrical when describing the reactions of the land forces of the Athenians to the efforts of their fellows at sea, as they swayed between optimism and despondency.

Eventually the Athenians were routed and the brief description given is sufficient to indicate that the Syracusan victory was total. Athenian vessels made for shore at whatever point was immediately accessible. Their land forces came to give support wherever necessary and more importantly to man the walls, which they thought would be the subject of attack. The Athenians were now wholly on the defensive. The Athenians did not even ask for the deliverance of their dead in this battle.[30] This is a highly unusual occurrence in Greek warfare and signifies their utter demoralisation. Demosthenes went to Nikias to propose that they man what was left of their fleet and try to force their way out of the harbour at daybreak. The Athenians still had more seaworthy ships available to them than the Syracusans. Nikias agreed. It is illuminating that Demosthenes sought his agreement in the matter. It seems that Nikias was in the position of having the final say and that the other commanders deferred to him.

The moment had passed. The Athenian crews refused to man the vessels, they were so dispirited. So it was that the only alternative was adopted, an overland retreat. With such huge loss of morale, the Athenian leaders had lost that tenuous thread so essential between a command structure and those commanded; trust. The army now controlled its fate and, while the general wish was to leave the vicinity of Syracuse as soon as possible, this had to be by land. Individuals therein would only follow a commander who agreed with their collective desire and, as will be seen later, individual needs destroyed the protection that collaboration and unity of purpose give. It is no exaggeration to state that from this moment on, the Athenian commanders no longer enjoyed sufficient confidence among their forces to permit the proper exercise of their command.

The retreat could have got off to an auspicious start. The Syracusans needed rest after the exertions of such a great battle and it so chanced that a festival to Herakles was to be celebrated at this time. Hermokrates realised that it would be highly unlikely that he or his fellows could persuade the citizenry to take up arms immediately to stop the Athenian evacuation. He resorted to the tactic of disinformation which has already been alluded to. Sending horsemen to the outskirts of the Athenian camp, he was able to persuade them not to make their move on that night, suggesting, falsely, that the Syracusans were already guarding the roads and suggesting that after careful and full preparation the Athenians should withdraw from the area by daylight. The ruse succeeded. Possibly the reason for its success is revealed in Thucydides' comment:

> These rode up close enough to be heard and called upon certain persons by name, as though they were friends of the Athenians – *for there were some who regularly reported to Nikias all that went on in Syracuse* and bade them tell Nikias not to lead his army away that night, since the Syracusans were guarding the roads, but to withdraw at his leisure, in the daytime, after having made full preparations. (Author's italics, VII. 73. 3)

The inference from this in a footnote by Charles Forster Smith, the translator of the Loeb edition, is that Nikias regularly derived intelligence from the disaffected section of the Syracusan populace. But the present author would argue that this is evidence that Hermokrates' acivities in dissimulation were bearing fruit and that those 'who regularly reported to Nikias' were Hermokrates' men. In all that is reported of him, Hermokrates stands head and shoulders above those around him. His initial analysis of actions to be taken prior to the arrival of the Athenian forces shows his military appraisal to be vastly superior to that of his fellows and certainly better than that of Nikias.

So the Athenians delayed their overland retreat. Once again, Nikias appears to have been the instigator. Undoubtedly he had persuaded his fellow commanders that his intelligence sources were good, although thus far their results had been far from fruitful. For how much longer could the Athenians rely upon them?[31]

Not only did the Athenians not move off immediately but they also spent the next day preparing for their retreat. This gave Gylippos and the

Syracusans ample time to set up road blocks and obstacles at fords and river crossings along the routes available to the Athenians.

Three days after the sea battle, the Athenians moved off, a cowed assembly, provisioned with only those items to satisfy immediate needs. The degree to which their spirits had fallen is measured in the report of unburied corpses of comrades left where they were. Such neglect was tantamount to sacrilege. There is no evidence that the commanders had ordered their burial in the normal way. If they so ordered, as was customary, an even worse scenario prevailed: orders being ignored.[32] At the same time as their preparations were going on, the Athenians had allowed Syracusan ships to come to the shore-line to tow away the remainder of their vessels unhindered. Some had been burned as planned, but this course of action had obviously been abandoned, another pointer to the mental condition of the men.

The wounded and sick were left behind and Thucydides paints a lurid picture of their leave-taking. Desertion of slaves and even mercenaries had taken place throughout the last year's hostilities and this was to increase following the final defeat. This led to hoplites unusually carrying their own supplies, either having no servant or slave to do so, or if they had, fearing that he too might desert taking the precious supplies with him.

This was still a formidable number of men on the move. For not only were there the army, their attendants, the artisans, stonemasons, smiths and merchants who had accompanied the expeditions, and all others necessary to a lengthy campaign, but also perhaps as many as 15,000 oarsmen. The muster could well have been well in excess of 30,000 men.

On the march Nikias tried to raise the spirits of the men by holding out the prospect of provisions being supplied by the Sikels, to whom messages for this purpose had already been sent. He also saw to it that order was maintained on the march. The formation chosen was the usual hollow square adopted when non-combatants needed protection. The line of march was due west, which meant they had to force a crossing of the Anapos river. As they marched on they were subject to missile attacks from Syracusan light infantry and cavalry. This slowed the advance and eventually the Athenians made camp on a hill. Their first day's march had covered some five miles which, considering the circumstances, was a notable achievement. The following day's march was started early but only took them half the distance to a plain wherein they took provisions from the local inhabitants and collected water supplies in readiness for the next part of their journey, where water was in short supply.

The Syracusan force had wisely moved on ahead while the Athenians were refreshing themselves and built a wall in the ravine through which the Athenian army had to pass. On the resumption of the march the Syracusan cavalry and light forces, possibly reinforced, continued their harassment to such a degree that the Athenians returned to their second camp. Here, the Syracusan cavalry continued their attacks and it was impossible for the Athenians to forage.

Once again an early start was made the following day and this time the Athenians managed to reach the point fortified by the Syracusans. There they found a considerable body of hoplites ranged against them behind the wall. The ravine is described as narrow and, with the steep heights occupied by javelineers, slingers, and other missile throwers, the Athenians were unable to force their passage. Bad weather did little to raise their spirits and, having broken off their attack on the Syracusan position, they took the opportunity to rest.

Syracusan observers must have kept Gylippos informed of the early progress of the Athenian withdrawal. His programme would have been to allow the Athenians to distance themselves sufficiently from the relative safety of their camp near Syracuse before commencing any significant hostilities. It was not in his interests to risk all in a pitched battle. The contested river crossing was to be anticipated, and can be seen as a necessary token. To have no one guarding this point would have aroused Athenian suspicions. Once the crossing had been made, the Syracusan commitment escalated considerably, with heavy and light infantry in front of the Athenians and an ever-present cavalry force harassing the advance.

During their rest period it became known to the Athenians that Gylippos had ordered part of his army to build a wall to their rear. They were lucky enough, through the timely despatch of a section of their own forces, to stop its completion and reopen the road down which they now returned to the plain where once more they made camp.

Yet again they were subject once more to attack on the march. This time, however, these attacks seem to have had more serious results for the Athenians and their allies. It is likely that Gylippos had brought increasing numbers of troops to the area. The marchers are described as being surrounded and suffering significant casualties. The tactics of the Syracusans were to retreat if any pursuit was made and then to return to the attack when the Athenians rejoined their ranks. These are the typical tactics of light infantry and cavalry. They may well have had the support of hoplites to threaten any over-eager pursuit of their light-armed comrades but sufficiently far from the Athenian army to avoid contact with the main body. Thucydides gives no evidence for such a presence but in the light of the obvious success enjoyed by the Syracusans it seems likely. The hope was to create panic in the Athenian forces and the reported preponderance of attacks on the rearguard was a classic means to create disruption (VII. 79. 5). Such was the intensity of the harassment that the Athenian army was still within the plain when it was decided to encamp. It had travelled a mere two-thirds of a mile.

The condition of the Athenians was desperate. They now had no supplies, many were suffering wounds and were totally dispirited. All was going to plan for Gylippos. His men were well provisioned, fresh, and morale was excellent.

To Nikias and Demosthenes it had become clear that the route they had initially chosen was now impossible to follow with any hope of success. In desperation they devised a plan by which they would change the direction of their withdrawal. Ordering the lighting of many fires, they led their army in an overnight march from their camp towards the sea. They hoped that they would be able to put sufficient distance between themselves and their enemy to gain relief from harassment. This was an unlikely prospect considering the efficiency of the large numbers of Syracusan cavalry and demonstrates that they, as commanders, were clutching at straws. The paucity of their options shows the extent to which they were at the mercy of their enemy. The only way they could have avoided the damaging attentions of the enemy would have been to travel through terrain unsuitable for cavalry.[33] This they were not proposing to do.

Needless to say, when they embarked on this change of direction at night some confusion ensued and the van soon lost touch with the remainder of the army. The distance between the two sections increased as the march went on. It would appear that Nikias kept his men in better order than Demosthenes and yet it is the latter who had more experience in night operations.

Nonetheless, both sections of the army made good progress and, at first light, the van had reached their initial objective, the sea, just over six miles away. They now turned south on the Elorine road hoping to follow the river valley of the Kakyparis inland to reach the Sikels. It would seem that the guides changed their minds for, after reaching the Kakyparis and forcing a crossing against a Syracusan-garrisoned defensive wall, the army pushed on farther south with the intention now of following the Erineos river inland. We do not know the reasoning behind the change of routes.

By now the Syracusans had discovered the flight of the Athenian army and accused Gylippos of allowing it to escape. What grounds they had are not given and the accusation may well have been made merely for the sake of laying blame at someone's door. Suffice to say that Gylippos remained firmly in command. It can be assumed that he had set observers in place and the fact that the Athenians were able to leave undetected says much for their discipline, engendered by fear and the desperate hope for security.

Immediately in pursuit, later in the day the Syracusans caught up with the part of the army under Demosthenes. His forces were moving much more slowly and in worse order than those of Nikias, who were pressing ahead. Thucydides (VII. 81. 3) indicates that Nikias was more than five miles ahead of his colleague and the Syracusans had little trouble in impeding Demosthenes' progress. He had stopped and formed in battle line to confront his pursuers, only to be harassed by cavalry to such an extent that he took up a position behind a wall. Now immobile, the

Athenians became sitting targets for the javelins and other missiles the enemy poured into their ranks. The refusal of Gylippos to come to close quarters but to rely on a tactic which was not only securing the safety of his own men but also producing the desired result of causing significant distress to the enemy, shows astute leadership.

The barrage continued for much of the day. At length Gylippos and the Syracusans offered freedom to those islanders among the Athenian forces willing to change sides. Thucydides says that only a few took up the offer. This is surprising considering that these were coerced 'allies' of the Athenians. At length the exhausted remnant of Demosthenes' force agreed to surrender on condition that none would suffer death. After giving up such possessions as they had, the 6,000 survivors were taken to Syracuse as prisoners.

During this time Nikias had reached and crossed the Erineos river and had made camp on a high position. His forces were overtaken the following day, certainly by Syracusan cavalry, who brought news of Demosthenes' capitulation and urged Nikias to consider doing the same. Initially he did not believe the news but, under truce, Nikias sent a horseman to verify the claim. On being convinced of the truth of the matter Nikias offered, on behalf of Athens, to repay all costs incurred in the war by the Syracusans, pledging to leave as hostage one man for every talent expended. This offer was rejected and Gylippos ordered the resumption of hostilities, once more using his tactic of missile barrage and avoidance of hand-to-hand combat.

Lack of food was now taking a severe toll on the Athenians. It was decided that another night march should be attempted. On this occasion they were observed and only 300 managed to break through the Syracusan lines, the remainder staying where they were. The group of 300 were later pursued and dealt with.

Nikias attempted to continue his retreat the following day and was again subject to constant missile attack. He managed to bring his forces to the Assinaros river a little farther south on the Elorine road. The remaining puzzle is why he had not yet taken any of the river valleys he is reported to have intended to follow as a route to the interior. Was it because they were blocked by Syracusan forces? This would have been unlikely when he was well ahead of the pursuing Syracusans.

On arrival at the Assinaros it may well have been Nikias' intention to cross over and make it difficult for the majority of his pursuers to do so, thereby gaining momentary respite. However, this did not take full account of the condition of those serving under him. They were plagued with thirst, and would have had little rest on the previous night and on this, the seventh day of the retreat, they would be exhausted.

A combination of circumstances brought disaster to the Athenians. At the banks of the river increased enemy pressure made some eager to reach the other side while others were desperate to take the opportunity to drink. The Athenians were, by necessity, in extremely close order and many lost their footing, falling foul of their own weaponry, or stumbling over those who had fallen before them. Some were swept away and those struggling either to cross or drink were the targets of the missile throwers. Mention is made of Syracusans on the *other* bank, which seems to suggest that a force of cavalry had reached the other side ahead of the Athenians. Indeed, VII. 85. 1 confirms this to have been the case. The Athenians, trapped in the river bed, sustained appalling casualties not only from missiles but from Peloponnesian hoplites coming down the river banks to add to the slaughter at close quarters. On Nikias surrendering his person to Gylippos and entreating him to stop the carnage, the latter ordered prisoners to be taken. These, too were marched back to the city. Mention is also made that *many* of the captives were clandestinely taken by members of the Syracusan soldiery. They were probably sold as slaves or kept as such in individual households.

Later (VII. 87. 4), Thucydides declares that the total number of prisoners taken was at least 7,000. But this number includes the 6,000 under Demosthenes who surrendered earlier. So as catastrophic as the disaster at the river must have been, Thucydides' πολλοί – *many* – cannot be an understatement. If the survivors from the river were a mere 1,000, this would make it the greatest loss of life ever to have been experienced in Greek history up to this time.

Gylippos and his Syracusan colleagues in positions of command had used their resources well. They impeded the enemy's route at suitable points, maintained pressure with a constant artillery barrage, forced a change of direction to the march to an area even better suited to the deployment of their own forces, denied rest and provisioning opportunities to their enemy, and attacked more vehemently when the opportunity for dealing with a divided enemy presented itself; all this with little or no loss to their own forces. A truly classic and virtuoso display of leadership, and this from a Spartan whose background would suggest automatic reliance on hoplite forces and not those other arms, which continued to be neglected by his countrymen until the time of Agesilaos.

The prisoners were kept in the stone quarries for just over two months and given barely enough to keep them alive. The survivors of this ordeal were then sold into slavery.[34] Despite the protestations of Gylippos, Nikias and Demosthenes were executed.

This was the major section of Thucydides' description of the Peloponnesian War. While he may have sought to demonstrate that the *hybris* of the Athenians was the cause of the disaster, and to write this episode up as a great tragedy, he nonetheless gives us extremely useful insights into the day-to-day operational aspects of an attempted siege of a coastal city. The practices and expectations of the Athenians at Syracuse can be transposed to those sieges about which we have little information. In highlighting those areas in which the Athenians were thwarted in their conventional operations by the unexpected and up to that time, unique form of resistance offered to them by the Syracusans, we learn much about what was the usual practice of siege warfare.

The description of the Athenian retreat from Syracuse is treated in epic style by Thucydides and must have made a powerful impact on those who knew of it in the years following, and who exercised their minds on military matters. Those survivors who returned would also have their tales to tell.

The problem of achieving a secure retreat with a large body of fighting men, encumbered as they were by the necessity of protecting even greater numbers of technical noncombatants, was daunting. There were many suggestions as to how much better it could have been done, and what was incorrect in the tactics or strategy of Nikias and Demosthenes, much in the manner of today's 'armchair generals'.

Just over a dozen years later, the theories emanating from such deliberations would be brought to the test. In Xenophon's *Anabasis* we have the account of the successful Greek retreat from the heart of the Persian Empire lasting *months* and not a mere few days. Their situation was initially not dissimilar. They had no cavalry, few provisions, they too were encumbered by a large number of camp followers, and were facing an enemy much stronger in cavalry than had been the Syracusans. Even worse, their command structure had been removed by a treacherous act. What was an even bleaker prospect was that, even if they were to escape the Persians, they would have to traverse arduous terrain, where peoples would undoubtedly challenge their passage with tactics and weaponry as yet unknown.

As the 'historian' – in fact more of a memoirist – who continued Thucydides' narrative, Xenophon would have been extremely well versed in Thucydides' writings and so the problems of the retreat. When he was elected a general of the Greek army after Kounaxa, he made constant proposals to his colleagues and to the men themselves to improve the security of the entire force. His proposals having been enacted, they represent a well thought-out methodology: securing heights, protecting flanks, advances uphill in columns, the use of light infantry, of a small cavalry force, special forces, reserves and combined forces, systems for river crossings, a myriad of tactical ploys.

This is not to say that he would have succeeded had he been a commander during the attempted withdrawal from Syracuse; rather that, as in all things, knowledge of those decisions made by others which have led to disaster – and their avoidance – often brings success.

Here is an early example of the benefits derived from the study of Thucydides.

Notes

1. Essential background reading is *The Peace of Nikias and the Sicilian Expedition.* D Kagan.

2. Athenian intentions in the earlier expeditions to Sicily are not wholly clear. In the fifth century there were three major areas which exported grain, the Black Sea, Egypt and Sicily. As long as Athens controlled the Hellespont, the first was secure, but there was always the threat of a Persian resurgence. Egypt revolted from the Persian empire and was greatly helped by Athenian forces. Their disastrous defeat by the Persians at Prosopitis in the Nile Delta in 454 BC was chastening and closed that area as a possible source of grain for the foreseeable future. In 444 Athens founded a colony, Thouria, in southern Italy, possibly for its abundant timber required for ship building but also as a base from which it might hold the emerging power of Syracuse in check. Around 443 Rhegion, also in southern Italy, and Leontini in Sicily, were brought into alliance with Athens.

   At III. 86. 4, Thucydides gives his opinion that the expedition under Laches, sent by the Athenians to Sicily early in the war in 427 BC ostensibly to support their brother Ionians against Dorian Syracuse, was, in reality, despatched to impede the export of grain to the Peloponnese and to assess whether Athens could gain control in Sicily. Thucydides' opinion must be given great weight. He was at the heart of Athenian decision making at this time and was soon to be one of the ten generals. As it was, little was achieved by this expedition other than the renewal of an old alliance with the city of Egesta on the north-west coast of Sicily.

   The second expedition of 425 BC was sent to attempt to regain Messene, a city on the north-east coast of Sicily. That fleet of forty ships was the one that carried Demosthenes to Pylos (see Chapter IV). The Syracusans had taken Messene for fear that it was too convenient a base for any future Athenian attack on their city (IV. 1. 2). The second Athenian expedition implies they were right. The great Syracusan statesman Hermokrates eventually persuaded the warring Sicilians to make peace at a gathering held at Gela in 424 BC and thereby gave the Athenians no excuse for a continued presence in the area. See Chapter 4 in *The Greek World 479–323 BC* by S. Hornblower.

3. S Hornblower, op.cit., p.56 regards the lack of direct evidence as a hindrance to establishing the true motivation for Athenian involvement in Sicilian affairs.

4. Meiggs and Lewis, *Greek Historical Inscriptions to the end of the Fifth Century*, 37, 63 and 64.

5. See S Hornblower, *The Greek World 479–323 BC*, p.136.

6. Perikles' force consisted of 4,000 hoplites, 300 cavalry, 100 Athenian triremes and fifty more from Chios and Lesbos together with their soldiery. Horse

transports were available for the first time (II. 56). They were constructed from old galleys. Their availability early in the war makes the lamentable, and in a sense decisive, lack of cavalry forces in the early stages of the Sicilian campaign all the more puzzling.

7. With the eventual failure of the policy to bring about a permanent disruption of the Peloponnesian League, Athens had to look, perforce, to another avenue. The war would continue whether openly or covertly and to break the impasse, Athens must win on land against the Spartans. To do this she needed manpower and the means to bring the Peloponnese to its knees by denying it imported foodstuffs. The subjection of Sicily seemed the solution to both problems.

8. See Plutarch, *Nikias* and *Alkibiades*.

9. Plutarch, *Alkibiades* 17 and *Perikles* 20. 4.

10. A herm was a rectangular column in bronze, marble or stone, topped with a sculpted head. It was placed at the entrance to a house or at the intersection of streets. Its positioning was important to the continued welfare of those living in the area.

11. The armed forces, plus the oarsmen of the triremes and transports, puts the manpower on the expedition significantly above 30,000 men. A trireme had 170 oarsmen on its three levels, a force of ten to fifteen marine hoplites, and up to sixteen additional marine personnel for steering, rigging and support duties.

12. Hermokrates is to be found later in the war commanding in the Aegean (Xenophon, *Hellenika*. I. 1. 27, 30 and 31, and I. 3. 13).

13. P B Kern *Ancient Siege Warfare*, (p.123) is of the same opinion about Lamachos' proposal. However, he is probably incorrect in claiming that the Syracusans did not possess a fleet. At VI. 50-52 the Athenians find that no fleet was manned against them; but this does not mean that there was no fleet, merely that the Syracusans were reluctant to engage them at sea. Indeed, Hermokrates had suggested a plan to send the Syracusan fleet out to disrupt the Athenian armada on its journey to Sicily.

14. This was surely the product of an intelligence structure and not accident. While it is admitted that scouts and observers were not then used consistently and intelligence gathering was of variable quality, much the same can be said of armed forces today. To the best of commanders this aspect of warfare would be important regardless of period.

15. See Peter Krentz, 'The Salpinx in Greek Warfare' 110 ff, in *Hoplites* (ed. Victor Hanson).

16. Alkibiades' speech was made during the winter of 415/414 BC. It was not until 413 BC that Sparta acted on his advice and occupied Dekeleia.

17. M M Sage in *Warfare in Ancient Greece* quotes Pindar, *The Nemean Odes*, I. 15–19 on the superiority of Syracusan cavalry.

18. G Busolt observed (*Griechische Geshichte* III pt. 2, 1340) that the Athenians could build a wall at the rate of just over a mile in two weeks.

19. The capture of Labdalon was the prime reason for Nikias seeking to make another secure base on Plemmyrion. It proved to be a mistake and serves to show that, despite having been in the area for a considerable time, Nikias' knowledge of such basics as water supply was sadly lacking.

20. See also Chapter V, where the attempt on the Peiraeus was modified because of the unseaworthiness of the available triremes.

21. The Neodamodeis were a relatively new level of citizen without voting rights. They were formerly helots or state slaves emancipated for service in war. Such was the reward for those who had served with Brasidas. The helots on this expedition could look forward to a similar reward at the end of their service.

22. Konon was to figure significantly as a commander in the latter stages of the war.

23. After Delion the Athenian refusal to contest the war openly on the mainland is a reversion to its original land force policy. However, while fortress Athens continued to be secure, and its fleets commanded the control of the seas, its manpower could effectively be committed to overseas operations.

24. The *paean* was an invocation of the gods expressed in song. They are usually associated with the advance into battle. However, a supplicatory example is described in Xenophon (*Hell*. IV. 7.4). In 388 BC, during an invasion of Argive territory, the Spartan army experienced an earthquake. The immediate reaction to this was to raise a paean to Poseidon, the god of earthquakes. Other paeans may have been used on the march to assist in keeping spirits high and regulate step. The Spartans used a double reed instrument, the *aulos*, to keep their marching to a standard pace, often singing a paean at the same time. Further discussion can be found in chapter VII of *The Greek State at War*, Part I, by W K Pritchett, and in 'A Study of the Greek Paean' by A Fairbanks, *Cornell Studies in Classical Philology*, (12. 19–24).

25. By this stage the Syracusans were clearly confident enough at sea.

26. To be fair, this very aggressive type of defence had not been faced, up to this time, by any other commander.

27. For battlefield sacrifices see *Hoplites*, ed. Victor Hanson, pp 197–227 and for religious practices concerned with warfare, see the sections on Piety in *Xenophon and the Art of Command* by Godfrey Hutchinson.

28. If this includes the usual four to six archers and ten marines on each vessel, the loss of life would have been 3,348 men. However, in the enclosed waters of the harbour it is highly likely that that the Athenians had put many more combatants on each ship, leading to a much greater loss of life.

29. P B Kern in *Ancient Siege Warfare*, (p.133) considers Nikias' greatest mistake was not removing his forces immediately it became clear that his siege operations would not succeed.

30. See 'Identification and Retrieval of Hoplite battle dead', Pamela Vaughn, in *Hoplites*, ed. V D Hanson.

31. Had Thucydides given more details of the sources, methods of transmission, and use to which this intelligence was put, we would have a better understanding of why Nikias' colleagues apparently deferred to him.

32. The tradition of a general's responsibility to the fallen is clearly stated in Onasander's *Strategikos* XXXVI. 1–2. To those of the ancient world, Nikias and Demosthenes acted outrageously in their neglect. Though there may well have been a refusal by those under their command to carry out the necessary duties. There certainly is evidence of insubordination at this time.

33. A constricted area such as a rocky river valley would have sufficed where it would have been difficult for mounted but unshod horses to move with ease and comfort, or with the requisite speed for advance and retreat. It would have been necessary to secure the adjacent heights to the line of march to avoid attacks from enemy light infantry or missiles. Nikias seems to have wished to follow such a route to make contact with the inland Sikels. Why he did not do so when the first opportunity presented itself is difficult to understand. Had he done so, however, there is no evidence that he possessed the tactical skills to complete such a retreat successfully in such terrain.

34. Possibly dating to 412 BC, the honorific Decree of Epikerdes, *Inscriptione Graeciae* (II^2 No. 174, edit. Kirshner) names a foreign resident in Athens (metic) who gave 100 minas, a considerable sum of money, for the ransom of Athenians in Sicily.

VIII

The Elusive Checkmate

After the disaster for the Athenians at Syracuse, the Greek world must have anticipated a speedy end to the war. Many states which had been ambivalent in taking sides hitherto now committed themselves firmly to the cause of the Peloponnesians (VIII. 2. 1). Syracuse was now expected to sail east immediately with its victorious fleet and join a blockade of the Peiraeus. But this was not a realistic prospect. The expenditure incurred during the siege had left Syracuse drained of resources and there was a need for retrenchment. Nonetheless, in 412 BC, a year after the Athenian defeat in Sicily, we find a contingent of twenty-two Sicilian ships joining the Peloponnesian fleet. Unsurprisingly, Hermokrates was a prime instigator in the matter and was himself part of the expeditionary force (VIII. 26. 1).

During the winter of 413/412 BC Agis led Spartan forces from the fortress, Dekeleia, in northern Attika to the Malian Gulf farther north where he subjugated the Oitaians and much of Pthiotis. Hostages and funds were taken from the Thessalians whom he tried to bring over to the side of the Peloponnesians. Sparta required the League to build a new fleet of 100 ships in readiness for a spring offensive.

What surprises most is the resilience shown by the Athenians. One of the biggest threats they had to face was the revolt of some of their 'allies'. When it became a choice between sending aid to either Chios or Euboia, the Spartans eventually decided on the former, no doubt considering that their presence at Dekeleia was causing enough problems for the Athenians at that time. Now that Sparta had effectively blocked Euboian supplies coming overland from Oropos, Attika had to be circumnavigated for supplies to arrive in Athens. The Athenians built another fleet and continued to prosecute the war at sea.[1]

The next two years are characterised by naval skirmishes and tactical manoeuvring with the Peloponnesians encouraging and aiding revolt and the Athenians attempting to quell those of their allies who dared to change sides. Persia had now come into the reckoning. First Tissaphernes, then Pharnabazos, satraps to the Great King, solicited assistance from Sparta in the hope that they would regain control of the Greek cities on the Asian littoral.[2] During this time Alkibiades busied himself in the politicking between Tissaphernes and the Spartans. Eventually Sparta realised that he was not acting in their interests. Indeed, his continued dissimulations toward both oligarchic and, later, democratic elements in Athens appear solely to have been made for the purpose of securing his recall and elevation to a position of command. There is little detail by which the actions and abilities of participating commanders can be assessed during this period, until towards the abrupt close of Thucydides' account.

In 411 BC, the last year to be chronicled by Thucydides, two actions stand out from the rest in being described in more detail.

The first, occurring at a time of significant political unrest in Athens, was the foray of an allied Peloponnesian fleet of forty-two ships. These sailed from their rendezvous in Lakedaimon to Epidauros, then to the island of Aigina – which was pillaged – and back to Epidauros. The democrats in Athens, whose initial intelligence had suggested that the enemy fleet was bound for Euboia in support of a likely rebellion there, were dismayed by this incursion into the Saronic Gulf. They became convinced that it was coming at the behest of the oligarchs, who had fortified part of the entrance to the Peiraeus when the Peloponnesian fleet under the command of Hegesandridas moved north from Epidauros to Megara. The fortification was demolished and shortly after news came that the Peloponnesian fleet was now sailing along the coast of Salamis (VIII. 94. 1). It is not clear which coast, the western, out of sight of Athens, or more likely, the more threatening east coast, between the mainland and Salamis, passing Peiraeus. The present author suggests the latter route for two reasons. First, with the greater part of the Athenian naval resources deployed in the eastern Aegean there were insufficient warships at the ready in Peiraeus to pose a problem for the Peloponnesian fleet. Second, this fleet is described (VIII. 95.1) as skirting the shore of Attika before rounding the cape at Sounion.

It has been generally accepted that Book VIII was set down in note form for revision into a final version. This would explain the unusual lack of specifics in this book compared to what had gone before. We must accept that whatever further notes followed the abrupt end in 411 BC, covering the remainder of the conflict, are irrecoverable. Thucydides' usual careful cross-checking of all possible sources of information, both Spartan and Athenian, had probably been completed but had not yet been applied to a final version.

A hesitancy in parts of the text suggests that these were matters which had to be clarified for any final version and that Thucydides in treating them in this way was setting down 'markers' for himself on what should be checked. One such 'marker' section which resonates with caveats is:

Now it may well be that Hegesandridas was acting in accordance with some prearranged understanding when he hovered about Epidauros and that neighbourhood, but it is possible that in tarrying there he also had regard to the dissension prevailing among the

Athenians, and was hopeful that possibly he might arrive in the very nick of time. However this may be... (VIII. 93. 2-3)

After coming to an anchorage between Thorikos and Prasiai just north of the silver mines on the eastern seaboard of Attika, the fleet proceeded northward to Oropos. This had been captured by the Boiotians in the winter of 412/411 BC. The intention was obvious: to assist in a revolt of Euboia. This caused consternation at Athens where all possible naval resources were mobilised. To lose Euboia was to lose supplies close at hand. The squadron already in the area was much too small to afford protection. The Athenian commander Thymochares, following on, managed to rendezvous with the Euboian squadron at Eretria. He now had a fleet of thirty-six ships under his command.

The battle zone would favour the Peloponnesian ships. Sea room was fairly restricted. The unimpeded view of the opposite shore-line would make any move by the enemy immediately obvious. The very approach of the ships under Thymochares would have been clearly seen from some distance away; Hegesandridas used the time of approach to breakfast his forces.

The newly arrived Athenians had obviously disembarked and dispersed to seek their own refreshment. There is evidence of a well-laid plan, the intent of which was not merely the defeat of the Athenian fleet but also the annihilation of the crews.

But they [the Athenians] chanced to be providing themselves with food for their breakfast, not in the market place – for by design on the part of the Eretrians nothing was being offered for sale there – but from the houses in the furthest parts of the town; and this had been so arranged that while they were manning at their leisure the enemy might surprise them by their attack and force them to put to sea in haphazard fashion. (VIII. 95. 4)

Further, it had been arranged that Hegesandridas would be given a signal when the dispersal of the crews was most complete. This signal was obviously visual and, on its sighting, the attack started. Modern Eretria covers much of the ancient site. It is a relatively flat area rising inland towards the theatre and the slope to the acropolis. The ancient shore has silted up and the old harbour area is now well back from the present coastline. It is probable that the Athenian ships were drawn up on the shore rather than being in the rather restricted harbour area. Presumably fairly relaxed as they searched for food, it is highly unlikely that entire crews remained together. Hegesandridas would benefit from the time it would take for all the Athenian crewmen to return to their posts by cutting down the sea-room available for the Athenian ships to deploy. Given that the distance between Oropos and Eretria is just under seven miles, the Peloponnesian fleet may well have been at the halfway point before the first of the Athenian ships was launched to meet them. In the scramble to man their ships the Athenians evidently put to sea in no semblance of order. Before they could do so the Peloponnesian fleet would have reached a point where any chance that the Athenian vessels could run for safety was lost. The action probably took place a mile and a half offshore. Thucydides mentions (VIII. 95. 5) that the Athenians did put up reasonable resistance before being put to flight and chased to the shoreline from where they had come.

Their return to what they would have considered to be relative safety was met by the citizens of Eretria who were waiting to slaughter all who came ashore. Some did, however, escape to an Athenian fort inland and the surviving Athenian ships managed to make their way north to the narrows at Chalkis.

Twenty-two Athenian ships were captured with the crews either killed or made prisoner. A massive defeat, and the inevitable loss of Euboia followed, the Athenians only holding on to a position in the very north of the island at Oreos. This was a magnificently organised and executed action for which Hegesandridas must be applauded. (See map, page xxiii.)

What strategy was Sparta following? Obviously winning the war or achieving a peace was the aim, but the strategy itself is not wholly clear. There seems to be an ignorance of Spartan policy at this time on Thucydides' part.[3] Perhaps this was something which he would have sought to address had book VIII received its expected revision.

In the initial manoeuvres around Epidauros, Aigina, Megara and Salamis, Hegesandridas had posed a threat to Athens itself. It appeared that, given the opportunity, he might well have attempted an attack or blockade of Peiraeus itself. It is therefore difficult to understand why Hegesandridas, after his successful action off Eretria, did not immediately sail first south to round Sounion and then up to the port of Athens. The Athenians were now without sufficient naval defence and, with both sea and landward approaches blocked, Hegesandridas could well have achieved the result that Lysander was to achieve some seven years later. The war could well have been decided much earlier. The knowledge that an Athenian Aegean fleet still existed should not have been a deterrent, considering that a Peloponnesian fleet of similar or greater size was in the same waters. It would seem that the Spartans proceeded from one objective to the next in a disjointed fashion, the next stage or target being decided upon *after* the achievement of the first. It is almost as if their commanders, kings apart, needed to be directed to a singular objective, the completion of which necessitated recourse to Sparta for further orders.[4] If true, this is effectively an *absence* of strategy.

Initiative, with some exceptions such as Brasidas, appears limited. Even the eminently successful Gylippos merely completed the requirements of his mission. His initiative was circumscribed by that mission – the defence of Syracuse and the prosecution of the war in Sicily against the Athenians.

Apart from serving as a subordinate to Lysander and being ordered by him to take the captured finances of the Athenians after the battle of Aigispotamai to Sparta, there is no record of his ever having been given a further command in the remaining years of the war. Perhaps his talents were recognised more as a land commander than as a potential Admiral.

> ...the Lakedaimonians proved the most convenient people in the world for the Athenians to make war upon. (VIII. 96. 5)

The ultimate victory achieved by Lysander was the destruction of the Athenian fleet and the closing of the grain routes from the Black Sea area to Athens. The difference here was the continued existence of a strong Athenian fleet. Had Hegesandridas attempted a blockade of Athens, it is likely that he would have drawn the whole Athenian Aegean fleet back to defend its homeland or created a division in Athens' naval strength. Part would have come to attempt the liberation of Athens despite the internal political dissension, and part would have remained to defend interests in the northern Aegean. Either outcome would have been preferable to doing nothing to threaten Athens. Hegesandridas' action can be admired for its immediate success and for the secession of Euboia from Athens that followed. But there does at first sight appear to be a missed opportunity to build further on this success. A closer analysis of the activities of the Spartans and their allies, however, might lead to a different conclusion: that Spartan strategy was to deprive Athens of supplies from both Euboia *and* the Black Sea area.

Thucydides hints that Mindaros, the admiral of the Aegean Peloponnesian fleet, moved towards the Hellespontine area at the invitation of the Persian Satrap Pharnabazos (VIII. 99). But the timing of that move had links to what was going on in Greece itself. The northward move to the bottle-neck from the Black Sea was made soon after the sea action off Eretria. Mindaros had eventually been persuaded that the reinforcing Phoenician fleet promised by the rival satrap Tissaphernes would never come. The acceptance of Pharnabazos' long-standing invitation to join with him in actions against Athenian-held cities had much to do with Tissaphernes' vacillation, but perhaps there was another motive behind Mindaros' move north. Although there is no proof that the two operations, Eretria and the Hellespont, were planned in conjunction, the sequence of events appears rather too 'structured' and effective not to have been so. If, indeed, it was planned, the criticism of Spartan strategy made above is ill-founded. Unfortunately, there is no direct evidence to support this and Thucydides' unchanging view that the Spartans were 'convenient' enemies must stand – except for the following clue:

> Meanwhile the Peloponnesians on their part left Abydos and sailed to Elaeus, where they recovered such of their captured ships as were

sound – the Elaeusians had burned the rest – *and sent Hippocrates and Epicles to Euboia to fetch the ships that were there.* (Author's italics, VIII. 107. 2)

This proves that Mindaros knew of the successful action of Hegesandridas or of his intention to sail to waters adjacent to Euboia. Hegesandridas' threatening manoeuvres in the Saronic Gulf prior to his move on Eretria are explicitly ignored in the statement. Mindaros knows where the ships are and sends Hippokrates to Euboia. A variety of conflicting conclusions are possible; that communications between the mainland and the Spartan Aegean fleet were secure and regular; that Mindaros was to keep Athenian ships fully occupied while the Euboian campaign was carried out; that this information concerning the whereabouts of the Euboian fleet was received *after* the battle of Kynossema (see below); that both operations were part of a single, developed plan to deprive Athens of ready supplies. If the last is true, the attempt to win the war by securing control of both Euboia and the Hellespontine area proves that Sparta did indeed have a well developed strategy. To occupy Dekeleia was not enough. Even to capture Euboia, although very damaging to Athens, would never achieve victory. All seaborne supplies had to be cut off.

That the Athenian fleet held firm and continued to block the Spartan fleet from moving north to the Hellespont while Sparta was having its successes in Euboia could have been in part caused by the disaffection of the 'democratic' forces based at Samos with the oligarchic government at Athens.[5] It proved to be the correct decision (or even outcome of indecision). To have sailed home would have been to leave the enemy to take control of the empire and of their lifeline through the Hellespont (VIII. 96.4).

To return to the movements leading up to the battle of Kynossema:

Mindaros put off from Miletos in good order and, giving his fleet *the command without previous notice* that his move might not become known to the Athenians at Samos... (Author's italics, VIII. 99)

This may well have been normal practice when seeking to preserve secrecy, but whether it was or wasn't, such an order could steal a head start for a fleet which required time to reach an objective unanticipated by the enemy. From the Spartan base at Miletos, Mindaros' task was to sail past Samos and then Lesbos with seventy-three ships. Earlier that year sixteen vessels had been sent to ravage the Chersonnesos adjacent to the Hellespont and these were now on station at Abydos on the opposite shore. Again, it must be asked whether these had not been sent ahead as part of a greater enterprise. To the Athenians they were merely a nuisance and represented no real problem. The larger fleet was a different matter. It was a definite threat to the waterway itself.

The Athenian admiral Thrasyllos had managed to arrive at Lesbos from Samos with fifty-five ships while the Peloponnesian fleet was at Chios. He was in a good position to thwart any further movement north. There is no suggestion of tardiness on either side, but the Peloponnesians had been delayed by early adverse weather and had taken shelter farther west of Samos at Ikaros. This had allowed Thrasyllos to take up his position at Methymna in advance of the enemy. There he set up observers on both the island and the mainland to give warning of any sighting of the Peloponnesian fleet. His position at Methymna at the north of Lesbos was an ideal point from which to intercept Mindaros on whichever side of Lesbos he chose as his route north. Thucydides suggests (VIII. 100. 2) that Thrasyllos had decided to attack the Peloponnesians if they were to stay for any length of time at Chios. The situation on Lesbos had been complicated by an earlier attack on Methymna by a small force of 300, made up of fifty exiles and mercenaries led by Anaxarchos, a Theban. This small army had been unsuccessful in its attempt to bring over Methymna to the side of Sparta and had moved to the south-west of the island to successfully bring Eresos to revolt against the Athenians.

Presuming that his corps of observers would give him warning of any approach of the Peloponnesian fleet, Thrasyllos decided to move against Eresos. He was joined by Thrasyboulos with five triremes and arrived at Eresos with assault engines and a fleet further increased to sixty-seven ships by five Methymnian vessels and two Athenian ships returning to Athens from the Hellespont.[6]

Descriptions of Mindaros seeing that the provisioning and payment for his men was in order suggest that he accounted morale as important as haste. He had stayed only two days at Chios.

Had the Peloponnesian fleet attempted to sail past in open sea the Athenians would have given battle. Mindaros obviously had intelligence of the Athenian position and had chosen to pass between the mainland and the eastern side of the island. This proved to be a most successful move and by sailing from before dawn until midnight from Arginousai, he was able to reach Rhoiteion and Sigeion at the southern entrance to the Hellespont. Mindaros had outwitted the Athenians by the timing of his sailings and the route taken. It is obvious from VIII. 101. 2–3 that a considerable part of his voyage past Lesbos was undertaken before daylight.

Although Mindaros proved himself later to be a much more enterprising admiral than the majority of his predecessors, reasons for taking this route seem fairly obvious when viewed with hindsight. The Peloponnesians still feared Athenian naval skills and avoided open waters as much as possible. They had avoided action even when they had significant naval superiority in numbers. The choice of this route allowed them the possibility, if discovered, to either take refuge onshore or to engage in restricted waters. (See map, page xxiv.)

Halfway up the Hellespontine waterway, on the opposite coast, lay Sestos, where a squadron of eighteen Athenian ships was stationed. They were alerted by signals, presumably fires, that the Peloponnesian fleet was entering the Hellespont. Naturally their commander did not wish to be caught in enclosed waters and proceeded south along the coastline in an attempt to gain the open sea before their passage was blocked. They did succeed in passing the Peloponnesian squadron on the opposite shore at Abydos referred to above. The commander of those sixteen ships was aware of the Athenians' movements but was correct in not attempting to confront them, knowing that Mindaros' fleet would inevitably make contact farther south. Four Athenian ships were captured before the remainder outstripped their pursuers and made landfalls at the islands of Lemnos and Imbros.

Joined by the Abydos squadron, Mindaros' fleet now numbered eighty-six ships. With these he threatened Elaios at the southernmost tip of the Chersonnesos. The town refused to capitulate and the fleet moved north to anchorage at Abydos. To all intents and purposes the Peloponnesians now held control of Athens' lifeline and it would only have been a matter of time before Athenian-held towns on the coast of the narrows were subjugated. The only hope for the Athenians was to wrest back control by coming to battle.

Thucydides mentions that it was the failure of the Athenian observers that allowed the Peloponnesian fleet to move around Lesbos, leaving the Athenian commanders Thrasyllos and Thrasyboulos bypassed on the opposite side of the island. No blame can be levelled at Thrasyllos for the Peloponnesian fleet eluding him. In moving from an ideal position at Methymna for interception by either route he had set up what must have been assumed to be a secure signalling system, which could have allowed him to move back to Methymna to forestall any further move north by the enemy.[7]

Abandoning their siege, it took the Athenians the best part of two days to reach Elaios. There, five days were spent in making preparations for battle and making further enlargement of the fleet by incorporating the ships from those which had earlier taken refuge at Imbros.

The opening move was made by the Athenians. Their fleet of seventy-six vessels deployed in column and moved north along the coastline towards Sestos into narrowing waters. The Peloponnesian fleet of eighty-six ships moved out and south from Abydos to meet them. The width of the available channel in this area is between one and three miles, with the narrowest point being between the promontory of Kynos sema (Dog grave, from where the name, Kynossema, of the battle is derived), and the opposite shore. Thucydides is quite clear about the extent of the opposing lines. When both lines were engaged, the Athenian fleet was between Idakos and Arrhiana on the European coastline and that of the Peloponnesians from Dardanos to Abydos on the Asiatic (VIII. 104. 2).

However, much had happened before these parameters were achieved. Thrasyllos on the left was faced by the Syracusans, and Thrasyboulos on the right by Mindaros. As the Peloponnesian fleet advanced in line the Syracusans enjoyed a significant overlap. With the Athenian fleet still proceeding in column in an attempt to improve its overall position before facing the enemy, Thrasyllos passed Kynossema and was lost to view by the remainder of the Athenian fleet. His quick extension of the line on the left to avoid being outflanked by the Syracusans stretched the overall line but weakened the centre, which was obviously not moving quite as quickly as the ships under Thrasyllos. He was unaware of the plight of the centre and was caught up soon thereafter in a skirmish, away from the main battle, with the Syracusans, out of sight of both sides beyond the headland. Meantime the Athenian centre was routed and driven to the shore.

It was the intention of Mindaros to contain the entire opposing fleet within the confines of the narrows and to seek to inflict a decisive defeat on an Athenian fleet of lesser numbers. This accounts for his attempt to outflank Thrasyboulos at the start of hostilities. Both the Peloponnesian centre and right would have engaged prior to Mindaros, there being less water to be covered by the attacking ships in these areas of the contest. It may well be that Thrasyboulos attempted to cover this outflanking attempt by extending his wing a little distance back in the direction from which it had come. This would have had the effect of further weakening the Athenian centre as both Athenian wings moved in opposite directions. With victory won early by the Peloponnesians in the centre, some confusion ensued as individual pursuits took place. Similarly, Mindaros' wing, in full knowledge of the success of their centre, allowed some indiscipline to appear in its own formation. With the integrity of line thus disturbed, Thrasyboulos turned from his southerly move to face his pursuers. Having put Mindaros to flight, Thrasyboulos continued to roll-up the disorganised Peloponnesian centre. Around the headland Thrasyllos had gained the upper hand over the Syracusans. These last broke and fled when they saw the remainder of their fleet making for safe haven.

This was a fortunate victory for the Athenians. Although Thrasyllos had more than held his own against the Syracusans, he must take responsibility for the weakening of the fleet's centre. His success in negating the overlap which might have been enjoyed by the Syracusans had he not rounded Kynossema can be balanced against the fact that he lost contact with the remainder of the Athenian fleet, leaving it to Thrasyboulos to seize victory. Mindaros' attempted *periplous* with his left flank was initially thwarted by Thrasyboulos, who merely extended the distance to be sailed to achieve the objective. In so doing he was calling for some supreme seamanship from his men. They would have to retrace some of the waters already crossed. To do this in good formation, whilst keeping sufficient distance between themselves and the enemy, would not be easy. In the jockeying for positional advantage while on the move, with both sides probably in parallel column, each seeking to out-row the other, Thrasyboulos read the battle well and took his opportunity to move from a reactive to an active role. But he must take some responsibility for the disaster which beset the Athenian centre whose commander is not named in the account. With his preoccupation for lengthening his section of the line, his initial manoeuvre may well have given Mindaros the impression that he was running for safety following the collapse of the centre. It seems highly likely that he found himself in a position to achieve a *periplous*, or sailing around, on Mindaros' line. Having perceived the break-up of the formation of the successful Peloponnesian centre and its preoccupation with the destruction of the opposition, he took the opportunity to engage the Peloponnesian left wing before it could be reinforced by a regrouped centre. The element of surprise in his switch to aggression is not to be underestimated.

Diodoros (XIII. 39.5) mentions each side manoeuvring to try to gain the advantage of not having to row against 'the current' and that this 'was of no little hindrance where the strait was narrow'. (See map, page xxv.) The manoeuvres he describes being employed by the Athenian pilots make for a better understanding of what took place.

For although the Peloponnesians had the advantage in the number of their ships and the valour of their marines, the skill of the Athenian pilots rendered the superiority of their opponents of no effect. For whenever the Peloponnesians, with their ships in a body, would charge swiftly forward to ram, the pilots would manoeuvre their own ships so skilfully that their opponents were unable to strike them at any other spot but could only meet them bows on, ram against ram. Consequently Mindarus, seeing that the force of the rams was proving ineffective, gave orders for his ships to come to grips in small groups, or one at a time. But not by this manoeuvre either, as it turned out, was the skill of the Athenian pilots rendered ineffective; on the contrary, cleverly avoiding the oncoming rams of the ships, they struck them on the side and damaged many. And such a spirit of rivalry pervaded both forces that they would not confine the struggle to ramming tactics, but tangling ship with ship fought it out with the marines. Although they were hindered by the strength of the current from achieving great success, they continued the struggle for a considerable time, neither side being able to gain a victory. While the fighting was thus equally balanced, there appeared twenty-five ships which had been dispatched to the Athenians from their allies. The Peloponnesians thereupon in alarm turned in flight toward Abydos. (Diodorus XIII. 40. 1–4)

Diodoros is probably correct to emphasise the superiority of the Athenian pilots as being a decisive factor. The detail of the manoeuvres is useful and plausible. It is, however, unlikely that the battle on this wing lasted as long as he suggests. Time would have brought a re-formed Peloponnesian centre to the support of Mindaros and Thucydides' description of Thrasyboulos' opportunism is far more convincing. The 'twenty-five ships' do not figure in Thucydides' description and may be Diodoros muddling this battle with that of Abydos (see below).

Obviously this victory raised the morale of the Athenian fleet. Twenty-one of the Peloponnesian fleet were captured for the loss of fifteen of their own. The battle could well have been more disastrous for the Peloponnesians had the shore not been so close to the action, affording places for retirement.[8] They later recovered some of their vessels at Elaios and, as has been discussed above, sent for the fleet which was presently off Euboia.

The importance to Athens of this victory is impossible to overstate. To have been defeated would have been to lose the food supply from the Black Sea area, and to cede control of the sea to the enemy with the consequent defection of 'allies'. Following as closely as it did on the loss of Euboia, the war could quickly have come to a close. Any significant loss of ships would have been difficult to replace given the state of Athenian finances. Thrasyboulos' victory was momentous.

This is the last action reported in Thucydides' account; the following narratives are taken from Xenophon and Diodoros. Problems arise when dealing with their accounts. Often they are at variance one with another and common sense must be applied in the handling of these sources.

Mindaros was still in the Hellespontine area and was awaiting reinforcements. Despite his lack of success he had shown courage and tenacity and was proving that Sparta was at last producing commanders who would prosecute the war more vigorously at sea. The Athenians, although buoyed up by their victory at Kynossema, still faced the problem of dislodging him and this was not to be a straightforward matter. Their victory had not been decisive.

The case for the existence of a concerted Spartan strategy to deny foodstuffs and supplies to Athens is proven, in the opinion of the present author. Looking at their achievements and their reported intentions it is clear that the Hellespont was an early target for Sparta after the Athenian disaster in Sicily. (Their choice of Astyochos as *navarch*, however, was not a good one.) Sparta had forced Athenian supplies to be taken from Euboia by sea rather then the quicker and more convenient overland route. In 411 BC, with the greater part of the Athenian fleet obliged to be in the eastern Aegean, Sparta had successfully taken Euboia. In preparation for a move against the Hellespont a small army under Derkyllidas had gone north from Miletos overland to support the revolt of Abydos and Lampsakos. As early as summer 412 BC, at an allied meeting in Corinth, it was decided to send ships first to Chios, then to Lesbos, and then on to the Hellespont under Alkamenes who, on arrival, was to pass over their command to Klearchos. He was then to operate in the region in conjunction with the Persian satrap Pharnabazos (Thuc. VIII. 8. 2). During the following winter twenty-seven ships were requisitioned for an expedition in the Hellespont. They carried eleven Spartiate advisers with them to encourage a more positive approach to the war than had been shown by the timorous Spartan *navarch* Astyochos (VIII. 39. 1–2).

The long overland route of Derkyllidas and his army has been described as inevitable because of the Peloponnesian fear of Athenian seapower.[9] But while there can be little dispute that the Spartan *navarch* was extremely reluctant to engage, the circumstances make the decision a sound one even so. The seamanship of the Athenians really was infinitely better at this time than that of the Peloponnesians, so it was a healthy fear. To attempt to transport land forces by sea in waters controlled by the enemy would have been to court disaster. The transport ships would have been slower and less manoeuvrable. In addition, the land route sent a powerful psychological message to the Greek communities on the Ionian littoral. A Peloponnesian army marching unimpeded demonstrated that, while the sea was in the control of Athens, the land was always likely to be under the control of the Peloponnesians when and where they so wished. Contacts with communities on that march would have been invaluable. An unhindered passage through areas assumed to be allies of Athens or within her empire would have sent a powerful message to the Greek world.

Returning to the aftermath of Kynossema, both sides sought to regroup for the inevitable next contest. The Athenians moved north to retake Kyzikos, which had revolted against them earlier that year. Mindaros attacked Elaios and retook the ships captured from his fleet. He had also requested Hegesandridas' fleet at Euboia to join him in the Hellespont. As we near the end of Thucydides' narrative we encounter an example of the kind of problem of interpretation periodically faced in the sources.

We learn from Xenophon (I. 1. 1) that had Hegesandridas' flotilla not encountered storms near Mt Athos, the combined Peloponnesian naval forces would have had an overwhelming advantage. With the remnant of his fleet Hegesandridas defeated a larger contingent of Athenian vessels before joining with Mindaros. Diodoros, on the other hand, makes no mention of this minor battle and states that the Spartan commander was Epikles (XIII. 40. 1–3). Thucydides also makes no mention of the storm or the engagement, though we are right at the end of his work. He also states that the commanders of the Peloponnesian reinforcements from Euboia were Hippokrates and Epikles. It seems likely that the storm did occur, otherwise the number of Peloponnnesian ships at Kyzikos (see below) would have been greater.

The next encounter was the product of chance and not planning. Dorieus, a Rhodian commander of ships allied to the Peloponnesians, had managed to sail north to attempt to join Mindaros. Xenophon gives the number of ships under Dorieus as fourteen (I 1.2 ff) and his account states that these were initially attacked and driven ashore near Rhoeteon by an Athenian squadron of twenty vessels. Dorieus managed to repulse the Athenian attack on his shore position and the Athenians retired to rejoin their fleet at Madytos. Mindaros had been making sacrifice at Ilion and hurriedly returned to his base from where, with his entire fleet, he set out to escort Dorieus' small fleet to safety. The Athenian fleet then came out to engage the Peloponnesians off Abydos. The battle was evenly contested for much of the day until Alkibiades appeared with eighteen additional vessels, at which point the Peloponnesians disengaged and ran for the shore where they made a barrier with their fleet and fought from the shoreline. The Athenians captured thirty ships – without their crews – recovered their own previously captured ships and retired to Sestos. The Athenians must have been successful in hauling the enemy's triremes from their positions in the barricade. These would still be afloat, with too little time to beach them.

The bare bones of Diodoros' narrative show some agreement with Xenophon's but in its detail and hyperbole needs cautious attention. At XIII. 45 he has the entire Athenian fleet make the attack on Dorieus, who had enlisted the local troops to help in his defence of the ships and shore. The ships had not engaged at sea in Diodoros' version. Mindaros then comes to Dorieus' support with eighty-four ships and with Pharnabazos' land forces onshore. Diodoros gives the disposition of the naval commanders and it seems likely that he was correct in putting the commanders-in-chief, Mindaros and Thrasyboulos, on their respective right wings and the Syracusans and Thrasyllos on each left wing. The two major fleets engage with ninety-seven Peloponnesian ships to the Athenians seventy-four. Diodoros has obviously added thirteen of Dorieus' ships to the Peloponnesian total, even though Xenophon states that the squadron numbered fourteen. Although Diodoros does not give the size of Dorieus' contingent at the outset, the one vessel which appears missing could well have been an early casualty. In any case the numbers are sufficiently close to be accepted. There follows a description of the battle which closely resembles that of Kynossema in terms of close-quarter tactical manoeuvring, the Athenians turning their bows at the last instant to meet those of the enemy with combat following on deck by the marines of both sides. Diodoros states that the battle lasted for a long time. Rather than the twenty ships under Alkibiades, Diodoros gives eighteen. He adds the detail of both sides hoping that the newcomers are coming to reinforce them and that Alkibiades raised a purple flag as an agreed signal of his arrival. Where the arrangement for that signal was made is not explained.

The Peloponnesians fled for the shore and on the way lost ten ships. A storm rose and its high winds caused problems for the pursuit or attack. Diodoros describes the difficulties:

... for because of the high waves the boats would not respond to the tillers, and the attempts at ramming proved fruitless, since the ships were receding when struck. (Diod. XIII. 46. 4)

Onshore, the Peloponnesians with the support of Pharnabazos' forces beat off the attempts of the Athenians to capture more of their ships. This description is followed by a passage in which Diodoros once more muddles Tissaphernes, his actions and motives, with Pharnabazos. This undermines the author's credibility elsewhere but should not deter us from seeing in some of the detail, particularly the weather conditions, reasons why the Athenians were not more successful on this occasion.

Between the two sources the initial phases of the engagement are more likely to have been in line with what Xenophon describes. It is unlikely that the Athenians would have launched their entire fleet to deal with thirteen or fourteen enemy ships. They had always been confident in their superior tactical prowess at sea and twenty triremes were more than enough to deal with this small squadron. Only when Mindaros appeared to rescue Dorieus was it deemed necessary to commit the entire fleet.

Diodoros indicates that 'it was already night' (XIII. 47.1) when the Athenians retired to Sestos and collected their damaged vessels the following day. Xenophon puts the Peloponnesian losses at thirty ships (I. 1. 7) and later indicates that all but forty Athenian ships set out from Sestos to gather funds while Thrasyllos went to Athens to request further men and triremes. Payment for troops and oarsmen was now a critical issue for the Athenians.

Xenophon (I. 1. 11) has the remaining forty Athenian ships leaving Sestos under cover of night and sailing to Kardia, which lay on the northern coast of the Chersonnese because they had intelligence that Mindaros planned to attack them with sixty ships. Mindaros, unlike most of his predecessors, was intent on prosecuting the war at sea vigorously. This probably occurred in the spring of 410 BC after Mindaros had spent the winter gathering more ships. Diodoros (XIII. 49. 2–3) states that the Athenians vacated Sestos at the end of winter because they feared an attack and adds that from Kardia they sent to Thrasyboulos, Theramenes and Alkibiades to bring the fleets under their control to join them. Thrasyboulos is identified by Diodoros as being the commander-in-chief (XIII. 49. 1), whereas in Xenophon's account of what follows the impression given is that Alkibiades is in supreme command and that it was he who issued the instruction for all Athenian forces to gather. Here Diodoros is preferred. Thrasyboulos was a naval commander of proven ability and it is extremely unlikely that the Athenians would have placed him in a subordinate position at such a critical time. This correct indication of command probably more than anything else lends authority to Diodoros' treatment of the battle that followed. His description is the more detailed. The reader, however, needs to be aware of information in Xenophon's terse account that does not appear in Diodoros but does add to our understanding of the action.

Mindaros, in the meantime, had moved north from Abydos and, with Pharnabazos, had taken Kyzikos after a brief siege. Both sources are agreed on this.

Xenophon gives the number of Athenian ships as eighty-six (I. 1. 13) and both he and Diodoros record that this large force sailed north under cover of night past Abydos and to the north-west of Kyzikos to anchor at Prokonnesos. Their approach could have been well away from the eastern coastline in the wider waterway of the Sea of Marmara, and for even better concealment, between the islands of Marmara and Haloni. The fact that the Peloponnesians and Pharnabazos' land forces remained unaware of such a large force to their north-west and of its approach can possibly be explained by reports of the heavy rains that followed, right up to shortly before the battle (Xen.I. 1. 16). Plutarch in *Alkibiades* 28 also refers to sudden rainstorms of such magnitude that the Athenians themselves, on embarking, did not think that any fighting would take place under such conditions. Alkibiades is reported (Xen. I. 1 15) to have ensured that no ship already at anchor in the harbour could leave to report the arrival of the Athenian fleet to the enemy. Any lookouts set by either Pharnabazos or Mindaros would, in any case, have been looking to the west.[10] Diodoros says a land force under the command of Chaireas was disembarked and ordered to attack Kyzikos, presumably at the same time as the hoped-for naval engagement. The location of the landing of this land force is not known.

The approach even in the unsettled conditions would not have been unduly hazardous for the Athenian fleet. It would have been made in relatively sheltered waters between the mainland and the island of Haloni, then skirting the mainland shore. A sub-peninsula lies almost due east of Kyzikos and this provided concealment for the two squadrons under Thrasyboulos and Theramenes.[11] Just off it lies the small island of Artaki and, between it and the mainland, the waters would have been conducive to a speedy attack.

Both Xenophon (I. 1. 16) and Plutarch (*Alk.* 28) have the weather conditions radically improving. At this point in the narratives there are differences. In Xenophon Mindaros is already well outside the harbour and conducting training exercises with sixty ships. In his pursuit of Alkibiades the other Athenian vessels came between the Peloponnesian fleet and its anchorage. Mindaros' only option was to make for the nearest shoreline some way from the city.

Plutarch has Alkibiades sailing with forty ships towards Kyzikos and offering battle. Mindaros manned his much larger fleet and, while both sides were engaged, the remainder of the Athenian fleet came in support of Alkibiades and their enemy made for the shore.

While Xenophon's narrative is plausible, Plutarch's is not. Plutrach is not guileful enough to appreciate that the Peloponnesian fleet needed to be cut off from its base.

Diodoros has the fleet being divided into three sections, one each commanded by Alkibiades, Theramenes and Thrasyboulos. He describes the outline of their plan, which was to use the force under Alkibiades to lure Mindaros out into open waters where the other two fleets could cut off any retreat back to the anchorage and, by encirclement, destroy the Peloponnesian fleet. Mindaros fell for the ploy and pursued Alkibiades' twenty ships with his fleet of eighty. When sufficiently distant from Kyzikos, Alkibiades raised a signal, presumably like the one he gave when he arrived in the Hellespont (see earlier). His squadron turned and threatened the enemy and the other two Athenian squadrons sailed directly towards the city, denying the Peloponnesians any possibility of gaining refuge there. They turned in face of greater odds and made a landfall at Kleroi where Pharnabazos could give them support with his land forces. There, the Athenians under Alkibiades attempted to haul away the beached Peloponnesian ships and a battle ensued.

Thrasyboulos then disembarked his marines to help Alkibiades and instructed Theramenes to land and join with Chaireas' force as soon as possible. Mindaros, meantime, had despatched Klearchos with a mixed force of Peloponnesians and mercenaries from Pharnabazos' army to block the attempted union of Thrasyboulos' men with those of Alkibiades. This meant that there were two separate engagements occurring simultaneously in both of which the Peloponnesian and Persian forces held numerical superiority. After resisting for what must have been a considerable time, Thrasyboulos' men were heartened by the appearance of Theramenes leading both his and Chaireas' troops. These hitherto uncommitted forces soon broke the resistance of the men under Klearchos and then went on with Thrasyboulos to give aid to Alkibiades. Mindaros, seeing their approach, sent half of his troops against the newcomers while he continued the fight at the ships. When he was killed his men lost heart and fled. Pursuit was curtailed by the news of Pharnabazos' approach with a strong force of cavalry. All Peloponnesians appear to have abandoned Kyzikos and taken refuge in Pharnabazos' camp. The Athenians captured both the Peloponnesian fleet and the city. Xenophon (I.1.18) says that the Syracusan ships were burnt by their own crews to stop them falling into the hands of the Athenians.

The greater detail given by Diodoros is not at odds with Xenophon's short description and permits a fairly clear reconstruction to be made of the sequence of the sea and land manoeuvres. True to form Mindaros had shown great courage, although his decision to pursue Alkibiades' squadron was precipitate. Only his death brought about the final defeat of his forces. His dispositions as the land engagements unfolded were logical and could well have saved the day had his untimely death not occurred before Pharnabazos' cavalry came up in support. The forlorn message sent to Sparta by Mindaros' second-in-command, Hippokrates, which was intercepted and taken to Athens, denotes the despair felt by the remaining Peloponnesians. 'Ships lost. Mindaros dead. Men starving. We do not know what to do.'

It is impossible to identify who it was from among the Athenian commanders who decided upon the naval ruse. Perhaps it was the outcome of joint discussion. All went to plan at sea until the Peloponnesian fleet made for the shore. Perhaps it had been hoped that hostilities would have been confined within the bay of Artaki and that the Peloponnesian fleet would have been largely destroyed afloat. Needless to say the encirclement could not have been complete, otherwise the Peloponnesians would have had to break through to reach landfall. Both of the sources indicate that they were pursued there. Thrasyboulos read the developing land action well and it was his decisions that eventually brought about the tremendous success enjoyed by the Athenians. Even so, he could not have known of Chaireas' position when he suggested that Theramenes' men join with them. Chaireas' relative proximity, like the early weather conditions, turned out to be fortunate.[12]

Sparta made overtures to Athens to bring an end to hostilities. It is easy to see why the Athenians would reject the offer made, with its central proposition that, apart from the exchange of Dekeleia for Pylos, all else would remain unchanged. Athens had lost considerable territory, not least Euboia. Many of her former 'subject allies' had revolted or been drawn to the Spartan side. Although many would have wished for peace, it would not have given the demagogue Kleophon much trouble to persuade the Assembly to reject the offer. They had after all seen the annihilation of the Spartan fleet following a series of stunning victories.

Athens would have done herself a service if she had accepted the terms. The problem of revenue still remained, her manpower and the availability to her of ship-building materials were greatly depleted. Her commanders had been fortunate at Kynossema, Abydos and Kyzikos; but in order to continue to prosecute this phase of the war they had been obliged to suspend hostilities in order to collect monies to support their efforts. Sparta, by comparison, now had the financial support of Persia, even if the Treaty of Miletos of 412 BC had sacrificed the freedom of the Greeks on the Asian littoral.[13]

From the battle of Kyzikos in 410 BC down to 407, Athens held control of the waterways to the Black Sea and her supplies were assured. The Peloponnesians with increasing difficulty continued to hold land bases with the support of Pharnabazos but could do little to cause Athens discomfort. When Byzantion came under Athenian control, Spartan fortunes were at a very low ebb. A general characteristic during these years was the Athenian return to land-based operations using significant forces, for example against Pygela, Kalchedon, Selymbria and Byzantion. With Carthaginian interference in Sicily, further help from the west for the Peloponnesians became a remote prospect. However, all was to change and that change was brought about by two intriguing personalities.

In the same year (407 BC) that Alkibiades finally returned to Athens and was made commander-in-chief, Lysander was appointed *navarch* of the Peloponnesian fleet. Kyros, a son of Darius, was given supreme control of the western satrapies. While the first two appointments were in no way unusual, that of Kyros indicates that the Great King wished to prosecute the war with Athens to a conclusion and to circumvent the machinations of Tissaphernes in particular.[14]

One of Lysander's first decisions was to make Ephesos his base rather than Miletos. This placed him to the north of the main Aegean Athenian base at Samos rather than to its south at Miletos. He could thus move north to the Hellespont without having to run the gauntlet past an Athenian fleet at Samos. He had gathered together a fleet of perhaps seventy ships (Xen. I. 5 1; Diod. XIII. 70. 2). With the arrival of Kyros at Sardis, Lysander and the Spartan envoys with him went inland to meet him.

Complaints were laid against Tissaphernes. In the course of the negotiations, a strong friendship was forged between Lysander and Kyros. At those talks the Spartan ambassadors requested that the payment for oarsmen should be doubled from 3 obols per day to an Attic drachma (Xen. I. 5. 4). This they argued would persuade the rowers within the Athenian fleet to desert. The strategy had been propounded by the Corinthians prior to the start of the war in 432 BC in a speech to the League Assembly.

> ...we shall be able to equip a fleet, not only with the means we severally possess, but also with the funds stored up at Delphi and Olympia. For by contracting a loan *we can use the inducement of higher pay to entice away from them their mercenary sailors; for the forces of the Athenians are made up of hirelings rather than their own citizens.* (Author's italics, Thuc. I. 121. 3–4)

Kyros demurred and declared that the agreement had set payment at 3 obols per day for each oarsman irrespective of the size of the Spartan fleet.[15] Later, however, Lysander's charm had obviously worked wonders on the teenage prince who asked: '...by what act he would gratify him most, Lysander replied: " By adding an obol to the pay of each sailor."' (Xen. I. 5. 6–7).

Kyros agreed and the payment was now set at 4 obols per day. He also cleared all arrears owed to the men of the fleet and gave a month's advance payment. He had brought significant funds with him to sustain several months of naval activity and had given every indication that financial support would be ongoing.

To many at that time it may have appeared that Athens was going to win the war at the last gasp. A change of support by Persia from Sparta to Athens would not have been surprising, but this had not happened. Kyros had come with sufficient finance to maintain the Spartan fleet over several months and there was the prospect of more. The key difference between the two sides lay in the Spartan agreement to permit the Greek cities of Asia Minor to revert to Persian suzerainty. Another, and personal factor, was Kyros' need for land forces in the dynastic struggle which was to come. He, and those who supported him, rightly concluded that a phalanx of Peloponnesian mercenaries was far superior to any other and it was this more than anything else which led him to give full support to the Peloponnesians.[16]

Diodoros describes Lysander's activities on his return to Ephesos. Summoning the influential men from the surrounding area and hinterland he persuaded them that, when successful in bringing the war to a conclusion, he would see to it that they were placed in positions of authority within their communities. In so doing he established a docile political power base eager to support him in all that he wished for.

> And it came to pass for this reason that these men, vying with one another, gave greater aid than was required of them and that Lysander was quickly supplied with all the equipment that is useful in war. (XIII. 70. 4)

All our sources, Plutarch included, give evidence of Lysander's powers of persuasion. There also comes across the picture of a man who brooked no indiscipline and possessed tremendous organisational ability. Xenophon indicates (I. 5. 10) that he dragged the fleet, now numbering ninety ships, ashore so that it could be dried out and put in good order. Lysander took no aggressive action, content to develop the supporting resources for his fleet and to further build his client base. He had no reason for haste. His men were in good spirits, he had a guaranteed source of finance, and time would allow the increase in the oarsmen's pay to have its effect. Desertions from the Athenian fleet would permit him to increase his naval strength. The Athenians, by contrast, were still faced with the problem of raising revenues to support their forces and had to either acquire these by collection from coerced donor cities or by booty from raids. Lysander could focus his efforts wholly on organising and training his forces in relative comfort while the Athenians were forced to deviate from the prime objective of bringing about a naval engagement.

A sea battle was a necessity for the Athenians but if Lysander refused to engage there was little they could do. Alkibiades seems to have wasted some time in attacking Andros, Cos and Rhodes before settling his base at Notion just to the north of Ephesos. Any attempt by Lysander to move to the Hellespont would bring on the desired confrontation. Alkibiades, having left twenty ships with Konon at Andros, was now outnumbered; but with the confidence of past naval successes the Athenians would not have been unduly perturbed. Diodoros has Alkibiades sailing up to Ephesos to invite an engagement and when this was refused going on to Notion (XIII. 71.1). Frustratingly for Alkibiades, Lysander's continued avoidance of contact led to his attention being drawn elsewhere, possibly in support of Klazomenai, a city to the north, now back in Athenian control but beset by attacks from exiles who had brought about its earlier defection from the Athenian empire. This was the location indicated by Diodoros (XIII. 71. 1), whereas both Xenophon and Plutarch suggest Phokaia. Xenophon has Alkibiades going to meet Thrasyboulos who had sailed from the Hellespont to set up a blockade of Phokaia. This is the preferred location and the journey might well have been made for two reasons: to bring additional forces to Thrasyboulos in order to achieve a quick end to hostilities at Phokaia and to discuss the problem of bringing Lysander to battle. Thrasyboulos' ships would have been a welcome addition to counter the gradual but inexorable increase of the Spartan navy.

Alkibiades was without his deputy, Konon, left at Andros. He put the command of the fleet into the hands of his pilot, Antiochos, with instructions not to make any attack on the enemy (Diod. XIII. 71. 1; Xen.Hell. I. 5. 11).

It would seem a straightforward enough order: but why leave the pilot Antiochus in command? There were other subordinate commanders. These were Aistokrates and Ademantos, whom Xenophon describes as being chosen as generals to operate on land (I. 4. 21). With an order not to engage in a naval battle in his absence, it would seem to have been more sensible to have given command to one or other of these land deputies. It has been suggested that these generals went with Alkibiades.[17] However, it would have surely been tactically safer to have placed command into the hands of a proven commander. In the unlikely case of an attack on their position by Lysander a land commander would have been more competent than a helmsman to marshal forces to fight from the shore. The mode was to be defensive until Alkibiades' return. There appears to be no sensible reason for his choice of deputy and the fact that Antiochos would appear not to have followed his instructions shows a failure of character assessment on the part of Alkibiades, a severe handicap for any commander-in-chief.

Diodoros (XIII. 71. 2), following the historian of the *Hellenica Oxyrhynchia* (IV. 1), suggests that Antiochos had a plan to entice Lysander well away from his anchorage. Diodoros follows this by saying that Antiochos was impetuous and wished to accomplish some great deed of his own. This smacks of wisdom after the event. Whereas it has been commonly accepted that this was his intention, the evidence suggests otherwise and will be considered after the description of the action. [18]

According to Diodoros, Antiochos gave orders to his fleet to be in readiness for battle and then took ten of his best ships (Xenophon I.5 12, and Plutarch *Alk.* 35, say two ships, his own and one other), sailing to the enemy and challenging them to battle; at which Lysander launched his whole fleet, sank Antiochos' vessel and pursued the remainder. The Athenian captains gave a general order for all ships to come to their support and were defeated not far from the coastline, losing twenty-two ships. The Oxyrhynchos historian (IV. 1) states that Antiochos had ordered the rest of the fleet to lie in wait until the Peloponnesians had moved sufficiently away from land, suggesting that a repetition of the Kyzikos ploy was indeed the intention.

Both Xenophon and Plutarch have Lysander launching a *few* ships against Antiochos and only committing the whole fleet when some of the Athenian ships came up in poor order to give support when the pursuit was observed. So we have two distinct narratives, with Xenophon's being the more plausible.

The different number of ships in both traditions can make sense if the squadron consisted of ten ships but in two units, Antiochos' vessel and one other sailing some distance ahead of the other eight. Indeed it may well have been the case that the eight were lying hidden on the coast between Notion and Ephesos while the commander's ship and its companion sailed on to the Spartan anchorage. This could account for the initial skirmish as the Athenian eight came up in support of their fleeing companions when the few ships that Lysander had sent to attack the two Athenian vessels pursued it. It could also account for Lysander's quick response in launching his entire fleet. As these Athenian vessels are described as some of the best (Diod. XIII. 71. 2) the pursuit may have been over several kilometres before the tiring Athenians were overtaken in sight of Notion.

Xenophon's brief description rings true:

> Antiochus, however, with his own ship and one other sailed from Notion into the harbour of Ephesus and coasted along past the very prows of Lysander's ships. Lysander at first launched a few ships and pursued him, but when the Athenians came to the aid of Antiochus with more ships, he then formed into line of battle every ship he had and sailed against them. Thereupon the Athenians also launched the rest of their triremes at Notion and set out, as each one got a clear course. From that moment they fell to fighting, the one side in good order, but the Athenians with their ships scattered, and fought until the Athenians took to flight, after losing fifteen triremes. (Xen. *Hell.* I. 5. 12–14)

The flaw in the Diodoros/Oxyrhinchos description lies in the report that Antiochos had ordered the remainder of the fleet to be in readiness for a possible engagement. Had they been so, their order of battle would surely have been much better. The impression given by both suggests that they were totally unprepared. '... he (Lysander) chased them until the Athenian captains manned the rest of their vessels and came to the rescue, but in no battle order at all.' (Diod. XIII. 71. 3–4.)

> But the remaining Athenians, seeing the Spartans had sailed away and were pursuing their force of ten ships, embarked quickly, hurrying to come to the aid of their own ships. But as the enemies were already approaching quickly they could not get the triremes manned before they arrived; but having advanced a little from the harbour of the Kolophians (i.e. Notion) with most of them, the ones sailing in the vanguard...they in confusion without fighting...retreated from the enemy in confusion. But the Spartans seeing the Athenians fleeing pressed on and destroyed or captured twenty-two ships, and blockaded the rest in Notion. (Oxyrhinchia IV. 3–4)

If the Athenians were so unprepared, did Antiochos actually have a plan to bring Lysander to battle? Lysander's later attack on the enemy position is unexpected. The readiness of the Athenians to be expected in anticipation of action was nowhere in evidence. In which case it must be assumed that there never was a battle plan. As Xenophon's account lacks any suggestion of such a plan but does convey, as do the other sources, the impression of good order in the Spartan fleet and confusion in that of the Athenians, he is to be preferred. Add to this the comment at *Oxy*. IV.3 concerning the Athenians: 'But as the enemies were approaching quickly they could not get the triremes manned before they arrived'; this shows that the Spartan fleet had covered almost the entire eight miles between the respective anchorages.

It is possible that Antiochos was seeking to do a little damage to the Spartans by enticing a few ships to pursue him to a point where they could be attacked by the eight and underestimated the response. His squadron would have been too small to cause a problem to the entire Spartan fleet and would not have been able to cut the Spartan ships off from their harbour when they put out into more open waters. To suggest that this was a plan modelled on Kyzikos is to ignore the fact that the Athenian force committed to the operation was wholly inappropriate.

Had there been a plan as suggested by the Oxyrhynchos historian and Diodoros, those described by the former as having been instructed to 'lie in wait until those of the enemy should have moved far off from the land' (IV.1) would surely have been in place. Again, if an engagement had been planned it may well have been the case that the Athenian ships needed a little time to 'get into battle order' but the ships are described as not even being manned (*Oxy*. IV.3) and, at the same reference, as still being at Notion.[19] Lysander was aware that Alkibiades was not present and possibly deserters had informed him also of the identity of the temporary commander. On sinking Antiochos' vessel, which probably had some identifiable insignia of command, he took the opportunity to launch an immediate attack on the main fleet. That immediacy itself speaks volumes for the proof of which side was the better prepared for action.

A fine victory, not in terms of the damage done to the Athenian fleet, but in tipping the psychological balance and for the repercussions. Xenophon (I. 5. 14) indicates that the Athenian losses were fifteen ships, Diodoros XIII. 71. 4 and *Oxy.* IV. 3, twenty-two.[20]

Although the Athenian combined fleets still markedly outnumbered Lysander's, the losses must have been an added inducement to that of pay for deserters. Alkibiades tried to redeem the setback by later offering battle just off the Spartan anchorage at Ephesos, but Lysander was not going to be drawn into conflict against a numerically superior fleet even if the morale and seamanship of his men were the better. Alkibiades' reputation suffered increasingly in the weeks which followed and eventually he was forced once again into exile, retiring to one of his fortresses on the Chersonese. New generals were elected and Konon, on taking over the fleet at Samos, is said to have discovered it in poor spirits with morale at a low ebb (Xen. I. 5. 20).

So, in a few months, Lysander had transformed the situation in the Aegean. Sparta and her allies now had a fleet which, though inferior in number was much the superior in seamanship. His winning for his men of better pay had improved their morale and led to a haemorrhage of mercenaries from the Athenian fleet. So much so that at times they had not been able to man all ships which were available to them. His victory had contributed to a much needed boost in confidence in the Peloponnesian League. All this had been done by a man who weighed risk carefully, organised thoroughly, achieved a level of competence in his forces so that action could be swift and effective and did not permit his enemy any initiative, meantime improving and steadily increasing the forces at his disposal. Perhaps the most significant result of his activities was the discredit which he brought upon Alkibiades, which led to his removal from the position of commander-in-chief, thereby denying Athens one of its more imaginative generals. Imaginative, yes, but apart from his near success in depriving Sparta of its power base in the Peloponnese and bringing them to chance their all at the battle of Mantineia, he had shown competence but not brilliance as a commander. His brilliance was in political persuasion and less so in action. His military record on land and sea has been inflated

Lysander's term of office of one year came to an end and with it the appointment of a young successor, Kallikratidas. With his appointment comes the opportunity to understand two opposing views on the methods by which the war was to be conducted. Some, like Lysander, did not worry about their reliance on Persian finance so long as it brought Sparta ultimate victory. Others like Kallikratidas baulked at the idea, believing still in the brotherhood of Greeks and in the time-honoured morality of the Lykourgan tradition. Unfortunately for those with the latter view those in current ascendancy in Sparta required commanders to follow a strategy of expediency. One must therefore question this appointment on the grounds that those who made it must have known of the opinions of Kallikratidas. Unless, of course, those who favoured receiving help from Persia relied on his obedience and sense of honour to follow the orders of the state whatever the circumstances. Those in his camp would no doubt be pleased that one of their own was now in a position to limit such reliance to bare necessity.

Lysander may have felt aggrieved at being replaced despite the fact that he must have known that his command was only for a year.[21] Certainly the transition of command was uncomfortable and here we have evidence of a similarity between Lysander and Alkibiades in that they thought as much, if not more, of their own glory and reputation as they did for the success and security of their state.

Xenophon is our source for this (I. 6. 1–12). Lysander boasted that he was passing over the fleet as master of the sea. His bluff was called. Kallikratidas told Lysander to deliver the fleet to Miletos by a route which he knew would oblige him to pass the Athenian fleet base on Samos. If he did this Kallikratidas would acknowledge Lysander's mastery of the sea. Lysander demurred and declared that as he was no longer in a position of command he would not do so.

Kallikratidas also found that Lysander had returned unused funds to Kyros and that his authority was being questioned. Lysander's friends were spreading it abroad that Sparta had made an error in replacing him. All in all, the evidence strongly suggests great resentment on Lysander's part at being replaced.

Kallikratidas was obliged to call a meeting of all Spartans present with the fleet to ask their advice, offering to relinquish his command if necessary. No one present suggested anything other than that he carry out the orders of the state. His problems did not end there. Being obliged to go for money to Kyros, he found himself being made to wait for two days for an audience; upon which he sailed to Miletos from where he dispatched three ships to bring funds from Sparta. While at Miletos he addressed the assembly there and told it of the financial problems he faced. Xenophon records that some of those present who were guilty of being actively pro-Lysander made personal contributions to the monies offered to Kallikratidas.

Rivalry and resentment had their place in the war and those who showed splendid qualities of leadership could also descend to the petty. To put all at risk for the sake of personal feelings shows an unacceptable character trait. To put one's own interests above those of the state is unacceptable in a commander. Despite his ultimate success this must deny Lysander a place in the first echelon of great generals.

Kallikratidas took over 140 ships from Lysander, a significant increase in number. The expansion of the fleet may have been Lysander's constant preoccupation in preparation for a decisive move north to the Hellespont in overwhelming force. He may have seen this as a priority over and above an immediate exploitation of his success at Notion. Kallikratidas, however, energetically sought to use the present resources. His future finances were insecure and the time when the fleet would fall back to its previous level of lesser competence might well have been not too distant.

In the absence of any further threat from Lysander, Konon may in part have countered the threat of desertion by keeping the Athenian fleet very busy. He is described by Xenophon (I. 5. 20) as making several plundering raids in enemy territories. This would produce additional and much needed finance and bring his men up to a good state of fitness and morale.

Kallikratidas attacked and secured Methymna on Lesbos when some citizens gave him entry. There, after capturing the Athenian garrison, he gave the city back to the Methymnians, now as Spartan allies, and is reported by Xenophon (I. 6. 14) as having declared that he would not have Greeks sold as slaves. This marked a return to the sentiments of Brasidas and was no doubt intended for public consumption among those reluctant members of the Athenian empire.

Konon was wise not to seek a direct confrontation with Kallikratidas. The fleet under his command was almost half the size of his enemy's. He was faced by an opponent who, unlike previous Spartan commanders, now actively searched for the Athenian fleet. Konon's move north with his fleet of seventy ships to attempt the relief of Methymna came too late and for initial security he was obliged to seek anchorage in the Hekatonnesoi Islands (Hundred Islands) adjacent to the mainland. He was sufficiently distant from Methymna to have hoped to be unobserved before returning south to the Athenian base on Samos. His presence became known to Kallikratidas, seeking to cut off Konon's expected route south through the Strait of Mytilene the two sides caught sight of each other at dawn. What followed is described with stark differences by Xenophon and Diodoros.

From XIII. 77. 2., Diodoros has Konon devising a plan to lure some of the enemy's ships in pursuit so that he could engage them off Mytilene where, if victorious, he could pursue the remainder or, if in difficulties, retire to the city harbour. Diodoros then describes Konon as setting a slow-ish pace so that the Peloponnesians would gradually overtake. The latter eventually tired in their efforts to make contact with the Athenian ships to the rear and on seeing this, Konon gave the signal by means of a red flag, upon which the Athenian fleet turned to attack. The Peloponnesians backed water, had no room for manoeuvre because of the following ships coming up to them and were subject to damage from the Athenians. The left wing of the Athenian fleet pursued their opposition until the bulk of the Peloponnesian fleet appeared, on which Konon sailed to Mytilene with forty ships. There he had great difficulties, outnumbered as he was, and abandoning his ships he took refuge with his men in the city.

This all sounds very heroic and can be dismissed as fanciful. If, as Diodoros continues, 'Kallikratidas, by the capture of thirty ships, was aware that the naval power of the enemy had been destroyed, but he anticipated that the fighting on land remained', why was it necessary for Kallikratidas to blockade Mytilene with fifty ships under the command of Eteonikos prior to the battle of Argunisai, unless there was a significant Athenian squadron remaining?

Indeed, if we follow Xenophon's more believable account (I. 6.15–17), we find Konon just managing to evade being cut off from his intended route and reaching Mytilene. He was pursued by all 170 Peloponnesian ships and forced to come to battle at the mouth of the harbour. Forty of his seventy triremes were able to be drawn up ashore under the protection of the city and the crews of the other thirty ships, which were either damaged or fell into enemy hands, reached the safety of the shore. The distance of the pursuit was just under twenty miles.

Kallikratidas had increased the size of the fleet by another thirty ships since his assumption of command, a clear sign that desertions of mercenary oarsmen from the Athenian fleet were continuing. Diodoros (XIII. 78. 4 –XIII. 79. 7) plausibly describes a battle for control of the harbour entrance which may well have occurred and is omitted by Xenophon. The description contains defensive details which add to our knowledge of ancient warfare although one has to wonder how Konon found time, under the pressure of his circumstances, to complete them. The harbour breakwaters were protected by triremes on both seaward and landward sides. Small boats filled with rocks were sunk in the shallower parts of the harbour; merchant ships were stationed in deeper water with their yard-arms loaded with stones to be used as missiles thrown from above onto enemy ships or on those who attempted a landing. All ships including the merchantmen were stationed with their prows facing the enemy and fully manned, blocking the passage. The ensuing struggle is described more like a land battle.

A blockade of Mytilene ensued with Kallikratidas ferrying his land forces from Chios and summoning the Methymnians to come overland in support. Konon was in dire straits and Athens was unaware of his plight. His only hope was to send news of his position as soon as possible. This was to be no easy matter and Xenophon alone of our sources describes how it was achieved (I. 6. 19–22). Refloating two ships from those on shore and known to be the fastest of those remaining, Konon manned them with his best oarsmen. Side screens were set up and marine hoplites spent the daylight hours on board, only going ashore in darkness. This practice was continued for four days during which the enemy would no doubt have become accustomed to their presence. On the fifth day, presumably before daylight, food was put aboard. In the early afternoon, when most of the Peloponnesians were taking the time-honoured siesta common to Mediterranean peoples, the two ships sailed out of the harbour, one making for the open sea, and the other in a northerly direction towards the Hellespont. Pursuit was made and here it seems that, in following and overhauling the ship on a direct route to Athens, the Peloponnesians had let the other Athenian vessel escape unnoticed, presuming both had taken the anticipated direct route to Athens.

One of the other Athenian commanders, Diomedon, arrived in the Mytilene Strait with twelve ships, though how he supposed he could assist Konon is difficult to understand. He had probably been alerted by the trireme bound for the Hellespont and may have come to the vicinity on the presumption that other squadrons would soon arrive to establish a viable force. Kallikratidas, however, acted swiftly and in a surprise attack captured all but two of them.

Money now arrived from Kyros, which was reluctantly accepted by Kallikratidas for the payment of the men only because of the agreement between Sparta and Persia. He is reputed to have declined a personal gift of money from Kyros.[22]

Athens received the news of the blockade. While it continued there was hope but without intervention Mytilene would fall. Lesbos would be lost and their base at Samos would be under great threat. Any further success by the enemy would lead to defections among the 'allies'. Speed was of the essence for both sides. The Spartans needed a relatively quick capitulation of Mytilene to sustain the impetus.

Both Xenophon and Diodoros make clear the feverish preparations made by the Athenians. As usual these sources differ in detail but are in general agreement that, with those of their allies, Athens mustered a fleet of over 150 vessels. Athens' biggest problem was manpower and she solved it by enrolling for service all men of military age, slave, resident alien, and even those whose duties were to serve as cavalry. This last class would not serve as oarsmen but more likely took up the role of a marine corps. All this Athens accomplished within thirty days (Xen. I. 6. 24) and the relief force set out around midsummer of 406 BC. The city had had to find almost 30,000 men in all, and that from a population which had suffered the effects of the plague and the Sicilian disaster.

Obviously, training for the crews was minimal and the fleet arrived at the Arginousai islands just off the coast of Asia Minor opposite Cape Malea on Lesbos south of Mytilene. They had arrived in time and Mytilene was still untaken. Here the accounts of our sources radically diverge. Xenophon's shorter account contains useful tactical and positional detail. That of Diodoros is fuller, containing implausible detail, and is short on tactical comment; it does throw light on the overall positioning of the Athenian fleet prior to hostilities although his designation of command is muddled.

Part of Diodoros' description, when taken together with the more believable detail of Xenophon, allows a tentative reconstruction of the battle.[23]

Knowing of the Athenian departure north from Samos, Kallikratidas sought to take the initiative in bringing on a battle. He was obviously unaware of the size of the enemy fleet, not that this should have caused him undue concern. His fleet was in prime condition, his men well-trained and their seamanship superior. The essence of the man dictated that he should take the earliest opportunity to destroy the vestiges of any Athenian opposition. His distaste for Spartan reliance on Persian finance further contributed to a desire to end such reliance by a quick and final victory. Tactically he recognised the need to engage the enemy well away from Mytilene, where his rear would have been exposed to attack by the blockaded Athenian ships.

Kallikratidas moved south to a position at Cape Malea on Lesbos, no doubt accompanied on land by a section of his army. From there, on the south-east tip of the island, he could threaten any attempted move up the Mytilene Channel towards the city made by the Athenians. Apparently, at the same time, the Athenian fleet had reached the islands of Arginousai near the opposite coast of modern-day Turkey, just over nine miles away across the channel. Their fires were spotted during the night and Kallikratidas made plans for a surprise night attack (Xen. *Hell.* I. 6. 28). A thunderstorm prevented him putting this plan into operation and his sailing was delayed until daybreak. Had his original intention not been thwarted by the weather the Athenians would probably have been severely mauled. The impression given by Xenophon is one of tactical preparedness, whereas the less reliable Diodoros describes his actions as reactive and hasty (Diod. XIII. 97. 30). In his version Kallikratidas is still at Mytilene when he hears of the Athenian fleet at Arginousai.

The differences between the two are important in that according to Diodoros the Spartan fleet would approach from the north-west, rather than from a position directly opposite and due west of the Athenian position as described in Xenophon. Both sources agree that the battle was delayed, Diodoros stating that strong winds caused the Athenians to refuse an engagement until the following day. This seems implausible because the Spartan fleet was unlikely to have deployed in such conditions.

Both agree there was a numerical disparity. Diodoros gives 140 ships for the Spartan fleet against 150 for the Athenian, while Xenophon gives the Spartan fleet at 120, having left fifty to continue the blockade at Mytilene, to more than 150 for the Athenians. This thirty-plus difference makes sense of Kallikratidas' pilot Hermon advising him not to engage (I. 6. 32), whereas Diodoros' difference of ten or so is not big enough for such a suggestion to have been made.

Analysis of the battle itself is fraught with problems. The assumption that the present-day conditions reflect those 2,500 years ago is wholly a matter of faith. Although the area is well away from the boundaries of the African, Arabian and Eurasian tectonic plates, the region has been subject to lesser seismic occurrences. It is therefore difficult to be fully confident of depths or the contours of islands and mainland. It is easy to assume that this coastline would silt up over time just as Thermopylai is now distant from the coast because of the continuous depositions of the Spercheios and Asopos rivers. However, Thermopylai and similar locations are in restricted waters, whereas the Arginousai islands face open sea with only the southern tip of Lesbos nine miles to the west.

Navigational maps of the last two hundred years have shown virtually no change in depths and, with the nearest significant river outlets being more than thirty miles to the north into the Straits of Mytiline and about twenty-eight miles to the south, alluvial deposits in the vicinity would have been unlikely. In addition, the islands are immediately adjacent to a large promontory, the bays on either side of which show depths of 38 and 78 metres respectively. These would be subject to any deposition long before the area around the islands.

The most interesting aspect of this battle is the formation adopted by the Athenian fleet. Xenophon is quite specific:

> The Athenians stood out to meet him, extending their left wing out to sea and arranged in the following order: Aristocrates, in command of the left wing, led the way with fifteen ships, and next in order Diomedon with fifteen more; and Pericles [the Younger] was stationed behind Aristocrates and Erasinides behind Diomedon; and beside Diomedon were the Samians with ten ships, drawn up in single line; and their commander was a Samian called Hippeus; and next to them were the ten ships of the taxiarchs, also in single line; and behind these the three ships of the navarchs and also some ships of the allies [see below] and the right wing was under the command of Protomachus, with fifteen ships; and beside him was Thrasyllus with fifteen more; and Lysias, with the same number of ships was stationed behind Protomachus, and Aristogenes behind Thrasyllus. The ships were arranged in this way so as not to give the enemy a chance of breaking through the line; for the Athenians were inferior in seamanship. (Xen. *Hell*. I. 6. 29–31)

Here, unlike modern terminology, 'ships in line' can also be 'ships abreast'. The thinking behind this battle line was that it nullified the possibility of a successful *diekplous*. An enemy ship sailing through the line to attempt an attack on the stern or midship of an Athenian vessel would itself be subject to attack from the second Athenian line.[24]

In this case, the second line need not have been 'abreast.' Rather, each squadron of fifteen ships may have been subdivided into small groups of two or three vessels patrolling to the rear of the front line waiting for any opportune bow-on-bow attack or *diekplous* attempted by the enemy.

The Spartans deployed in a single line of 120 ships and this would certainly be line abreast. Hereafter, we enter an area of hot debate which only common sense and knowledge of the possibilities afforded by the geography and the snippets within our sources can help us.

Given that the Athenians by virtue of their inferior seamanship had chosen a defensive battle-order, if their front was continuous, it would have only have been eighty ships (15+15+10+10+15+15) and would have given the Spartans an overlap on one or both wings. However, it has been suggested that the distances between each ship of the Athenian front line was greater than normal, the gaps being covered by the line to the rear.[25]

This would explain why, in Xenophon, the pilot Hermon spotted the disparity in numbers and Diodoros states that Kallikratidas could not make his line equal to that of the enemy (Diod. XIII. 98. 4). However, Diodoros immediately goes on to say that the reason for being unable to do so was because of *'the large space occupied by the islands'* (XIII. 98. 4). He uses the plural. It should also be noted that in Xenophon's description of the Athenian battle lines it seems that no mention is made of a centre, only details of each wing.

Scrutiny of the islands themselves suggests that the Athenian fleet was divided; and for very good defensive reasons. The two main islands stand one in front of the other near the Asian littoral. The present depth between the two diminishes from just over 17 metres at their south to less than a metre near their northern points and is unlikely to have been deeper in the past. This would not afford sufficient draught for any vessel passing between the islands. Added to which, the space between the islands is very narrow. Victory by the Spartans on one flank could not lead to an attack on the other Athenian flank to its rear if it had positioned itself screened by the seaward island.

Xenophon's description of the Athenian battle order suggests two wings without an active centre, the centre being possibly the seaward of the two islands (but see below). He first describes the left wing and then the right wing and omits any mention of a centre, although some have located the Samians and the navarchs in the centre. (See maps, pp xxv-xxvi.)

If, indeed, the Athenians had a long left wing, the front line of which was fifty ships covering almost the usual space of eighty and stretching seaward at the south, and a right wing with a front line of thirty ships covering the distance of fifty, it is possible that both wings had their innermost points adjacent to either of the islands. Here the depths at each end are great enough for navigation, and the shorter right wing would have had the benefit of its right flank being protected by a small promontory less than a mile to its north. A front of thirty on the right with about forty-five yards between each vessel would certainly be sufficient to set up a defensive holding position. In this way the Athenian centre was made up of the islands. This gives credence to the fact that Diodoros describes Kallikratidas as dividing his fleet into two to fight battles against each of the Athenian wings (XIII. 98. 4).[26]

The Athenians had probably acquainted themselves with local conditions by taking soundings of the depths around the islands and gleaning knowledge from the local population. Although there appears to be no evidence in ancient sources for taking soundings, this practice in coastal waters is likely to have been used in antiquity.

It is likely in such circumstances that the Athenians put their best seamen in their longer left flank and attempted to gain victory there by outflanking the enemy while their right held its own against the Spartan left. Xenophon indicates at I. 6. 29 that it was the Athenian left wing which threatened by extending out to sea to outflank the Spartan right.

Of significance was the arrangement of manageable units of ten or fifteen ships under its own commander. This lent flexibility to the Athenian fleet, each unit having its own responsibility depending on its place in the lines.

Under the circumstances the only option for Kallikratidas on the right wing and his colleague the Theban Thrasondas (Diod. XIII. 98. 4) on the left was to attempt to outflank on both wings This would be more difficult for Thrasondas given the restrictions of the suggested location. More likely the battle on this wing developed into a struggle at close quarters with the Peloponnesians attempting prow-on-prow attacks and the Athenians throwing grappling irons onto their enemy's ships to restrict further movement. Kallikratidas would have had open sea but is unlikely to have succeeded considering the extension of the Athenian left. His death (falling overboard while ramming, Xenophon, worn down by numbers as Athenians swarmed over his grappled ship, Diodoros) was the signal for a Spartan retreat. Under such circumstances the pursued are extremely vulnerable and this accounts for the huge losses on the Spartan side (Xenophon says nine out of the ten Spartan ships along with more than sixty allied vessels, i.e. more than seventy; Diodoros puts the Peloponnesian losses at seventy-seven).

The Athenian ploy of causing disturbance of the line of their opponent and holding on the right in a position where both flanks of this wing were protected by land, while attacking with an outflanking movement on the left, was imaginative. Technically the battle was won on this wing. The Athenian right probably had its success after that of the left, there being no indication that it came in support of its left wing.

The sources do not give us sufficient detail to offer anything other than a purely conjectural reconstruction but it must be concluded that Kallikratidas was, this time, obliged to give battle on his enemy's terms. Had he not engaged and waited until a better opportunity arose, the debacle of Arginousai would not have led to an extension of the war.

Since the example of Syracuse, Peloponnesian fleets had strengthened the prows of triremes so that a successful prow-on-prow attack could be made. However, the Athenian battle line was well calculated to counter this. Having already by their dispositions negated the *diekplous*, they could also threaten to take Peloponnesian ships amidships if a prow-on-prow atttack was made. This could easily be done by ships of the second line as a Peloponnesian vessel disengaged and disentangled itself from its target by backing water. As the attacked ship grappled its opponent the task of the ship of the second line was even easier.

This second line operating in the manner described makes an active centre to the Athenian line irrelevant. The idea of some that an Athenian centre was established as a single line with the seaward isle to its rear can be dismissed. With no active support to the rear those ships would have been a sitting target for prow-on-prow attack. If there was a reason for the Athenian battle line to use only the islands and not ships as a centre, this would seem the most convincing and explains why Kallikratidas had to divide his fleet. Diodoros is following the Oxyrhynchos historian or Ephoros in factual detail and reserving his poetic licence for the description of the battle.

> And since he [Kallikratidas] was unable to make his line equal to that of the enemy by reason of the large space occupied by the islands, he divided his force, and forming two fleets fought two battles separately, one on each wing. Consequently he aroused great amazement in the spectators on many sides, since there were four fleets engaged. (XIII. 98. 5)

After the battle the survivors of the Peloponnesian fleet made south for either Chios or Phokaia. The Athenians, meantime, made arrangements to pick up the survivors of their wrecked ships and to sail against Eteonikos at Mytilene. The decision to divide the fleet to complete these two important tasks was a sound one. They would still have been numerically superior to the Spartan blockading fleet. The forty-seven triremes designated to undertake the rescue were under more than competent command. Thrasyboulos and Theramenes whose task this was were present as captains and not as generals. Their wealth of experience was surely enough to achieve the objective, but this does not take into account the weather conditions. Xenophon (I. 6. 35) and Diodoros (XIII. 100. 2) refer to a storm that not only prevented the rescue but also the attack on the Spartans at Mytilene. A Peloponnesian ship had managed to bring Eteonikos news of the battle.

> As for Eteonicos, the dispatch-boat reported to him the whole story of the battle. He, however, sent the boat out again, telling those who were in it to sail out of the harbour in silence and not to talk with anyone, and then to sail back immediately to his fleet, wearing garlands and shouting that Kallikratidas had been victorious in battle and that all the ships of the Athenians had been destroyed. This they pro-

ceeded to do; and when they were sailing in, Eteonicos began to offer sacrifices for the good news, and gave orders that the soldiers should take their dinner, that the traders should put their goods into their boats in silence and sail off to Chios (for the wind was favourable), and that the triremes also should sail thither with all speed. And he himself led his land forces back to Methymna after setting fire to their camp. Konon now launched his ships and, since the enemy had stolen away and the wind was quieter, went to meet the Athenians, who had by this time set out from the Arginusae. (Xen. I. 6.36–38)

Why did the Athenians fail to pick up their survivors? If in the aftermath of the battle, there was sufficient time for the merchantmen at Mytilene to load their vessels, sail off and then to be followed by Eteonikos' fleet, and all this in good sailing conditions, why was this time not also used by the Athenians to save their fellows? No valid reason emerges and one must come to the conclusion that no plans had been made for this eventuality and the arrangements for rescue were made some time after the conflict. The Athenian assembly was correct in expressing its concern on the matter and attempting to establish the truth. The unfortunate outcome, no doubt assisted by the natural human desire of the many who had lost relatives to claim retribution against those deemed responsible, led to the execution of six of the eight generals who returned to Athens. The remaining two generals had chosen not to return.

Athens had deprived herself of the services of Alkibiades and the eight generals who had served in achieving the great victory. Admittedly the outstanding Thrasyboulos and Konon and the capable Thrasyllos were still available but, apart from Konon, these did not figure in later commands at sea. At Arginousai Athens seemed to have departed from giving seniority to a commander-in-chief and moved to a command structure made up from a board of generals. Probably the role hitherto taken by a commander-in-chief was now a matter of a day-by-day rotation among the generals. However, decisions made by 'committee' can often be too slowly arrived at for unfolding events.[27] On a human level those elected into a position of command would be more than a little circumspect given the treatment meted out to their predecessors despite the outstanding success of Arginousai. Although conjectural, it may well be that the more able sought to avoid such appointment. It becomes evident in the following two years that strategic thinking and day-to-day safety measures expressed in the actions of Athenian commanders having to work under consensus lack positive direction. The Athenians appear much more reactive in consequence and this surely was their downfall. Although not mentioned in either of our two main sources, there would appear to have been a further Spartan offer of peace after the battle. Aristotle, in his *Athenian Constitution* 34, claims that Sparta offered to evacuate Dekeleia as part of the peace arrangement. Many of the assembly were inclined to negotiate but the demagogue Kleophon persuaded them against the proposition. Thus it would appear that Athens not only lost another opportunity to achieve an honourable peace but set itself on a course of self-destruction with commanders, mostly of lesser ability than hitherto, probably fearful of the consequences of any action they might take.

Although the Peloponnesian losses had been great at Arginousai, they still had a fleet of possibly ninety ships under Eteonikos based on Chios. A meeting of the Spartan Aegean allies at Ephesos sent an embassy to Sparta requesting that Lysander be appointed navarch. Sparta circumvented the law which did not permit the same man to be admiral more than once by appointing him as vice-admiral under Arakos with the proviso that the ships were actually under the command of Lysander. All our main sources are in agreement concerning this arrangement.

Lysander sailed across to his former base at Ephesos with thirty-five ships. From there he summoned Eteonikos' fleet to join him and ordered allied vessels to make this their base. Once again he set up a programme of shipbuilding and improving the quality and training of the crewmen. In a quite unprecedented manner Lysander also found himself given the tribute from those cities under the personal control of Kyros. He was requested by Kyros not to make any attack on the Athenians until such time as he outnumbered them.

Lysander's activities thereafter are not wholly clear from the available and conflicting evidence. Diodoros has him behind the insurrection at Miletos, attacking Iasos in Karia, and even sailing across to Attika. Xenophon only records the raid on Kedreiai in Karia, but both agree on the brutal outcome for the populations.

What may puzzle is the impression that Lysander seemed able to sail where he wished. He was still heavily outnumbered. The Athenians had 180 ships (Xen. II. 1. 20) and Lysander possibly 140. It should have been imperative for the Athenians to bring about a battle at the earliest opportunity before their lack of resources caused desertions and their opponent's fleet became larger. It may well be that their raiding farther north of their base at Samos was to gather finance through booty. Xenophon reports that they also 'sailed against Chios and Ephesos' (II. 1. 16) but follows this by saying that they were also making preparations for battle, which seems to contradict their approach to Chios and Ephesos. Nonetheless, it shows the Athenians to have been busy, if unfocused. For some unknown reason they had chosen three additional generals.

Lysander then made his crucial move north to the Hellespont. That he could do so is encapsulated in two phrases in Xenophon: 'Lysander sailed along the *coast* of Ionia to the Hellespont...' and 'the Athenians likewise set out thither from Chios, *keeping to the open sea; for Asia was hostile to them*' (author's italics, II. 1. 13–18).

The Athenian fleet, or part of it, was away from Samos at Chios when Lysander made his move. The operational objective could well have been set by the Spartan assembly or ephors before his departure; to establish control of the Athenian grain route through the Hellespont. He could sail with impunity near the Asian littoral knowing that, if challenged, he could take refuge on a friendly coastline. The Athenians by comparison had to take the slightly more circuitous route north in open waters. This brings into focus another of Lysander's skills, that of ensuring that his relations with key men throughout the area were firm. He had in modern parlance taken it upon himself to arrange a secure political interface.

Whatever the Athenian battle plan had been, it had been overtaken by events and may have been the casualty of the 'talking shop' of the generals' 'committee'. Lysander had taken his opportunity and moved north to his intended position where he could threaten Athens' grain supply. The speed of Lysander's operations once in Abydos should be noted. It indicates sequential planning of his operations from the point of his departure north. Using land forces raised locally under Thorax, an attack was made from both land and sea against Lampsakos, which was in a position to intercept merchantmen coming out of the Propontis. The distance to be covered for such an attack was about twenty-two miles. The city was taken and the citizens allowed to leave unharmed, unlike those of Lysander's operations to the south earlier in the year. He achieved his objectives before the arrival in the Hellespont of the pursuing Athenian fleet. The Athenian commanders had been out-thought and out-manoeuvred. Their nearest substantial base was at Sestos but this was a little too far south to maintain realistic observation of the enemy. Any move from Sestos against Peloponnesian vessels coming out from Lampsakos would have been to no avail. The narrow channel would permit the Peloponnesians to seek refuge either by a return to harbour or by making for the friendly coastline nearby before Athenian vessels had covered the distance to make contact.

There seems no reason to believe that conditions in the area have materially altered over time. Today there is a fairly strong mid-current flowing in a southerly direction through the Dardanelles, together with a north-easterly breeze sometimes exacerbated by the funnel-like natural features of the region as a whole. Therefore no criticism can be made of the Athenian generals in establishing their fleet directly opposite Lampsakos, where reaction to a move made by the enemy could be immediate. Where criticism can be levelled is that they made no significant arrangements for food supplies to be regularly delivered to them from Sestos, nor do they appear to have established a market for their men or to have set up a food reserve. They were also without land forces and this factor will be enlarged upon after the treatment of the eventual action.

Lysander had provided the Athenians with a quandary. If the Athenians feared that Lysander's intention was to make his way into the Propontis and the Bosphoros up to Byzantion, a base farther north within the Propontis, such as Kyzikos or Perinthos, would still not ensure that Lysander did not slip by them in the wider waters. Had they protected grain ships in convoy past Lampsakos, they would have been subject to attack without the necessary sea room for effective deployment. Time was against them. The longer Lysander refused battle the greater the financial cost to the Athenians and the greater the likelihood of defections when that finance was exhausted.

All the Athenians could think of doing was to row across the strait and offer battle every morning. With little more provocative to offer it was easy for Lysander to refuse an engagement. He was not in the same position as Kleon (see Chapter V). His men were unlikely to grumble about inactivity following as they did a man of proven record who had procured for them all that they needed both in terms of welfare and booty. Their morale was high, their position secure, they were well prepared and they had a commander they could trust not to risk their lives unnecessarily. There would seem to be nothing to be gained by fighting against superior odds. Technically Lysander held the initiative.

Although Xenophon and Diodoros agree on some details, the former (as usual) is to be preferred when it comes to the description of the so-called battle. Both remark on the increasing difficulty for the Athenians in gathering supplies and both record the visit made to the Athenian camp of Alkibiades from one of his strongholds nearby. Xenophon indicates that Alkibiades pointed out the poor supply position of the Athenians and his advice to them to make Sestos their base was rejected (II. 1. 25). Diodoros (XIII. 105. 3–4) has Alkibiades claim that he could bring a large army of Thrakians supplied by his friends, the kings Medokos and Seuthes, so that Lampsakos could be attacked by both land and sea. This was conditional on his being given a share of the command. The Athenian generals rejected his offer on the grounds that if successful all credit would go to him and not be shared by them. The proposal, if indeed it was made, was tactically sound and reminiscent of Kyzikos where joint land and sea operations brought success. But could Alkibiades produce an army and, if so, why had he not brought it with him? No doubt it would have taken some time to raise and by that time the battle which occurred within days would be over. Was it the opportunist at work again or was there truth behind his claims?

In the preferred account of the action, Xenophon has Lysander preparing for battle from the very morning after the arrival of the Athenians.[28] The men embarked after breakfast and the side screens were raised. All in readiness, the captains were told not to leave the harbour but to hold their positions. The Athenians arrived in battle line outside the harbour and, having met no reaction from the Peloponnesians, returned to their base. Lysander then had some of his swiftest vessels follow to observe what the Athenians did after disembarking. Only on their return were his own men allowed to stand down. The same procedure was followed by each side for four days with Lysander receiving intelligence that the Athenians were foraging farther and farther away from camp (II. 1. 27). On the fifth day his observation vessels were instructed to sail back to mid-channel after they had assured themselves that the enemy was disembarked and well scattered. From there a signal using a shield was to be made. This would not be the flash of the sun on burnished bronze. The time of Athenian retirement is described as being late in the day (Xen. II. 1. 23). The Peloponnesian ships would be returning towards base eastwards with the sun *behind* them. It is more likely that a shield was raised to a position where it could be observed from the shore.

On receipt of the signal Lysander gave the order to the fleet to set out at full speed. It carried Thorax and the land forces. The short distance of just under two miles was covered before the Athenians could properly man their ships. Some are described as having men for only one or two banks of oars and some as being totally unmanned when Lysander attacked (Xen. II. 1. 28). Konon managed to escape with eight ships including his own together with the state trireme, the *Paralos*. He wisely did not return to Athens but went into self-imposed exile to his friend Evagoras in Kypros and the *Paralos* took news of the defeat to Athens.

The defeat was total. Although Xenophon does not do more than say that all the remaining ships were captured, it was not necessary for him to go into detail on what was a predictable course of events. His readers would know what would follow. It is clear that as Thorax and his men were put ashore to attack the camp the Peloponnesian ships laid hold of the enemy vessels by grappling irons and pulled them off the shore. Thorax's men rounded up those who were not killed or could not escape and all were brought over to Lampsakos. Given that our two major sources do not give any figures for the prisoners and that Plutarch (*Alk.* 37) and Pausanias (IX. 32. 9) give 3,000 and 4,000 respectively, it can be assumed that the dispersal of the Athenian forces was quite widespread. If fully manned the total force can be calculated as follows: 180 ships each carrying 170 oarsmen, ten marine hoplites and six archers plus helmsmen and other necessary artisans. This would give a figure of just over 34,000 men of whom 2,880 were soldiers. It seems likely that the majority of the prisoners were from this last group who would have attempted some resistance and who would have had less mobility than crewmen unencumbered by arms. The great disparity between the overall total and those who were taken prisoner may be explained by crewmen not being counted as belligerents in this case. Xenophon's comment (II. 1. 28) that almost all the crews were captured except for those who managed to reach safe haven in neighbouring fortifications and Diodoros' claim (XIII. 106. 6) that the majority of the soldiers managed to reach Sestos are incompatible.

The Athenian generals had not made due provision for security. It is significant that the best of them, Konon, was able to escape with his squadron and shows that he alone appeared to be in some state of readiness with direct control of his men. He too is reported to have attempted by signal to summon a return of those scattered to their ships (Xen. II. 1. 28). Alternatively, it may have been Konon's duty that late afternoon to remain in a state of readiness. If so, his signal came too late for the widely dispersed men to react successfully.

The root of the Athenian failure lies with a neglect of logistics, and here Lysander can be given credit for posing the problems his opposition faced and causing, to use a modern military term, their dislocation. Remaining at Lampsakos forced the Athenians to make the choice between establishing their base to the south at Sestos or, as they did, a good distance to the north opposite the Spartan camp. Having chosen the latter, the Athenians should have set in place a secure camp and possibly built sea protection for their ships. Even more important was an arrangement for a sufficiency of supplies to limit the necessity for foraging. The Athenian commanders' only hope in neglecting to do so was to bring about an early engagement, but knowledge of Lysander's past record as a sea commander should have dissuaded them from thinking he would act in such a straightforward manner. The Athenians gave themselves no options. Their position lacked sustainability. They had been forced into a reactive role from the time of Lysander's move north. Comparison between the arrangements made for the Sicilian expedition and their total lack in this case for a force of similar size, a mere few miles north of the base at Sestos, is indicative of a serious lack of responsible leadership.

In Lysander's campaign his control of tempo was impeccable. His movement from one operational area to the next led to responses from his opponents which were much too late and finally brought them to an uncomfortable location. Had Lampsakos held out a little longer, that tempo would have been slowed a little, but the feasibility of the overall operation would not have been compromised. The Athenian fleet had no adequate land forces with which to mount a joint assault on any shore position taken by Lysander. The Athenians had come with a force which was not adequate for the task. They were clearly the victims of dislocation in that their strength became an irrelevance. There is no evidence that they had any alternative course of action in mind. So at the tactical level Lysander had pre-empted his enemy.

A meeting is reported by Xenophon (II. 1. 31–32) at which Lysander asked his allies to decide the fate of the Athenian prisoners. Such had been the atrocities committed by them and in particular under the leadership of one of the generals, Philokles, that it was decided to execute all prisoners except for one of the Athenian commanders, Ademantos. He was known to have been the lone voice opposed to a decree of assembly to cut off the right thumbs of any taken alive following a successful naval action (Plut. Lys 9).

Thereafter, there is additional confusion in our sources and again Xenophon is to be preferred except for the detail of the attack by Lysander on Sestos (Diod. XIII. 106. 8). There the surviving Athenians were permitted to leave under truce and this fits well with the policy described by Xenophon at II. 2. 2, that Lysander allowed all Athenian garrisons to return to Athens and to no other place, knowing that the more people the city had to accommodate the more acute the shortage of food would be. Instead of going on to lay siege to Samos as suggested in Diodoros, Xenophon has Lysander going to Byzantion and Kalchedon where again the Athenian garrisons were allowed to leave with only Athens as their destination. The latter course is the more probable because this would have given Sparta complete control of the grain route.

Athens then became the object of siege by both land and sea, with Lysander blockading entry to the Peiraeus and the Spartan kings Agis and Pausanias bringing the army near the city walls. There was no need to attempt an assault. The passage of time brought the inevitable capitulation. During the course of the remainder of 405 and into 404 BC Athens made proposals for peace but Sparta's insistence on the destruction of part of its Long Walls led to two rejections by the Athenians. A ridiculous decree was passed by the Athenian Assembly which forbade anyone from proposing peace on these terms. In all probability this was engineered by Kleophon. In face of this domestic impasse Theramenes asked to be sent to Lysander to clarify issues. He is likely to have been sent by Lysander to Sparta as the only place where negotiations could realistically take place and remained there for three months. The reason for this inordinate length of time has never been satisfactorily explained.[29] Circumstances in Athens further deteriorated and Theramenes and nine others were given full powers to negotiate terms

The war was over. Xenophon gives us an interesting insight into the attitudes of members of the Peloponnesian League.

> When they [Theramenes and his nine colleagues] arrived, the ephors called an assembly, at which the Corinthians and Thebans in particular, though many other Greeks agreed with them, opposed making a treaty with the Athenians and favoured destroying their city. The Lacedaemonians, however, said that they would not enslave a Greek city which had done great service amid the greatest perils that had befallen Greece. (Xen. II. 2. 19–20)

Sparta's will prevailed in the matter and Athens became an ally on the usual terms; that she would follow where Sparta chose to lead. From II. 65. 6–13 Thucydides lists the factors which led to Athens' defeat: Perikles' early death and the departure from Periklean strategy made by political leaders whose self-interest was damaging to the state; the debacle of the Sicilian expedition followed by the revolt of allies; active support for Sparta by Persia, and finally Athens' own inner dissension late in the conflict. To these can be added a significant loss of manpower and income and the refusal to accept Sparta's offers of peace. However, in the final analysis, the Peloponnesian League proved to be much more durable than the Athenian empire and produced commanders of outstanding ability in Brasidas, Gylippos and Lysander.

Notes

1. The original Periklean strategy included a requirement for a reserve fund to be held in case of dire emergency and a reserve fleet of 100 ships. Where were those ships now? Obviously they had been committed for use elsewhere. Some may have been part of the armament which went with Demosthenes to Syracuse.

2. Of the main sources for the period following on from the point at which Thucydides narrative ends, Diodoros confusingly ascribes the actions of Tissaphernes to Pharnabazos. Indeed, his history seems to ignore the presence of the former altogether.

3. Thucydides at V. 68. 2 comments on the secrecy of the Spartan government.

4. When in the field, the Spartan kings held supreme power and could decide upon action without needing to consult the home authorities.

5. Plutarch. *Alk.* 25–27 graphically describes Alkibiades' vacillations with both political factions.

6. The Loeb translation is incorrect in giving the total of ships as sixty-five. The text clearly states ʽεπτὰ καὶ ἑξήκοντα. (VIII. 100. 5) indicating sixty-seven.

7 In his chapter on 'Scouts', *The Greek State at War* Part I, Pritchett cites the haphazard nature of scouting and placing lookouts but indicates a more methodical approach being adopted shortly after the Peloponnesian War. He takes as evidence references from Xenophon's writings, e.g. *Hell.* I. 4. 18 and II. 4. 31; *Hipp* 7. 6; *Anabasis* V. 1. 9 and VI. 3. 14; and *Cyr.* III. 2. 1. It could well be that as the war progressed the Spartans became more meticulous in this area than the Athenians. In the writings of Xenophon which cover the next half century, we see much more consideration being given to intelligence gathering and the need to know the position of the opposition. For a description of these developments see the relevant extended sections in *Xenophon and the Art of Command*, Godfrey Hutchinson.

8. Although the waters in the area of the battle were narrow, it should be noted that the Spartans preferred to fight in restricted waters where, if necessary, they could rely on the support of their land forces in times of emergency.

9. *The Fall of the Athenian Empire,* D Kagan, p.101, speaks of the Spartans being 'compelled to send their army to the Hellespont by land'. Later, he gives the obvious advantages of doing so, which perhaps negates the implied criticism for not making this expedition seaborne.

10. Rain clouds in any highland area often roll over the high points obliterating visibility. As the highest points on the peninsula are over 2,000 feet, had any lookouts been posted there, their efforts would have been fruitless. In such conditions they may well have descended to a lower position on the western side of the high ground, which would have given them a very restricted view to the west and north.

11. Frontinus *Stratagems* II. 5. 44–45 mentions such a small peninsula.

12. For a plausible but slightly different reconstruction of the battle see *The Fall of the Athenian Empire,* D Kagan, pp 237–46. He rightly awards Thrasyboulos the laurels for this victory for his successive actions which led to the division of the Peloponnesian forces and for relieving the pressure upon Alkibiades, allowing him to continue his attacks on the enemy fleet onshore.

13. By giving in to the demand of the Great King that control of these communities should revert to Persia, the Spartans had set the clock back almost a century. All that had been achieved in the Persian War and the later activities of the Delian League was set at nought. The claim that Sparta and the Peloponnesian League were seeking the liberation of the Greeks was turned on its head. Sparta may have correctly believed that the lot of the Greek cities would be no worse under Persia than it had been under the Athenian-led Delian League. In its desperation to make headway in the struggle, where finance was a major key to success, Sparta may have viewed this as a matter of temporary expediency. Soon after the Peloponnesian War was concluded Sparta made significant efforts to wrest control of the cities away from Persia.

14. It is no surprise, therefore, that Tissaphernes figures significantly as an enemy of Kyros in the record of the latter's attempt on the throne of Persia, Xenophon's *Anabasis.*

15. This treaty of 412/411 BC was the third to be negotiated between Sparta and Persia.

16. Covert Spartan support for Kyros' attempt to usurp the Persian throne is undeniable. See J K Anderson, *Xenophon.*

17. D Kagan, *The Fall of the Athenian Empire,* p. 314.

18. See D Kagan and the authorities he cites. Kagan suggests that Antiochos had as his model Kyzikos.

19. Kagan, ibid, p. 118. A Andrewes *Journal of Hellenic Studies* (1982) is particularly informative on the battles of Kyzikos and Notion.

20. George Cawkwell's footnote on p.76 of *Xenophon A History of My Times* offers a succinct and plausible account of the action and how it developed. It also offers an explanation for the difference in the number of ships between sources of Antiochos' approach fleet. 'The account of Diodoros XIII.71, plainly derives from *Hell. Oxy.* 4, for the understanding of which the key word is the partially preserved word for a sea-ambush, *[nau] lochein*. Antiochos did not disobey orders. He took a small squadron of ten ships, put eight of them behind a headland, and tried to lure out the 'three ships' which Lysander had used previously as a patrol. The plan miscarried; the eight Athenian ships, Xenophon's 'more ships', were chased home and the Athenian fleet forced suddenly to get out and try to rescue them, with disastrous results.'

21. Sparta appointed an admiral for the term of one year only. With Lysander's later recall the Spartans circumvented this by appointing him deputy commander in title but allowed him to express overall command in practice.

22. Kagan, pp.337-8. In a highly perceptive passage Kagan remarks that the success of Kallikratidas made Kyros aware that he could not alienate the Spartan without damaging his own plans for the future, i.e. his need for a Peloponnesian phalanx for his attempt to gain the Persian throne. Kagan cites Plutarch *Moralia* 222E as the reference for the exchange between Kyros and Kallikratidas which must have been conducted by messengers.

23. Kagan, pp. 340–53 provides an ingenious but implausible solution to the difficulties presented in the sources. His description of the Athenian centre as being a single line is surely incorrect (see note 26) as are the distances given in his description. He gives the distance between Cape Malea and the islands as two miles instead of the true distance of just over ten miles. Scrutiny of Admiralty Chart No. 1061 is helpful in presenting other options. The present author offers an alternative version of the battle line of the Athenians based on the same information but is in no way firmly confident that his description of the action is correct. One such option considers the landward island of the group that is given no consideration in Kagan's treatment.

24. A similar order of battle is reputed to have been seen in a naval engagement between the Karthaginians and the Greeks of Massilia off the coast of Spain, see F Jacoby, *Die Fragmente der Griechischen Historiker* 176; 1, vols I & 2 B

25. Kagan p.346. *The Fall of the Athenian Empire* cites Busolt, *Griechische Geschichte* III 2, 1594.

26. Kagan's description has an Athenian centre deployed in a single line in front of the seaward island. It takes no part in the battle but is described as being

fresh at the end of the struggle and is used in the pursuit of the defeated Peloponnesians even though there is no evidence for this. Had the battle proceeded in the manner Dr Kagan describes, a divided Spartan fleet would have been subject to flank and rear attack from such a centre. He does allude to this danger and suggests that the inactive centre unnerved the Spartans as the battle progressed. However, Kallikratidas did indeed divide his fleet and his reason for doing so was because there was no centre to the Athenian line other than the islands. Kallikratidas was obliged to divide his fleet because that of the Athenians was already divided. To cite Xen. *Hell.* I. 7. 30 in his note 82 on page 351 as proof that the entire Samian squadron and other ships of his centre survived through non-engagement is to overlook the possibility outlined in the present author's description, based on Xenophon's enumeration of the left wing: that they would be positioned nearest to the islands. The desperate part of the fighting would be at the other end of this wing that was seeking the overlap. With the loss of Kallikratidas, resistance was likely to crumble early and those ships well within the extremities of both wings would suffer much less than their more exposed fellows. This could well account for the survival of these contingents.

27. Prior to the battle of Nemea (394 BC) the allies opposed to Sparta wasted much valuable time in debate and lost the opportunity that a quick movement south would have given them to deprive Sparta of additional forces.

28. Kagan, pp.390–3 follows in part the possible but less plausible and more convoluted account of Diodoros and cites Ehrhart, *Phoenix* XXIV, 1970, in his support. It may well be that the Athenians were devising some plan to lure Lysander into a trap. But Lysander's record shows that, at sea, he only moved when he was convinced he could do damage to the enemy with little to his own forces. The fact that he set up observation vessels to monitor the movements of his enemy indicates that he was unlikely to be misled. In choosing Diodoros' version, Xenophon's critics may well have over-reacted to the discoveries of the Oxyrhynchus papyrii and Diodoros' reliance upon the history behind them. Are we then to overlook the gross errors in the history of Diodoros? The obsession with ruses and plans does little to persuade one away from the fact that indiscipline and unreadiness ashore was the cause of the Athenian downfall.

29 Xenophon II. 2.16 has Theramenes staying with Lysander for the three months. It is possible that Lysander kept him against his will so that the privations of the Athenians would increase. Other suggestions have been made. Cawkwell's footnote in Xenophon *A History of my Times*, pp 106–7, suggests that Theramenes may well have been at Sparta and the delay was caused by the need to summon allies from far afield to a peace conference. This does not convince since Theramenes had no power to negotiate a peace. More plausible is the treatment given to this issue by Kagan, *The Fall of the Athenian Empire*, pp 402–9, in which Theramenes sails to Lysander on Samos, his prime aim to save the city and its people and to point to the increasing belligerence of Thebes.

APPENDIX 1

An Outline of the Pentecontaetia

The actions scrutinised in this book – chosen to be analysed in detail for what they reveal about command – are better understood if their context is clarified by a review of the years prior to the outbreak of the hostilities which became known as the Peloponnesian War. Here is an outline of the main events leading up to the conflict.

The Pentecontaetia (period of fifty years) is the name generally given to the time between the end of the Persian War and the beginning of the Peloponnesian War. Thucydides deals with this period in Book I, chapters 89–118, of his history. As it is not his main historical concern, a broader picture of this period can only be achieved by using other sources often of lesser worth.[1] Until his narrative approaches his main concern, the Peloponnesian War, military actions are reported with scant detail.

Following the withdrawal of the Persians from much of mainland Greece after the Battle of Plataia, the leadership of the Hellenic League passed from Sparta to Athens. The reasons for this are variously given in sources and there may be a kernel of truth in the view that the arrogant behaviour of Pausanias, the Spartan commander-in-chief of the league, led to his recall, together with the unwillingness of the allies to accept a substitute commander from Sparta. Whatever the truth of the matter, Sparta left Athens with the task of leading the allies in the attempted liberation of their Ionian cousins on the Aegean littoral.[2]

Probably under the leadership of Aristeides, the allies met on the island of Delos in 478 BC. The decision to carry on the war was taken, its aims being to seek revenge and to ravage the Great King's territories. No doubt the prospect of plunder would be an attraction.

So it was that the Delian League was set up with arrangements being made for allies to contribute either finance or ships for the furtherance of the hostilities. The treasury for this purpose was established on the island of Delos.

In the early days of the alliance members were independent, but as time went on, Athens, with varying degrees of coercion, prevented states from leaving the League and made them subject to her. At the outset it was clear that Athens would be the leader (hegemon) because she had the largest fleet. It was Aristeides who made the assessment of contributions and ten Athenian officials who made the collection.[3]

Between 476 and 468 BC, Athens used the League to prosecute the war against Persia and to gain control of Aegean waters. Byzantion was liberated in 478 BC, thereby reopening the trade route to the Black Sea. Thereafter, Kimon's successful operations led to the expulsion of the Persians from Eion on the Strymon river (476-5 BC). He eventually won a great victory outside the mouth of the Eurymedon river (468 BC.), which destroyed Persian naval power and control of the coast of Asia Minor passed into the hands of the League.[4] Thus it would appear that the work of the Delian League was virtually complete.

All this would be considered laudable and in line with the main interests of the Delian League had it not been that attendant activities suggest that Athens was not slow to act in her own interests. The expulsion of the pirates holding the island of Skyros (474–473 BC) allowed Athens to set up its own colony (cleruchy) there. It is significant that its location is a strategic one on the route from Athens to Thrace and the Black Sea.[5] Similarly in 472 BC, Karystos, a city at the extreme south of Euboia which had not joined the League, was attacked and subjugated. Again its position was highly strategic in securing the eastern sea approaches to Attika. However, to attack a neutral state was not an honourable or acceptable practice to the majority of the Greeks at this time.

Thuydides highlights the disquiet and reports that the allies brought about their own problems to a certain degree:

> Now while there were other causes of revolts, the principal ones were the failures in bringing in the tribute or their quota of ships and, in some cases, refusal of military service…for most of them, on account of their aversion to military service, in order to avoid being away from home got themselves rated in sums of money instead of ships, which they should pay in as their proportionate contribution, and consequently the fleet of the Athenians was increased by the funds which they contributed, while they themselves, whenever they revolted, entered on the war without preparation and without experience. (I. 99)

The actions against Naxos in the early years of the 460s are defensible on the grounds that the islanders attempted to leave the League. This it could not be permitted to do while hostilities with Persia were ongoing. It was forcefully brought to heel and served as an example to others within the alliance. However, around 465 BC, Thasos withdrew from the League after a quarrel with Athens over trade issues and the goldmining of the nearby coast of Thrace from which Thasos derived much of its revenues. It is possible that Athens made unreasonable demands for a share of these revenues but, whatever the reason, Thasos had been one of the major contributors to the League and its attempted departure from the alliance could not be tolerated by Athens.

However, at this time, some three years after the victory at Eurymedon, Persia was no longer the threat it had been nor would it be for some time to come. It can be argued that Thasos and all other members of the Delian League should have been at liberty to withdraw from the alliance and devote their revenues to other purposes. After a sea battle and a siege which lasted for almost three years, the Thasians were forced to destroy their defensive walls, surrender the remnant of their fleet, pay an indemnity, give up the mines and mainland possessions and become subject to Athens. It is significant that Athens obliged the forces of the League to act against one of its members. From this time it becomes increasingly obvious that the League had moved from the position where all members were autonomous to that of a developing Athenian empire.

Athens attempted to establish a cleruchy with 10,000 colonists at a place called Nine Ways on the Strymon river. This proved unsuccessful and the Thrakians destroyed the settlers when they attempted to advance farther inland. It was to be almost thirty years later that the Athenians proved successful in the establishment of Amphipolis in the region. It would appear that Athens was seeking to consolidate its control of the coastal regions along the north Aegean seaboard to exploit the resources of the area and achieve the establishment of a network of safe anchorages.

The Thasos episode is interesting for another reason. At the time of the siege an appeal for help was made to Sparta. That appeal came in the form of a request for the Spartans to invade Attika to cause a major diversion to the Athenians. Athens was unaware that Sparta had agreed to do as the Thasians wished. The Hellenic Alliance (481 BC) of the Persian War was still in place and within its terms Athens and Sparta were allies. Had events gone as planned Greek history might well have been very different. As it was Sparta itself was devastated by a massive earthquake followed immediately by an opportune revolt of the slaves (helots) and some dependent but technically free communities (perioikoi) and was too preoccupied to assist.

What of Sparta between the Persian War and the mid-460s? This appears to be a period in which a lack of positive direction characterises Spartan foreign policy. The obvious evolution of Athens as a counter-balancing power in the Greek world would no doubt be disturbing to some. The fact that the exiled king Demaratos had been with Xerxes during the Persian invasion of Greece, his co-ruler Kleomenes accused of activities against the state[6], Pausanias, the victor at Plataia recalled and later charged with treason[7] and Leotychides banished for taking bribes[8] left the royal houses with a considerable loss of prestige. That loss was translated into greater powers for the magistracies, particularly those of the ephors.

A dilemma faced the ruling Spartiates. The most conservative, and these were in the ascendant, did not want further disgrace emanating from the activities of Spartan commanders serving far from home. Nor did the possibilities offered by the increase in wealth from the continuation of the Persian War appeal to them. They constantly feared an uprising of the helots. Rather than adopt an emancipatory approach to the problem as a means of increasing available and willing military manpower, thereby acquiring a safer society by an evolving constitution, they chose to withdraw as much as possible from involvement in anything outside the Peloponnese and entrench themselves in what they regarded as a safer tradition. There is a stark difference between those who pursued a policy of using helots militarily, later to be emancipated by way of reward and sometimes termed *neodamodeis*, a practice advocated by Pausanias (I. 132. 4) and later pursued by Brasidas and Lysander, and the outright brutal suppression of the serf population followed by other Spartiates.[9]

Much to Sparta's annoyance Themistokles had overseen the rebuilding of the defensive walls of Athens. He had also blocked the Spartan proposal that those states which had medised (gone over to the Persians) or had remained neutral be expelled from the Amphictyonic Council which controlled Delphi. These included Thessaly, Thebes and Argos and their removal would have given Sparta, as head of the Peloponnesian League, control of the majority of the available votes. When, and here the date is uncertain but possibly in 472 BC, Themistokles was ostracised (exiled for ten years) he made his home in Argos, Sparta's long-term enemy in the Peloponnese. There he is reputed to have been behind a variety of anti-Spartan activities. The arrangement made by Elis, the guardian of Olympia, to form some of its village populations into a city around 471 BC, was not an acceptable outcome to Sparta. It may well be that the same process (synoikism) was achieved at about this time at Mantineia.[10] These events are regarded as the outcomes of Themistokles' activities and he was the man to whom the Spartans had given great honours.

Evidence of the fomentation of considerable anti-Spartan feeling is found in Herodotos in Book IX.36, where mention of five battles is made which were to be of the greatest import for Sparta, namely Plataia, at Tegea against the Argives and Tegeans, at Dipaees against all Arkadians except Mantineia, against the Messenians at Mount Ithome, and against the Athenians and Argives at Tanagra. The second and third indicate the tensions within the Peloponnesian League during these years, and the fourth points up the instability of the times.

Being aware of Themistokles' anti-Spartan stance before his ostracism, Sparta warmed to Kimon's policy of maintaining cordial relations between Athens and Sparta. It was largely due to this relationship that Sparta regained her poise, demonstrating her authority in the Peloponnese. Kimon saw the security of Greece as the responsibility of a partnership, that partnership being between Athens and Sparta. Kimon, the conservative, found himself opposed by Ephialtes and Perikles. Ephialtes' policies were radically democratic and he viewed Sparta as a potential enemy. Perikles may well have shared those views.

The earthquake at Sparta (465 BC), with its attendant loss of citizen life, was followed by the revolt of the helots and the *periokoi* of Thouria and Anthaia. The dissidents made their stand at Mount Ithome in Messenia, a naturally strong location. The rebels must have fortified this place as this is the reason why Sparta invited Athens to come to its aid because 'they were reputed to be skilled in siege operations, whereas the long continuance of the siege showed their own deficiency in this respect; for otherwise they would have taken the place by assault.'[11] Despite opposition Kimon was successful in the Athenian Assembly and procured a positive vote for support to be sent to the Spartans. However, the army of the Athenians may well have contained elements of the new radical thinking that was pervading Athens and the Spartans were sufficiently alarmed to request the withdrawal of the Athenian force shortly after its arrival.

Obviously this did Kimon's reputation no good at all. Thucidides (I. 102. 4) states categorically that this was regarded as an affront and caused the breakup of the alliance between Sparta and Athens. The conservative element which Kimon led in Athenian politics and which had favoured maintaining good relations with Sparta was forced to retreat in the face of the democrats led by Ephialtes and Perikles. An alliance with Argos and with the Thessalians in direct opposition to Sparta was the outcome.

There could well have been a connection between the Thasos and Ithome affairs. Sparta must have been aware of the growing radicalism in Athens which sat uneasily with the control of her own subordinate population. She probably recognised that Kimon was becoming a spent force. Ephialtes is described by Plutarch quoting Plato (Perikles 7) as having 'poured out neat a full draught of freedom for the people and made them unmanageable', so that they 'nibbled at Euboia and trampled on the islands, like a horse which can no longer obey the rein' (trans. Ian Scott-Kilvert). Kimon's inevitable ostracism, in 461 BC, saw the radical democracy of Ephialtes and Perikles given room to grow.

Compare the two prospective opposing alliances. By 461 BC, it is difficult to call the Delian League an alliance. The power exercised by those remaining as so-called independent states was muted. Athens was paramount and woe betide a member who gainsaid the indicated direction of the leader. Sparta, by contrast, still led a League which concentrated on preserving stability within the Peloponnese. There was a check in the voting procedures. Decisions were taken within two forums: first, that of the allies, each of which had a single vote with the majority carrying the verdict, the second, the Spartan Assembly. Only if a vote was carried out in both places could a decision be made and acted upon.

After 460 BC, Athens continued to expand and increase control over the Delian League and, more importantly, attempted to build a land empire on mainland Greece. She was able to do so because the monies contributed by her allies in lieu of men or ships, permitted the Athenian navy and armaments to grow apace. In turn that power was used to bring any backsliders to heel. At the time of the first assembly of the Peloponnesian League to debate the issue of whether or not to go to war with Athens (432 BC) an Athenian diplomat was visiting Sparta. He had come on unrelated matters and was given permission to speak.[12] His words throw into relief the basic problem which had beset both sides throughout this period.

> ...indeed we did not acquire this empire by force, but only after you had refused to continue to oppose what was left of the barbarian forces, [i.e., the Persians] and the allies came to us and of their own accord asked us to assume the leadership. It was under the compulsion of circumstance that we were driven at first to advance our empire to its present state, influenced chiefly by fear, then by honour also, and lastly by self-interest as well; and after we had incurred the hatred of most of our allies, and several of them had already revolted and been reduced to subjection, and when you were no longer friendly as before but suspicious and at variance with us, it no longer seemed safe to risk relaxing our hold. For all seceders would have gone over to you. And no man is to be blamed for making the most of his advantages when it is a question of the gravest dangers. (Thuc. I. 75. 2–5)

Thus the ill-feeling among the coerced and subject allies was enhanced by the pressure brought upon them by Athens to fight against fellow Greeks, in particular the Spartans.

In the early years of what is described as the First Peloponnesian War (460-446 BC) with the democrats in unassailable power, Athens embarked on an unprecedented period of expansion. Megara was brought into alliance with Athens and Aigina reduced to subject status, thus securing the Saronic Gulf. The geographical position of the Megarid shows that Athenian influence here was a severe impediment to any moves members of the Peloponnesian League wished to make overland to central and northern Greece.[13]

The alliance with Megara followed a border dispute between the Megarans and Corinth. Megara had two ports, one on the Gulf of Corinth at Pegai and the other on the Saronic Gulf at Nisaia. The position was further exacerbated by the Athenians building walls which connected the city of Megara to Nisaia. The placing of an Athenian garrison there was an additional provocation and the possible threat to easier access to the Corinthian Gulf from Pegai was to be a matter of grave concern to Corinth.

Athens had already taken Naupaktos from the Ozolian Lokrians and thus commanded the entry to the Corinthian Gulf. Shortly afterwards, in the tenth year of the conflict between the Messenian helots at Ithome and the Spartans, the latter permitted those under siege to leave with their families, providing they left the Peloponnese forever. The Spartans had received an oracle instructing them to allow the supplicants at Ithome to leave. While acknowledging the fact that the Spartans were one of the most careful of the Greek peoples in terms of religious observance and response to oracles, it must have been a relief to them to be rid of this potential source of danger in their hinterland. It is significant that it was the Athenians who took them into their care and settled them at Naupaktos.

It was Corinth which took the lead in provoking hostilities against Athens. Sparta remained relatively unengaged until 457 BC, the point at which Athens started to build the long walls to Phaleron and the Peiraieus. In response to a plea from their 'homeland' Doris, which was under attack by the Phokians, the Spartans committed 1,500 of their citizen hoplites together with 10,000 allied troops to aid their fellow Dorians. This appears to be a very large force to send out of the Peloponnese, particularly at a time when the Ithome problem still had two years to run before its resolution. Some clues appear to point to the Spartans' desire to pursue other interests. In the confused chronology of events, Diodorus Siculus says that the Thebans were helped by the Spartan army to gain control over the other Boiotian communities in return for their promise to threaten northern Attika.[14] Another clue appears in Thucydides in his comment at I.107.3 that to return over the Corinthian Gulf could be difficult because of the Athenian naval presence.

Following the break-up of the old alliance with Sparta the early years of the so-called First Peloponnesian War saw an attempt by Athens to extend her influence over central Greece. Initially, this attempt was muted by a heavy defeat inflicted upon them by the Spartans and allies at the battle of Tanagra (457 BC) who were returning from their successful freeing of Doris from the Phokians. Thucydides comments: 'the Athenians went out against the Lakedaimonians with their whole force and with one thousand Argives and contingents of the several allies.' (I. 107. 5.)

However, two months later, Athens achieved her objective when her general Myronides defeated the Boiotians at Oinophyta before going on to raze the fortifications of nearby Tanagra, and bringing Phokis and Opountian Lokris under control.

Elsewhere in land battles, for example the actions prior to and including the Battle of Mantineia, Thucydides identifies the main allied contingents on both sides. Argos could truly be said to be in genuine alliance with Athens, but at this stage one must question the status of others conveniently bundled under the word *allies*. It is obvious that the founding principles of the Delian League had been left behind and such maritime states that had been independent allies were now subject to the will and deployment of Athens.

After the surrender of the island of Aigina, the Athenian admiral Tolmides raided the coastline of the Peloponnese. He destroyed the Spartan naval dock-yards at Gytheion and entered the Corinthian Gulf to seize the small city colony of Chalkis on the northern shore near its outlet to the Ionian sea, a good strategic position, which in conjunction with Naupaktos gave the Athenians unassailable control of the waterway. From there Tolmides sailed along the Gulf towards Corinth where at nearby Sikyon he made a raid on the territory, defeating those Sikyonian land forces sent out to meet him.

This frenetic activity of the Athenians is all the more surprising when their earlier commitment in Egypt is remembered. As a continuation of their policy of aggression against the Persians, they had responded to a request from Inaros, the king of Libya, to support him in sustaining the revolt of the Egyptians from the Great King Artaxerxes. Two hundred ships were despatched from Cyprus in 460 BC and were almost wholly successful in their objective. The Persians offered the Spartans money as an inducement to invade Attika, which would force the Athenians to withdraw from Egypt, but nothing came of this. The war went on until 454 BC at which point a large Persian army was dispatched to Egypt, successfully dislodging the Greeks from their stronghold at Memphis and blockading them on the island of Prosopitis. After a siege of a year and a half the Persian commander drained the canal waterway by creating a diversionary channel and, having the advantage of a land approach which had left the Greek ships land-locked, he dislodged the Athenian force. Few escaped, and, to make matters worse, a fleet of fifty ships coming to relieve the forces in Egypt was caught, in ignorance of what had happened, at the Mendesian mouth of the Nile between Persian land forces and a Phoenician fleet. Much of the Athenian fleet was destroyed with only a few vessels escaping.

In this same year of 454 BC the treasury of Delos was moved to Athens on the excuse that Athenian interest in Egypt did not end thereafter. Sixty ships were sent (perhaps in 451 BC) in support of Amyrtaios, the king of the Egyptian marshland peoples who had continued to be independent of Persian rule. Only the death of their admiral Kimon caused them to retire to their base in Cyprus where later they were to defeat a combined fleet of Phoenicians, Cypriots and Cilicians.

Now to the question of the interest that Athens had in Egypt. Other than the obvious declared objective of the Delian League of pursuing an attritional war against the Persians, it should be noted that Attika was possessed of relatively poor land, incapable of sustaining its population in basic foodstuffs. While Athens had control of the entrance to the Black Sea and the subsequent benefits of the grain production of its neighbouring regions, Egypt could be looked upon as another breadbasket. The commitment of its forces there was no less significant than its later commitment in the Syracusan expedition during the Peloponnesian War.

In 454 BC an Athenian opportunist attempt to gain influence in Thessaly made in support of Orestes, the son of the exiled King Echekratidas led to an Athenian expedition to Pharsalos supported by Boiotian and Phokian allies. The attempt failed but is indicative of Athens' aims at this time.

Another interesting aspect of the removal of the Delian treasury to Athens is that henceforth the Congress of allies ceased to meet and the Athenians alone decided how the revenues were to be used and the direction of foreign policy. From this time on the embellishment of Athens as an imperial city began apace. Thereafter, the judicial systems of 'subject allies' which had been 'persuaded' to become democratic found themselves under pressure to refer not only political cases to the courts in Athens but others of less apparent importance.

The establishment of garrisons was not unusual and after about 450 BC cleruchies, or settlements of Athenian citizens overseas, became relatively commonplace. Dispossessed islanders obviously became disenchanted when they saw their most fertile land worked by incomers who had been placed there by such men as Perikles in an attempt to alleviate unemployment at home. In such a way the hitherto unemployed Athenians were elevated by these land grants to hoplite status, thereby increasing the numbers available under a levy. But at what cost? The islanders often became the poorer after losing the more productive parts of their land. This could only increase their disenchantment.

448 BC saw a five-year truce with Sparta and an agreed end to hostilities with the Persians. A Panhellenic meeting was called in Athens to plan the rebuilding of temples and sacred places ravaged during the Persian wars, but the Peloponnesian states did not attend. Not too much weight should be placed on their absence considering that the material assets of the Peloponnese had not suffered during the Persian invasion.

In this time of temporary peace Perikles saw the opportunity to direct the thousands of soldiers and sailors, now redundant, to building programmes within the city. Athens had been ruined by the Persian invasion and this was an opportunity to replace not only the temples but also public buildings by using this reservoir of manpower and the surplus of revenues.

In 447/446 BC both Megara and the large island of Euboia revolted (I.114.1). Megara, with the help of the Sikyonians, Corinthians and Epidaurians, ousted the Athenian garrison, the remnant of which escaped to Nisaia. Perikles had already gone to Euboia but returned quickly to the mainland. Following an indecisive raid by the Spartan King Pleistoanax on the western fringe of Attika from where he returned to the Peloponnese, Perikles went back to Euboia and subdued the whole island, but Megara was lost to the Athenian side.[15] In 446 BC Athens made a peace treaty with Sparta as the head of the Peloponnesian League which was to last thirty years and gave up its remaining bases in the Megarid and the Peloponnese, e.g. Nisaia, Pegai, and Troezen in the Argolid.

The peace itself laid bare the established fact and nature of the Athenian empire. Some powerful island states such as Miletos are seen to be missing from the tribute lists of 448 BC, and this led to the decree of Kleinias a year later by which Athens informed its 'allies' of her decision to continue to make collection of tribute. Should any refuse or desire a reduction, their representative would have to plead the case in an Athenian court. Shortly after, Athens issued a decree requiring the use only of Athenian currency within her empire. All city state silver coins were to be melted down and their mints closed.[16] Undoubtedly this facilitated trade but the allies had lost their sovereignty.

The increasing Athenian stranglehold on her subjects' commerce and foreign policy along with the 'encouragement' to democratic government, and placement of cleruchies and garrisons within their territories was soon to be felt as a price too great to pay for the subsequent increase in prosperity. This became all too obvious at the time of the altercation between Samos and Mytilene at about 441 BC. Both were supposed to be independent members of the Delian League and would not have expected Athenian interference in their personal dispute. Athens, however, demanded that Samos should cease hostilities and accept her arbitration and Perikles went to Samos with forty ships. Samos was too near Persian-held territory to count on a lack of interference from that quarter. Indeed it is reported that Pissuthnes who governed Sardis sent help to the revolutionaries. In Samos Perikles established a garrison and set up a democratic government. After his departure the opposition returned, overthrowing his puppet government. Byzantion had also revolted and taken control of the Bosphoros (I. 115. 5), the very important corn route for the Athenians.

This could not be tolerated by the Athenians. They defeated the Samians at sea (c. 440 BC) and laid siege to Samos. After nine months, with the siege ending in Athens' victory, the Samians were made to destroy their walls, surrender their fleet and pay a large indemnity of over 1,200 talents. Further, and this is the most significant part of the outcome, they were obliged to swear an oath of fealty to Athens. Byzantion, too, was forced to come to terms. In the early years of the Peloponnesian War, Thucydides (II. 63. 2) reports a public statement by Perikles: '...for by this time the empire you hold is a tyranny, which it may seem wrong to have assumed, but which certainly it is dangerous to let go', admitting the de facto situation that the so-called Delian League, by that time defunct, had evolved into empire.

We come now to the period prior to the outbreak of hostilities in the Peloponnesian War. The causes of the war have been hotly debated by scholars but it can be seen that Corinth was the main protagonist in promoting those hostilities. Hitherto it had been a great commercial centre and over the years its rival Athens had usurped its position. Now, after the middle of the 5th century, it found itself surrounded by Athenian satellites. Its trading routes were threatened by Athenian stations at the mouth of the Corinthian Gulf with the shores of that seaway either neutral Achaia or in alliance with, or under the control of, Athens (most of the northern shore). When Megara had been under Athenian control its port of Pegai was at the eastern end of the Gulf. The Saronic Gulf, with Aigina subject to Athens, was now totally under Athenian control. It had been the custom for vessels to be moved from the Corinthian to the Saronic Gulf across the land bridge of the Isthmus via the *diolchos*, a stone paved road for the purpose. It was difficult for Corinthian vessels to continue to use the latter with full confidence.

Notes

1. Although written about AD100, Plutarch's Lives, *Themistokles, Aristeides, Kimon,* and *Perikles* offer a great deal of information often garnered from lost sources and from Athenian political pamphleteers. One such is still in existence and was possibly written just after the outbreak of the Peloponnesian War. The content of *The Constitution of the Athenians* is anti-democratic, its writer being given the name 'The Old Oligarch' or Pseudo-Xenophon. The plays of Aristophanes and Aischylos resonate with contemporary opinions. Diodorus Siculus' *History* is helpful if used guardedly. Born at the beginning of the first century BC, his strong reliance on written sources could have given rise to a truly authoritative study had he been possessed of critical insight. As it is, the summaries of his source material often omit detail and his pro-Athenian standpoint leads him to distort the truth in her favour. Inscriptions on stone prove an extremely valuable source. The vast majority are Athenian and include public accounts, decrees, tribute lists, casualty lists, dedications to the gods, etc.

2. Plutarch, *Kimon* 6, *Aristeides* 23; Thuc. I. 95.

3. Thuc. V. 18. 5.

4. See Plut., *Kimon* 13.

5. Plut., *Kimon* 8 suggests that it was at the behest of Thessalian merchants that the Delian League took action against Skyros. See also the brief reference at Thuc. I. 98. 2.

6. Herodotos, Book VI recounts much of the behaviour which came into question.

7. See Thuc. I. 95; and Book I. Chapters 131–134.

8. Herod. VI. 74.

9. See Thuc. IV. 80. The execution of 2,000 helots under the pretext that they were to be given their freedom is evidence of the extreme paranoia experienced by the ruling class at this time.

10. Strabo claims at 337 that this was engineered by Argos.

11. Thuc. I. 52. 2.

12. Thucydides states (I. 72. 1) that an Athenian embassy was present that had come on 'other business'. It was present to hear the complaints of the Corinthians as Thucydides indicates. It seems highly likely that Perikles, knowing that matters were coming to a head, had sent his diplomats with the express purpose of making a strong case for avoiding war. The reference to the likely 'long drawn out' nature of any conflict (I. 78. 2) reflects the prospective strategy of Perikles as does the request for arbitration in the settlement of the dispute (I. 78. 4). This would have been in accordance with the current treaty between Athens and Sparta. Significantly the Athenian speech is followed by the address to the assembly of King Archidamos. He and Perikles were long-term friends. It is unlikely that the one would be ignorant of the views of the other. Echoes of the points made by the Athenian can be heard in his speech. At I. 81. 6 he re-emphasises the likely longevity of the impending war, 'I fear rather that we shall even bequeath it to our children', and at I. 85. 2 asks that arbitration should be pursued. He demonstrates the different power bases of the two leagues, one a land power, the other a sea power capable of sustaining itself through imports and the avoidance of a major land engagement. His urging of the assembly to take two or three years to prepare by acquiring finance and ships appears sensibly to be playing for time. With time and a closer parity between the opposing sides it was probable that better counsels would prevail. When he did march at the head of an army into Attika, the damage done was minimal initially, suggesting he hoped that even at that late stage some accommodation could be achieved. It suggests that Archidamos was pursuing a face-saving policy against the odds in order to preserve the peace between the two leagues. It would not be surprising if Perikles was also party to this strategy.

13. This was the area through which ran the only overland route to central and northern Greece. Athenian control of the Megarid effectively hampered Sparta's contact with Boiotia and her other northern allies.

14. Diod. XI. 81. 2–3.

15. Pleistoanax was thought to have been bribed into abandoning the invasion and suffered banishment.

16. An asset in terms of easing trading problems but a symbolic loss of sovereignty for those forced to lose their currency. Such is the dilemma faced by the United Kingdom today with the prospect of joining the 'Euro' and abandoning Sterling, although the degree of coercion is a little less in the present case.

APPENDIX 2

Speeches

In setting a standard in his time for checking and rechecking sources Thucydides can be trusted to give a balanced report on what his principal characters said. It is unlikely that the speeches were set down verbatim but their content and tone of delivery can be accepted as a true reflection of what was delivered to particular audiences.

> As to the speeches that were made by different men, either when they were about to begin the war or when they were already engaged therein, it has been difficult to recall with strict accuracy the words actually spoken, both for me as regards that which I myself heard, and for those who from various other sources have brought me reports. Therefore the speeches are given in the language in which, as it seemed to me, the speakers would express, on the subjects under consideration, the sentiments most befitting the occasion, though at the same time I have adhered as closely as possible to the general sense of what was actually said. (I. 21. 1)

Speeches are set pieces from which we can derive valuable insights into matters of policy, strategic and tactical thinking, motivation, character and personal ambition as reportedly expressed by an individual. Thucydides often gives a more rounded character to the speaker than would be the case if only his actions were recorded.

The respect in which Thucydides' work was held by his contemporaries must attest to the overall accuracy of the content of the speeches. Those Athenians who knew his work would have heard some of the speeches and those who had not knew others who had been present at their delivery. Many were given on occasions when large numbers were present. If one includes those speeches in which the content is recorded but not given verbatim the total reaches 141. Leaving aside those speeches already examined in this book, samples of the remaining speeches are given below. Therefore, it is in those chapters in which figures such as Brasidas, Nikias, Hermokrates, etc. appear that the reader will find their words. Several bring humanity to the personages who would otherwise only be names.

Speeches early in the dispute

Prior to the start of the war the Corinthians, exasperated by the Athenian siege of their colony Potideia, requested that the members of the Peloponnesian league meet at Sparta to address the Spartan Assembly (432 BC). Many of the allies had grievances against Athens. Megara, for example, had been denied access to all sources of trade within the Athenian empire, and Aigina had been denied her independent status. After these had been permitted to make complaint, the representatives of Corinth added theirs (from I. 68). Sparta is accused of allowing the Athenians to build her empire and as a consequence of inactivity, tacitly giving licence to Athens to enslave hitherto free states. Comparison is made between the Spartan and Athenian characters. The Spartans are charged with having a limited view on foreign policy, of being slow to react to events and over-cautious to the extent of preferring the status quo. They are labelled as having no initiative and being averse to risk. The Athenians, on the other hand, are described as a mirror image of the Spartans; risk-takers, quick to make decisions, confident in their judgements, impulsive and adventurous.

Such a list of comparisons can be regarded as a thumb-nail sketch of the supposed cultural differences between the Dorians and the Ionians, but later the Dorians of Syracuse were to demonstrate that such dichotomy in the characteristics of Dorian and Ionian could not easily be made.

What proved to be the decisive point made in the speech of the Corinthians comes at I. 71. 4., with the threat that, if Sparta continued to procrastinate, Sparta's allies might be obliged to seek a place within another alliance.

Some Athenian envoys happened to be at Sparta on other state matters and heard the attack made by the Corinthians against their city. It is interesting that the Assembly of allies at Sparta proved to be open to others, particularly when the complaints of the members could not have been wholly unexpected by the Spartans. The Athenians' request to speak was acceded to by the Spartans. One might have expected that in the circumstances the speech of the Athenian spokesman to have been conciliatory but this was far from the case.

In stressing the contribution made by Athens to the war against the Persians, and attributing the birth of their empire to a reluctance by Sparta to prosecute that war to its conclusion, the spokesman proved boastful and arrogant. Finally, he suggested that the Spartans should think very carefully before they came to any decision and to submit any differences they might have to arbitration as agreed under the provisions of the existing treaty of 445 BC between Athens and Sparta.

In closed session, the Spartans now discussed the issue. It is obvious from what follows that the Spartan Assembly was split. The more cautious party sought a peaceful outcome, having as their spokesman Archidamos, one of the kings, and Sthenelaidas, an ephor, was the speaker for the faction which wanted war.

Archidamos was the first to speak. He is described as a wise and moderate man (I. 79. 2) and a friend of Athens' premier citizen, Perikles (II. 13. 1). He urged caution and his is the most important contribution of any within the deliberations at Sparta. With almost forensic accuracy he identified the problems of conducting a war wherein the participants were so different in resources. He recognised that such a war would be long and arduous because of this. A war between an unrivalled naval power against an overwhelming land power could not be easily resolved. He recognised that the Athenians needed to be defeated at sea and that without control of that element Athens could continue to support herself both in revenues and in fundamental resources, not least in foodstuffs, from her empire. He urged, therefore, a more conciliatory approach, to use the continual Athenian call for arbitration in the dispute to gain time to build a navy and new alliances. Such preparations, perhaps over two or three years and being recognised in Athens, would go a long way to defuse the hard line which was being taken by the Athenians. He recommended that the grievances of the allies should be first presented.

In distinct contrast Sthenelaidas' brief speech called for swift action, regarding any further discussion of the matter as superfluous. In many ways the speech of the ephor epitomises the laconic. The war party won the vote.

After sending to Delphi for approval of their intent to make war the Spartans called the Assembly of allies to debate and take a formal vote on the issue. Corinth had been busy canvassing support for immediate action prior to the meeting in the hope that a positive outcome would help the Potideians. The Corinthians were the last to speak at the Assembly. The points they made appear logical but, as time was to prove, some were disingenuous; to borrow money from the treasuries of Delphi and Olympia with which to offer greater payment to Athens' foreign seamen, to achieve an early naval success, to achieve a parity in naval skills.[1] A more cogent suggestion was that fostering dissent among the cities within the Athenian empire could bear fruit. Not least is the proposal to establish fortifications within Attika, not followed until nearly twenty years later, and that following the urgings of Alkibiades. They warn of Athens' intent to bring all Greece piecemeal into servitude and urge the coalition to act firmly. A majority of the League voted for war and, within a year, in 431 BC, Attika suffered its first invasion of the conflict.

Archidamos' viewpoint was realistic and his opinion was based on a well considered analysis of the resources available to both sides. When hostilities finally broke out, his initial actions were those of a commander who appeared to hope that some accommodation could still be found between the two sides. When the Peloponnesians and their allies had gathered at the Isthmos in preparation for an invasion of Attika, he addressed them. They must at all times be disciplined and aware that caution within an enemy's territory is a self-preserving virtue. He reminded them that they were going against a strongly defensible position but that the Athenians would fight when they saw their properties outside the walls of the city ravaged. He reminds his men that the Athenians were usually the perpetrators of such depredation and unaccustomed to having this done to their own lands. In consequence he declares that they will be sufficiently incensed to offer battle.

There is more than a suggestion here that Archidamos was doing the best he could under the circumstances. He had given his analysis to the assembly and had his suggestion of caution rebuffed. He was now leading the army in an invasion of Attika earlier than he would have wished and his tactical options were limited. In his decisions that followed, two tactical threads can be seen. It is possible to extrapolate the policy advocated in his speech to the Spartan assembly to the actions he undertook.

The first tactical echo was the hope that the threat of force might bring the Athenians to make terms. He obviously hoped that by initially limiting damage and allowing the period of the threat of further damage to be prolonged, the Athenians might well have a change of heart. He was, after all, aware that a vote in the Athenian Assembly could overturn the previously held position. Archidamos had sent a herald to Athens after his speech to the troops in the hope that there might indeed have been a change of mind. This had been forestalled by an earlier motion of Perikles which denied access to the Athenian Assembly of any such messengers. On the herald's return Archidamos commenced the slow advance. His first target, the fortified town of Oenoe, is revealing It lay towards the Boiotian border in the north of Attika and attacking it could not be described in any way as being a threatening move against Athens itself. Thucydides remarks (II. 18. 2) that much time was wasted in this location. There then follow the reasons for the later censure of Archidamos: his delay at Oenoe, his tardiness in supervising the original levy of men for the army, his delay at the Isthmos, and his slow advance. All these had allowed the communities of Attika to move with their portable property to the protection of Athens. A direct attack, thought his critics, would have led to disruption in the population and the capture of much property. Thucydides goes on to say what must be obvious to the reader, that Archidamos hoped to wring some concession from the Athenians before any damage to their property had been done (II. 18. 5). It was now midsummer and nothing of substance had been achieved.

The second tactical thread followed on as a natural consequence of the failure of the first, but can still be seen as an attempt to bring about an early resolution, this time by the time-honoured practice of provoking a battle by laying waste to the crops and properties of the opposition. His initial operations were, in a sense, a continuation of his first tactic in that the areas of Eleusis and Thria were sufficiently distant from Athens to persuade the Athenians that the advance would not come any nearer the city (II. 21. 1). It reminded them of the invasion some fourteen years earlier under the subsequently exiled king Pleistoanax, which had advanced no farther. During this period the people of Attika continued to move into the safety of Athens. Archidamos was later censured for this. It was when Archidamos moved his forces to Acharnai, some seven miles north of Athens and in clear view from the city, that dissension among those within the walls appeared. The people of the deme of Acharnai were the most vociferous in wishing to make a sally in defence of their territory and, as they contributed about a sixth of the hoplite force available to Athens, their opinion almost won the day. Perikles, however, refused to countenance either engaging the enemy or, more significantly, calling an assembly to debate the matter.[2]

So Archidamos failed in his enterprise, but his failure can be regarded as an honourable one. His tactic of delay was clearly to give time for the Athenians to reconsider their position and when this bore no fruit his clever choice of Acharnai as an area to ravage put great psychological pressure on the Athenian populace. His was an attempt to bring about a quick resolution to what he correctly saw could develop into a protracted and very damaging conflict.

The speeches of Perikles

In Archidamos' failure the controlling hand of Perikles was ever present. His advice to the Athenians and his policy for the war is detectable in the speeches reported by Thucydides. The first recorded speech of Perikles (from I. 140) was made possibly in the winter of 432 to 431BC prior to the outbreak of hostilities. His main points were that no concessions should be made because Sparta was refusing arbitration on the differences. To accede to any of Sparta's demands would lead to others following. War was preferable. The Peloponnesians did not have the capital funds to sustain a prolonged conflict. They were farmers and would not be able to leave their land untended for long periods of time. Here he is necessarily speaking of Sparta's allies and not of Sparta. They were no match for Athens at sea. Unlike Athens they did not have a single council chamber where decisions could be made speedily. Each contributory state would be seeking to pursue its own interest which in all likelihood would lead to hesitation or inactivity. This last point was probably made more for effect than for its veracity.

Once the Peloponnesian League voted for war, reaching decisions for action was quickly done. Sparta led and the allies followed. Perikles continued saying that Athens had resources overseas which could not be reached by Sparta until she acquired a navy and even then she could never match Athens in this element. The people of Athens should leave their properties in Attika and come into their well-fortified city, which they should regard as an island supported by the resources of its empire. They should avoid any land engagement in the knowledge that nothing would be gained by the probable succession of defeats they would suffer at the hands of the Peloponnesians. They should not worry over the loss of property but safeguard their population. If Attika was invaded by land the Athenians would raid the Peloponnese by sea. The most significant argument was for the need not to make further conquests during the course of the coming war. This has provoked continuing debate particularly in connection with the Sicilian expedition (see Chapter VII). Whether that expedition was made with the intention of subjugating Syracuse and thereafter the whole island of Sicily, or as a pre-emptive strike at a likely source of direct support for the Peloponnese, or for reasons of greed and ambition, will continue to exercise the minds of scholars.

The clear strategy outlined by Perikles at the time of that speech was held to for the course of the next two and a half years until his death and a little thereafter. His hope at that time must have been that the Spartans would tire of achieving little with their annual invasions of Attika while suffering themselves from coastal raids by the Athenian navy. This could have led to an eventual majority in the Spartan assembly and ephorate which would have sought peace. From 431 BC Athens invaded Megara annually until the capture of one of its ports, Nisaia. The first occasion under the command of Perikles himself saw a massive operation involving the whole Athenian army levy, including resident aliens, together with the 100 ships that had returned from raiding the Peloponnesian coast. These operations, together with the huge armament sent against Epidauros in 430 BC, again led by Perikles, refutes the view that his strategy was passive.

Perikles' next reported speech is the funeral oration he made for those who had fallen in the hostilities up to the winter of 431/430 BC (from II. 35). Athens had achieved much in the year in terms of securing her defences. Euboia was now safe from surprise attacks through the activity of a fleet sent to raid Lokris and to fortify Atalanta. The island of Aigina was purged of its population which was soon after settled in the Peloponnese by the Spartans. A reserve fleet was established and raids were made on the enemy's coastline.

In this speech Perikles set out those aspects of Athenian life and custom that made the city great. It reminded the populace of the values for which they fought. In essence, it was a call for those who still lived to emulate the example of the fallen who had given their lives in order to protect that which all citizens held dear. He cited Athens' democracy and its meritocratic institutions, its culture and sophistication, its position as a model for all Greece; and it comforted the bereaved. The children of the dead were assured of state support until maturity. This was a speech which gave a value to what was at risk to the citizen in this war. It sought to elicit a communal pride in the sacrifice made by the dead for their city and strengthen the resolve of those remaining to continue the fight.

Within months, in the following summer, plague broke out in Athens very shortly after Archidamos commenced another invasion of Attika. This time much of Attika was ravaged. Perikles refused to allow the army to go out to meet the Peloponnesians and instead mounted the very substantial expedition to Epidauros mentioned above. Fatalities caused by the plague continued within the city and in the expeditionary force. Furthermore, after Perikles' return, the original expeditionary force was sent under Hagnon north to Chalkidike and to Potideia. This army took with them the plague and infected those already engaged in the siege leading to the loss of a quarter of the force.

In the dire circumstances of a more thorough devastation of their lands and the calamitous toll of the plague, it is unsurprising that Athenian morale slumped to the extent that they sent representatives to Sparta to discuss peace terms. This approach to Sparta was rejected. They blamed Perikles for their misfortunes and it was at this juncture that, as a general, he called the assembly to make his most assertive speech (from II. 60).

Perikles called for the people to put the good of the state before personal matters, for without a strong state there would be no hope for the individual. He claimed that while he had not changed, the Athenians who had voted with him for war had obviously altered their viewpoint following on from the misfortunes of the plague. While they were unchallenged at sea and had their freedom, material items could be easily replaced. This would not be the case if freedom was lost. Athens could expect her citizens to work to retain what she had won and to take pride in her glory. In a direct warning Perikles declared that Athens' empire was a tyranny and it would be dangerous to lose control of their possessions. He asked them not to be persuaded by those who sought to deflect them from their original decision to resist. He reminded them of what had led to the greatness of Athens and asked them not to give the enemy any sign of wavering.

Thucydides states (II. 65. 2) that Perikles' speech won the day and that the community at large supported the continuation of the war. The citizenry, however, fined him as an expression of their discontent but this did not stop him from being re-elected as general.

The war could well have come to a speedy close. Thucydides does not tell us of the reasons for Sparta's rejection of the Athenian approach. It seems likely that without Perikles' intervention further approaches would have been made to Sparta ceding much if not more than had been originally demanded prior to the outbreak of war. Perikles managed to keep the Athenians on course following the strategy which he had originally outlined.

With changing circumstances, a strategy can and often must change. There can be little doubt that none of the original participants, even Archidamos, can have expected the conflict to last for twenty-seven years. Finance was seen as the key. Athens held considerable reserves and had the advantage of the products of an empire, but these were not inexhaustible. The Peloponnesians could well borrow from the treasuries of Olympia and Delphi but they too had their limit. It is therefore difficult to argue that the Athenians lost the war by not holding to the original plan as outlined by Perikles. To have held to an unmodified and unwavering strategy for such a length of time would have been contrary to Perikles' thinking. His policy envisaged a few years in which the Peloponnesians would realise they were faced with a stalemate. His gamble was that he would be able to keep the Assembly in check and in a democracy, a significant risk. The fact that his policy was followed for several years after his death is proof of his powers of persuasion.

A key phrase appears in Perikles' first speech immediately prior to the section which dealt with the building of fortified bases. '...but the opportunities of war wait for no man' (I.142. 1).

It was incumbent on the political as well as the military leaders to recognise a moment that could be used to advantage. Such an opportunity arose with the blockade of the Spartans on Sphakteria and it was Kleon who recognised its significance and the necessity to act. If for little else, Kleon must be admired for his recognition of the moment and for the political courage to carry through what he had proposed. His success, in conjunction with Demosthenes, in acquiring a key bargaining counter to use against Sparta must be applauded. Such was an opportunity envisaged by Perikles and something which could have been used to bring hostilities to a close. However, the Athenians let the opportunity pass.

> But the Athenians constantly made greater demands and the envoys, although they came again and again, were always sent home unsuccessful. (IV. 41. 4)

Obviously, after his success at Sphakteria, Kleon and his followers would have been in the ascendant. Perikleans such as Nikias would not be in a position to take advantage of the leverage acquired by the capture of so many Spartiates. Their voices would be muted in the protracted negotiations that followed, which could well have brought an early peace.

In Periklean terms 'to win the war' was to bring the enemy to a position where it would sue for peace, thereby leaving Athens free to continue as she had before the conflict. In not accepting the opportunity presented by their success at Sphakteria the Athenians condemned the Greek world to another twenty-one years of conflict. This then can be identified as the point at which the departure from Periklean strategy begins.

Speeches of Commanders to their troops

A neat grouping of opposing speeches is given prior to the sea battle off Naupaktos (see Chapter I). These appear after the initial disaster suffered by the Peloponnesians at the hands of Phormio in their attempt to transport troops to the north-west. Three commissioners, Timokrates, Brasidas and Lykrophon, had been sent to the Spartan admiral Knemos to advise and ensure success in the next operation. On calling their men together, these commanders are said to have addressed them in the following terms. It is not clear who delivered the speech or whether it was given severally by the commanders.

Common sense suggests that a communication which was to be heard by several thousand men must be given either several times by the general to sub-groups of the total forces in turn or by the commander and his colleagues to smaller groups and to an agreed text (see below).Even Phormio's force would have been over 3,500 strong and it would have taken a very powerful voice to carry clearly to all concerned.

The recognition of the fears of the men following their earlier defeat is excused on the grounds of their inexperience hitherto and the fact that they were involved in an exercise which was best described as transportation. The men are exhorted to remember that they had had little preparation for their first encounter, but they had now. They were also not to excuse themselves on the grounds of inexperience but to accept that this was more than made up for by their bravery and the comfort of having the advantage of numbers. They should learn from their mistakes and be confident that their new commanders had made preparations. They should be confident fighting as they would be just off their own coastline where their land forces offered security. Punishment would be dealt out to anyone who was less than assiduous and rewards would be received by those who showed courage.

Phormio is reported to have often told his men not to concern themselves with any inequality in the numbers of ships but had observed that they were dispirited nevertheless. His address to them (from II. 89) started from this point and urged them to recognise that the opposition needed to present itself with greater numbers because of their previous defeat, not having the courage to meet the Athenians on equal terms. He further declared that the courage of the Peloponnesians was based on land experience. That courage was not enough to match the Athenian confidence born out of experience on water. He suggested that the Spartans were forcing unwilling allies to attempt another engagement. They had come with superiority of numbers because they trusted more in strength than resolution and feared the unpredictability of the Athenian character. The Athenians lacked neither courage nor skill, a fact which had led to smaller numbers overcoming greater odds in the past.

Having addressed the question of morale in the first part of his speech, Phormio turned to the tactical issues. Contact was to be avoided if possible in the narrows at the mouth of the Gulf so that sea-room could be used to advantage. Here, again with an eye to morale, the opposition was described as clumsy and ill-managed in contrast to the fast, ably-manned Athenian vessels. To fight within the narrows would deny the Athenians the opportunity to employ their tactical superiority and convert the battle into one which would resemble one on land. He exhorted his men to keep order and to maintain silence. This last point was critical. Rowers had to hear the rhythm set and orders. The aim of the fight is made clear:

> The contest is a momentous one for you – whether you shatter the
> hopes which the Peloponnesians have in their fleet, or bring closer
> home to the Athenians their fear about the sea. (II. 89. 10)

Finally, a return to morale-boosting in reminding his men that they were
to fight against men they had already defeated who were unlikely to face
a similar danger again with the courage they had first exhibited.

Both speeches necessarily devote attention to morale. It is significant
that in the shorter address of the Peloponnesians this appears to be the
sole theme and no mention of tactics is made, although in the ensuing
action it has obviously been discussed. Phormio, by contrast, reminded
his men of the tactics which were to be expected of Athenian warships in
open waters: the necessity of seeing the enemy at a considerable distance
so as to make the alignment for running the vessel down, for having
sufficient water to effect a disengagement if hard pressed, and to move
through the enemy line with enough room to attack his rear.

The close of Phormio's speech recognised that the Athenians must maintain their naval superiority at all costs. Even a success against the small
Athenian squadron would send the wrong signals to the Spartans. One of
the foundations of Periklean strategy was the continuity of Athenian naval
supremacy and, if the Athenians did depart later from the all-embracing
terms of his vision, this was one aspect that they never neglected. Even
after the naval defeats at Syracuse, fleets were built with confidence
and the years thereafter were dominated by naval actions in which the
Athenians more than held their own.

Prior to the Battle of Delion

The speech of Pagondas prior to the battle of Delion can be regarded as critical. Without it there would have been no engagement. The Athenians had
made their incursion into Boiotian territory, set up their fortified position
and their light armed forces had started on their return to Athens. The hoplites had halted just over the border and were technically once more in their
own territory. Hippokrates was still supervising the completion of the work
of the fortification when the Boiotian muster was completed near Tanagra.
There, on the news that the main body of the Athenians had already left
Boiotian territory, all but Pagondas of the eleven *Boiotarchs* were of the
opinion that to join battle was not appropriate now that the enemy was not
within their territory. However, as commander-in -chief, Pagondas called all
the assembled army to him and exhorted them to go against the Athenians.

Obviously with an army of several thousand men, to address them all
at the same time would have been a waste of time. Thucydides makes it
clear that they were summoned to him in smaller numbers, he 'called the
men by companies one after another, that they might not leave their arms
all at once' (IV. 91).

The burden of his argument was that the idea of not engaging the Athenians should never have even entered the minds of the Boiotian generals. By separating himself from his elected colleagues he was making a singular claim to the loyalty of the men. He reminded them that the enemy had made an incursion on their lands and had built a fortification so that wherever they might be at this time they were still enemies of the Boiotians. He urged them to look at the current situation of the subdued Euboians as an example of Athenian imperialism. He reminded them of their success at the battle of Koroneia in 447 BC which restored security to the Boiotians thereafter. From this example those who had fought in that momentous engagement should seek to equal their earlier exploits, while those who were younger and possibly the sons of those heroes should not disgrace their heritage but put their trust in the god whose sanctuary had suffered sacrilege. Their duty was to give battle against the Athenians to show that they could not assume that they could do as they wished against freemen. Indeed the sacrifices had shown that the signs were in their favour in the matter of helping the offended deity.

Pagondas was successful with his arguments. He could have alluded to the fact that the Athenian army was now outnumbered and was without its many unarmed camp-followers who might have acted as missile throwers, a significant advantage under the circumstances. However, one must look at the description of the topography over which the battle was fought. In one sense the superiority of the Theban numbers was negated by the fact that its wings could not operate directly in support of their main body. This, together with the fact that the Athenian line was in all likelihood longer than theirs because of the varying depths at which the various Boiotian contingents arranged themselves. The main conflict was initially restricted to the area within the watercourses and was almost wholly a hoplite engagement.

It is possible that, even under the duress of reacting in haste to the threat, Hippokrates or his subordinates picked terrain which was most suitable for the available forces, seeking to nullify the Boiotian cavalry and light infantry. He was obviously under pressure and is described as passing along the Athenian line giving his troops in turn the following exhortation. He claimed that by winning the battle they would be freed of future invasions by the Spartans who would not do so without the support of the Boiotian horse. In so doing they would be masters of Boiotia.

Hippokrates had addressed his men sequentially (IV. 94. 2) by going along the assembled army and had only reached the half-way point of his line when the Theban attack was launched. In his and Pagondas' speech we have the proof that a general at this time addressed his men company by company.

Before the last sea battle at Syracuse

When the Syracusans blockaded the Athenian fleet within the Great Harbour in the summer of 413 BC, Nikias sought to raise the spirits of this men following on from their unprecedented defeat at sea. The decision had been taken to attempt to breach the blockade and to defeat the Syracusan navy. If they failed to do so they would burn their ships and withdraw to Katana by land. This was a decisive moment and Nikias stressed to his men the importance of the coming action and the preparations made for it. He exhorted them to remember that if they were to win they would be able to reach their homelands, to have trust in their numbers, and to realise that fortune in war is rarely always on one side only. He defined the task ahead of them. This was not to be a sea battle in which the superiority of Athenian seamanship would give them the usual advantage. In the confined space of the harbour area this would be more akin to a land battle and, in preparation for this, each vessel would be carrying archers, javelineers and hoplites in numbers much greater than if the battle were to be in open waters with room for manoeuvre and any additional weight a disadvantage. To counter the change in prow construction made by the enemy, which was noted to have caused such mayhem in the previous engagement, each vessel was equipped with grappling hooks. Any enemy ship which charged would not be able to back water after impact, being held in place by this means.

Nikias was preparing his men for a battle at close quarters in which the victory lay in the hands of the troops aboard each ship. He advised them not to allow themselves to be driven ashore but to fight for the possession of the enemy's decks. He reminded them of the Athenian advantage in numbers of ships and of men, of the pride the allies should feel in having shared in the advantages of empire, and of the many times they had defeated the Corinthians now ranged against them with the Syracusan fleet which hitherto had chosen not to engage an Athenian fleet when it was at its best.

The last comment recognises the poor condition of that part of the fleet which had been at Syracuse from the start of the siege. There is a sense of desperation in his allusion to the sickness as he urged them to show their skills despite this factor. Here, the reference to skills is ambiguous, for Athenian skills were mainly in seamanship and Nikias' forces were in no position to employ these. All preparations had been made for an action in stark contrast with the usual Athenian practices.

Nikias reminded them that at home there were no more ships and no hoplites in their prime. *They* were the city of Athens going aboard their vessels, and failure to win this battle would mean the loss of their city.

After the balancing speech of Gylippos and the Syracusan generals, Nikias, such was his anxiety, and despite his own indisposition, is reported to have gone aboard a boat and sailed from ship to ship calling to each of the captains exhorting them to be true to their wives, children, tribes, ancestors, their freedom and their country.

To turn to the speech of Gylippos and his fellow commanders. Here again, there is the suggestion of an agreed text delivered by several in order to cover the large number of men to be addressed. After the obvious comment that if the Athenians had come to Sicily as the best seamen in the world and had been beaten, then the Syracusans and their allies as victors must have assumed the mantle. The damage to Athenian pride and confidence is noted as a consequence. There follows an interesting analysis of the coming conflict. The Athenians would be obliged to fight on terms dictated by the Syracusans and in a manner to which they were unaccustomed. The greater number of their vessels was of no consequence because their manoeuvrability would be hampered by the weight of the numbers taken aboard. Those they had put on their ship were landsmen wholly unused to discharging missiles from unsteady decks, and if the ships had to be kept still so that a discharge could be made, confusion in their fleet would occur. The dire current position of the Athenians was recognised as were the options open to them of either forcing their way out of the harbour or having to retreat overland. The Syracusans were urged to engage with anger remembering that the Athenians had come to enslave them and their dependants.

Speeches in Assemblies

Early in the war uncomfortable signs of the savagery which was to break out from time to time appeared. In the summer of 427 BC a Peloponnesian fleet, sent out ostensibly to support the revolt of Mytilene, arrived in Ionian waters too late to accomplish its assignment. Much of the blame for its tardiness must be laid at the feet of its commander, Alkidas. He displayed every sign of a navarch who, while taking pride in the position, sought to risk nothing and as a consequence Mytilene surrendered to Athens. The Athenian assembly urged on by Kleon voted that the prisoners should be put to death together with all other adult males, and the women and children be sold as slaves. A ship was sent off to Mytilene with orders to the commander Paches to carry this out. The appalling nature of their decision brought many Athenians to the Assembly requesting that the matter be reconsidered. The prime mover of the original motion, Kleon, again addressed the people (III. 37.1).

He berated the members for allowing themselves to be moved from their original position by compassion. Democracy he declared was not fully capable of running an empire. The Athenians should avoid being a danger to themselves by such changes of heart.[3] They should remember that they led the empire through strength and not from the loyalty of those who were obliged to follow. He adhered to his original proposition and challenged those who wished to reopen the matter. Any such person must either have been bribed to do so or have supreme confidence in their powers of rhetoric to persuade the people away from their original decision. Kleon made clear that Mytilene was not a subject state but one which had enjoyed autonomy and had now chosen to change sides and had not learned the lesson of others within the empire who had rebelled and who had been subjugated. Mytline should be dealt with severely. Any lesser punishment meted out to an ally than to a subject state would set a poor example.

Before setting out the reply of Diodotos it is necessary to examine the legality of this second debate. Whether the chairman of the Assembly for the day (*Epistates*) was within the bounds of the constitution in allowing a second vote to be held on a matter already decided is doubtful. Discussion, perhaps, but permitting a vote which could overturn a previous decision is questionable. Kleon makes no reference to any legal problem in his speech and the arguments he made were put in such strong terms as to suggest that such a second vote was a possibility. Another occasion (VI. 14. 2) has Nikias calling for a second vote on the Sicilian expedition five days after the decision to do so had been passed in Assembly. These occasions were so rare, however, and the fact that the decision of the Assembly was deemed to be final makes these debates extremely unusual.

Diodotos spoke next in favour of clemency to the Mytileneans as he had evidently done on the previous day. His first comments were in the nature of an attack on Kleon and his like who seemed unable to debate a matter dispassionately and who levelled accusations of susceptibility to bribery at those who opposed their point of view. In debate a good citizen should win by persuasion and not through any attempt at frightening his opponents.

He pointed to the difference between a court of law and the political institution of the Assembly. In outlining what brings cities to a state of revolt he questioned the level of sanctions which could be taken against such miscreants. Each level could come to be superseded and if that of death could come to be disregarded, what further sanction beyond this would act as a deterrent? The likelihood of death alone would make the besieged hold out to the end, for they had nothing to gain. With opportunities to make good their error, a rebel could reduce the expenditure incurred in a siege and continue to pay tribute thereafter. Moderation was the key to successful continuation of the empire. Vigilance and good administration would pre-empt any rebellion. In the case of Mytilene the people were not in revolt alongside the oligarchs. They were the friends of Athens and, as soon as they had acquired arms, they had seen to it that the city was surrendered to the Athenian forces. Now it was suggested that they should be punished alongside the guilty. Even if they had been guilty, abjuring any punishment of them would be to avoid alienating the class within the empire which gave Athens support. Savagery in dealing out retribution was no substitute for good policy.

Diodotos won the day by a narrow margin and another ship was sent after the first to countermand the initial decision. Fortunately, the second, having rowed non-stop, arrived before the first and injustice was averted.

So it was that the veneer of civilised behaviour was almost stripped from what has been recognised as the fountainhead of western civilisation. It also shows how vulnerable democracy was to the demagogue. The vacillations of an Assembly which could change its mind from one day to the next depending on the force of argument presented was not the most comfortable and secure forum from which to conduct a war. Sparta, by contrast, had periods when policy was carried out during which either the Peace or War party was in the ascendant and was not subject to mercurial changes of policy.

The elation felt by the Athenian Assembly when presented with Spartan offers of peace in the Dekelean War led them to throw commonsense out of the window and presume that, because they were momentarily in the ascendant, a final 'push' would win them the war. In one sense the democracy of Athens was its downfall. Only when it was firmly led by a forceful personality such as Perikles were the aim and means to achieve it pursued without deflection. That being the case it can be argued that Periklean Athens was not a true democracy. After his death, Nikias, a man of merit but of much lesser significance, did his best to pursue the Periklean strategy but in the face of personalities such as Kleon had to await the latter's death at Amphipolis to eke out an unstable truce. That there were orators such as Diodotos preaching moderation active in the early years of the war must have been comforting to those of the populace who disliked the strident calls of the more extreme.

In the Spartan Assembly, we have the strange situation of an Athenian advising those who had been his enemies of the best way forward to achieve victory over his mother city.

Alkibiades (See Chapters VII and VIII) had evaded the party which had come to Sicily to secure his attendance in Athens to answer charges laid against him and had eventually arrived in Sparta under the guarantee of safe conduct. He was naturally nervous that his former fomentation of the Peloponnese against Sparta, which had culminated in the Battle of Mantineia, would set the Spartans against him.

Thucydides (VI. 88. 8) states that the Corinthian and Syracusan envoys on their arrival in Sparta found Alkibiades already there. He had come from Thurii in a merchant vessel to Kyllene in Elis and from there had travelled overland to the heartland of his former adversaries. Initially, the Corinthians, Syracusans and Alkibiades, in their attempts to cajole the Spartans into prosecuting the war more openly at home against Athens and sending help to Syracuse, were successful in persuading the Assembly, but were opposed by the ephors and presumably the *gerousia* (an elected body of thirty Spartiates over 60 years of age) from doing more than sending envoys to Syracuse to exhort them not to surrender to the Athenians. The word 'presumably' is used in the case of the *gerousia* because Thucydides' text does not name this body ('The ephors and others in authority'). In the Spartan constitution those others could only be the *gerousia* or the kings. As the latter were not elected it seems reasonable that the magistracies were behind the decision. There is no description of the first speeches at this meeting and it is significant that Alkibiades was allowed to make a second representation to the Assembly.

His first comments reminded them of his attempts to act on their behalf in negotiations as their *proxenos*, particularly in the case of Pylos. Their choice to ignore him and use his political enemies at Athens for that role had weakened his position there. He therefore sought to justify his actions thus far in the war against Sparta, particularly in his activities in the Peloponnese which had culminated in the battle of Mantineia. He declared himself against democracy but said that he, among others, had sought to give the commons leadership. The intention of the Athenians in Sicily was no less than its total conquest to be followed by that of Italy and Carthage. Success in these endeavours would allow the Athenians to build numerous ships and allow them to bring into their armies the human resources of their extended empire together with additional mercenary forces from Iberia. The newly conquered areas would provide foodstuffs and capital sufficient to allow Athens not to have to use its own revenues. With these forces the aim was to blockade the Peloponnese by sea and reduce the cities one by one with their land armies. The outcome would be the subjection of the whole Hellenic world.

This declaration of Athenian aims may well have expressed those of Alkibiades whose ambitions appear boundless. Such a view would be shared by those in Athens who hoped to profit from the opportunities offered by new acquisitions, but this attitude was not shared by all. Perhaps Alkibiades was attempting to inflame the Spartans by the alarming parameters he set as the aims of the expedition and, in doing so, was overstating those aims. However, the scenario he defines may well have been his own strategy for the winning of ultimate victory when he took up his position of command at the outset of the expedition. Now in exile that strategy could be declared as that of the Athenian state.

Alkibiades moved on from this depiction of the dire threat to the liberties of the Hellenes to those things which the Spartans must do to avoid impending calamity. Syracuse must be given help. Sicily, if united, could resist the Athenians, but if Syracuse fell all Sicily would succumb. He urged them to send hoplites to Sicily on ships that they rowed themselves and with them a Spartiate to take overall command of the forces there. This made extremely good sense. To have troops rowing themselves to Sicily would save money that would otherwise be paid to oarsmen and maximise the number of hoplites who could be sent. Although Syracuse had generals of its own and certainly one of talent in Hermokrates, it made sense to have a Spartan commander-in-chief who could establish discipline and training.

He continued by telling the Spartans to press the war more openly in Greece itself and to fortify Dekelea giving as reasons that Athens would be denied its countryside the whole year round and, among other things, be deprived of its produce from the silver mines at Laurion. This having been done, Athens' allies would be less inclined to pay their dues when they saw Sparta's successes and be less able to send reinforcements and supplies to Sicily.

Dekelea commanded one of the passes in northern Attika and was in sight of the city. The consequence of establishing a permanent base there deprived Athens of easy access to the produce of Euboia which had then to be transported by sea. It will be remembered that the Corinthians had suggested the establishment of permanently manned fortifications in Attika at the meetings prior to the outbreak of hostilities.

Alkibiades now gave his reasons for seeming to be an enemy of his own country. His main point was that he was seeking, as a patriot, to regain his country from those who had wrongfully driven him from it. He urged the Spartans to use his talents on their behalf. His speech swung the balance toward those whose inclination had been to openly move against Athens, and Sparta followed his advice.

Why was a fortification such as Dekelea not put in place after it was first mooted? The seeming reluctance of Archidamos to prosecute the war aggressively in its early years may have been a factor as was the notion that the conflict would, in any case, be short-lived. Perhaps the onset of the plague in Athens dissuaded the Peloponnesians from carrying out the plan. Certainly, after the Spartan disaster on Sphakteria they would not wish to endanger the lives of the prisoners held by Athens by anything so provocative as making a permanent base in Attika. Had such a base been in place *before* Sphakteria this could well have been a useful bargaining counter. With the death of Archidamos and the intervening years of the Peace of Nikias it is easy to see how the changing drift in hostilities, even within the agreed terms of that truce, made such a base a little too provocative to establish. Particularly when Sparta's allies were to a greater or lesser degree disaffected.

Dramatic dialogue

At the end of Book V, Thucydides departs from his normal practice and sets out in theatrical terms a debate between the Athenians and the Melians. The background to this was the second expedition against the island of Melos in 416 BC. Melos, although traditionally a colony of Sparta, had sought to remain neutral and to retain its freedom. At a time of particularly aggressive activity on the part of Athens, the refusal of this small and insignificant island to come under her control was not to be tolerated.

The leaders of the Melians entered into a debate with the Athenians on the subject of the status of independence and freedom. Thucydides uses the exchanges to display the arrogant and aggressive attitude adopted by the Athenians and contrast it with the firm rebuttal of the Melians who wished to have no part in the greater conflict. The cruder and more brutal aspects of imperialism are presented in this reflection of *Realpolitik*. It is difficult to find any valid reason for Athens to seek to subjugate the island other than it was there, not yet under their control, and that they wished to make a show of force. This was naked power politics as the extracts below indicate:

Athenians But that is for the benefit of our empire that we are here, and also for the safety of your city that we now propose to speak, we shall make plain to you, since what we desire is dominion over you without trouble to ourselves, and that you should be saved to the advantage of both.

Melians And how could it prove advantageous for us to become slaves, as it is for you to have dominion?

Athenians Because it would be to your advantage to submit before suffering the most horrible fate, and we should gain by not destroying you.

Melians And so, you mean, you would not consent to our remaining at peace and being friends instead of enemies, but allies of neither combatant?

Athenians No; for your hostility does not injure us so much as your friendship; for in the eyes of our subjects that would be proof of our weakness, whereas your hatred is a proof of our power. (V. 91. 2–95)

And a little later:

Athenians Rather the question before you is one of self-preservation – to avoid offering resistance to those who are far stronger than you. (V. 101)

The tenor of the exchanges displays a firmness on both sides, the Melians to resist and retain their freedom to the end, and the Athenians to take control of the island whatever the circumstances. Thucydides uses the debate to express moral issues, honesty, hope and justice in terms which show the Athenian position as being cynically realistic. They were aware of the unlikelihood of the Spartans coming to the aid of the Melians.

Athenians Do you not think, then, that self-interest goes hand in hand with security, while justice and honour are practised with danger – a danger the Lacedaemonians are in general the least disposed to risk? (V. 107)

The outcome was that the Melians resisted and were put under siege. Inevitably, they were defeated and all surviving adult males of military age were executed, the women and children sold into slavery, and the island settled by an Athenian cleruchy.

Historically the Melian episode comes at a time just before the Sicilian expedition. Thucydides uses the occasion to prepare his readers for the coming Athenian tragedy. The overweening arrogance of 'might is right' pervades this episode and the savagery with which the Melian population is treated prepares us for the misfortunes to come for the Athenians. *Dike* (ordered justice) had given way to *hybris* (excess).

The unusual form in which this small but powerful episode is related serves to give it a moral prominence which remains with the reader of Thucydides' history throughout the two books which cover the central tragedy for Athens.

Needless to say, although a minor operation in terms of the war in general, the subjugation of Melos was unarguably out of line with Periklean strategy.

Notes

1. The question of payment to oarsmen was to become a major issue in the closing years of the war. It was very much to the fore in the minds of the Spartan envoys who held negotiations with Kyros the Younger, and only through the charm of Lysander was a higher rate than that paid by the Athenians secured for the Spartan fleet.

2. The dexterity with which Perikles minimised open debate within the Athenian Assembly proved crucial to the continuation of his policy. He used what powers he had, backed by his reputation, to mute the usual forms of democratic practices. Technically he was acting unconstitutionally. He had not been voted additional powers such as those used later by the Roman Senate but, to all intents and purposes, his activities in this respect are reminiscent of those of a Roman dictator.

3. Kleon, like Perikles, recognised the weaknesses of democracy. He, however, used those weaknesses for his own ends whereas Perikles sought to limit any damage to the state which they might provoke.

   For further reading on speeches the commentaries on Thucydides by Simon Hornblower and that of P Rhodes are useful. Speeches at times of battle are treated by Hansen, *Historia* 1993.

APPENDIX 3

Calendar of the Peloponnesian War

The Archidamian War 431–421

431 Outbreak of hostilities. The Thebans are thwarted in their attempt to take Plataia, a Boiotian city allied to Athens.

King Archidamos at the head of the Peloponnesian League invades Attika.

Perikles orders Athenian inhabitants to leave their homes and come to Athens.

Perikles sails with fleet around the coasts of the Peloponnese making raids on Methone in Lakonia and Pheia in Elis. Later the fleet makes raids to the north-west taking the Corinthian colony of Sollion and also Astakos bringing over Kephallenia to their alliance. Another Athenian fleet ravages the seaboard opposite Euboia, capturing Thronion and defeating the Lokrians at Alope. The Athenians establish a base at Atalanta.

The Spartans give Thyrea in Lakonia to the Aiginetans dispossessed by Athens.

Athens enters into alliances with Perdikkas of Makedonia and Sitalkes, King of the Odrysians.

In the autumn Perikles leads an army to ravage Megara.

The Corinthians capture Astakos in winter but are unsuccessful against the Kephallenians.

430 Invasion of Attika by Spartan army. A large area of Attika is ravaged.

Perikles attacks various coastal areas of the Peloponnese.

The plague appears in Athens.

Collapse of resistance at Poteidaia and the end of the siege (see Appendix I).

429 Perikles dies of the plague.

The Spartans attempt to take Plataia by storm before finally settling to a siege.

Athenian actions against the Chalkidians.

Peloponnesian attack against Akarnania.

Phormio with the twenty Athenian ships at Naupaktos defeats a larger Peloponnesian fleet.

Mixed fortunes for both fleets in later actions within the area.

A daring plan to capture the port of Athens, the Peiraeus, fails to come to fruition.

A winter invasion of Makedonia by the Odrysians.

Winter expedition of Phormio to Akarnania.

428   Invasion of Attika by Spartans.

Mytilene revolts from Athens and sends envoys to Sparta.

Asopios, son of Phormio, ravages the coastal areas of Lakonia. He later makes an incursion into Akarnania but fails in his objective.

Planned second invasion of Attika abandoned by Spartans due to reluctance of allies to conduct war at the time of harvest.

Athens at her greatest in naval strength having employed 250 ships in action during the year without counting the reserve of 100 vessels.

427   Plataia surrenders and the city is destroyed

Spartan led-forces invade Attika and send a fleet to Mytilene which never arrives.

Without material support from Sparta, Mytilene is forced to surrender.

Much civil unrest in Kerkyra with both Sparta and Athens attempting to exert influence in this area.

Athens sends fleet to Sicily under Laches to impede the supply of grain to the Peloponnese and to investigate the possibility of helping their allies defeat Syracuse.

The winter sees the return of the plague to Athens.

426   The annual invasion of Attika by the Spartans, this time under Archidamos' son Agis, is abandoned in the face of regular earthquakes.

Athenian attacks on the island of Melos and against mainland Tanagra.

Sparta assists Doris, their supposed homeland, and founds Herakleia in Trachis.

Demosthenes attacks the island of Leukas and is then persuaded to make an expedition against the Aitolians. This ends in defeat for Demosthenes.

Aitolians, together with a force from Sparta under Eurylochos, attack Naupaktos.

Demosthenes with some Akarnanians brings relief to Naupaktos.

Eurylochos joins the Ambrakiots attacking Amphilochia.

Demosthenes defeats both the Peloponnesian and Ambrakiot forces during a winter campaign.

425   Agis leads the annual invasion of Attika.

A further forty Athenian ships are sent to Sicily.

An Athenian fort is established at Pylos more by accident than design.

At the news Agis returns to the Peloponnese after a campaign of only fifteen days.

The Spartans blockade Pylos by land and sea and occupy the island of Sphakteria opposite the Athenian position.

In the north the Athenian general Simonides is driven from Eion by the Chalkidians and their allies.

After the defeat of the Peloponnesian fleet at Sphakteria isolates their forces, the Spartans conclude an armistice with the Athenians so that negotiations can proceed. Kleon opposes the peace offer in Athens and hostilities are resumed under Demosthenes and Kleon until the surrender of the Spartiates.

All Greece is amazed, having assumed that the Spartans would have fought to the last man. This act was to prove damaging to the reputation of Sparta.

An Athenian attack on Corinthian territory eventually leads to an Athenian victory.

The Athenians establish a base at Methana, between Epidauros and Troezen.

Further Athenian activities in Kerkyra.

The Athenians force the citizens of Chios to dismantle their walls.

424 Lesbian exiles from Mytilene together with hired mercenaries capture cities on the coast of Asia Minor to be better positioned for attacks on Lesbos.

Athenian attack on the island of Kythera to the south of Lakonia. Sparta raises, for the first time ever, a force of archers and 400 cavalry as a mobile unit to defend against coastal incursions.

Hermokrates of Syracuse warns that continued warfare among the Sicilian cities will only weaken them thereby making them easy prey for the Athenians. On their return from an expedition to Sicily the Athenian generals are prosecuted for allegedly taking bribes.

Megaran democrats offer to open their gates to Athens.

Athens takes the long walls of Megara but fails to take the city.

Athens takes the Megaran port of Nisaia.

Brasidas, the Spartiate, thwarts the Athenians and occupies Megara before he pursues his original objective of going to the north.

Athens plans attacks on Boiotia.

Brasidas marches through Thessaly to Makedonia.

His even-handed dealings with cities gain him an enviable reputation.

Brasidas wins over Akanthos.

In the winter the plan of Demosthenes and Hippokrates to invade Boiotia by a pincer movement fails in its timing. The battle of Delion sees the Athenians well beaten.

The destruction of Delion with the aid of a flame thrower.

Amphipolis secured by Brasidas.

Thucydides, the author of the history serving as admiral, arrives too late from Thasos to save Amphipolis but secures its port of Eion.

More success for Brasidas later in the year. His appeal to Sparta for reinforcements is ignored.

423   A year-long armistice is agreed between Athens and Sparta. Both sides are to hold their acquired territories.

Brasidas brings over the city of Skione before news of the armistice is received and plans also to bring over Mende and Poteidaia.

On calculating that the date on which Skione had been taken was later than that on which the armistice had been concluded, Athens refuses Sparta's request for arbitration on the issue and prepares an expedition to the north.

Brasidas secures Mende.

Joint expedition against Lynkestis by Brasidas and Perdikkas.

Repulse of first Athenian attack on Mende. It is taken and sacked next day.

Skione is besieged.

Spartan reinforcements, finally on their way to Brasidas, are prevented from crossing Thessaly. Their leaders, Ischagoras, Ameinias and Aristeus however, join Brasidas.

Thebes dismantles the walls of Thespiai which is no longer able to resist after heavy hoplite losses at the battle of Delion.

Mantineia and Tegea fight an inconclusive battle.

Brasidas fails to take Poteidaia.

422   End of the period of armistice.

Kleon takes forces first to Skione then to Torone which he takes.

Phaeax is sent by Athens to Sicily and southern Italy to organise a coalition of cities against the growing power of Syracuse.

Further Spartan reinforcements for Brasidas are delayed at Herakleia.

The Athenians are routed by Brasidas' forces at Amphopolis. Both Kleon and Brasidas die.

Peace negotiations throughout the winter. Some Spartan allies are reluctant to make peace. Athens and Sparta enter into a fifty-year alliance. This alliance was to last just short of seven years and is to prove an unsettled period with violations on both sides before open hostilities break out once again.

The unsettled Peace, or the Peace of Nikias 421–416

421   Corinth advises Argos to build alliances. Mantineia, Elis, Corinth and some Chalkidians ally with Argos in opposition to Sparta. This is a significant threat to the Peloponnesian League.

Athens captures Skione.

Pleistoanax, king of Sparta invades and frees Parrhasia from the Mantineians.

Helots who served under Brasidas are freed by the Spartans.

Return from Athens of those Spartans captured at Sphakteria.

Both Athens and Sparta fail to fully fulfil the terms of their treaty.

Newly appointed ephors, Kleobolos and Xenares secretly advise Corinth and Boeotia to join with Argos and bring the latter into alliance with Sparta.

The Boiotarchs recommend the proposal to their assemblies who vote it down.

420   There follows several months of diplomacy in which proposals for realignments were made. Significant among the personalities is Alkibiades who tricks Spartan envoys to Athens and uses them for his own political end.

Athens agrees a hundred-year alliance with Argos, Mantineia and Elis.

Corinth refuses to be involved.

419   Alkibiades, with the Argive army, marches through the territories of their allies and Achaia cementing the alliance.

Argos attacks Epidauros to try to effect Corinth's neutrality and to give Athenian forces a more direct sea route for reinforcements to be brought to the Argolid.

Spartans under their king, Agis, return home from their intended expedition after adverse sacrfices. The object of this enterprise is not known.

Argos withdraws from Epidauros at Corinth's request but reinvades when no agreement is reached. Sparta's army gathers at her border but desist from any further action when border sacrifices are again unfavourable.

Spartans send aid to Epidauros in the winter.

Alkibiades persuades Athenians to return the helots to Pylos to harry the Lakonians.

418   The full resources of Sparta and her allies, Boeotia included, gather at Phleious to destroy the Argive alliance. Unbeknown to them, the Argive army is surrounded on all sides. Negotiations between their leaders and King Agis lead to the acceptance of arbitration. The Spartan army retires.

Alkibiades arrives in Argos and eventually persuades the alliance to continue hostilities.

Spartan anger at Agis leads to a new arrangement whereby the power of the king in making war is limited by ten Spartiates who are to be in his entourage as advisers.

Spartans and allies win the first battle of Mantineia.

In the winter Argos allies herself with Sparta who brings into the alliance Perdikkas and the Chaldikian cities. Peace is restored between Sparta and Mantineia.

417   The oligarchic party in Argos loses power and the democrats court favour with Athens. Argos builds long walls to the sea.

Sparta invades Argos and destroys the long walls. On the Spartan retiral Argos ravages Phleious in reprisal. Athens blockades Makedonia.

416   Alkibiades removes 300 Argive sympathisers of Sparta from the city to islands.

Athenians begin siege of the island of Melos, a Spartan colony, which had remained neutral.

An intended Spartan winter invasion of Argive territory is abandoned because of unfavourable winter sacrifices.

Melos surrenders. All men are killed and women and children sold as slaves.

The Sicilian Expedition 415–413

415   Decision of Athenians to subjugate Sicily. The plea for aid from the Egestan envoys proves a convenient excuse. Nikias attempts to dissuade the Athenians from undertaking such an enterprise.

Nikias, Alkibiades and Lamachos elected generals of the expedition.

The desecration of the Hermai in Athens. Alkibiades is suspected. He demands a trial before the departure of the expedition. The fleet sails.

Hermokrates warns the Syracusans of the intentions of the Athenians.

The majority of Italian cities refuse support to the Athenians who arrive at Rhegion where they contact Egesta and discover that their envoys have lied about the extent of their wealth.

Syracuse makes defensive preparations.

Nikias suggests, under the circumstances, displaying the power of Athens in the area and returning home. Alkibiades wishes to enlist support from cities and to encourage a revolt of the Sikels from the Syracusans.

Lamachos suggests an immediate attack on Syracuse while the city is still unprepared.

Alkibiades is ordered home to face trial but goes instead to the Peloponnese.

Initial battle takes place in a thunderstorm. Syracusans are defeated but their retreat is covered by their cavalry. Hermokrates calls for a reform leading to a reduction in the number of generals.

Syracusans extend city walls and fortify sensitive areas.

Alkibiades, now in Sparta, suggests aid should be sent to Syracuse.

Corinth sends help. Sparta sends Gylippos with a force to help Syracuse.

414 Athenians in Sicily take some cities.

Sparta invades the Argolid but returns after an earthquake.

The Syracusans are defeated by the Athenians in an attempt to secure the Epipolai.

Walls and counter-walls are built by both sides.

Gylippos, having acquired allies, marches overland to Syracuse.

The arrival of Gongylos, a Corinthian, with the news that help is at hand, restores Syracusan morale.

Gylippos captures the Athenian fort at Labdalon.

The construction of a counter-wall by the Syracusans. Nikias fortifies several locations and sends twenty ships to report on the approach of the Corinthian fleet.

Successful operations of Gylippos. Arrival of Corinthian fleet. Gylippos' activities force the Athenians onto the defensive. Nikias requests reinforcements from Athens and asks for his recall on grounds of ill-health.

413 Spartans invade Attika and fortify Dekeleia.

Peloponnesian reinforcements succeed in evading Athenian ships and arrive in Sicily.

Athens reconfirms Nikias' command and sends reinforcements under the command of Demosthenes.

Gylippos, with the support of Hermokrates, persuades the Syracusans to challenge the Athenians at sea.

A combined attack on Plemmyrion by both land and sea is planned by Gylippos.

The Athenians gain a narrow victory at sea after the capture of Plemmyrion by the Syracusans.

Athenian coastal raids of the Peloponnese continue.

Taxes introduced in Athens to support the war.

Demosthenes sails around the Peloponnese making coastal raids before proceeding to Kerkyra where he takes on board more of the allies. He then sails to Akarnania to engage further forces.

Konon stationed at Naupaktos requests additional ships to face the increasingly belligerent Corinthian fleet.

Corinthian success with strengthened prows, which would prove to be a critical modification.

The Syracusans adapt their ships in the same manner as the Corinthians.

Syracusan success in their harbour.

Demothenes arrives with the reinforcements and seventy-five ships.

Demosthenes' attack on the Epipolae is unsuccessful.

Demosthenes suggests withdrawal. Strangely, Nikias disagrees.

Demosthenes suggests retiral to a more defensible location.

Gylippos returns to Syracuse with a new army of allies.

Another Syracusan naval victory. Athenian commander Eurymedon is killed.

The Syracusans blockade their harbour.

Defeat of Athenian fleet in the harbour of Syracuse. A second Athenian attack is aborted after the refusal of the men to man the triremes.

Athenian withdrawal eventually leads to the surrender of Demosthenes' forces and then those of Nikias.

The Spartan King Agis orders ships to be built by the allies.

In the winter Athens also builds more ships.

Lesbos and Chios revolt from Athens.

Persians request that a Peloponnesian fleet is directed to the Hellespont.

412   Athenian fleet intercepts and blockades Peloponnesian fleet sent to support Chios.

Alkibiades, in Sparta, persuades the ephors to give him five ships with which to sail to Chios.

An Athenian fleet mauls a smaller number of Peloponnesian vessels returning from Sicily.

Alkibiades and Chalkideos persuade the Chians, Erythraians and Klazomenians to revolt.

Alkibiades brings about the revolt of Miletos. The Peloponnesian fleet is always just ahead of that of the Athenians.

Treaty between the Peloponnesians and Persia.

The Samians overthrow their government and support Athens.

Revolts against thens in Ionia.

Mention of one of the *perioikoi*, Diniades, who is in command of a Peloponnesian fleet, and who causes the revolt of Methymna and Mytilene.

The Spartan commander, Astyochos, is too late to save the island of Lesbos from the Athenians.

Athenians blockade Miletus and defeat Chians.

Great naval activity in the northern Aegean with the balance of success in favour of the Athenians.

A new treaty is proposed between the Spartans and the Persians.

Astyochos' fleet is augmented by additional Peloponnesian vessels.

Spartan commissioners reject the proposed treaty with Persia.

Rhodes is persuaded to revolt from Athens.

Alkibiades, suspected by Sparta, is condemned to death. He takes refuge with Tissaphernes and plots now for the overthrow of the Peloponnesian cause. He advises reducing Persian financial aid.

Alkibiades suggests to Tissaphernes that the best policy for Persia is to let both the Spartans and Athenians fight to a stalemate.

Alkibiades tells Athenian commanders that the installation of an oligarchy at Athens would bring Persian help.

The siege of Chios goes on and the Athenians are not ready to believe Alkibiades.

Another treaty is proposed between Tissaphernes and the Spartans.

Tissaphernes increases the funds of the Peloponnesian fleet.

411   At the Hellespont the cities of Abydos and Lampsakos revolt from Athens.

The Athenian fleet refuses battle off Samos due to the fall of democracy at Athens.

Athens institutes oligarchies in place of democracies.

The oligarchs in Athens attempt to reach a peace settlement with Sparta.

Agis rejects the initial proposal and marches with an army on Athens. He is more responsive to their second proposal.

Athenian forces at Samos in favour of democracy against the home government.

Alkibiades persuades the Athenians to recall him. He is elected general.

Spartan distrust of Tissaphernes grows. His support has been derisory.

Alkibiades manages to dissuade the democratic Athenian forces at Samos from sailing to the Peiraeus.

Vacillation of Tissaphernes with regard to bringing the Phoenician fleet over to the support of the Spartans. This fleet of 147 ships would have been a decisive factor.

The oligarchs, worried about their position at Athens, send another peace delegation to Sparta.

Theramenes accuses the oligarchs in Athens of wishing to give over the city to Sparta rather than have a restoration of democracy.

Spartan fleet win a victory off Eretria in Euboia. Except for Oreos all Euboia revolts from Athens.

Oligarchs are swept from power at Athens. Their leaders seek refuge at Dekeleia.

Problems with pay for both fleets.

Athenian naval victory at Kynossema. Thrasyyboulos and Thrasyllos are the successful commanders.

Tissaphernes tries to improve relations with the Peloponnesians.

Here the writings of Thucydides stop and we are mainly reliant on the writings of Xenophon and Diodorus Siculus for the following.

410   Athenian naval victory at Kyzikos.
        Restoration of democracy at Athens.

409   Athens loses Nisaia and more, importantly for the Spartans, Pylos.

408   Kyros the Younger is appointed by the Great King to rule the western provinces of the Persian empire. From this point on Spartan financial resources are assured.

407   Alkibiades is recalled to Athens.

406   Alkibiades is appointed admiral. Spartans win the sea battle of Notion against Alkibiades' lieutenant who, in his commander's absence, engaged the Spartan fleet, despite strict orders not to do so.

        Alkibiades is dismissed from his command.

        Athens wins a naval victory over the Spartans at Arginousai but the majority of the commanders are tried and executed in Athens for supposed neglect in picking up survivors during the storm which followed the battle.

        In this year the Athenians lose some of their most able commanders, a commodity they could ill afford to be without.

405   Lysander defeats Konon's fleet at Aigospotamoi.

404   Death of Darius II and the succession of Artaxerxes II.
        Blockade and surrender of Athens to Lysander.
        Destruction of Long Walls.
        Oligarchy set up in Athens by Sparta.

Select Bibliography

The list below is by no means exhaustive. It offers suggestions for further reading. (JHS = Journal of Hellenic Studies.)

Adcock, F E, *Thucydides and his History*, Cambridge, 1963.

—, *The Greek and Macedonian Art of War*, Berkeley and Los Angeles, 1957.

Anderson, J K, *Military Theory and Practice in the Age of Xenophon*, University of California, 1970.

Barron, J P, *Silver Coins of Samos*, Athlone Press, University of London, 1966.

Barry,W D, 'Roof Tiles and Urban Violence in the Ancient World', Greek and Byzantine Studies 37(1), 1996.

Cartledge, P, 'Hoplites and Heroes', JHS, 1977, pp. 11–27

—, *The Greeks*, Oxford, 1993.

Cawkwell, G L, Classical Quarterly 33, 1983.

Connors, W R, *Thucydides*, Princeton NJ, 1984.

Delbruck, H, *The History of the Art of War*, Vol. I, Warfare in Antiquity (trans. W J Renfroe), Bison Books, 1990.

de Romilly, J, *Thucydides and Athenian Imperialism* (trans. P Thody), Oxford, 1963.

de St Croix, G E M, *The Origins of the Peloponnesian War*, London, 1972.

Fairbanks, A, Cornell Studies in Classical Philology 12, 1900

Finley, M I, *Ancient Sicily*, London, 1980.

—, *Three Essays on Thucydides*, Oxford, 1973.

Forrest, W G, *A History of Sparta*, London: Hutchinson, 1968.

Gomme, A W; Andrewes, A and Dover, K J, *A Historical Commentary on Thucydides* (5 vols), Oxford, 1945–8; Vol. IV, 1970.

Grundy, G B, *Thucydides and the History of His Age*, Oxford, 1948.

Hammond, N G L, *Studies in Greek History*, Oxford, 1973.

Hanson, V D, 'Hoplite Obliteration. The case of the town of Thespiae', in *Ancient Warfare*, eds J Carman and A Harding, Sutton, 1999.

—, *War and Agriculture in Ancient Greece*, Pisa, 1983.

—, *The Western Way of War*, New York, 1989.

—, The *Wars of the Ancient Greeks*, Cassell, 1999, p.115.

—, 'The War to Begin all Wars', New Criterion, Vol. 21, 2003.

Holladay, A J, 'Sparta's Role in the First Peloponnesian War', JHS, 1977, pp. 54–63.

Hornblower, S, *The Greek World 470–323 BC*, Methuen, 1983.

—, *A Commentary on Thucydides*, Vol. I, Oxford, 1991; Vol. II, 1996.

—, *Thucydides*, Baltimore, 1986.

Kagan, D, *The Outbreak of the Peloponnesian War*, Ithaca NY, 1969.

—, *The Archidamian War*, Ithaca NY, 1974.

—, *The Peace of Nicias and the Sicilian Expedition*, Ithaca NY, 1981.

—, *The Fall of the Athenian Empire*, Cornell University, 1987.

Kern, P B, *Ancient Siege Warfare*, Souvenir Press Ltd., 1999.

Keen, A G, 'Athenian Campaigns in Karia and Lykia during the Peloponnesian War', JHS, 1993, pp. 152–7.

Krentz, P, 'Casualties in Hoplite Battles', Greek, Roman and Byzantine Studies, No. 26, 1985, pp. 13–21.

Lateiner, D, 'Heralds and Corpses in Thucydides', Classical World 71, 1997, pp.97–106.

Lazenby, J F, *The Spartan Army*, Aris & Phillips, 1985.

—, *The Peloponnesian War*, Routledge, 2004.

McKechnie, P R and Kern, S J, *Hellenica Oxyrhinchia*, Aris & Phillips, 1988.

May, J M F, *Coinage of Abdera 540–345 BC*, OUP, 1966 (Special Publication No. 3.

Meiggs, R, *The Athenian Empire*, Oxford, 1972.

Meigga, R and Lewis, D M, *A Selection of Greek Historical Inscriptions to the end of the Fifth Century BC*, Oxford, 1988.

Morrison, J S, Coates, J F and Rankov, N B, *The Athenian Trireme*, Cambridge, 2000.

Pritchett, W K, *The Greek State at War* (5 vols), University of California, 1971–91.

—, *Studies in Ancient Topography* Vols I–IV, Berkeley and Los Angeles, 1965–.

Rich, J and Shipley, G, *War and Society in the Greek World*, London, 1993.

Rubincam, Catherine, 'The Topography of Pylos and Sphakteria and Thucydides' measurement of distance', JHS, Vol. 121, 2001.

Runciman, W G, 'Greek Hoplites. Warrior Culture and Indirect Bias', Journal of the Royal Anthropological Institute, Vol. 4, 1998.

Sage, M W, Warfare *in Ancient Greece: A Sourcebook*, Routledge, 1996.

Salmon, J, 'Political Hoplites', JHS, 1977, pp. 84–101.

Sealey, R, *A History of the Greek City States 700–338 BC*, University of California, 1976, pp. 297–385.

Sidebottom, H, *Ancient Warfare. A Very Short Introduction,* Oxford, 2004.

Stewert, P. 'The Ephebic oath in 5th-century Athens' JHS, 1977, pp. 102–11.

Strassler, R B, 'The harbour at Pylos, 425 BC', JHS, 1988, pp. 198–203.

Sun Tzu, *The Art of War*, translated by Lionel Giles, London, 1910.

Tod, M N, *Greek Historical Inscriptions*, Clarendon Press, Oxford, 1933.

Toynbee, A J, *Some Problems of Greek History*, Oxford, 1969, pp. 376–7.

Vaughan, P, 'Identification and Retrieval of Hoplite battle dead' in *Hoplites*, ed. Hanson, Routledge, 1991.

Warry, J, *Warfare in the Classical World*, New York, 1980.

Westlake, H D, *Individuals in Thucydides*, CUP, 1968.

Whitby, M, 'Two shadows: images of Sparta and the helots', *The Shadow of Sparta*, eds. A Powell and S Hodkinson.

Winter, F E, *Greek Fortifications*, University of Toronto, 1971.

Worley, L J, *Hippeis: The Cavalry of Ancient Greece*, Westview Press, 1994.

About the Author

Godfrey Hutchinson is a classical historian, educated at the universities of Durham and Newcastle upon Tyne, whose main area of expertise is warfare in the Classical and Hellenistic periods. He has travelled extensively in Greece examining the topography of the battlefields, defensive systems and possible routes taken by armed forces. These inform him of the range of tactical options available to commanders. His study, *Xenophon and the Art of Command*, dealt with a wide range of leadership issues such as tactics, piety, secrecy, spies, morale and training in the earlier part of the 4th century BC.

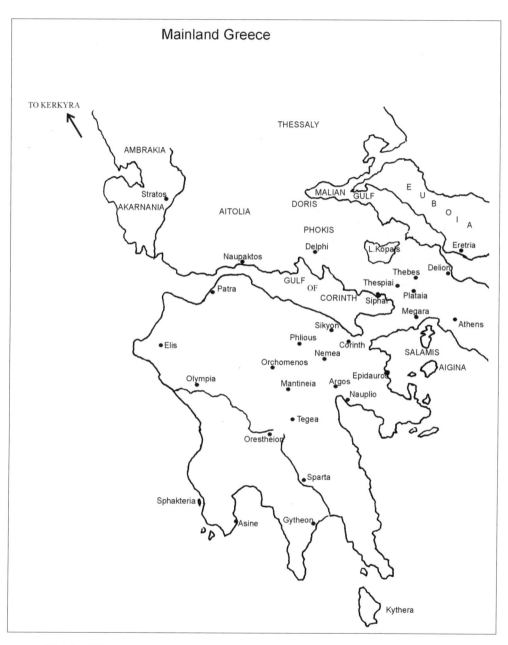

Mainland Greece

TO KERKYRA

THESSALY

AMBRAKIA

Stratos

AKARNANIA

AITOLIA

DORIS

MALIAN GULF

E
U
B
O
I
A

PHOKIS

Delphi

L.Kopais

Eretria

Naupaktos

Thebes

Delion

Patra

GULF OF

Thespiai

Plataia

CORINTH

Siphai

Megara

Sikyon

Phlious

Athens

Corinth

Elis

Nemea

SALAMIS

Orchomenos

AIGINA

Olympia

Epidauros

Mantineia

Argos

Nauplio

Tegea

Orestheion

Sparta

Sphakteria

Asine

Gytheon

Kythera

Mainland Greece

Index

Abydos 184, 188
Ademantos 191, 209
Agarthachidas 13
Agarthachos 160
Agesilaos 166
Agesipolis 156
Agis 101-107, 111-114, 116, 143, 172,
    210, 247-248, 250-251, 253-254
Aisimides 6
Aistokrates 191, 200
Alexarchos 143
Alkamenes 182
Alkibiades xv, 99-101, 105, 121-122,
    124-126, 131-132, 143, 169-170, 172,
    184-187, 189-191, 193-195, 204, 207,
    211, 212, 229, 241-243, 250-255
Alkidas 20-22, 24, 69-70
Alkiphron 104
Ameinias 86, 249
Ammeas 32
Amyrtaios, King of Egyptian marsh
    peoples 215-216, 225
Anaxarchos 178
Antiochos 191-194, 212, 213
Arakos 205
Archidamos, Spartan king vii, xii, 20,
    27-28, 31-33, 102, 226, 228-233, 243,
    246-247
Aristeides 215-216, 225
Aristesteis 86, 249
Aristogenes 200
Aristokles 113-114
Aristokrates 200
Ariston 148-149
Aristonymos 83

Arrhabaios 71, 76
Artaxerxes, Great King of Persia 222
Asopios 19
Astyochos 182-183, 253-254
Athenagoras 124
Athenaios 83
Autocharidas 93

Battles:
  in Aetolia 37-39
  Aigospotami 206-209
  Arginousai 197-204
  Delion ix, 46-51, 79, 83, 100, 121,
    236-237
  Mantineia viii-ix, 112-114, 119, 121-
    122
  Kynossema 177-182, 188
  Kyzikos 186, 188, 192-193, 207, 213
  Notion 191-194, 196, 213
  on Sphakteria Chapter IV passim
  near Sybota 5-8
  Brasidas viii-x, 2, 15-16, 19, 22, 24, 36,
    45, 56, 61, Chapter V passim, 100,
    121, 170, 175, 196, 211, 218, 227,
    234, 248-250
Bromeros 76

Chalkideos 253
Charikles 143, 146
Chaireas 186-188
Chromon 39

Demaratos, exiled Spartan king 217
Demosthenes viii-x, 36-39, 41-43, 45-
    46, 51, 53-56, 59, 61, 63, 70, 72-73,

75, 95-96, 143, 146-147, 150-155,
157-160, 164-168, 171, 211, 234, 247,
248-249, 252-253
Derkylidas 182-183
Diemporos 25
Diniades 253
Diototos 240-241
Diomedon 198, 200
Diomilos 133
Diphilos 146
Dorieus 183-184

Ekkritos 143
Epameinondas 47
Ephialtes 219
Epikles 183
Epikydidas 93
Epitadas 55, 59-60
Erasinidas 200
Eretria 174-5
Eteonikos 197, 203-205
Eukles, (Athenian) 79
Eukles, (Syracusan) 138
Eupompidas 31, 33
Eurylochos 247
Eurymedon 53, 62, 121, 143, 146-147,
150-151, 157, 160, 253
Euryvatos 6
Euthydemos 143, 160
Eurylochos 39-43, 45
Evagoras 208

Gylippos ix, 132, 138-142, 144-145,
148, 150-155, 157, 159-161, 163-166,
175, 211,
238-239, 252-253
Gongylos 252

Hagnon 93, 233
Hegesander 143
Hegesandridas ix, 173-177, 183
Herakleides 130, 138
Hermokrates of Syracuse 120-121,
123-124, 130-131, 133-135, 138,
144-145, 155, 161, 168-169, 172, 227,
242, 248, 251-252
Hermon 199, 200
Hippagretas 60

Hippaos 200
Hippokrates, (Athenian) 46-48, 50,
72,-73, 236-237, 249
Hippokrates, (Peloponnesian) 183, 188
Hipponoidas 113-114

Inares, King of Egypt 222
Iphikrates 2
Ischagoras 86, 249
Isokrates 13

Kallikratidas 194-199, 201-203, 213-214
Kimon 30, 216, 218
Klearchos 183, 187
Klearidas 86, 89-92, 94
Kleinias 224
Kleobolos 250
Kleomedes 36
Kleomenes, Spartan king 20, 217
Kleon x, 53-54, 58, 61, 63, 84, 88-92,
100-101, 207, 234, 239-241, 245,
248-249
Kleophon 188, 205, 210
Knemos 9-12, 14-17, 19, 23, 66, 68, 234
Komon 60
Konon 146, 170, 191, 194, 196-198, 204,
208
Kratesippidas 2
Kyros theYounger 189-190, 195, 198,
205, 212-213, 245, 255

Laches 105, 120, 168
Lamachos 121-122, 126-127, 130, 135-
137, 155, 251
Lakedaimonios 6
Leotochides, Spartan king 217
Lykrophron 15, 19, 24, 66, 234
Lysander vii-ix, 2, 65, 98, 175-176, 189-
196, 205-211, 213-214, 218, 255
Lysias 200
Lysikles 20
Lysistratos 80

Machaon 13
Makarios 39, 42
Medokos, King of the Thrakians 207
Menander 143, 151, 160
Menedaios 39, 42

Mikiades 6
Mindaros ix, 176-186
Myronides 221

Naukleides 25
Naupaktos 12-19, 234-236
Nichomachos 46
Nikias 2, 36, 58, 61, 72, 86-87, 100, 119,
    121-128, 130, 132-142, 144, 147-148,
    150-151, 154-156, 158-162, 164-166,
    169-171, 227, 234, 238, 240-241, 243,
    251-253
Nikon 143
Nikostratos 69, 86, 105

Paches 21, 239
Pagondas ix, 47, 49-50, 5..2, 236
Pasitelidas 86, 88,-89, 95
Pausanias Spartan king   210
Perdikkas, King of Makedon 10, 71,
    75-76, 79, 84-85, 89, 93, 249, 251
Perikles vii, x, xii, 9, 27, 53-54, 118-120,
    122-123, 169, 210, 219, 223-226, 229-
    234, 241, 245-246
Perikles the Younger 200
Pharnabazos 170, 176, 183—188, 211
Philokles 209
Phormio viii, 9-16, 18-19, 66, 68, 70,
    234-236, 247
Phrynichos 95
Pissuthnes 21, 224
Pleistoanax, Spartan king 115, 223,
    226, 230, 250
Polydamidas 84, 86-88
Prokles 36, 39
Protomachos 200
Pythangelos 25

Pythen 138, 160
Pythodoros 121

Ramphias 93

Salaithos 21
Sargeos 143
Seuthes, King of the Thrakians 77, 207
Sikanos 130, 154, 156, 160
Sitalkes 77
Sokrates 99
Sophokles 53, 62, 121
Sthenelaidas 228-229
Styphon 60

Tellias 138
Tesias 36
Teutiaplos 21
Theainetos 31
Themistokles 119, 218, 225
Theramenes 185-188, 203, 210, 214,
    254
Thorax 206, 208
Thrasondas 200
Thrasyllos 104-105, 178-180, 184-185,
    200, 204, 255
Thrasyboulos 178-182, 184-188, 191,
    203-204, 255
Thymochares 174
Timokrates 15, 18, 66, 234
Tissaphernes 172, 176, 185, 189, 211-
    212, 254-255

Xenares 250
Xenon 143
Xenokleides 5